CONSTITUTIONAL LAW
Individual Rights

Examples and Explanations

CONSTITUTIONAL LAW

Individual Rights

Examples and Explanations
Second Edition

Allan Ides

Professor of Law and William M. Rains Fellow
Loyola Law School

Christopher N. May

James P. Bradley Professor of Constitutional Law
Loyola Law School

ASPEN LAW & BUSINESS
A Division of Aspen Publishers, Inc.
Gaithersburg   New York

Permissions
Aspen Law & Business
1185 Avenue of the Americas
New York, NY 10036

Printed in the United States of America

1 2 3 4 5 6 7 8 9 0

Library of Congress Cataloging-in-Publication Data

Ides, Allan, 1949-
    Constitutional law — individual rights : examples and explana-
tions / Allan Ides, Christopher N. May. — 2nd ed.
        p. cm. — (The examples & explanations series)
    Includes index.
    ISBN 0-7355-2031-3
    1. Civil rights — United States. I. May, Christopher N.
II. Title. III. Series.

KF4749 .I34 2001
342.73'085 — dc21
                                                            00-053610

About Aspen Law & Business
Legal Education Division

With a dedication to preserving and strengthening the long-standing tradition of publishing excellence in legal education, Aspen Law & Business continues to provide the highest quality teaching and learning resources for today's law school community. Careful development, meticulous editing, and an unmatched responsiveness to the evolving needs of today's discerning educators combine in the creation of our outstanding casebooks, coursebooks, textbooks, and study aids.

ASPEN LAW & BUSINESS
A Division of Aspen Publishers, Inc.
A Wolters Kluwer Company
www.aspenpublishers.com

For Cindi and Barbara

Summary of Contents

Contents

Preface

Most of us arrive at law school with at least a minimal awareness of our constitutional system of government. We know generally that the national government is divided into three branches and that the Bill of Rights protects our fundamental freedoms. That awareness probably began with elementary school Thanksgiving Day pageants, developed substance through various American history and government classes in high school, and finally, for some of us, is topped by an undergraduate course in constitutional law. Outside the educational setting, constitutional law issues ripple through the popular media with frequent references to abortion, free speech, religion, racial and gender discrimination, gay rights, and so forth.

As law students, however, we learn very quickly that the study of constitutional law is anything but a meditation on the commonplace. And therein lies the treachery. The familiar quickly blends with the arcane and we are forced to grapple with a tumult of doctrines, distinctions, and qualifications. Indeed, the familiar may soon disappear as we trek through justiciability, the commerce power, state action, and various other subjects that never seem to make the headlines. Even those topics that strike a common chord are presented with a treatment that is most uncommon. Add to this a bevy of wavering doctrines, concurring or opposing opinions, and the changing personnel of the Court, and the complexity can become overwhelming.

We're here to help. We have written two volumes designed to give you a foundation in the doctrines and methods of constitutional law and constitutional argument. The first, *National Power and Federalism,* covers the powers of the federal courts, Congress, and the President; the doctrines of separation of powers and federalism; and some of the limitations that the Constitution imposes on state power. This second volume, *Individual Rights,* covers the provisions of the Constitution that protect us against the government, including the Takings and Contracts Clause; the Due Process and Equal Protection Clauses; as well as the Speech, Press, and Religion Clauses of the First Amendment.

These books try to provoke you into thinking about the larger issues of constitutional law with some depth and perception. They are not outlines. Nor are they research treatises on all the nuances of constitutional law. Rather, they present a problem-oriented guide through the principal doctrines of constitutional law — those covered in typical constitutional law courses — with an emphasis on how one might think about issues that arise within the various contexts in which these doctrines operate. Lawyers, after all, are problem solvers. These books are tools for constitutional law problem solvers (and students confronted with the reality of final exams).

We must include the usual caveat. Our books are not a substitute for your constitutional law class or for a basic casebook. Nor are they a substitute for reading those cases. We hope, however, that they will make the classroom experience richer and more accessible. In fact, our experience is that students who have read these materials along with traditional case reading have found the cases more understandable and more easily digested. They have also found that class participation is less threatening and more fruitful. We are confident that you will have the same experience.

The approach we suggest is quite simple. As you begin a new topic in your constitutional law course, read the related chapter in either *National Power and Federalism* or *Individual Rights*. This will give you an overview of the area and a preliminary sense of how doctrines are applied within the area. In reading the chapters, however, don't just *read* the problems, *do them*. In other words, consider the problem and try to anticipate how it will be solved before you read the accompanying explanation. This will develop your analytical skills. Next, as you read your cases refer back to the related chapters and chapter sections and assess how each case fits into the overall framework developed by the Court. See if the case comports with the problems and explanations. Be critical. Finally, when you complete the coverage of a topic, review the chapter again. This will give you confidence that you know the material. Students have also found these materials useful as study aids when preparing for their final exams. After all, finals are simply problems to be solved. In any event, don't just read these books; use them to develop your understanding and your skills.

Good luck in your studies and in your careers as problem-solving students of the Constitution.

Allan Ides
Christopher N. May
December 2000

Acknowledgments

We would like to express our appreciation to several people who provided assistance in the preparation of these books, beginning with a special thanks to our student research assistants at Loyola Law School and Washington and Lee University: Lilly Kim (LLS '98), Lauren Raskin (LLS '98), Eric Enson (LLS '99), James V. DeRossitt IV (W&L '96), Ashley DeMoss (W&L '97), Lawrence Striley (W&L '95), Kristen Strain (LLS '01), and Kasha Arianne Harshaw (LLS '02). We are also indebted to a number of colleagues who either read and commented on parts of the original manuscript or otherwise provided inspiration and support for this project: Lash LaRue, Calvin Massey, David Millon, and Brian Murchison. Thanks also to our secretaries, Ruth Busch and Diane Cochran. In addition, we gratefully acknowledge the financial support provided by the Frances Lewis Law Center at Washington and Lee University and by the James P. Bradley Chair in Constitutional Law at Loyola Law Schoool. Finally, Anne Brunell, Renee Cote, and Lai T. Moy provided helpful professional editorial assistance for which we are indebted.

CONSTITUTIONAL LAW
Individual Rights

Examples and Explanations

1

Introduction to Individual Rights

§1.1 Introduction and Overview

In one sense, the entire body of the Constitution is designed to protect individual rights. In fact, many of the Framers believed that the political structure created by the Constitution was the primary and essential vehicle through which to protect the liberty of the people. Such structural devices as the separation of powers, checks and balances, bicameralism, enumeration of powers, and federalism, among others, were thought to provide a substantial bulwark against governmental tyranny. Alexander Hamilton went further and argued that a detailed bill of rights would be affirmatively dangerous in that it "would contain various exceptions to powers which are not granted; and, on this very account, would afford a colorable pretext to claim more than were granted." *The Federalist No. 84*, at 513 (Clinton Rossiter ed., 1961).

The text of the original Constitution reflects this structural bias by including only a few specific protections for what we now commonly consider individual rights. See, e.g., Art. I, §9, cls. 2 & 3 (privilege of the writ of habeas corpus, proscription against bills of attainder and ex post facto laws); Art. III, §2, cl. 3 (right to trial by jury in criminal cases). Yet Hamilton's confidence in political structure was not universally shared. The absence of a bill of rights was perceived by many as a major flaw in the proposed Constitution, and a number of states premised their ratification of it on a recommendation that the Constitution be amended to include such a statement of rights. See, e.g., 3 Jonathan Elliot, *The Debates in the Several State Conventions on the Adoption of the Federal Constitution as Recommended by the General Convention in Philadelphia in 1787*, at 657-661 (proposed amendments by Virginia). Two states, North Carolina and Rhode Island, did not ratify the Constitution until a proposed Bill of Rights had been approved by Congress and submitted to the states for ratification.

In response to these concerns and others, James Madison introduced a series of proposed amendments to the Constitution during the first session of Congress. The Bill of Rights, which was approved by Congress in 1789 and ratified by the states in 1791, was a direct product of Madison's proposals. It includes ten amendments to the Constitution, nine of which address individual rights; the tenth reiterates the limited nature of the government created by the Constitution. In practical effect, the Bill of Rights limits the power of the federal government to transgress the rights described therein. In other words, the rights enumerated in the Bill of Rights act as a trump on the exercise of federal power.

The Supreme Court held early on that the Bill of Rights limits only the authority of the national government and not that of the states. *Barron v. Mayor & City Council of Baltimore,* 32 U.S. (7 Pet.) 243 (1833). Thus, although the body of the Constitution contains a few specific individual rights limitations on state authority—e.g., the Privileges and Immunities Clause of Article IV and the Contracts Clause of Article I, §10 — by and large the protection of individual rights against state encroachment was to be found, if at all, in the respective constitutions of the several states. At least that was the case throughout much of the nineteenth century.

The adoption of the Fourteenth Amendment in 1868, however, radically changed both the Constitution's and the national government's role in the protection of civil rights against state interference, essentially establishing federal supremacy within this realm of civil rights. As we will see below, through a process of incorporation the Fourteenth Amendment became the constitutional vehicle through which courts now apply most provisions of the Bill of Rights to the states. In addition, the Equal Protection Clause of the Fourteenth Amendment eventually came to operate as a powerful and judicially enforceable principle of equality. Finally, the Fourteenth Amendment vested Congress with a broad authority to enforce civil rights against state encroachment. Thus, with the adoption of the Fourteenth Amendment, accompanied by subsequent judicial and congressional interpretations, the Constitution now provides substantial protection against both federal and state encroachments on individual liberty.

In the chapters that follow, we will examine the substantive and procedural reach of a number of the more important and frequently litigated individual rights limitations on governmental authority. This chapter, however, addresses several preliminary matters. It begins with a brief historical and descriptive perspective on the Fourteenth Amendment. This is designed to provide a foundation for the multitude of doctrines that are built on and around that amendment. Although the provisions of the Bill of Rights merit their own individual consideration, the Fourteenth Amendment stands alone in its radical transformation of our system of government. Next, the chapter examines three preliminary doctrinal matters directly related to the protection of individual rights—namely, the incorporation doctrine, the state action doctrine, and the scope of congressional enforcement powers under the Thirteenth, Fourteenth, and Fifteenth Amendments, otherwise known as the Civil War Amendments.

§1.2   The Fourteenth Amendment: An Introductory Overview

The Text of Section 1 of the Fourteenth Amendment

Section 1 of the Fourteenth Amendment consists of two sentences. The first sentence provides: "All persons born or naturalized in the United States and subject to the jurisdiction thereof, are citizens of the United States and of the State wherein they reside." This sentence accomplishes two things: First, it creates a definition of U.S. citizenship ("All persons born or naturalized"); second, it provides a definition of state citizenship ("reside"). Neither point is controversial today, and there is general agreement that the language of this sentence means exactly what it appears to say. The phrase "subject to the jurisdiction thereof" requires further investigation. That investigation would reveal that the phrase was designed to exclude two classes of persons —children of alien enemies in hostile occupation and children of diplomatic representatives of foreign states. We could also quibble about the word "reside," but without too great an effort, a workable and relatively noncontroversial meaning would be discovered, namely, domicile or place of permanent residence. In short, the first sentence defines citizenship at both the federal and the state levels in relatively clear terms and with only a minimal need to look beyond the specific language used.

Despite the relative clarity of the first sentence, some reference to history is beneficial. Prior to the Civil War, the U.S. Supreme Court had held that an African American sold as a slave is not a citizen of the United States. *Dred Scott v. Sandford*, 60 U.S. (19 How.) 393 (1857). The *Dred Scott* decision, which denied the status of citizenship to slaves, former slaves, and their descendents, was viewed by Republicans as a precipitating and an infamous cause of the Civil War, and the first sentence of §1 was designed to repeal that decision. This specific purpose would have been clear to contemporary observers, though it is a bit obscure to the modern reader. Even given that underlying purpose, however, the language of the Amendment is much broader than would have been necessary to simply overrule *Dred Scott*. It covers *all* persons born or naturalized in the United States, not just former slaves. In other words, it creates a general definition of citizenship, and we need not look beyond the actual words to discover that definition.

The second sentence of §1 is both more complicated and less clear. It is divided into three parts. The first part provides: "No State shall make or enforce any law which shall abridge the privileges or immunities of citizens of the United States.¹ . . ." The text does not define the "privileges or immunities of citizens of the United States." One immediately thinks of the Privileges and Immunities Clause of Article IV, which protects the "Privileges and Immunities of Citizens in the several States." See Christopher N. May & Allan Ides, *Constitutional Law: National Power and Federalism*, ch. 9 (2001). At the time the Fourteenth Amendment was adopted, judicial decisions had given some content to the "fundamental rights" protected by Article IV. See *Corfield v. Coryell*, 6 F. Cas. 546, 552 (C.C.E.D. Pa. 1823). Do both clauses refer to the same fundamental rights, or is there a distinction between the privileges or immunities held by citizens of the United States and the privileges and immunities held by citizens in the several states? In other words, has a new category of fundamental rights been created to coincide with the newly created definition of U.S. citizenship? And if so, what are those rights? The text, standing alone, does not provide an answer to these questions.

The next part of the second sentence provides, "[N]or shall any State deprive any person of life, liberty, or property, without due process of law. . . ." This sounds a little easier. Before a state can take away a person's life, liberty, or property, it must provide something called due process of law. Implicitly, the rights to life, liberty, and property are not absolute. A deprivation of these rights is permissible as long as due process is satisfied. The word "process" suggests procedures; the word "due" suggests appropriate, proper, or reasonable. A person, therefore, is entitled to appropriate procedures before being deprived of life, liberty, or property. Presumably reference to accepted practices will provide guidance as to what procedures will be deemed to satisfy due process. Note also that the category "person" appears to be broader than the category "citizen." All citizens are persons; all persons are not necessarily citizens. The Due Process Clause protects the more inclusive category.

Finally, §1 provides, "[N]or [shall any State] deny to any person within its jurisdiction the equal protection of the laws." The phrase "equal protection of the laws" suggests at the very least that otherwise neutral laws must be enforced in an evenhanded manner for the benefit of all who fall within the letter of their protection. But does it mean, in addition, that state laws may not discriminate or classify? In other words, does it require that the law itself be evenhanded? Assuming that this is the case and keeping in mind that all laws classify in some manner, is this potential ban on classifications limited to certain types of discriminations? If so, what types of discriminations are banned? Again, the text does not answer these questions.

This cursory examination of the text of §1 should make at least one thing clear: A reading of a constitutional text begins, but rarely resolves an inquiry into meaning. The language must be placed in a context that includes the surrounding historical events as well as the specific matters that led to the enactment. Certainly this is borne out by the obscure language of the second sentence of §1. These observations are also true with respect to language that appears clear. The clarity may be an illusion caused by our lack of appreciation for the historical context. For example, we may think we know what equal protection of the laws means, but the authors of the text may have been writing from a very different understanding of the phrase. In short, the text cannot be read in a historical vacuum. A deeper understanding of the text requires at a minimum a passing familiarity with the historical milieu in which the Fourteenth Amendment was adopted.

A Brief Historical Survey

The context surrounding the adoption of the Fourteenth Amendment can be succinctly described as slavery, the abolition movement, the Civil War, and the Reconstruction response to events in the post-Civil War South, including the adoption of the Black Codes. The authors of the Fourteenth Amendment and those who supported it, both in Congress and in state conventions, were immersed in these events. They lived them and were responding to them.

The Thirteenth Amendment, which abolished slavery, had been ratified in 1865, but it was evident (and believed to be evident) that the institution of slavery was being replaced by a system that was designed to keep the former slaves in a condition of virtual servitude. The Black Codes, enacted by most of the southern states, severely restricted the civil rights of former slaves, including the rights to enter into contracts, to purchase property, and to sit on juries. In addition, there was evidence that former slaves were not being given full and impartial protection of otherwise neutral laws. Both formally and informally the former slaves were being treated as noncitizens.

In response to these conditions, Congress passed the Civil Rights Act of 1866, which provided in pertinent part:

> That there shall be no discrimination in civil rights or immunities
> . . . on account of race . . . but the inhabitants of every race . . .
> shall have the same right to make and enforce contracts, to sue, be
> parties, and give evidence, to inherit, purchase, lease, sell, hold and
> convey real and personal property, and to full and equal benefit of
> all laws and proceedings for the security of person and property, and
> shall be subject to like punishment . . . and no other.

President Andrew Johnson had vetoed the Civil Rights bill on the ground that it was unconstitutional, and though Congress overrode the veto, a number of Republicans who supported the measure were concerned that the Act exceeded the enumerated powers of Congress. This concern provided the initial impetus for the Fourteenth Amendment. One of the primary purposes of that Amendment was to ensure that Congress possessed the power to enact legislation such as the Civil Rights Act of 1866. Section 5 of the Fourteenth Amendment does precisely that. It grants Congress the power to enforce the provisions of the Fourteenth Amendment, including the so-called substantive provisions of §1 described above. See §1.5.

Proponents of the Fourteenth Amendment, therefore, probably understood §1's Privileges or Immunities Clause as encompassing the "civil rights or immunities" described in the Civil Rights Act of 1866. Those rights are remarkably similar to the fundamental rights associated with Article IV's Privileges and Immunities Clause, and like that Clause, the Civil Rights Act prohibited discriminatory treatment of citizens exercising those rights. If this interpretation is correct, one purpose of the Fourteenth Amendment's Privileges or Immunities Clause was to prevent states from denying U.S. citizens, as defined in the first sentence of §1, the equal exercise of those fundamental civil rights and immunities described in the Civil Rights Act.

The legislative history of the Fourteenth Amendment supports this interpretation. That history is replete with cross-references to the Civil Rights Act, suggesting a close affinity between the Act and the proposed Amendment. This interpretation also comports with the notion that Congress, through the Fourteenth Amendment, was attempting to construct a constitutional provision that would validate the prior enactment. In fact, immediately after the adoption of the Fourteenth Amendment, the Civil Rights Act of 1866 was reenacted as an enforcement of §1 rights.

A second strand of history suggests that the Privileges or Immunities Clause may have been intended to have an even wider application. The Court, in *Barron v. Mayor & City Council of Baltimore*, 32 U.S. (7 Pet.) 243 (1833), held that the Bill of Rights limits only the power of the federal government and not the power of the states. Prior to the Civil War, abolitionists rejected the soundness of *Barron*. For a variety of reasons, they believed that the first eight amendments to the Constitution either were or should be fully applicable against the states. This view was shared by a number of Republicans, many of them former abolitionists, who participated in the drafting and passage of the Fourteenth Amendment. Moreover, even those Republicans who did not expressly subscribe to the complete incorporation theory probably thought that the Privileges or Immunities Clause protected at least some additional fundamental rights beyond those listed in the Civil Rights Act of 1866. For example, the freedoms of press and speech were widely accepted as being fundamental rights held by all U.S. citizens. One cannot say definitively, however, that the purpose of the Privileges or Immunities Clause was to incorporate all or part of the first eight amendments. The surrounding history is certainly consistent with that possibility, but the available information is far from dispositive. See Raoul Berger, *Government by Judiciary* (1977) (arguing that the first eight amendments of the Bill of Rights were not incorporated against the states via the Privileges or Immunities Clause); Michael Curtis, *No State Shall Abridge* (1986) (arguing precisely the opposite). Here, we are left with an ambiguous record and an indeterminate meaning.

If the Privileges or Immunities Clause was in fact designed to prevent the denial of certain fundamental rights, what purpose can be assigned to the Due Process and Equal Protection Clauses? The independent significance of the Due Process Clause is not difficult to envision. It provides procedural protection against the taking of life, liberty, or property. Again, the Republicans were convinced, with some justification, that individuals—in particular, former slaves and Union sympathizers—were being deprived of basic civil rights without proper procedures. The Due Process Clause specifically addressed that concern.

Similarly, the independent purpose of the Equal Protection Clause appears to have been to ensure that all laws would be applied to individuals in an evenhanded manner. Consider the language of the Civil Rights Act: "[I]nhabitants of every race . . . shall have the same right . . . to full and equal benefit of all laws and proceedings for the security of person and property, and shall be subject to like punishment . . . and no other." The Equal Protection Clause speaks directly to this concern—equal *protection* of the laws. The fact that segregation was actively practiced in the North as well as in the District of Columbia at the time the Fourteenth Amendment was adopted suggests that the Equal Protection Clause was not seen as a general prohibition against racial discrimination. The Privileges or Immunities Clause, on the other hand, did provide protection against racial discrimination in the context of the rights protected by the Clause.

Taking the foregoing together, what can be said of §1 of the Fourteenth Amendment? First, the Privileges or Immunities Clause was seemingly intended to prevent state discrimination with respect to fundamental civil rights, such as those protected by Article IV's Privileges and Immunities Clause. Second, the Privileges or Immunities Clause probably was thought to include certain other fundamental rights found in the Bill of Rights, such as freedom of the press and freedom of speech. Third, the Privileges or Immunities Clause may have been designed to incorporate all the provisions of the first eight amendments to the Constitution. Fourth, the Due Process Clause required states to provide fair or reasonable procedures prior to the deprivation of life, liberty, or property. Fifth, the Equal Protection Clause was probably designed merely to remedy a state's unequal enforcement of the laws.

Early Judicial Trends in Construing
the Fourteenth Amendment

Four years after the ratification of the Fourteenth Amendment, the Supreme Court decided the *Slaughter-House Cases*, 83 U.S. (16 Wall.) 36 (1872). At issue was a Louisiana statute that granted a monopoly over the butchering trade in three parishes in Louisiana. The butchers who challenged the statute claimed, among other things, that the monopoly violated the Privileges or Immunities Clause of the Fourteenth Amendment. The premise of the butchers' argument was that §1 of the Fourteenth Amendment had incorporated the substantive privileges and immunities previously protected by Article IV's Privileges and Immunities Clause, among which was the right to engage in a common calling.

The majority of the Court rejected this argument, reasoning that since the Fourteenth Amendment draws a distinction between citizens of the United States and citizens of a state, the content of the Fourteenth Amendment Privileges or Immunities Clause, which specifically protects the privileges or immunities of U.S. citizens, must differ from the content of the Article IV Privileges and Immunities Clause, which protects the rights of the citizens of one state while visiting in another state. The federal privileges or immunities would not, therefore, replicate the basic liberty and property rights protected by Article IV. Instead, the federal privileges or immunities would be those that pertained to the Union as a whole, such as the right to petition the federal government. The Court's conclusion here was contrary to the original understanding of those who wrote §1 of the Fourteenth Amendment. The net effect of this interpretation was to severely limit the utility of the Fourteenth Amendment Privileges or Immunities Clause. For a discussion of a potential resurrection of the Privileges or Immunities Clause, see Christopher N. May & Allan Ides, *Constitutional Law: National Power and Federalism,* §9.3.1 (The Fourteenth Amendment Privileges or Immunities Clause); and in this volume, §7.4 (The Right to Travel).

The decision in the *Slaughter-House Cases* had several significant effects on subsequent judicial interpretations of the Fourteenth Amendment. First, beginning in the late nineteenth century, the Court began using the Due Process Clause as a vehicle for incorporating various provisions of the Bill of Rights against the states. In this manner, due process came to signify something more than a protection for procedural rights. The "selective incorporation" of the Bill of Rights continued throughout the twentieth century such that most of the Bill of Rights has now been incorporated into the Fourteenth Amendment. See §1.3. In this manner, the Due Process Clause has functioned as a partial surrogate for the moribund Privileges or Immunities Clause.

At about the same time, the Court also began interpreting the Due Process Clause as providing protection for substantive rights not necessarily found in the Bill of Rights. The liberty of contract, for example, was deemed a fundamental right that could not be invaded by the states without sufficient justification. *Allgeyer v. Louisiana,* 165 U.S. 578, 589 (1897). Again, this "substantive" approach to due process operated as a substitute for the judicially eviscerated Privileges or Immunities Clause.

Finally, in the late nineteenth century, the Court began to apply the Equal Protection Clause as something more than a provision for equal enforcement of the law. In *Strauder v. West Virginia*, 100 U.S. (10 Otto) 303 (1880), for example, the Supreme Court struck down a statute that prohibited African Americans from serving on juries. This interpretation of the Equal Protection Clause filled another gap created by the questionable decision in the *Slaughter-House Cases* by putting teeth into the concept of equality in the context of basic civil rights. In addition, the Court interpreted the Equal Protection Clause as applicable to all races, *Yick Wo v. Hopkins*, 118 U.S. 356 (1886), despite what one could characterize as the more narrow focus of the precise circumstances leading to the adoption of the Amendment. The scope of this antidiscrimination thrust was, however, limited by the separate but equal doctrine announced in *Plessy v. Ferguson*, 163 U.S. 537 (1896).

In short, by the end of the nineteenth century, the foundation for the modern law of the Fourteenth Amendment was established. That foundation consists of a combination of the text, the pre- and post-ratification history, the legislative intent, and a developing jurisprudence of interpretation and application. The foundation includes a commitment to the judicial protection of both substantive and procedural rights as well as to an emerging concept of equality under the law.

§1.3   The Incorporation Doctrine

As was noted above, the Bill of Rights by its own force applies only to action by the federal government. However, most of the provisions of the Bill of Rights are now fully enforceable against state or local government action by virtue of the incorporation doctrine, a doctrine through which specific provisions of the Bill of Rights have been absorbed into the Due Process Clause of the Fourteenth Amendment. Thus, if public school students claim a violation of their rights of free speech, the First Amendment, as incorporated by the Due Process Clause of the Fourteenth Amendment, will provide the students with a constitutional basis for their claims. This is so because the First Amendment in effect now operates as a limitation on state and local power by virtue of the Fourteenth Amendment.

The process of absorption began in the late nineteenth century, when the Court held that the taking of private property for public use without just compensation violates "the due process of law required by the Fourteenth Amendment." *Chicago, Burlington & Quincy Railroad Co. v. Chicago*, 166 U.S. 226, 241 (1897). The *Chicago, Burlington* Court did not, however, describe the Takings Clause as having been incorporated by the Fourteenth Amendment; rather, it concluded that the principle of just compensation was "fundamental" to our system of civil liberties and that the Due Process

Clause of the Fourteenth Amendment embraced all such fundamental principles. The question in any case, therefore, was not whether in some technical sense a provision of the Bill of Rights had literally become part of the Fourteenth Amendment, but whether the claimed right was fundamental under our system of justice. Under this approach, not all provisions of the Bill of Rights qualified for inclusion as part of due process. See *Hurtado v. California*, 110 U.S. 516 (1884) (Fifth Amendment requirement of a grand jury indictment not included in Fourteenth Amendment right of due process).

The fundamental rights approach to due process was reaffirmed in *Twining v. New Jersey*, 211 U.S. 78 (1908), where the Court declined to consider whether the Bill of Rights, in its entirety, had been incorporated by the Fourteenth Amendment. Id. at 98. The Court deemed the "weighty arguments" in favor of total incorporation foreclosed by prior decisions applying the fundamental rights model. According to the *Twining* Court, a right is protected by the Due Process Clause "not because [it is] enumerated in the first eight Amendments, but because [it is] of such a nature that [it is] included in the conception of due process of law." Id. at 99.

One of the most articulate and often-quoted descriptions of the fundamental rights approach to due process incorporation is found in Justice Cardozo's opinion for the Court in *Palko v. Connecticut*, 302 U.S. 319 (1937). By the time of that decision, the Court had already recognized that several provisions of the Bill of Rights were enforceable against the states via the Fourteenth Amendment, including the freedoms of speech and religion, the right of assembly, and, to some extent, the right to counsel. At issue in *Palko* was whether the Double Jeopardy Clause of the Fifth Amendment should be included within this panoply of fundamental rights. In particular, the defendant argued that consistent with due process a state could not appeal an acquittal after a jury trial. In rejecting this contention, the Court attempted to draw a principled distinction between those rights included and those rights excluded from due process protection.

> The right to trial by jury and the immunity from prosecution except as the result of an indictment [both of which were excluded from due process at the time *Palko* was decided] may have value and importance. Even so, they are not of the very essence of a scheme of ordered liberty. To abolish them is not to violate a "principle of justice so rooted in the traditions and conscience of our people as to be ranked as fundamental." Few would be so narrow or provincial as to maintain that a fair and enlightened system of justice would be impossible without them. What is true of jury trials and indictments is true also, as the cases show, of the immunity from compulsory self-incrimination. This too might be lost, and justice still be done. . . .
>
> We reach a different plane of social and moral values when we pass to the privileges and immunities that have been taken over from the earlier articles of the federal bill of rights and brought within the

> Fourteenth Amendment by a process of absorption. . . . If the Four-
> teenth Amendment has absorbed them, the process of absorption
> has had its source in the belief that neither liberty nor justice would
> exist if they were sacrificed. This is true, for illustration, of freedom
> of thought, and speech. Of that freedom one may say that it is the
> matrix, the indispensable condition, of nearly every other form of
> freedom.

Id. at 325-327. Applying these principles, the Court concluded that at least insofar as double jeopardy was implicated by the facts before it, no funda-mental principle of justice had been violated. Id. at 328. "The state is not attempting to wear the accused out by a multitude of cases with accumulated trials. It asks no more than this, that the case against him shall go on until there shall be a trial free from the corrosion of substantial legal error." Id.

Justice Cardozo's principled approach to due process does not neces-sarily lead to bright-line conclusions. Quite obviously some degree of sub-jective judgment must be exercised in determining whether any particular right is essential to an ordered system of liberty. And later decisions by the Supreme Court have disagreed with Cardozo's conclusion that the right to a jury trial and the privilege against compulsory self-incrimination were nonfundamental. As the application of the fundamental rights principle in *Palko* indicates, however, the initial tendency of the Court was to be some-what chary of finding an "absorption" into the Fourteenth Amendment.

A very different approach to incorporation was urged by Justice Black. In his famous dissent in *Adamson v. California,* 332 U.S. 46, 68 (1947), Black argued that the authors of the Fourteenth Amendment intentionally designed §1 of that Amendment to make all provisions of the first eight amendments to the Constitution applicable to the states; in other words, one purpose of §1 was, according to Black, to overturn *Barron v. Mayor & City Council of Baltimore* and make the entire Bill of Rights fully enforceable against the states. Black backed his argument with detailed references to the legislative history of the Fourteenth Amendment that tended to support his total-incorporation view. See 332 U.S. at 92-123 (Appendix to Black, J., dissenting). He also challenged the constitutional legitimacy of the funda-mental or "natural" rights model of incorporation, seeing that approach as vesting the judiciary with an unwarranted authority to pick and choose rights according to the fashion of the day. Id. at 86-89. The net result of the Court's approach, according to Black, was that the judiciary was free to ignore vital provisions of the Bill of Rights and at the same time create new rights that had no constitutional warrant. Both practices were, in Black's view, contrary to the principles of limited government and to the very idea of a written Constitution.

During the Warren Court era, Justice John Marshall Harlan became the chief proponent of a variant of the fundamental rights model described in *Palko.* See *Duncan v. Louisiana,* 391 U.S. 145, 171-193 (1968) (Harlan, J., dissenting). In his view, Fourteenth Amendment due process embodied an evolving constitutional standard dependent only on concepts of fundamental fairness and ordered liberty, neither of which was defined or restricted by the provisions of the Bill of Rights. For Harlan, any overlap between the Bill of Rights and due process was "accidental." Id. at 177. Even if the Fourteenth Amendment's Due Process Clause were found to protect some of the same rights protected by the Bill of Rights, the comparable Bill of Rights provision would not be deemed literally "incorporated" into the Fourteenth Amendment. Instead, the two sets of rights would still exist separately, perhaps closely resembling each other, but still separate and distinct. In addition, Harlan's model of due process included the possibility of embracing rights nowhere mentioned in the Constitution. See *Poe v. Ullman*, 367 U.S. 497, 522, 539-555 (1961) (Harlan, J., dissenting) (right of privacy).

Since the early 1960s, the Court has followed a process of incorporation that has increasingly focused on the specific provisions of the Bill of Rights as providing at least a minimal definition of what is fundamental within the American system of liberty and justice. See *Benton v. Maryland*, 395 U.S. 784, 793-796 (1969) (overruling *Palko* and holding that protection against double jeopardy is fundamental for purposes of due process). For example, in *Duncan v. Louisiana*, 391 U.S. 145 (1968), the Court described the inquiry as one focused not on a theoretical system of ordered liberty, but on whether the claimed right was "fundamental to the American scheme of justice." Id. at 149. In this way, the fundamental rights model and the total incorporation model began to converge. As a result, most provisions of the Bill of Rights, particularly those in the context of criminal procedure, have been incorporated into the Fourteenth Amendment through what has been described as a process of selective incorporation. Essentially, the Court concluded, on a case-by-case basis, that each of the incorporated provisions is fundamental within the American system of justice and liberty.

As matters currently stand, the following provisions of the Bill of Rights have been incorporated into the Fourteenth Amendment Due Process Clause:

- the First Amendment in its entirety;
- the Fourth Amendment in its entirety;
- the Fifth Amendment, except for the requirement of a grand jury indictment for criminal prosecutions;
- the Sixth Amendment in its entirety; and
- the Eighth Amendment proscription against cruel and unusual punishments.

The Court has also held that neither the Second Amendment right to bear arms nor the Seventh Amendment right to a jury trial in civil cases is incorporated into the Fourteenth Amendment. See *Presser v. Illinois*, 116

U.S. 252 (1886) (right to bear arms); *Walker v. Sauvinet*, 92 U.S. 90 (1876) (right to a jury trial in civil cases). The Court has not ruled on the incorporation of the Third Amendment's proscription against the quartering of soldiers or the Eighth Amendment's proscriptions against excessive bail and excessive fines.

Although the Court has not been completely consistent on this issue, the standards for measuring the constitutionality of state action potentially inconsistent with an incorporated provision of the Bill of Rights are essentially identical to the standards applied when invoking that same provision as a direct limitation on federal power. See *Benton v. Maryland*, 395 U.S. 784, 795 (1969); *Malloy v. Hogan*, 378 U.S. 1, 10-11 (1964). Justice Harlan, among others, objected to this "jot-for-jot" importation of federal doctrine into the Fourteenth Amendment, see *Duncan v. Louisiana*, 391 U.S. at 181; however, Justice Harlan's call that a more flexible standard of due process be applied against state action has not been followed.

§1.4   The State Action Doctrine

The Fourteenth Amendment expressly limits the power of a "State" to transgress the substantive and procedural rights created by §1 of the Amendment. In other words, the Fourteenth Amendment operates as a limit on "state action," i.e., activity undertaken by a state or local government. Its Due Process and Equal Protection Clauses do not, however, impose any constitutional restraints on purely private activities. Thus, while the term *state* is defined broadly to include all aspects of state and local government, that definition stops short of including activity that is more properly characterized as private in nature. For example, while a public school may not discriminate on the basis of race by virtue of the Equal Protection Clause, there is no such *constitutional* limitation on the activities of a purely private school. The reason is simple: A private school is not the state. (Of course, state and federal civil rights statutes may make discrimination by private schools unlawful.)

The state action requirement of the Fourteenth Amendment is not unique. It follows the pattern of most constitutional limitations. The Bill of Rights, for example, limits the authority of the federal government; it does not impose limitations on private parties. Similarly, limitations on federal and state government power found in the text of the Constitution impose no impediments to private activity. See Art. I, §§9 & 10 (describing various limits on federal and state power). The one notable exception to this pattern is found in the Thirteenth Amendment, which abolishes slavery in both the public and the private spheres. The Fourteenth Amendment, however, follows the general rule and not the exception. In short, the state action requirement of the Fourteenth Amendment mandates that the generally recognized constitutional distinction between government and private activity be followed in all cases applying the restraints imposed by the Fourteenth Amendment, including those incorporated by the Due Process Clause.

Because our focus here is on the application of the Fourteenth Amendment, the problem that we confront is one of "state action." However, you should bear in mind that the same "state action" problem may arise with respect to application of the constitutional provisions that apply to the federal government. In other words, there are times when the conduct of private actors will be deemed to be action of the federal government and, therefore, subject to the constraints of the Bill of Rights.

The principle of state action is easily satisfied when the state or any of its subdivisions, such as a state agency or a city or county, either directly or through an officer or employee, is the perpetrator of the challenged activity. In most such cases, the state action doctrine merits at most a passing reference. Activity undertaken by the state, directly or indirectly, is quite simply state action for purposes of the Fourteenth Amendment. Suppose, for example, that a city police officer, while on duty, engages in what is arguably an unreasonable search. In a Fourteenth Amendment challenge to that activity, the state action requirement is easily satisfied, since the activity at issue was undertaken by an agent of the state under the authority of state law. Moreover, the state action requirement remains satisfied even if the officer acted in violation of state law when conducting the search. *Adickes v. Kress & Co.*, 398 U.S. 144, 152 (1970). As long as the officer acts in an official capacity, the state action requirement is satisfied. (There is one narrow exception to the general rule described in this paragraph. That will be addressed at the end of §1.4.2.)

The state action doctrine is not, however, as simple as the foregoing example may suggest. Although the Fourteenth Amendment does not directly limit private activity, the distinction between state activity and private activity is sometimes quite elusive, and problems of state action tend to arise in situations in which that distinction may be critical. For example, although a private school is not generally considered a state actor, that conclusion might be altered if the state were intimately involved in the day-to-day operations of the school. In such circumstances, the question becomes whether the state is sufficiently implicated in the private activity to transform the latter into state action. Similarly, if a state delegates its governmental powers to a private entity or a private person, that entity or person may, depending on the scope and nature of the delegation, become a state actor for purposes of the Fourteenth Amendment.

Unfortunately, the tools created by the Court for examining these issues are relatively unfocused and are at times as elusive as the distinction they are supposedly designed to assess. This murky jurisprudence is attributable partly to an unresolved philosophical clash between the Warren Court and the later

Burger and Rehnquist Courts. While the Warren Court took an expansive view of state action, thereby increasing the circumstances under which the constitutional protections of the Fourteenth Amendment would apply, particularly in the context of race, the Burger and Rehnquist Courts have tended to apply a version of state action that curtails the realm within which the Fourteenth Amendment operates. Yet despite these very different philosophies, the approach of the latter Courts has been not to overrule prior decisions, but to create distinctions of a more or less ephemeral quality, thus contributing to doctrinal confusion. Add to this mix occasional decisions seeming to go in opposite directions, on the basis, in part, of the underlying constitutional claims and, in part, of policy judgments regarding the scope of judicial review, and you should have a fair idea of the potential confusion that lurks beneath the surface of the state action doctrine.

But one need not despair. The state action doctrine is not completely inaccessible or incoherent. The underlying question in any state action case is relatively simple: Is the state sufficiently implicated in the challenged activity to warrant an application of the Fourteenth Amendment? Moreover, significant landmark decisions provide some guidance in the resolution of that question, at least in the particular contexts to which those decisions may apply. Do not, however, expect complete consistency or mathematical certainty. As the Court has often observed, the state action inquiry is largely fact bound, and therefore each case can be expected to present unique considerations.

One effective way to develop a facility for applying the state action doctrine is to begin by examining four patterns of state action problems that emerged from the Court's efforts to grapple with the underlying doctrine during the post-New Deal and Warren Court eras. Each pattern or category focuses on a particular type of state action problem and at the same time provides insight into the larger state action inquiry. Having considered these somewhat distinct categories and their evolution, the next step is to examine the more generalized approach the modern Court now employs to determine whether the requisites of state action have been satisfied. This latter approach also operates as an overlay on the categorical approach by rationalizing the four patterns into a somewhat unified model that focuses on the responsibility of the state for the challenged action. The discussion that follows is organized around these principles.

One final preliminary point: Many state action cases involve a construction of 42 U.S.C. §1983, the federal civil rights statute that provides a private remedy for action taken "under color of state law." The phrases "state action" and "under color of state law" have been treated as being synonymous. *American Manufacturers Mutual Ins. Co. v. Sullivan,* 526 U.S. 40, 50 n.8 (1999); *Lugar v. Edmondson Oil Co.,* 457 U.S. 922, 928-929 (1982). We will do the same.

§1.4.1   *The Categorical Approach*

The categorical approach to state action focuses on four contexts in which state action has been found. Each category presents a particular type of state action problem, and within each category, special doctrinal rules have developed to help shape the scope of the category. The categories are not, however, completely distinct from one another. They share a common thread of seeking to determine the relationship between the state and the underlying challenged activity. In addition, cases arising in the real world often involve elements of more than one category. Indeed, you may find it useful to view potential state action problems from the perspective of several categories.

Private Performance of a Public Function

The private performance of a public or governmental function may under some circumstances qualify as state action. Stated somewhat differently, if a state permits a private party to exercise what is clearly governmental power, then the activity of the private party will be treated as state action for purposes of the Fourteenth Amendment. This principle is variously referred to as the public function doctrine, the governmental function doctrine, or the sovereign function doctrine. As we will see from the cases, while in theory the scope of this doctrine may appear quite expansive, in practice the actual scope is relatively modest.

One of the leading public function cases is *Marsh v. Alabama*, 326 U.S. 501 (1946). In that case, a Jehovah's Witness claimed a First and Fourteenth Amendment right to distribute literature on the streets and sidewalks of a town that was completely owned and governed by a private company. As described by the Court, "[T]he town and its shopping district are accessible to and freely used by the public in general and there is nothing to distinguish them from any other town and shopping center except the fact that the title to the property [including title to the streets and sidewalks] belongs to a private corporation." Id. at 503. Despite the private ownership and private governance of the town, the Court agreed that the First and Fourteenth Amendments were fully applicable under the circumstances presented. Essentially, by monopolizing all governmental functions within the town, the company had taken on the character of a governmental actor and was, therefore, subject to the same First Amendment restraints applicable to state and local governments. As the Court later described *Marsh,* "[T]he owner of the company town was performing the full spectrum of municipal powers and stood in the shoes of the State." *Lloyd Corp. v. Tanner,* 407 U.S. 551, 569 (1972).

The public function doctrine was also applied successfully in *Smith v. Allwright,* 321 U.S. 649 (1944), a case in which African-American voters from Texas challenged their exclusion from participation in primary elections conducted by the Democratic Party. The Party conducted the primary elections under state statutory authority. Moreover, the results of the primary dictated who could appear on the state's general election ballot. As such, the primary was an integral part of the general election machinery. Given these facts, the Court concluded that the Democratic Party was performing a governmental function as an agent of the state. The racial discrimination practiced by the Democratic Party was, therefore, state action. Id. at 664. See *Terry v. Adams,* 345 U.S. 461 (1953) (similar conclusion with respect to a privately conducted "pre-primary" that, as a practical matter, controlled access to state ballots).

The Court appeared poised to expand the public function doctrine further in the late 1960s, when it held that a privately owned shopping mall is subject to the constraints of the First and Fourteenth Amendments. *Amalgamated Food Employees Union v. Logan Valley Plaza,* 391 U.S. 308 (1968). The Court reasoned that the mall was the "functional equivalent of the business district" at issue in *Marsh v. Alabama.* Id. at 318. The requirement of state action was, therefore, satisfied. The decision in *Logan Valley* was, however, short-lived. Four years later in *Lloyd Corp. v. Tanner,* 407 U.S. 551 (1972), the Court distinguished *Logan Valley* in a manner that cast serious doubt on the continuing legitimacy of the earlier decision. In refusing to find state action on roughly similar facts, the *Lloyd* Court emphasized the unique nature of the facts in *Marsh,* particularly the pervasive scope of the company's authority in that case, suggesting a narrow ambit for the public function doctrine. Finally, in *Hudgens v. NLRB,* 424 U.S. 507 (1976), the Court expressly overruled the decision in *Logan Valley* and again underscored the limited reach of the decision in *Marsh* and of the public function doctrine in general. Id. at 518.

The Court also declined to apply the public function doctrine in *Jackson v. Metropolitan Edison Co.,* 419 U.S. 345 (1974). There, the plaintiff sought to invoke the protections of the Fourteenth Amendment against Metropolitan Edison, a privately owned utility company that had terminated her services. She argued, among other things, that since Metropolitan provided an "essential public service," it performed a public function subjecting its activities to scrutiny under the Fourteenth Amendment. Id. at 352. The Court disagreed: "We have, of course, found state action present in the exercise by a private entity of powers *traditionally exclusively* reserved to the State." Id. (emphasis supplied). The italicized language was meant to and did effectively limit the scope of the public function doctrine. While many municipalities provided public utility services and while even the private provision of such services was marked with a strong public interest, the provision of utility services was not "traditionally exclusively" reserved to the states, but was associated with both the public and the private spheres. By way of contrast, the Court noted that "[i]f we were dealing with the exercise by Metropolitan of some power delegated to it by the State which is traditionally associated with sovereignty, such as eminent domain, our case would be quite a different one." Id. at 352-353. See also *American Manufacturers Mutual Ins. Co. v. Sullivan*, 526 U.S. 40, 54-57 (1999) (private insurer's decision to withhold payment of claim for medical services pending review of claim's validity not traditionally exclusively a public function); *Flagg Bros. v. Brooks*, 436 U.S. 149, 160 (1978) (private sale of stored goods under state law permitting such a sale is not state action, since the resolution of disputes in the commercial world is not the "exclusive prerogative of the sovereign"). The message of *Jackson* was clear: The concept of "public function" is not to be read broadly.

In addition, the fact that the government has funded a private operation for public purposes or public benefit will not necessarily establish that the private operation performs a public function. From the perspective of the modern public function doctrine, the question is not simply whether the government has funded the private activity, but whether that private activity can be fairly characterized as traditionally and exclusively the prerogative of the state. Thus, in *Rendell-Baker v. Kohn*, 457 U.S. 830 (1982), the Court held that although a privately owned school for maladjusted high school students received 90 percent of its operating budget from the state in order to educate children who have been removed from public school, it was not performing a public function. The provision of special educational opportunities for such students is not a traditional and an exclusive function of the state. Id. at 842. See *Blum v. Yaretsky*, 457 U.S. 991, 1011-1012 (1982) (privately owned nursing facility that receives state funding does not perform a public function).

EXAMPLE 1-A

State X requires all persons under the age of 16 residing within the state to attend an accredited elementary or secondary school. The state itself provides an extensive system of public education operated through taxpayer-funded local school districts. In addition, numerous private groups, both sectarian and nonsectarian, provide private education that meets the state's accreditation standards. Mary, who is 15 years old, attends Good Values Prep, a private school accredited by the state. Mary claims that Good Values violated her First and Fourteenth Amendment rights when it punished her for wearing an armband protesting the expulsion of a fellow student. Does Good Values perform a public function by providing students with a state-accredited education?

EXPLANATION

One could certainly argue that schools such as Good Values perform a public function by acting as a surrogate for public schools and by providing a service through which one may comply with the state's mandatory education requirement. Yet given the current status of the public function doctrine, a court is not likely to find that Good Values performs a public function under the given circumstances. While the provision of education through the private sector can be fairly characterized as a public service, perhaps even as an essential public service, education itself has not been *traditionally and exclusively* reserved to the states. Indeed, the "tradition" of public education is a relatively recent phenomenon. In addition, applying the cases, private education seems more like the private utility at issue in *Jackson* than it does the privately run primary election in *Smith v. Allwright*. Education and utility services have long been provided by the private sector. Primary elections, on the other hand, represent a quintessential governmental function as part of the very process of governing. Moreover, the authority exercised by a private school is certainly not as extensive as the quasi-governmental authority exercised by the company-owned town in *Marsh*. Rather, a private school is more like a private shopping mall, both of which exercise authority over a limited private domain. In short, given the Court's relatively strict application of the public function doctrine, Good Values Prep does not perform a public function.

EXAMPLE 1-B

Jails R Us, Inc. (JRU), is a private corporation that owns and operates jails on behalf of municipal governments that wish to privatize their jail operations. The JRU facility accepts prisoners from these municipalities on a contractual basis for a set per diem fee. When an inmate is housed in a JRU facility, he or she is subject to all JRU regulations and to the JRU disciplinary system. Geoffrey, a convicted shoplifter who was transferred to JRU by the City of Metrolex, claims that JRU's disciplinary procedures violate the Fourteenth Amendment. Do the activities of JRU qualify as state action under the public function doctrine?

EXPLANATION

By entering into a contract with JRU to house Geoffrey, Metrolex delegated its governmental authority to JRU, and as a consequence, the corporation operates as an agent for the municipality, i.e., the state. Moreover, since the punishment for crimes has been *traditionally and exclusively* reserved to the states, the housing of prisoners on behalf of a municipality is a public function within the meaning of the public function doctrine. Indeed, operating a prison is akin to conducting primary elections or governing a company-owned town in the sense that all three represent quintessential governmental operations. See *Street v. Corrections Corp. of America*, 102 F.3d 810, 814 (6th Cir. 1996) (private prison under contract with state held to be a state actor performing a public function).

The Judicial Enforcement of Private Agreements

The second category involves the judicial enforcement of private action, which may, under relatively limited circumstances, satisfy the state action requirement. The leading case is *Shelley v. Kraemer*, 334 U.S. 1 (1948). There, the Court considered a Fourteenth Amendment challenge to the judicial enforcement of a covenant that restricted the sale of real property to members of the Caucasian race. The Court recognized that the private agreement to discriminate did not violate the Fourteenth Amendment, since the agreement was between private parties. Id. at 13. The enforcement of the covenant by a judicial officer, however, brought the power of the state into the transaction, and the Court concluded that this state involvement was sufficient to establish the presence of state action. Id. at 19-20. In other words, the judicial enforcement of the private agreement transformed that agreement into state action.

If, as one might assume, the critical element in *Shelley* was the act of judicial enforcement, then presumably whenever a judge enforces a private agreement, the private agreement will be attributed to the state. Thus, in any case in which a party seeks to enforce the provisions of a private contract, the party against whom the contract is being enforced can demand that the enforced contractual provisions comply with the Fourteenth Amendment. The private contract is, by virtue of the judicial involvement, transformed into an act of the state. Similarly, under this theory, a private decision to eject a trespasser may well become the action of the state if the property owner resorts to the judicial process. As a consequence, a decision to eject solely on the basis of the religious beliefs of the trespasser would be unenforceable as contrary to the First and Fourteenth Amendments.

Shelley has not, however, developed along these lines. See *Bell v. Maryland*, 378 U.S. 226, 326-335 (1964) (Black, J., dissenting) (describing *Shelley* as limited to circumstances in which the judiciary intervenes to prevent a property owner from exercising rights guaranteed by the Fourteenth Amendment). The judicial enforcement of a private agreement or private decision does not automatically transform the underlying private activity into state action. To hold otherwise would be to constitutionalize an almost infinite array of private affairs from contracts, to wills, to the testamentary disposition of property. In fact, the critical element in *Shelley* was not simply the judicial enforcement of a private agreement in the abstract, but also the judicial enforcement of a particular type of private agreement, namely, a racially restrictive covenant that limited a willing seller's right to convey his or her property to a willing purchaser. The interposition of the judiciary between these parties, essentially forcing the seller to discriminate on the basis of race, provided the critical factor in the finding of state action. By forcing the seller to discriminate, the court, i.e., the state, became complicit in the otherwise private act of discrimination.

EXAMPLE 1-C

In 1911, General Wallstone bequeathed in trust a large tract of land for use as an all-male military school. Under the terms of the trust, if the school were ever to admit women, the property would revert to General Wallstone's heirs. The trustees have concluded that the all-male admissions policy can no longer be sustained, and they have voted to admit women in the upcoming term. Would a state court order enjoining the trustees from violating the terms of the trust satisfy the state action doctrine as applied in *Shelley v. Kraemer*?

EXPLANATION

Yes. Like the court order in *Shelley*, the order here interposes the judiciary between parties who wish to enter into a legal relationship, and it requires one of the parties to discriminate in a manner that would violate the Fourteenth Amendment if engaged in by the state. See §6.6. Applying *Shelley*, such a judicial order to discriminate satisfies the state action doctrine.

Suppose, however, that the court in Example 1-C applied neutral principles of state law that required it to enforce the reverter clause in General Wallstone's will, thereby returning the property to the general's heirs. Would state action be satisfied under such circumstances? Unquestionably the court's order is state action. The court, after all, is an official representative of the state. But the court's order is itself neutral; it does not discriminate, and it does not require anyone else to do so. Thus, although state action is satisfied with respect to the court's order, there is no violation of the Equal Protection Clause. The more precise question is whether the court's order will transform General Wallstone's private discriminatory intent into state action. The answer is no. As long as the court itself does not discriminate or require discrimination, the enforcement of the terms of General Wallstone's bequest, under otherwise neutral principles of law, will not transform that private activity into state action. See *Evans v. Abney*, 396 U.S. 435, 445-446 (1970). The distinction between this hypothetical and the circumstances presented in *Shelley* is that only in the latter case would the court actually participate in the act of discrimination.

The principle of *Shelley* seems also to have been applied in the context of the First Amendment freedoms of speech and press, although not explicitly so. For example, in *Cohen v. Cowles Media Co.*, 501 U.S. 663 (1991), the Court found that state action is satisfied in a case in which a private party sues a newspaper for breach of a promise of confidentiality. The newspaper raised a First Amendment defense. In a brief discussion of state action, the Court explained, "Our cases teach that the application of state rules of law in state courts in a manner alleged to restrict First Amendment freedoms constitutes 'state action' under the Fourteenth Amendment." Id. at 668. As in *Shelley,* a court order restricting First Amendment freedoms would itself violate the asserted constitutional right.

EXAMPLE 1-D

The *National Snooper* published an article in which it described the police chief of a "northeastern metropolis" as heavily involved in organized crime activities. The allegation was apparently made in reference to Chief Kanner of New York City. Kanner sued the *Snooper* for libel. At trial, Kanner did not submit any evidence that the allegations were false. Nevertheless, the court awarded Kanner $500,000 in damages, holding that under state law, given the egregious nature of the allegations made by the *Snooper,* falsity would be presumed. Would a judicial decree enforcing this judgment satisfy the state action requirement?

EXPLANATION

Yes. Application of state rules of law in state courts in a manner alleged to restrict First Amendment freedoms constitutes state action under the Fourteenth Amendment. Under *New York Times v. Sullivan,* 376 U.S. 254 (1964), the award of damages in *"Kanner v. The National Snooper"* violates the "actual malice" standard required by the First Amendment in cases involving the defamation of public figures. See §8.3.4. Therefore, enforcement of the judgment would constitute state action.

Joint Activity between a State and a Private Party

If a private party and a state engage in joint activity that results in the deprivation of another's constitutional rights, the activity of the private party may be deemed state action, thus subjecting the otherwise private actor to the same restrictions and remedies under the Fourteenth Amendment as are applicable against the state. See *Dennis v. Sparks,* 449 U.S. 24, 27-28 (1980); *Adickes v. Kress & Co.,* 398 U.S. 144, 152 (1970). The determining factors are the nature and the scope of the relationship between the private party and the state. There are two general patterns under which such joint activity has been deemed sufficient to impute state action to otherwise private activity. The first involves concerted or conspiratorial activity between a state actor and a private actor directed toward depriving another individual of his or her constitutional rights. The second involves the creation of a mutually beneficial relationship between a state and a private actor in which the private actor takes action that would violate the Fourteenth Amendment if undertaken by the state. In both cases, the private activity is treated as state action. We will consider each form in turn.

The first form is relatively easy to spot and apply. If a state actor and a private actor undertake concerted activity that operates to deprive another person of his or her constitutional rights, the activity of the private actor will be treated as state action. The presence of the state actor triggers the state action doctrine, while the "joint" nature of the activity brings any accompanying action undertaken by the private actor within the scope of the doctrine. Thus, in *Adickes v. Kress & Co.*, the Court held that allegations that a Kress employee had conspired with a police officer to deprive a schoolteacher of her Fourteenth Amendment rights were sufficient to assert a cause of action against Kress, a private company, for violation of those rights.

EXAMPLE 1-E

Harrison is a reporter for a syndicated "police reality" show. As part of his job, he engages in "ride alongs" with city police officers while the latter are performing their official duties. During one of these ride alongs, Harrison convinces Officer Lucas to break into the hut of Jabba, a suspected gang leader. After the two break in, Harrison films Lucas rummaging through Jabba's hut in search of incriminating evidence. Jabba has now filed suit against Harrison and the officer, claiming that the two engaged in an unlawful search of his hut in violation of his Fourth and Fourteenth Amendment rights. Is the state action requirement satisfied with respect to Harrison?

EXPLANATION

Yes. As a city police officer, Officer Lucas is a state actor, and any activity undertaken by him in his official capacity qualifies as state action. Under the given facts, Lucas's break-in and search of Jabba's hut is, therefore, state action. Moreover, although Harrison is a private citizen, his participation in the break-in and search will also be deemed state action, since Harrison acted in concert with a state actor.

EXAMPLE 1-F

Dr. Livesay sued Captain Flint in order to prevent the latter from removing certain valuable artifacts discovered on property over which Livesay claimed an ownership interest. Flint, however, bribed the presiding judge, the Honorable L.J. Silver, to dismiss the suit with prejudice. After the dismissal, Flint absconded with the goods. Livesay has now sued both Silver and Flint, claiming that the two conspired to deprive him of his property without due process of law. Is the state action requirement satisfied with respect to Flint?

EXPLANATION

Yes. Judge Silver is a state actor acting in an official capacity. His dismissal of Livesay's suit is, therefore, state action. Flint's bribery of Silver makes Flint complicit in that state action, thereby subjecting Flint to the restraints of the Fourteenth Amendment. See *Dennis v. Sparks,* 449 U.S. 24 (1980) (holding that a private party under similar facts remained subject to the Fourteenth Amendment even though the judge who had accepted the bribe was absolutely immune from civil liability).

Private action may also be treated as state action if a state and a private party enter into a mutually beneficial or "symbiotic relationship" within which the private party takes action that would violate the Fourteenth Amendment if undertaken by the state. The classic example of this form is found in *Burton v. Wilmington Parking Authority,* 365 U.S. 715 (1961). There, the Supreme Court found a symbiotic relationship between a city that owned and operated a parking structure and its lessee, a restaurant located within the parking structure that discriminated on the basis of race. Critical to the finding of state action was the fact that the restaurant "constituted a physically and financially integral and, indeed, indispensable part of the State's plan to operate its project as a self-sustaining unit." Id. at 723-724. Furthermore, in the words of the Court,

> [i]t cannot be doubted that the peculiar relationship of the restaurant to the parking facility in which it is located confers on each an incidental variety of mutual benefits. Guests of the restaurant are afforded a convenient place to park their automobiles. . . . Similarly, its convenience for diners may well provide additional demand for the [state's] parking facilities.

Id. at 724. In short, the interdependent and mutually beneficial relationship between the state and the restaurant was sufficient to identify the racially discriminatory practices of the privately owned and operated restaurant as state action. In essence, the state was deemed a "joint participant" in the otherwise private acts of discrimination. Id. at 725.

Not all relationships between a state and a private party will transform the activities of the private party into state action. The critical element is the interdependence of the state and the private actor. In *Moose Lodge v. Irvis,* 407 U.S. 163 (1972), for example, the plaintiff challenged certain racially discriminatory practices of a private club as violative of the Equal Protection Clause. He argued that the private club's state-issued liquor license created a sufficient relationship between the state and the private club to warrant treating the activities of the club as state action. The Court disagreed and, in so doing, distinguished its decision in *Burton:*

Here there is nothing approaching the symbiotic relationship between lessor and lessee that was present in *Burton*, where the private
lessee obtained the benefit of locating in a building owned by the
state-created parking authority, and the parking authority was en-
abled to carry out its primary public purpose of furnishing parking
space by advantageously leasing portions of the building constructed
for that purpose to commercial lessees such as the owner of the
[private restaurant].

Id. at 175. Although in *Moose Lodge* both the state and the club derived some
mutual benefit from the state's licensing and regulatory scheme, that alone
was insufficient to establish the requisite interdependence needed to satisfy
the state action doctrine.

The *Moose Lodge* Court further emphasized that the mere presence of
state regulation or a state licensing scheme will not, standing alone, suffice
to transform private action into state action. Id. at 175-176. Only if the state
regulation mandates the specific activity being challenged will the otherwise
private activity be treated as state action. Id. at 178-179; accord *American
Manufacturers Mutual Ins. Co. v. Sullivan*, 526 U.S. 40, 52 (1999). Thus,
in *Moose Lodge*, the Court found state action to be present because state law
required the club to adhere to its bylaws, which were racially discriminatory;
once that law was enjoined, however, the club's discriminatory practices were
no longer mandated by the state and, therefore, no longer constituted state
action.

EXAMPLE 1-G

Example 1-A considered whether a private secondary school performed a
public function by providing a private school option for satisfying the state's
mandatory education requirement. In that example, Mary argued that the
school violated her First and Fourteenth Amendment rights when it punished
her for wearing an armband. We concluded that the public function doctrine
for finding state action was not satisfied. Considering the same facts, however,
is the relationship between such a private school and the state sufficient to
establish state action under the theory applied in *Burton v. Wilmington
Parking Authority*? In other words, is the relationship between the state and
the private school mutually beneficial to the extent that the activities of the
private school can be imputed to the state?

EXPLANATION

One can certainly argue that the state and the private school mutually benefit
from one another. The state's mandatory education law creates a potential
market for the private schools, and the private schools reduce the overall
expense of public education incurred by the state by taking students out of
the public system. Thus, the case in favor of finding a symbiotic relationship

is stronger than that present in the licensing scheme at issue in *Moose Lodge*, where the state merely licensed and regulated the private actor. On the other hand, the relationship here is not nearly as interdependent as the mutually beneficial economic relationship at issue in *Burton*. In that case, the private restaurant operated as an "indispensable part of the State's plan to operate its project as a self-sustaining unit." 365 U.S. at 723-724. And in the absence of such an interdependent relationship, a court is unlikely to find state action. As a consequence, the more abstract mutual benefit enjoyed by the state and the private school will not be adequate to treat the activities of the school as state action.

Moreover, since the state did not require the school to regulate the wearing of armbands for expressive purposes, state action could not be found on this ground either.

The potential reach of *Burton* in the context of governmental funding of private activity has also been somewhat limited. The mere fact that the government pays for or subsidizes private activity will not establish a symbiotic relationship between the government and the private actor. In *Rendell-Baker v. Kohn*, 457 U.S. 830 (1982), for example, the Court rejected a symbiotic relationship argument in the context of a private school for mal-adjusted high school students that received 90 percent of its funding from the state. Although the state and the school were in a mutually beneficial relationship, there was no showing that the state derived any benefit from the precise activity being challenged, namely, the school's personnel policies. In distinguishing *Burton*, the Court emphasized that the state in that case "profited from the restaurant's discriminatory conduct." Id. at 843. In *Rendell-Baker*, although the state benefited from its relationship with the school, the state derived no particular benefit from the challenged personnel policies.

The *Rendell-Baker* Court's interpretation of *Burton* is somewhat strained, since there was no showing in *Burton* that the state derived any benefit from the discriminatory practices of the restaurant. This reinterpretation is, however, consistent with the modern Court's insistence that private activity be imputed to the state only when the state is somehow responsible for the precise activity being challenged. See §1.4.2. It is also supported by the Court's policy concern that to hold otherwise might subject a vast array of private actions—including that of government contractors and all persons who receive any form of governmental aid — to the constraints of the Constitution.

EXAMPLE 1-H

State T's Department of Agriculture entered an arrangement with Brea University, a private institution, under which the state agreed to fully fund research by the university's agriculture department regarding the effects of certain food additives on pregnant women. The purpose of the research was to provide the Department of Agriculture with information useful to the promotion of agribusiness within the state. The details and method of the research project were left to the discretion of the university. The women subjected to these experiments, although volunteers, were not informed of potential dangers to their health and to the health of the children they were carrying at the time of the experiments. Now, several years later, a number of these women and their children have suffered severe consequences as a result of the experiments. They claim that the university's failure to fully inform them of potential risks violated the Due Process Clause of the Fourteenth Amendment. Did the action of the university constitute state action for purposes of the Fourteenth Amendment?

EXPLANATION

Probably. Unlike the circumstances present in *Rendell-Baker v. Kohn,* the state here directly benefited from the specific program being challenged. Thus, while the state in *Rendell-Baker* had no stake in the personnel policies of the private school, here the state had a strong interest in the actual experiments being undertaken. Indeed, those experiments were undertaken specifically for the benefit of the state. This would seem, therefore, to present a strong example of a symbiotic relationship between the state and a private party. See *Craft v. Vanderbilt Univ.,* 18 F. Supp. 2d 786 (M.D. Tenn. 1998) (so holding under similar facts).

State Endorsement of Private Conduct

The fourth category involves state authorization or encouragement of private conduct that would violate the Fourteenth Amendment if engaged in by the state. The leading case is *Reitman v. Mulkey,* 387 U.S. 369 (1967). At issue in *Reitman* was a provision of the California Constitution that legalized private acts of racial discrimination in the sale or rental of housing. The effect of the provision was not only to repeal then-existing fair housing laws, but also to immunize racial discrimination in housing from all future "legislative, executive, or judicial regulation at any level of the state government." Id. at 377. The question before the Court was whether a private act of discrimination undertaken pursuant to this provision constituted state action. The Court held that it did, relying largely on the California Supreme Court's conclusion that the provision at issue "significantly encourage[d] and involve[d] the State in private discriminations." Id. at 381. Indeed, the history of the provision indicated that its purpose was to authorize and immunize such discriminations.

The key factor in establishing state action in *Reitman* was the finding that the provision at issue affirmatively authorized and encouraged acts of racial discrimination. Id. Had the statute merely repealed existing civil rights legislation, thus leaving the state neutral on the issue of race discrimination in housing, state action would not have been found. Id. at 376. The affirmative endorsement of otherwise private acts of discrimination, however, sufficiently implicated the state in the discriminatory acts to satisfy the state action requirement.

EXAMPLE 1-I

A statute of State Q requires cable television operators within the state to ban "indecent" programming on commercial cable channels, i.e., channels leased to commercial programmers (e.g., HBO, The Movie Channel). CTO owns a cable franchise within State Q, and pursuant to the above statute, CTO has attempted to regulate the "indecent" content on its access channels. Several commercial programmers affected by CTO's actions have filed suit against the company, claiming a violation of their First and Fourteenth Amendment rights. Do the actions of CTO constitute state action?

EXPLANATION

Yes. The state here has not only encouraged but required the particular action being challenged. In other words, the state has not taken a neutral stand, but has affirmatively commanded cable operators to ban indecent programming. Thus, if the ban violates the First Amendment, the private action enforcing the ban is attributable to the state.

The issue of "state endorsement" may also play a role in the finding of state action in other categories. For example, an underlying concern in both *Shelley v. Kraemer* and *Burton v. Wilmington Parking Authority* was the potential perception of state endorsement of private discriminatory action. In *Shelley,* a state court's enforcement of a racially restrictive covenant might be seen as a judicial approval of such covenants. 334 U.S. at 20. Similarly, the public nature of the parking structure in *Burton* seemed to lend the authority of the state to the discriminatory policies of the lessee restaurant. 365 U.S. at 720.

§1.4.2   The Two-Part Approach

In *Lugar v. Edmondson Oil Co.*, 457 U.S. 922 (1982), the Court attempted to distill the state action doctrine into its basic elements:

> Our cases have accordingly insisted that the conduct allegedly causing the deprivation of a federal right be fairly attributable to the

> State. These cases reflect a two-part approach to this question of
> "fair attribution." First, the deprivation must be caused by the exer-
> cise of some right or privilege created by the State or by a rule of
> conduct imposed by the State or by a person for whom the State is
> responsible. . . . Second, the party charged with the deprivation
> must be a person who may fairly be said to be a state actor. This
> may be because he is a state official, because he has acted together
> with or has obtained significant aid from state officials, or because
> his conduct is otherwise chargeable to the State.

Id. at 937. The *Lugar* two-part approach did not create a new test for state
action. Rather, the two-part approach was designed to highlight those factors
that have been deemed significant in what is essentially a fact-bound and
context-driven inquiry, namely, the extent to which any particular action can
or should be deemed attributable to the state for purposes of the Fourteenth
Amendment. The second part of this two-part approach encompasses the
four categories we previously considered, and the first part of the *Lugar*
approach was implicit in the cases around which the categories were constructed. The four categories thus describe specific contexts in which the
state action requirement has been met. For example, one can analyze *Shelley
v. Kraemer* through the lens of *Lugar.* The claimed deprivation in *Shelley* was
caused by a right created by state law, i.e., the right to create racially restrictive
covenants, and the party charged with the deprivation was a state actor
because he obtained significant aid from a state official, namely, the judge to
whom the request for an injunction was addressed. In short, *Lugar*'s two-
part approach synthesizes the earlier cases and focuses our attention on the
specific problem to be resolved in every state action inquiry: Is the state
sufficiently implicated in the challenged activity such that the activity may be
characterized as state action?

Both parts of the two-part approach are sufficiently malleable to allow
a wide latitude for the application of subjective judgment. As a result, one
can expect results under *Lugar* to be somewhat variable, depending on a
combination of the facts, relevant policy concerns, and judicial philosophy.
Of course, this was also true of the more compartmentalized approach under
the categories. Do not think of the two-part approach as a complete substitute for the categorical approach. The separate categories inform the elements of the two-part approach, particularly the second element, and courts,
including the Supreme Court, continue to incorporate the categorical approach when the facts so warrant. *American Manufacturers Mutual Ins. Co.
v. Sullivan,* 526 U.S. 40 (1999) (integrating categorical approach with
two-part approach).

EXAMPLE 1-J

Lowbar was indebted to Edmunson. Edmunson, seeking to secure the debt,
sought prejudgment attachment of certain of Lowbar's property, claiming
that Lowbar was disposing of that property to defeat his creditors. A state

statute allowed Edmunson to obtain an attachment by merely filing an ex parte petition alleging the facts described above. Acting on Edmunson's petition, a clerk of the state court issued a writ of attachment, which was executed by the county sheriff. Lowbar then filed suit in federal court, claiming that Edmunson had acted jointly with the state to deprive him of his property without due process of law. His claim was premised on two separate theories: Under the first, he challenged the constitutionality of the state's prejudgment attachment scheme itself; under the second, he claimed that Edmunson had abused the judicial process. Is the state action requirement satisfied?

EXPLANATION

Under the *Lugar* approach, we must first determine whether the claimed deprivation was "caused by the exercise of some right or privilege created by the State or by a rule of conduct imposed by the state or by a person for whom the State is responsible." *Lugar*, 457 U.S. at 937. Lowbar's first claimed deprivation challenges the attachment right created by the state statute. Therefore, the first element of *Lugar* is satisfied with respect to this claim. As to the second claim, however, this element is not satisfied. Edmunson's alleged *abuse* of the state's attachment process was not created by the state, nor was it imposed by the state or by a person for whom the state was responsible. Rather, the abuse of the state-created attachment scheme was the product of Edmunson's own independent action. Since the *Lugar* two-part approach is conjunctive, we can conclude at this point that Lowbar's second claim does not constitute state action.

Next, with respect to the first claim, we must determine whether Edmunson "may fairly be said to be a state actor. This may be because he is a state official, because he has acted together with or has obtained significant aid from state officials, or because his conduct is otherwise chargeable to the State." Id. Although Edmunson is not a state official, he did act together with, and did obtain significant aid from, state officials, namely, the clerk of the court and the county sheriff. Notice that this conclusion flows directly from the "joint activity" category discussed under the categorical approach. The second element is, therefore, satisfied. As a consequence, Lowbar has established state action with respect to his first claim, the challenge to the constitutionality of the state's prejudgment attachment scheme. See id. at 939-942 (similar conclusion under similar facts).

EXAMPLE 1-K

Brooks's goods were stored in Flagg's warehouse. After Brooks refused to pay the storage costs, Flagg informed her that her property would be sold pursuant to a state law that permitted the private sale of stored goods under such circumstances. Brooks filed suit in federal court, claiming that the threatened sale would violate the Due Process and Equal Protection Clauses of the Fourteenth Amendment. Would Flagg's sale of Brooks's property constitute state action?

EXPLANATION

First, was the claimed deprivation caused by the exercise of some right or privilege created by the state or by a rule of conduct imposed by the state or by a person for whom the state is responsible? Yes. Flagg's right to sell Brooks's property was created by the state. This element is, therefore, satisfied.

Next, was Flagg a state actor: i.e., was he a state official, did he act together with or obtain significant aid from state officials, or was his conduct otherwise chargeable to the state? No. He was not a state official, and the sale did not require the presence of a state official. Compare example 1-J, where the attachment required the participation of state officials. Thus, there is no joint activity here. Moreover, the fact that the right exercised was created by the state is not sufficient to hold that the state is chargeable with the conduct. A more affirmative showing of state complicity is required to satisfy this element. See *Reitman v. Mulkey* (state constitutional right to discriminate in housing implicates state in private action). Therefore, the second element being unsatisfied, Flagg's proposed sale does not constitute state action. See *Flagg Bros. v. Brooks*, 436 U.S. 149 (1978) (so holding on similar facts).

Of course, one could alternatively argue that the power exercised by Flagg was vested in him by the state and that the state should, therefore, assume responsibility for the exercise of that power on the theory that it involved the private performance of a traditional governmental function. This is especially so since the function exercised by Flagg is public in nature and, therefore, attributable to the state. See *Flagg Bros. v. Brooks*, 436 U.S. at 168-179 (Stevens, J., dissenting). The *Flagg* Court, however, rejected this argument, signaling a more restrictive approach to state action.

EXAMPLE 1-L

The National Collegiate Athletic Association (NCAA) is a voluntary association of approximately 960 public and private universities. The role of the NCAA is to adopt rules governing member institutions' recruiting, admissions, academic eligibility, and financial aid standards for student athletes. The NCAA's Committee on Infractions is expressly authorized to conduct investigations into alleged infractions of the rules, to make findings, and to impose sanctions. Member institutions agree contractually to abide by the committee's findings and to comply with any sanctions imposed. The committee conducted such an investigation of the men's ping-pong program at Casino University (CU), a state university and a member of the NCAA. The committee found that Jerry Sharkanian, CU's head ping-pong coach, had violated numerous recruiting rules. As a consequence, the NCAA imposed sanctions on CU and issued an order to show cause why further sanctions should not issue unless CU removed Sharkanian as head coach. The university decided to remove Sharkanian rather than risk further NCAA sanctions. Sharkanian filed suit against both CU and the NCAA, claiming that the committee's hearing procedures violated the Due Process Clause of the Fourteenth Amendment. Did the NCAA's actions constitute state action?

EXPLANATION

First, we must consider whether the claimed deprivation was caused by the exercise of some right or privilege created by the state or by a rule of conduct imposed by the state or by a person for whom the state is responsible. Although the procedures challenged by Sharkanian were created not by the state, but by the NCAA, the privilege to conduct the investigation was delegated to the NCAA by the state (i.e., by CU, a state university). Thus, in holding the hearings and imposing sanctions on CU, the NCAA was exercising a privilege that could not otherwise have been exercised without the approval of the state. Moreover, CU's delegation of authority over university personnel matters would seem to make the NCAA a "person for whom the state is responsible."

Assuming our first conclusion is correct, we must next consider whether the NCAA was a state actor. The NCAA did act together with state officials. The NCAA held an investigation and imposed sanctions. The university, which was contractually bound to the NCAA, adhered to the committee's findings and removed Sharkanian from his position rather than risk further sanctions. Thus, CU and the NCAA acted jointly to deprive Sharkanian of his job, much like a private litigant who bribes a state judge to rule against an opposing party and thereby deprives that party of his or her property. See *Dennis v. Sparks*, 449 U.S. 24 (1980) (discussed in §1.4.1, under Joint Activity).

It would seem, therefore, that the activity of the NCAA constituted state action. However, on facts similar to those described here, the Court ruled otherwise, finding no state action. *National Collegiate Athletic Assn. v. Tarkanian*, 488 U.S. 179 (1988). The five-person majority reasoned that the state university had not delegated its authority to the NCAA, since the university remained free to withdraw from the NCAA at any time. Moreover, the Court said that the fired coach, Jerry Tarkanian, was dismissed by the university and not by the NCAA. Since the final act was undertaken by the state, the preliminary acts of the NCAA would not be construed as state action, particularly since the state could ignore the NCAA's orders by simply withdrawing from the NCAA. Thus, in the majority's view, there was no joint activity between the state university and the NCAA. Id. at 191-199. In terms of the *Lugar* two-part approach, the claimed deprivation of due process was solely the product of private conduct, namely, the NCAA hearing procedures, and not the result of the exercise of a right or privilege created by the state. Nor was the NCAA a state actor. It did not act together with the state, the state being free at all times to withdraw from the NCAA.

The four-person dissent challenged the majority's assertions and argued that the factual pattern presented an unremarkable example of joint activity between a state and a private actor. Id. at 199-203 (White, J., dissenting). Indeed, a strong argument can be made that the state university and the NCAA were involved in a mutually beneficial symbiotic relationship. But, of course, the majority rejected this argument.

Example 1-L contains an important lesson. Under the facts given, one could argue both for and against a finding of state action. Neither the *Lugar* two-part approach nor the categorical approach will provide a definitive answer to the inquiry. Nor will reliance on precedent alone. At best these approaches help focus the discussion and thereby highlight the critical doctrinal differences between opposing views. But those doctrinal differences may belie the policy judgments that are often at the heart of state action decisions. The *Tarkanian* case presents a good example of this phenomenon. Had the Court found state action, a wide array of activities engaged in by the NCAA would have come under constitutional scrutiny, thus creating a new source of constitutional litigation of both uncertain dimensions and equally uncertain consequences. *Tarkanian* foreclosed that possibility on rather thin doctrinal reasoning, leaving one to ponder whether a desire to limit the scope of judicial review did not play a part in the Court's judgment.

EXAMPLE 1-M

A white criminal defendant who was charged in state court with assaulting an African American attempted to exercise his allotted peremptory challenges to exclude African Americans from his jury. The prosecution objected to the defendant's racially discriminatory use of peremptory challenges on the ground that it violated the equal protection rights of potential jurors. Does the use of peremptory challenges by a criminal defendant constitute state action?

EXPLANATION

First, both the existence and the scope of peremptory challenges are created by state law. Thus, the claimed deprivation of equal protection rights under the given facts was the product of a right or privilege having its source in state authority. The first part of *Lugar* is, therefore, satisfied.

As to the second part of *Lugar*, the defendant's exercise of peremptory challenges constitutes joint activity with the state, since it could not be accomplished without the assistance of the state judge. Indeed, the entire jury selection system is dependent on participation by state officers and the force of state law. As a consequence, a criminal defendant exercising peremptory challenges on a racially discriminatory basis will be deemed a state actor, and the state action requirements are, therefore, met. See *Georgia v. McCollum*, 505 U.S. 42, 50-53 (1992) (so holding on similar facts); see also *Edmonson v. Leesville Concrete Co.*, 500 U.S. 614 (1991) (private litigant exercising peremptory challenges is state actor).

Georgia v. McCollum, on which Example 1-M is based, also presents an example of policy playing a role in a finding of state action. As part of its *Lugar* analysis, the Court emphasized the negative consequences of permitting a criminal defendant to employ racially discriminatory peremptory challenges. "Regardless of who precipitated the jurors' removal, the perception and the reality in a criminal trial will be that the court has excused jurors based on race, an outcome that will be attributed to the State." 505 U.S. at 53. This is much the same policy concern that animated the Court in *Shelley v. Kraemer*, where the Court found that a state court's enforcement of a racially restrictive covenant violates the Equal Protection Clause. There, the "perception and the reality" would have been that the court was forcing private parties to discriminate on the basis of race. A similar perception problem may have played a role in *Burton v. Wilmington Parking Authority*, where the restaurant that discriminated on the basis of race was located in a building that bore the city's name and flew the state flag.

A State Actor Anomaly

As should be evident by now, problems in the context of state action focus largely on those circumstances under which the activities of a private party may be said to qualify as state action. When the party being sued is an officer or employee of the state, the difficulty disappears, and as Justice White observed in *Lugar*, the two-part inquiry collapses into a single principle. 457 U.S. at 937. A state officer, when operating in an official capacity, is a state actor whose activities stem from a right or privilege created by state law. Thus, state action is easily satisfied under such circumstances. There is, however, one narrow exception to this rule.

In *Polk County v. Dodson*, 454 U.S. 312 (1981), the Court held that the activities of a public defender undertaken in the normal course of representing a criminal defendant do not constitute state action. Although the public defender was a public employee, the Court explained that the public defender, as an attorney, was professionally independent from and in fact an adversary of the state in representing her client. In essence, the public defender's actions were a private matter that could not be attributed to the state. Id. at 319-324. Thus, the special nature of the attorney-client relationship altered the almost universally applicable rule that activities by state officers or employees constitute state action.

The Court has not applied *Polk County* beyond the specific context of that case. See *Tower v. Glover,* 467 U.S. 914, 920 (1984) (conspiracy between public defender and other state officials to secure criminal defendant's conviction constitutes state action). In *West v. Atkins,* 487 U.S. 42 (1988), the Court held that the activities of a doctor under contract with a state constitute state action despite the professional status of the doctor. The Court distinguished *Polk County* as involving the unique ethical obligations of a criminal defense attorney who was an adversary to the state. Id. at 50-52. In general, therefore, the activities of professionals employed by or under contract to a state are attributable to the state under *Lugar.* Id. at 52.

§1.5   Congressional Enforcement of the Civil War Amendments

The Thirteenth, Fourteenth, and Fifteenth Amendments each include a clause that grants Congress the power to enforce the provisions of the underlying Amendment. Much of this country's civil rights legislation is premised on these enforcement clauses. Their scope, therefore, can be of critical importance. Note, however, that civil rights legislation may also be premised on other granted powers, including those found in Article I, §8. *Heart of Atlanta Motel, Inc. v. United States,* 379 U.S. 241 (1964) (affirming use of Commerce Clause to validate the Civil Rights Act of 1964); *Katzenbach v. McClung,* 379 U.S. 294 (1964) (same); Christopher N. May & Allan Ides, *Constitutional Law: National Powers and Federalism,* ch. 5 (2001). In the sections that follow, however, our focus will be solely on the enforcement powers created by the Civil War Amendments. You should, nonetheless, cross-reference these materials with your understanding of the overall scope of congressional powers.

§1.5.1   *Enforcement of the Thirteenth Amendment*

The Thirteenth Amendment to the U.S. Constitution expressly abolishes slavery within the United States:

> Neither slavery nor involuntary servitude, except as a punishment
> for crime whereof the party shall have been duly convicted, shall ex-
> ist within the United States, or any place subject to their jurisdiction.

U.S. Const. amend. 13, §1. The abolition is self-executing, and unlike the
Fourteenth Amendment, its force applies to both state and private action.
Civil Rights Cases, 109 U.S. 3, 20-23 (1883). Thus, with the adoption of
the Thirteenth Amendment, all forms of slavery or involuntary servitude,
both public and private, were banned within the United States.

Despite the self-executing quality of the abolition, however, the authors
of the Thirteenth Amendment recognized that legislation would be required
to enforce the grant of universal freedom. To that end, §2 of the Thirteenth
Amendment provides that "Congress shall have power to enforce this article
by appropriate legislation." This grant of power "clothes Congress with
power to pass all laws necessary and proper for abolishing all *badges and
incidents* of slavery in the United States." Id. at 20 (emphasis supplied).
Given the scope of the Thirteenth Amendment, that power may be addressed
to both public and private conduct.

In the *Civil Rights Cases,* the Court provided a partial list of what it
considered to be the badges and incidents of slavery:

> Compulsory service of the slave for the benefit of the master, re-
> straint of his movements except by the master's will, disability to
> hold property, to make contracts, to have a standing in court, to be
> a witness against a white person, and such like burdens and incapaci-
> ties, were the inseparable incidents of the institution.

Id. at 22. Under §2 of the Amendment, Congress has the power to pass
legislation designed to eradicate all such practices.

The most important modern case interpreting and applying the Thir-
teenth Amendment is *Jones v. Alfred H. Mayer Co.,* 392 U.S. 409 (1968).
The controversy in *Jones* arose out of a private company's refusal to sell a
home to an African-American couple. The couple brought suit under 42
U.S.C. §1982, a statute passed pursuant to the Thirteenth Amendment.
Section 1982 provides:

> All citizens of the United States shall have the same right, in every
> State and Territory, as is enjoyed by white citizens thereof to inherit,
> purchase, lease, sell, hold, and convey real and personal property.

The lower courts dismissed the suit, having concluded that §1982 applied
only to state action. Two questions were presented to the Supreme Court:
First, did the statute apply to private action; second, if so, was the statute a
valid exercise of Congress' power to enforce the Thirteenth Amendment?

The Court first concluded that the plain language of the statute prohibited all racial discrimination, both public and private, in the sale or rental of
property. 392 U.S. at 422-436. Next, the Court explained that the authority

given to Congress under §2 of the Thirteenth Amendment included the power to enact laws that directly regulate the activities of private individuals. Id. at 438. This was so because the Thirteenth Amendment itself was directed at all forms of slavery, both public and private. Id. The only question, therefore, was whether Congress had authority to conclude that racial barriers to the acquisition of property were a badge or incident of slavery. In answering this question, the Court adopted a deferential rational basis test:

> Surely Congress has the power under the Thirteenth Amendment rationally to determine what are the badges and the incidents of slavery, and the authority to translate that determination into effective legislation. Nor can we say that the determination Congress has made is an irrational one. For this Court recognized long ago that, whatever else they may have encompassed, the badges and incidents of slavery — its "burdens and disabilities" — included restraints upon "those fundamental rights which are the essence of civil freedom, namely, the same right . . . to inherit, purchase, lease, sell and convey property, as is enjoyed by white citizens."

Id. at 440-441 (quoting *Civil Rights Cases,* 109 U.S. at 22). Later in its opinion, the Court observed, "If Congress cannot say that being a free man means at least this much, then the Thirteenth Amendment made a promise the Nation cannot keep." Id. at 443.

Under *Jones,* therefore, the scope of the congressional power to enforce the Thirteenth Amendment is measured by the rationality of a congressional determination that the activity being regulated or prohibited is a badge or incident of slavery. This is a deferential standard designed to recognize the broad latitude of the authority vested in Congress by §2 of the Thirteenth Amendment.

EXAMPLE 1-N

Title 42 U.S.C. §1981 provides that "[a]ll persons within the jurisdiction of the United States shall have the same right in every State . . . to make and enforce contracts . . . as is enjoyed by white citizens. . . ." By judicial construction, §1981 applies to private action. The African-American parents of a child who had been denied admission to a private school because of the child's race brought suit against the school under §1981. They argued that the school had refused to enter into a contract with them because of their race. The trial court first held that §1981 applied to the facts before it. The refusal to admit was a refusal to enter into a contract, and since the refusal was racially motivated, the proscription of §1981 applied. Given this construction, does §1981 represent a constitutional exercise of congressional power under the Thirteenth Amendment?

EXPLANATION

Yes. Like the right to purchase property, the right to make or enter into contracts is a basic civil right that was denied to slaves. As a consequence, both rights were recognized in the *Civil Rights Cases* as badges and incidents of slavery. 109 U.S. at 22. Thus, Congress could rationally conclude that a racial barrier to the making of a contract is a badge or incident of slavery. That being the case, §1981 falls squarely within the enforcement power granted to Congress by §2 of the Thirteenth Amendment. See *Runyon v. McCrary*, 427 U.S. 160, 179 (1976) (so holding under similar facts). The fact that §1981 regulates private activity does not alter this conclusion, since the Thirteenth Amendment limits both private and public activity.

EXAMPLE 1-O

John and Julia, both of whom are African-American college students, spent their summer vacation working as volunteers in a voter registration program in a large, rural county in Mississippi. One evening while they were driving along a country road, they were stopped at gunpoint by three local white residents. While two of the locals pointed guns at the couple, the third beat John and Julia severely and threatened to kill them if they did not leave the community. John and Julia have filed suit against their three assailants under 42 U.S.C. §1985(3), which provides a cause of action against anyone who conspires to deprive "any person or class of persons of the equal protection of the laws, or of the equal privileges and immunities under the laws." On the correct assumption that §1985(3) applies under the given facts, does the statute come within Congress' §2 powers under the Thirteenth Amendment?

EXPLANATION

Yes. John and Julia were engaged in the exercise of a basic civil right, namely, the right to use public highways and thoroughfares. This is a right that the law secures to all free members of society. Hence, a private conspiracy to deny that right to African Americans can be rationally described as a badge or incident of slavery.

The preceding example was based loosely on the facts of *Griffin v. Breckenridge*, 403 U.S. 88 (1971), where the Court observed:

[T]he varieties of private conduct that [Congress] may make criminally punishable or civilly remediable extend far beyond the actual imposition of slavery or involuntary servitude. By the Thirteenth Amendment, we committed ourselves as a Nation to the proposition that the former slaves and their descendants should be forever

> free. . . . We can only conclude that Congress was wholly within its powers under §2 of the Thirteenth Amendment in creating a statutory cause of action for Negro citizens who have been the victims of conspiratorial, racially discriminatory private action aimed at depriving them of the basic rights that the law secures to all free men.

Id. at 105.

The concept of a badge or incident of slavery is not, however, completely elastic. In *Memphis v. Greene,* 451 U.S. 100, 124-129 (1981), for example, the Court held that the closing of a street that incidentally set up a barrier between white and African-American communities was not a badge or incident of slavery. Yet the Court's conclusion may well have been different had there been evidence establishing that the street closing was purposefully designed to segregate these neighborhoods.

The Court has yet to hold that the Thirteenth Amendment enforcement power may be exercised beyond the context of racial discriminations. See *Bray v. Alexandria Women's Health Clinic,* 506 U.S. 263, 269 (1993) (declining to decide whether animus toward women falls within the proscription of §1985(3)). The Court has, however, construed statutes enforcing the Thirteenth Amendment as including discriminations against groups other than African Americans. See *Shaare Tefila Congregation v. Cobb,* 481 U.S. 615 (1987) (person of Jewish ancestry may state a cause of action under §1982); *Saint Francis College v. Al-Khazraji,* 481 U.S. 604 (1987) (person of Arab ancestry may state a cause of action under §1981); *McDonald v. Santa Fe Trail Transp. Co.,* 427 U.S. 273, 285-296 (1976) (white person may state a cause of action under §1981).

§1.5.2 Enforcement of the Fourteenth Amendment

Section 5 of the Fourteenth Amendment provides, "The Congress shall have power to enforce, by appropriate legislation, the provisions of this article." Pursuant to this grant of authority, Congress may adopt measures it deems necessary and proper to the implementation or enforcement of the provisions of §1 of that Amendment — specifically, the Privileges or Immunities, Due Process, and Equal Protection Clauses. Given the *Slaughter-House Cases'* relatively limited interpretation of the Fourteenth Amendment privileges or immunities, the primary, if not exclusive, focus of the Fourteenth Amendment enforcement power has been the enforcement of the due process and equal protection guarantees.

As a general matter, the scope of the Fourteenth Amendment enforcement power is as broad in its context as is the authority vested in Congress by the Necessary and Proper Clause in Article 1, §8. *Katzenbach v. Morgan,* 384 U.S. 641, 650 (1966). The Court's decision in *McCulloch v. Maryland,* 17 U.S. (4 Wheat.) 316 (1819), therefore, provides the guiding principles:

> Let the end be legitimate, let it be within the scope of the constitution, and all means which are appropriate, which are plainly adapted to that end, which are not prohibited, but consist with the letter and spirit of the constitution, are constitutional.

Id. at 421; see *Katzenbach v. Morgan*, 384 U.S. at 650-658 (applying *McCulloch* standards in context of Fourteenth Amendment enforcement power).

The standards of *McCulloch* do not, however, vest Congress with an unreviewable authority to interpret the Fourteenth Amendment. Rather, at least in the Court's view, §5 vests Congress only with a discretion, albeit quite broad, to select the "means" through which to enforce the underlying constitutional guarantees, the definition of which remains largely a judicial prerogative. In other words, the §5 enforcement power does not vest Congress with the authority to define the scope of Fourteenth Amendment rights; instead, it grants Congress the power only to enact measures designed to remedy or prevent violations of rights that are ultimately defined in the process of judicial review. Of course, in enforcing constitutional rights, Congress must engage in a process of interpretation, but whatever interpretation Congress may adopt will be subject to judicial review. As a consequence, before we can determine whether any particular exercise of the enforcement power is within constitutional bounds, we must first define the scope of the right to be enforced.

Problems surrounding the application of the §5 enforcement power can be seen as clustered around three types of remedial measures:

1. those that require the plaintiff to prove the violation of a judicially recognized Fourteenth Amendment right;
2. those that do not require plaintiff to prove a violation of a judicially recognized Fourteenth Amendment right, but which are nonetheless designed to remedy or prevent the violation of a judicially recognized right; and
3. those that purport to create Fourteenth Amendment rights not recognized by the judiciary.

The first category we will refer to as parallel enforcement, the second as nonparallel enforcement, and the third as congressional interpretation.

Parallel Enforcement

Parallel enforcement occurs when the congressionally created remedy encompasses all elements of the judicially recognized Fourteenth Amendment right. Essentially, the test here is one of rational basis. Could Congress rationally conclude that the adopted enforcement mechanism, e.g., a private action for money damages to remedy the violation of a constitutional right, was an "appropriate" measure to redress or prevent violation of that right? Consistent with the jurisprudence of *McCulloch v. Maryland,* a Court is quite unlikely to second-guess congressional judgment on this score. The creation of such "parallel" private rights of action represent a standard and constitutional exercise of the Fourteenth Amendment enforcement power.

Consider the equal protection proscription against racial discrimination. As we will discuss in further detail in Chapter 6, under the Equal Protection Clause, a state, including its agencies and officers, may not intentionally discriminate on the basis of race except under the narrowest of circumstances. In order to establish a violation of this equal protection principle, a victim of such discrimination must prove both state action and the prima facie elements of purposeful racial classification and disproportionate impact. In order to enforce this right, Congress could create a private civil remedy for money damages or equitable relief. As long as the statutory scheme required the plaintiff to prove all the elements of an equal protection claim—namely, state action, purposeful racial classification, and disproportionate impact — the congressionally created remedy would easily pass muster as an exercise of the Fourteenth Amendment enforcement power. Such a parallel measure represents a rational method for enforcing the underlying and judicially recognized constitutional right.

EXAMPLE 1-P

Eugene, a Japanese American, claims that he was dismissed from his position at State University because of his Asian heritage. He has filed a lawsuit against his supervisor, Smith, seeking reinstatement and back pay. In so doing, Eugene relies on a federal statute that creates a private civil action for the violation of civil rights. In order to prevail under the statute, Eugene must show that Smith acted "under color of state law" and that Smith's actions denied him "equal protection of the law." Does this statute represent a constitutional exercise of Congress's Fourteenth Amendment enforcement power?

EXPLANATION

Yes. If we assume that "equal protection of the law" means equal protection as defined by the judicial branch, then Eugene will be required to establish a prima facie equal protection violation in order to prevail. Moreover, the "color of state law" requirement is, as was noted above, the virtual equivalent of state action. Therefore, this federal statute represents an unremarkable application of the Fourteenth Amendment enforcement power through which Congress has provided a remedy for the violation of a judicially recognized Fourteenth Amendment right. There is nothing to indicate that this remedial scheme is irrational.

The Court has never held a parallel enforcement mechanism to be beyond Congress's §5 enforcement power.

Nonparallel Enforcement

Nonparallel enforcement occurs when Congress designs a remedy for the enforcement of a judicially recognized constitutional right, but allows that remedy to be invoked without requiring the plaintiff to establish a violation of the right. For example, Congress may not require the plaintiff to prove every element of the constitutional right, or Congress may create a completely new statutory right designed to insulate the constitutional right from violation. To establish the constitutionality of such measures Congress must show that the nonparallel enforcement mechanism is designed to remedy the violation of a judicially recognized constitutional right and that the remedy is tailored to accomplish that goal. The test is sometimes characterized as one of rational basis, though recently the Court seems to have adopted a somewhat closer level of scrutiny. The reason for this closer scrutiny stems in part from the current Court's concern for state sovereignty.

EXAMPLE 1-Q

Suppose that the statute described in Example 1-P provided that purposeful racial discrimination would be presumed if the plaintiff showed that he had been dismissed from his job, that he was a member of a racial minority, and that the person hired as a replacement was not a member of a racial minority. The state could rebut the presumption only by showing that race was not a factor in the dismissal. Thus, Eugene could prevail under this statute without proving a necessary element of an equal protection violation, namely, purposeful discrimination. Would such a statute be valid as an exercise of Congress' §5 enforcement power?

EXPLANATION

The constitutionality of this congressional action depends on whether Congress acted rationally in devising this remedial scheme. In other words, did Congress have reasonable grounds to believe that a presumption of intent under such circumstances was appropriate to the enforcement of a judicially recognized Fourteenth Amendment right? Possibly. Suppose that Congress concluded that proof of racially motivated intent in state employment discrimination cases was particularly problematic because such intent was rarely documented and could be easily hidden behind ostensibly neutral justifications. Moreover, suppose that Congress found that due to such problems of proof, the full vindication of equal protection rights in the state employment context was threatened. Under such circumstances, a court may well find that Congress had acted within its §5 enforcement powers. This is particularly so because the statute is narrowly focused on a particular type of problem, namely, racial discrimination in state employment, and because it provides a mechanism under which the state can rebut the presumption of intent. As a consequence, the remedy is not likely to be viewed as overly intrusive into state employment policies.

Another variation of this second category occurs with statutes that create federal rights that are not themselves embodied in the Fourteenth Amendment, but that are designed to ensure the full vindication of Fourteenth Amendment rights. This was the type of problem presented to the Court in *Katzenbach v. Morgan*, 384 U.S. 641 (1966). At issue there was a section of the Voting Rights Act of 1965 that prohibited states from denying the right to vote to certain Puerto Ricans who could not read or write English. In other words, the Voting Rights Act created a federal right to be free from literacy tests under specified circumstances. The Court had previously held that the Fourteenth Amendment did not itself create any such right. *Lassiter v. Northampton Election Bd.*, 360 U.S. 45 (1959). Nonetheless, the Court upheld this section of the Voting Rights Act as an appropriate exercise of the Fourteenth Amendment enforcement power. In the Court's words,

> It was well within congressional authority to say that this need of the Puerto Rican minority for the vote warranted federal intrusion upon any state interests served by the English literacy requirement. It was for Congress, as the branch that made this judgment, to assess and weigh the various conflicting considerations — *the risk or pervasiveness of the discrimination in governmental services,* the effectiveness of eliminating the state restriction on the right to vote as a means of dealing with the evil, the adequacy or availability of alternative remedies, and the nature and significance of the state interests that would be affected by the nullification of the English literacy requirement. . . . It is not for us to review the congressional resolution of these factors. It is enough that we be able to perceive a basis upon which the Congress might resolve the conflict as it did.

384 U.S. at 653 (emphasis supplied). In short, the Court deferred to the congressional judgment that the literacy test ban was a rational means to prevent violations of the equal protection guarantee against racial discrimination in the provision of governmental services.

Katzenbach was decided during an era in which the Court was highly deferential to exercises of congressional power, and particularly so in the context of civil rights. Although *Katzenbach* continues to be cited authoritatively, the current Court is, as you may be aware, much less solicitous of broad assertions of congressional power, especially when those assertions interfere with what the Court perceives as the traditional prerogatives of the states. See Christopher N. May & Allan Ides, *Constitutional Law: National Power and Federalism*, §4.2.7 (restrictions on congressional abrogation of Eleventh Amendment immunity); §5.3.4 (restrictions on commerce power). That less deferential judicial attitude has led to what may be described as a tightening of the standards under which nonparallel exercises of the §5 enforcement power are now measured. Under these new standards, if Congress creates a nonparallel statutory right, the exercise of power will be upheld only if the statutory right is "congruent" with judicially recognized constitutional rights and "proportional" in terms of the remedy it provides. In other words, it must be shown that the statutory right is truly designed to protect a judicially recognized constitutional right and that the remedy is in proportion to the scope of the perceived constitutional violation. As you will see, the judicial scrutiny of congruence and proportionality is not particularly deferential.

The Court first applied these principles in *City of Boerne v. Flores*, 521 U.S. 507 (1997). There the Court held that Congress had exceeded its §5 power in enacting the Religious Freedom Restoration Act (RFRA). RFRA was passed in response to the Court's decision in *Employment Division v. Smith*, 494 U.S. 872 (1990). In *Smith*, the Court had held that the Free Exercise Clause, as incorporated by the Fourteenth Amendment, does not prevent a state from punishing the use of peyote by a practicing member of the Native American Church. This is so even though the ingestion of peyote is an integral part of the church's system of worship. Since the law at issue was neutral from a religious perspective, i.e., it applied to all uses of peyote regardless of the user's religious beliefs or practices, the Court found no violation of the Free Exercise Clause despite the impact of the law on the practices of the Native American Church. According to the *Smith* Court, as long as a law is not purposefully directed at religious practices, i.e., as long as the law is neutral and of general applicability, it can be enforced without violating the proscriptions of the Free Exercise Clause. This remains true even if the law incidentally and substantially interferes with a religious practice. See §9.5. Under *Smith*, therefore, only laws designed to prohibit a religious practice because of the religious nature of that practice will run afoul of the First and Fourteenth Amendments.

RFRA was enacted to overrule *Smith* and to require the application of a compelling state interest test whenever any law, enacted at any level of government, substantially burdens a religious practice regardless of the law's perceived neutrality. For example, under RFRA, a neutral law banning the use of peyote could not be applied against a member of the Native American Church in the absence of a compelling state interest and a showing that the ban represented the least restrictive means to advance that interest.

Supporters of RFRA argued that the statute was remedial in nature and, therefore, within the scope of §5 as interpreted in *Katzenbach v. Morgan*. In their view, RFRA was designed to ferret out ostensibly neutral laws that were enacted for purposes of religious bigotry. As such, RFRA would in fact operate as a nonparallel remedial or preventive measure designed to enforce the precise free exercise right defined in *Smith*, namely, the proscription of laws purposefully designed to regulate or prohibit religious practices. The Court, however, did not accept this argument.

The Court began with the proposition that "[w]hile preventive rules are sometimes appropriate remedial measures, there must be a congruence between the means used and the ends to be achieved." 521 U.S. at 530. The Court then examined the legislative history of RFRA and found it bereft of examples of "modern instances of generally applicable laws passed because of religious bigotry." Id. Although that legislative history did include modern examples of neutral laws that adversely affected religious practices, there was no showing that those incidental burdens were the product of religious bigotry or bias. As the Court phrased it, "Congress' concern was with the incidental burdens imposed, not the object or purpose of the legislation." Id. From the perspective of this legislative history, therefore, RFRA seemed to be designed not to vindicate a judicially recognized right, but to create a new right, broader in scope than any free exercise right currently recognized by the judicial branch.

More important than the absence of legislative history, however, was the lack of what the Court described as "proportionality" between the "sweeping coverage" of RFRA — a permanent and undifferentiated proscription that applied to every facet and level of government — and the violation of any perceived Fourteenth Amendment right.

> Sweeping coverage ensures its intrusion at every level of government, displacing laws and prohibiting official actions of almost every description and regardless of subject matter. . . . RFRA has no termination date or termination mechanism. Any law is subject to challenge at any time by any individual who alleges a substantial burden on his or her free exercise of religion.

Id. at 532. The Court further noted that prior exercises of the §5 power had been carefully designed to address specific and sometimes notorious violations of Fourteenth Amendment rights. Thus, provisions of the Voting Rights Act subjecting states to Department of Justice review were limited in application to those states with a history of intentional racial discrimination in voting. As the Court observed,

> This is not to say, of course, that §5 legislation requires termination dates, geographic restrictions or egregious predicates. Where, however, a congressional enactment pervasively prohibits constitutional state action in an effort to remedy or to prevent unconstitutional state action, limitations of this kind tend to ensure Congress' means are proportionate to ends legitimate under §5.

Id. at 533.

In short, RFRA failed to pass constitutional muster because, in the Court's view, the broad remedy Congress created was substantially more intrusive on state prerogatives than was warranted by the undifferentiated fear that religious bigotry might be imposed through the adoption of ostensibly neutral laws. After *Boerne,* therefore, congressional remedies that do not require a party to establish a violation of a Fourteenth Amendment right, i.e., nonparallel remedies, must be congruent and proportionate to the perceived violation of Fourteenth Amendment rights. Factors to consider in this assessment include identification of the precise constitutional evil Congress seeks to remedy, the breadth of the remedy, the depth and pervasiveness of the problem being addressed, and any factors tending to limit the scope of the actual remedy to the precise problem Congress seeks to remedy. The more generalized the perceived evil and the congressional response to it and the more intrusive that response is on state prerogatives, the less likely it is that a Court will find congruence and proportionality satisfied.

The Court applied the *City of Boerne* congruence and proportionality test in two cases involving congressional efforts to abrogate a state's Eleventh Amendment immunity. In both cases, the Court found that the congressional measure failed the test. In *Florida Prepaid Postsecondary Education Expense Board v. College Savings Bank,* 527 U.S. 627 (1999), a case involving the enforcement of federal patent laws, the Court found a lack of congruence and proportionality between the abrogation of the state's immunity and any underlying constitutional right. Specifically, there was no showing of a pattern under which states were violating the constitutional rights of patent holders. Hence, the §5 enforcement powers were not an appropriate vehicle for abrogating the state's immunity. Similarly, in *Kimel v. Florida Board of Regents,* 120 S. Ct. 631 (2000), the Court found no congruence or proportionality between the provisions of the Age Discrimination in Employment Act (ADEA) and any underlying constitutional right to be free from age discrimination. Id. at 647. The state could not, therefore, be sued for statutory violations of the ADEA. The flaw in both cases was the failure of Congress to connect the remedy it was creating with the protection of a judicially recognized constitutional right. See Christopher N. May & Allan Ides, *Constitutional Law: National Power and Federalism,* §4.2.7 (2001).

EXAMPLE 1-R

Christy, a student at State University, was raped by a member of the university's varsity football team. Her assailant later publicly boasted of what he had done. Moreover, at a hearing before a university disciplinary committee, he admitted to having sexual contact with Christy even though she had twice told him "no." He was found guilty of sexual assault and suspended from school for two semesters. On appeal, the university rescinded his punishment as "too severe." Christy then filed a civil lawsuit against her assailant under a federal statute, the Violence Against Women Act (VAWA), that provided a federal civil remedy for the victims of gender-motivated violence. In order to establish a claim under VAWA, Christy would have to show by a preponderance of the evidence that she was the victim of a violent assault by the defendant and that the assault was at least in part motivated by her gender.

Prior to adopting VAWA, Congress held hearings that established a nationwide pattern of bias in state justice systems against the enforcement of gender-based crimes. Among other things, Congress found that this pattern of bias often resulted in insufficient investigation and prosecution of gender-motivated crime and unacceptably lenient punishments for those who are actually convicted of such crimes. While Congress did not survey every state, the information Congress gathered led it to conclude that the problem was pervasive. VAWA was designed to provide a partial remedy for this apparent pattern of gender discrimination in state law enforcement and judicial systems. Does the civil remedy created by VAWA represent a proper exercise of Congress's §5 enforcement powers?

EXPLANATION

In order to evaluate the constitutionality of VAWA's civil remedy, we must determine if the principles of "congruence" and "proportionality" have been satisfied. We begin with congruence and the underlying constitutional right, namely, the right to be free from gender discrimination in the administration of justice by the states. So described, the underlying right Congress seeks to redress appears to be congruent with the Court's standards for protecting against gender classifications under the Equal Protection Clause. See §6.6. State action is satisfied since the focus is on state criminal justice systems, and the basic elements of a gender discrimination claim seem to be met as well, i.e., purposefulness and impact. Thus, unlike the situation in *City of Boerne v. Flores* where Congress was seeking to protect a right the Court did not recognize, under VAWA Congress is trying to redress violations of a well-established constitutional right. Next, as to proportionality, the civil action remedy is broad-based and seemingly permanent, but it does not in any manner intrude into the processes of state government as did the remedy at issue in *City of Boerne*. Moreover, the breadth of the remedy, i.e., its nationwide availability, can be justified as a reasonable response to findings that indicated the presence of gender bias in the justice systems of a substantial number of states. By way of comparison, in *City of Boerne*, the breadth of the remedy easily outran any perceived constitutional violations.

On the other hand, one can also argue that congruence and proportionality are not satisfied. As to congruence, the absence of any state action requirement in the VAWA cause of action suggests that the actual congruence between gender discrimination in state justice systems and VAWA is illusory. For one thing, the remedy is not corrective of the underlying violation.

VAWA lawsuits against private individuals will not alter the patterns of discrimination in state justice systems. Moreover, the VAWA remedy can be imposed even if there is no underlying constitutional violation, i.e., even if the state fully prosecutes and punishes all acts of gender-based violence. In short, there is an apparent disconnect between the underlying right Congress seeks to protect and the remedy Congress has imposed. This brings us to proportionality. Since the VAWA remedy is available regardless of any underlying constitutional violation, to demonstrate proportionality one would arguably need to show that the pattern of gender bias is so pervasive that a more carefully circumscribed remedy would be ineffective. Congress made no such findings. It found only that there was a problem of gender bias in the justice systems of a substantial number of states. A more proportional remedy would be one that was directed only at those jurisdictions in which the presence of gender bias had been established, as was the case in *Katzenbach v. Morgan*. From this perspective, the VAWA civil remedy is not constitutional.

In *United States v. Morrison*, 120 S. Ct. 1740 (2000), under similar facts, and adopting reasoning similar to that in the preceding paragraph, the Court held that the civil remedy created by VAWA was beyond the §5 enforcement powers of Congress. Id. at 1754-1759. The *Morrison* Court also held that VAWA was not a valid exercise of the commerce power. Id. at 1748. See Christopher N. May & Allan Ides, *Constitutional Law: National Power and Federalism*, §5.3.4 (2001).

Congressional Interpretation

The third category of Fourteenth Amendment enforcement measures is, in a sense, as simple as the first. May Congress, pursuant to its §5 power, create independent Fourteenth Amendment rights, i.e., federal rights that are neither judicially recognized nor designed to enforce a judicially recognized right? In other words, may Congress interpret the Fourteenth Amendment to include rights not otherwise recognized by the judicial branch? For example, if the Supreme Court were to hold that women did not have a right to an abortion, could Congress, *relying solely on its §5 enforcement power*, establish a statutory Fourteenth Amendment right to an abortion? There is a reasonable argument that Congress does possess such a power. After all, the power to enforce the Fourteenth Amendment is vested in Congress, and in order to exercise that power, Congress must interpret the provisions to be enforced. Yet the post-*Boerne* answer appears to be in the negative. In the words of the *Boerne* Court, "Any suggestion that Congress has a substantive, non-remedial power under the Fourteenth Amendment is not supported by our case law." 521 U.S. at 526. Moreover, the Court explained,

> [i]f Congress could define its own powers by altering the Fourteenth Amendment's meaning, no longer would the Constitution be "superior paramount law, unchangeable by ordinary means." It would be "on a level with ordinary legislative acts, and, like other acts, . . . alterable when the legislature shall please to alter it." *Marbury v. Madison*, 1 Cranch, at 177. Under this approach, it is difficult to conceive of a principle that would limit congressional power. . . . Shifting legislative majorities could change the Constitution and effectively circumvent the difficult and detailed amendment process contained in Article V.

Id. at 529. To underscore these points, the *Boerne* Court gave no further consideration to the argument that RFRA reflected a congressional interpretation of the free exercise guarantee that was more encompassing than the Court's interpretation. Indeed, implicit in the Court's opinion was a conclusion that if that were the case, the creation of such a substantive right would be well beyond the legislative prerogative of Congress.

In short, congressional powers under the Fourteenth Amendment are remedial only. Congress may not use those powers to create rights not recognized by the judiciary. See also *Oregon v. Mitchell*, 400 U.S. 112 (1970) (majority rejects notion that Congress possesses plenary authority to interpret the Fourteenth Amendment without definitively holding that Congress was absolutely without power to create independent Fourteenth Amendment rights).

Finally, just as Congress may not expand Fourteenth Amendment rights, Congress may not use its §5 power to limit the scope of judicially recognized rights. Thus, in *Mississippi University for Women v. Hogan*, 458 U.S. 718 (1982), the Court rejected an argument that Title IX of the Education Amendments of 1972 could validly narrow the scope of the judicially recognized equal protection right to be free from gender discrimination. In the Court's words,

> Congress' power under §5, however, "is limited to adopting measures to enforce the guarantees of the Amendment; §5 grants Congress no power to restrict, abrogate, or dilute these guarantees." *Katzenbach v. Morgan*, 384 U.S. 641, 651, n.10 (1966). Although we give deference to congressional decisions and classifications, neither Congress nor a State can validate a law that denies the rights guaranteed by the Fourteenth Amendment.

Id. at 732-733. See also *Saenz v. Roe*, 526 U.S. 489, 507 (1999) ("Congress may not authorize the States to violate the Fourteenth Amendment").

§1.5.3   *Enforcement of the Fifteenth Amendment*

The Fifteenth Amendment was adopted because of concerns that the Fourteenth Amendment was not broad enough to prevent states from disenfranchising the recently freed slaves. The scope of the Fifteenth Amendment is limited to racial restrictions on voting. Section 1 provides:

> The right of citizens of the United States to vote shall not be denied or abridged by the United States or by any State on account of race, color, or previous condition of servitude.

Section 2 of the Amendment provides, "The Congress shall have power to enforce this article by appropriate legislation." This enforcement power has been interpreted in essentially the same fashion and with the same breadth as is the Fourteenth Amendment enforcement power.

Cases construing the scope of the Fifteenth Amendment enforcement power generally involve problems arising in the "nonparallel" category described in our discussion of the Fourteenth Amendment enforcement power. The standards for measuring the scope of both powers are identical. Thus, the Court in *City of Rome v. United States,* 446 U.S. 156 (1980), observed, "It is clear, then, that under §2 of the Fifteenth Amendment Congress may prohibit practices that in and of themselves do not violate §1 of the Amendment, so long as the prohibitions attacking racial discrimination in voting are 'appropriate,' as that term is defined in *McCulloch v. Maryland.* . . ." Id. at 177. Of course, as the foregoing quotation suggests, the context in which the Fifteenth Amendment power can be exercised relates exclusively to racial discrimination in voting.

EXAMPLE 1-S

The federal Voting Rights Act regulates the electoral laws of states and local communities that have a demonstrated history of racial discrimination in voting. The City of Hills, a regulated jurisdiction within the coverage of the Act, has recently revised its local electoral system on race-neutral grounds, but in a manner that has the effect of diluting minority voting strength. There is no evidence of purposeful discrimination in this revision. Nonetheless, the Voting Rights Act precludes implementation of the city's plan, since the plan has the "effect" of abridging the right to vote on the basis of race within the meaning of the Act. The city claims that as so applied the Voting Rights Act exceeds the power of Congress to enforce the Fifteenth Amendment. In support of this claim, the city argues that since the Fifteenth Amendment bars only purposeful discrimination, Congress may not use its enforcement power to bar electoral practices with only a discriminatory effect. Assuming that §1 of the Fifteenth Amendment bars only purposeful discrimination, does the Voting Rights Act exceed the Fifteenth Amendment enforcement powers of Congress?

EXPLANATION

No. Under the *City of Rome* standard quoted above, Congress may prohibit practices that do not themselves violate §1 of the Fifteenth Amendment as long as the prohibition is directed toward the enforcement of the underlying principles of that Amendment. Here, "Congress could rationally have concluded that, because electoral changes by jurisdictions with a demonstrable history of intentional racial discrimination in voting create the risk of purposeful discrimination, it was proper to prohibit changes that have a discriminatory impact." *City of Rome,* 446 U.S. at 177.

2

Substantive Due Process

§2.1   Introduction and Overview

The Origins of the Due Process Clause

There are two Due Process Clauses, one in the Fifth Amendment and one in the Fourteenth Amendment. The former operates as a limit on the power of the national government, while the latter operates against the power of the states. Both Clauses guarantee within their respective spheres that no person shall be deprived "of life, liberty, or property, without due process of law." Since both Clauses operate in essentially the same fashion, albeit against different governmental bodies, we will refer to them collectively as the Due Process Clause.

The basic notion behind the Due Process Clause derives from Article 39 of Magna Carta, in which the King of England promised in 1215 that "[n]o free man shall be taken, or imprisoned, or disseized, or outlawed, or exiled, or any wise destroyed . . . but by the lawful judgment of his peers or by the law of the land." While this guarantee severely narrowed the King's prerogative—barring him from depriving a person of life, liberty, or property except in accordance with the law — it placed no constraints on what Parliament might enact as "the law of the land." Magna Carta would thus not have been offended if, pursuant to an act of Parliament, the King imprisoned everyone whose mother's first name began with the letter "V."

While some early American state constitutions closely tracked the language of Magna Carta, the fifth article of the federal Bill of Rights replaced the words "by the law of the land" with the more ambiguous phrase "due process of law." It was possible to have read this Clause as going no further than Magna Carta. Under such a reading, a governmental deprivation of life, liberty, or property would automatically satisfy the Due Process Clause as long as it was in accordance with a law duly enacted by the legislature. However, the Supreme Court rejected such a reading of the Due Process Clause in *Murray's Lessee v. Hoboken Land & Improvement Co.*, 59 U.S. (18 How.) 272 (1856). The Court there ruled that the fact that a deprivation may occur "in conformity with an act of Congress" does not necessarily mean that it satisfies the Fifth Amendment Due Process Clause.

> It is manifest that it was not left to the legislative power to enact any process which might be devised. The article is a restraint on the legislative as well as on the executive and judicial powers of the government, and cannot be so construed as to leave congress free to make any process "due process of law," by its mere will.

Id. at 276. The same principle holds with respect to state legislation challenged under the Due Process Clause of the Fourteenth Amendment. *Davidson v. New Orleans*, 96 U.S. 97, 102 (1878) (rejecting notion that a state can "make any thing due process of law which, by its own legislation, it chooses to declare such"). In short, the Due Process Clause operates as an independent check on the exercise of governmental power.

Procedural versus Substantive Due Process

The limitations imposed by the Due Process Clause are of two distinct types —procedural and substantive. Procedural due process commands that when the government acts to deprive a person of life, liberty, or property, it must do so in accord with procedures that are deemed to be fair. As we will see in Chapter 5, procedural due process usually requires that a person be given notice and the opportunity to be heard before a deprivation occurs.

The current chapter examines substantive due process. In contrast to procedural due process, which is concerned with the procedures employed in enforcing a law, substantive due process insists that the law itself be fair and reasonable and have an adequate justification regardless of how fair or elaborate the procedures might be for implementing it. Thus, a law that comports with procedural due process because a person is given notice and a full opportunity to be heard might, nonetheless, violate substantive due process if it is substantively unfair or unreasonable. This substantive due process protection is independent of any other textual guarantees found in the Constitution or its Amendments. Thus, substantive due process protects "life, liberty, and property" even if no other textual right has been infringed.

EXAMPLE 2-A

A state law provides that anyone suffering from AIDS shall be incarcerated in a special state facility until he or she is cured of the disease. The law provides that no one shall be incarcerated until after there has first been a full judicial determination that the person is suffering from AIDS. The alleged victim is entitled to a trial-type hearing with appointed counsel, and an adverse determination by the trial court may be appealed as of right to the state supreme court. Does this law deprive an AIDS victim of liberty without due process of law?

EXPLANATION

As a matter of procedural due process, the law is constitutional. The measure provides notice and a full opportunity to be heard before any deprivation of liberty occurs. However, as a matter of substantive due process, the measure is probably unconstitutional. A challenger would argue that no matter how fair the procedures for enforcing it, the substance of the law is so unfair and unreasonable as to violate due process. While the state's goal of protecting the public against the spread of AIDS is an important one, there are arguably less drastic ways of achieving this goal that do not involve such a severe interference with personal liberty.

Executive Abuse of Power

Most procedural and substantive due process cases involve alleged deprivations of life, liberty, or property that result from legislative action, i.e., from action that was specifically authorized by a statute or regulation. In these instances, where we know that the government intended to cause the deprivation, the only issue is whether the deprivation violates the Due Process Clause. Sometimes, however, a deprivation of life, liberty, or property is caused by an executive official in a situation where no legislation approved the specific deprivation in question. For example, suppose a fire truck collides with an automobile and kills the driver, or a prison guard accidentally drops and destroys an inmate's television set. In these instances, though public employees were operating within the scope of their official duties, the deprivations of life and property were not specifically sanctioned by statute or regulation. Instead, they resulted from what may have been ordinary negligence on the part of a governmental official. Should such executive deprivations be actionable under the Due Process Clause? If so, the Due Process Clause would function like a system of tort law, providing a constitutional remedy whenever executive officials cause injury to persons or property.

The Supreme Court has rejected such a reading of the Due Process Clause, whose principal goal is "protection of the individual against arbitrary action of government." *Wolff v. McDonnell*, 418 U.S. 539, 558 (1974). As the Court has explained, "Our cases dealing with abusive executive action have repeatedly emphasized that only the most egregious official conduct can be said to be 'arbitrary in the constitutional sense'. . . ." *County of Sacramento v. Lewis*, 523 U.S. 833, 846 (1998). This distinction between legislative and executive action is necessary "to preserve the constitutional proportions of constitutional claims, lest the Constitution be demoted to what we have called a font of tort law." Id. at 847 n.8. The Court has thus held that "in a due process challenge to executive action, the threshold question is whether the behavior of the governmental officer is so egregious, so outrageous, that it may fairly be said to shock the contemporary conscience." Id. Otherwise, the deprivation is not the stuff of constitutional law and must be redressed through whatever statutory or common law remedies may exist.

Whether or not executive action is sufficiently arbitrary, egregious, or conscience-shocking to state a due process claim turns on the circumstances under which the government official was acting. In no case, however, will an allegation of mere negligence suffice: "the Constitution does not guarantee due care on the part of state officials; liability for negligently inflicted harm is categorically beneath the threshold of constitutional due process." Id. at 849. At the opposite extreme, "conduct intended to injure in some way unjustifiable by any government interest is the sort of official action most likely to rise to the conscience-shocking level." Id. Between these extremes, there may be occasions when "something more than negligence but 'less than intentional conduct, such as recklessness or "gross negligence"'" will suffice, depending on how much opportunity there was for deliberation, reflection, and forethought. Id. at 849, 851. In *County of Sacramento*, the Court held that only an allegation of "purpose to cause" harm would suffice to state a due process claim in a case involving a motorcycle rider who was killed during a high-speed police chase calling for split-second judgments. By contrast, the Court suggested that an allegation of "reckless disregard" or "deliberate indifference" might be enough to support a due process claim in a case concerning the medical treatment of prisoners or pretrial detainees.

Standards of Review

The determination of whether a law violates substantive due process because it is so arbitrary, unfair, or unreasonable as to lack an adequate justification depends almost entirely on what standard a court employs in assessing these criteria. The Court today generally uses one of two basic standards to decide whether a law violates substantive due process. If a *fundamental liberty interest* is infringed, the Court applies strict scrutiny, in which case a law will usually be struck down unless it is shown to be the least burdensome means of achieving a compelling governmental interest. On the other hand, where only property or a nonfundamental liberty interest is involved, the Court applies a rational basis test, under which a law will be upheld if there is any legitimate goal that a rational legislature *might* have thought the measure would further — whether or not this was actually the law's goal or whether the law actually furthers it. The strict scrutiny and rational basis tests constitute the Court's two basic approaches to substantive due process. However, in certain settings, such as abortion, the Court may employ a variation of the normal strict scrutiny test.

Economic versus Noneconomic Due Process

In thinking about substantive due process, it is helpful to distinguish between economic due process and noneconomic due process. Economic due process involves the Court's application of the Due Process Clause to protect real and personal property and to assess potential infringements of economic liberties, such as the liberty to contract and the liberty to pursue a trade or occupation. The standard of review in all economic due process cases is rational basis. Noneconomic due process deals with the Clause's application to laws that infringe on civil or personal liberties, such as the freedom to marry and the freedom from physical restraint. If the noneconomic personal liberty at issue is deemed fundamental, then the standard of review is strict scrutiny. Otherwise, a rational basis standard applies.

Though the Court's decisions in these two areas have taken divergent paths, there was initially no hint of a distinction between economic and noneconomic due process. Indeed, in one of the first decisions to recognize a substantive component to the Due Process Clause, the Court suggested that private property was entitled to the same level of due process protection as personal liberty: "[T]he rights of property are united with the rights of person, and placed on the same ground by the fifth amendment. . . ." *Dred Scott v. Sanford,* 60 U.S. (19 How.) 393, 450 (1857). Yet despite the fact that the text of the Due Process Clause gives liberty and property equal billing, the Court today does not treat property or economic liberty as fundamental rights. However, for roughly 50 years, spanning the period from the late 1880s through the late 1930s, the Supreme Court was far more protective of economic interests than it is today, placing them at least on a par with personal liberties. We will briefly examine that period, which is known as the *Lochner* era, before turning to the Court's current application of substantive due process in property and economic liberty cases.

§2.2   The Rise and Fall of Economic Due Process

§2.2.1   *Economic Due Process in the* Lochner *Era*

The Fourteenth Amendment and its Due Process Clause were ratified in 1868. Shortly thereafter the Court rejected a number of substantive due process challenges to state laws that interfered with property or economic liberty. See, e.g., *Munn v. Illinois,* 94 U.S. 113 (1877) (upholding state regulation of grain elevator rates); *Slaughter-House Cases,* 83 U.S. (16 Wall.) 36 (1872) (upholding Louisiana law conferring monopoly on butchering in New Orleans). In *Munn,* the Court declared that while state economic regulation may at times be excessive, "[f]or protection against abuses by legislatures the people must resort to the polls, not to the courts." Id. at 134.

By 1887, however, the Court's personnel and its thinking had undergone a dramatic change. In *Mugler v. Kansas,* 123 U.S. 623 (1887), the Court rejected a substantive due process challenge to an Iowa law that banned the future manufacture or sale of liquor. However, in sharp contrast to the hands-off approach of *Munn,* the Court declared that when states exercise their police powers, the judiciary has a "solemn duty to look at the substance of things"; if it appears that a law "has no real or substantial relation to those objects, or is a palpable invasion of rights secured by the fundamental law, it is the duty of the courts to so adjudge, and thereby give effect to the Constitution." Id. at 661. Federal and state courts were soon using substantive due process as a tool for striking down an array of Populist and Progressive reform measures that regulated corporations and businesses in the interest of farmers, consumers, workers, and children. Among the statutes declared unconstitutional were rate and price controls, measures protecting women and children in the workplace, wage and hour standards, and laws that promoted collective bargaining.

Liberty to Contract

While some of the courts' economic due process decisions hinged on a determination that the government had unreasonably interfered with property, many cases found that there had been a deprivation of an economic liberty, the liberty to contract. This liberty interest was first recognized by the Court in *Allgeyer v. Louisiana,* 165 U.S. 578, 589 (1897), which held that among the liberties protected by the Due Process Clause is the freedom "to enter into all contracts which may be proper, necessary and essential" to pursue a livelihood. The Court later suggested that liberty to contract is also implicit in the Due Process Clause's "right of private property," *Coppage v.*

Kansas, 236 U.S. 1, 14 (1915), for the freedom to enter into contracts is essential to acquiring, exploiting, and disposing of property.

The liberty to contract protected by the Due Process Clauses of the Fifth and Fourteenth Amendments involves the freedom to *enter into contracts* on terms and conditions of one's choosing. This liberty interest should not be confused with the Contracts Clause of Article I, §10, which prohibits a state from "impairing the Obligation of Contracts" by interfering with the terms of preexisting contracts. See Chapter 4.

The Decision in *Lochner v. New York*

One of the most revealing examples of the Court's approach to economic due process during the *Lochner* era is the case from which the era took its name—*Lochner v. New York,* 198 U.S. 45 (1905). In a five-to-four decision, the Court there struck down a New York law that sought to protect the health of bakers by outlawing their employment for more than 10 hours a day or 60 hours a week. The Court held that the law violated the Due Process Clause because it was "an unreasonable, unnecessary and arbitrary interference with the right of the individual to . . . enter into those contracts in relation to labor which may seem to him appropriate or necessary." Id. at 56. The approach taken by the Court in striking down the New York law embodied three key features that often characterized the Court's economic due process cases during the *Lochner* era.

First, the *Lochner* Court identified a particular aspect of liberty—liberty to contract—that is not enumerated or mentioned anywhere in the Constitution and elevated that liberty to a status where it received extraordinary protection. While the Court said that a law interfering with this liberty would be upheld if it was "fair, reasonable and appropriate," id., a seemingly deferential standard, the Justices very closely scrutinized the *means-end relationship* between New York's law and its alleged police-power goal. Despite an impressive body of evidence that linked the long hours bakers worked and their generally poor health, the Court ruled that "the limitation of the hours of labor . . . has no such *direct relation* to and no such *substantial effect* upon the health of the employee as to justify us in regarding [it] as really a health law." Id. at 64 (emphasis supplied). The Court also suggested that the New York statute was unnecessary because there were other ways to protect the health of bakers, even though the state had already implemented them. Id. at 61-62. Thus, according to *Lochner,* a law that interferes with liberty to contract will be found to violate the Due Process Clause unless the Court is convinced that the measure was necessary to directly advance an important governmental purpose. As the Court later explained, under this approach, "[F]reedom of contract is . . . the general rule and restraint the exception; and the exercise of legislative authority to abridge it can be justified only by the existence of exceptional circumstances." *Adkins v. Children's Hosp.*, 261 U.S. 525, 546 (1923) (invalidating minimum wage law for women and children).

Second, in deciding whether New York's interference with liberty to contract was justified by an important governmental interest, the Court was not interested in the actual facts, but relied instead on its own understanding of the situation. Despite abundant evidence demonstrating the adverse effect of long hours on the health of bakers, much of which was summarized in Justice Harlan's dissent, the Court declared that "[t]o the common understanding the trade of a baker has never been regarded as an unhealthy one." *Lochner*, 198 U.S. at 59. Several years later in *Muller v. Oregon*, 208 U.S. 412 (1908), the Court upheld a law that set maximum hours for women who worked in factories and laundries. In this case, the future Justice Louis Brandeis, then a prominent Boston lawyer, filed a 116-page brief, 113 pages of which were devoted to factual data showing the harmful effect of long hours of work on women. The difference between the outcomes of *Lochner* and *Muller* is often attributed to "the Brandeis brief." Yet the factual evidence may have been as irrelevant in *Muller* as it was in *Lochner*. For the Court in *Muller* suggested that all of Brandeis's data merely confirmed what the Justices already knew, i.e., the "widespread and long continued belief" that "woman has always been dependent upon man." Id. at 421. However, in *Lochner*, where the facts ran counter to the Justices' own intuitive judgment, the Court ignored those facts and invalidated the law as being an arbitrary and unreasonable interference with liberty to contract. Though the majority in *Lochner* denied that it was "substituting the judgment of the court for that of the legislature," 198 U.S. at 56-57, this appears to be exactly what the Court did.

Third and finally, *Lochner* rejected the legitimacy of governmental efforts to redress inequalities in wealth or bargaining power. In addition to finding that New York's health justification for regulating bakers' hours was insufficient to pass muster, the Court concluded that the health goal was a sham. "It is impossible for us to shut our eyes to the fact that many of the laws of this character, while passed under what is claimed to be the police power for the purpose of protecting the public health or welfare, are, in reality, passed from other motives." Id. at 64. Instead, said the Court, the measure was "a labor law, pure and simple," id. at 57, for its "real object and purpose were simply to regulate the hours of labor between the master and his employees . . . ," id. at 64. As such, the law was invalid.

What was wrong with a labor law? According to the *Lochner* Court, the only legitimate purpose of government is to promote the *public* good. Labor laws seek to redress inequalities between *private* individuals, in effect taking property from one person (the employer) and giving it to another (the worker). Yet "the interest of the public is not in the slightest degree affected by such an act." Id. at 57. Because such laws are beyond the legitimate scope of the state's police power, they lack a valid purpose and, therefore, violate the Due Process Clause. The Court in earlier dicta had said that a law that took property from A and gave it to B would be invalid both as a matter of natural law, *Calder v. Bull*, 3 U.S. (3 Dall.) 386, 388 (1798), and as a violation of substantive due process, *Davidson v. New Orleans*, 96 U.S. 97, 102 (1878). The *Lochner* Court viewed labor laws as falling squarely into this prohibited category.

In striking down New York's attempt to redress inequalities between bakers and their employers, *Lochner* adopted the Social Darwinist view that it is both wrong and futile for government to interfere with the process of natural selection, through which the strong will succeed and the weak must perish. New York had tampered with this process by seeking to assist those bakers who might be incapable of surviving on their own. As the *Lochner* majority candidly declared: "We do not believe in the soundness of the views which uphold this law." 198 U.S. at 61. The Court later expressed itself even more bluntly: "[I]t is from the nature of things impossible to uphold freedom of contract and the right of private property without at the same time recognizing as legitimate those inequalities of fortune that are the necessary result of the exercise of those rights." *Coppage v. Kansas*, 236 U.S. 1, 17 (1915) (striking state ban on yellow dog contracts, in which workers had to agree not to join a labor union).

In a strong dissent filed in *Lochner*, Justice Holmes objected to the Court's having enshrined in the Due Process Clause the views of Herbert Spencer, a prominent Social Darwinist. Holmes wrote that "a constitution is not intended to embody a particular economic theory, whether of paternalism and the organic relation of the citizen to the State or of *laissez faire*." 198 U.S. at 75. Instead, except in rare situations, "the word liberty in the Fourteenth Amendment is perverted when it is held to prevent the natural outcome of a dominant opinion. . . ." Id. at 76. In contrast to the *Lochner* majority, Holmes thus advocated a highly deferential standard of judicial review under the Due Process Clause.

§2.2.2 *The Demise of* Lochner

The approach to economic due process exemplified by *Lochner* was applied by the Court well into the 1930s. Some regulations of business were upheld. These included measures that were clearly necessary for health or safety, as well as laws regulating prices charged by monopolies, public utilities, and other businesses deemed to be "affected with a public interest." Yet many other statutes were invalidated because they interfered with liberty to contract; among them were wage and hour legislation, laws protecting collective bargaining, and price regulations in industries not "affected with a public interest."

The tide began to turn in the mid-1930s during the Great Depression. In *Nebbia v. New York*, 291 U.S. 502 (1934), the Court upheld a New York law that sought to rescue farmers by setting a minimum price for the sale of milk. Writing at the peak of the Depression, the Court rejected its earlier view that there is a "closed class or category of businesses affected with a public interest" whose prices may, therefore, be regulated; instead, price regulation is potentially valid with respect to any business, including the dairy industry. Id. at 531-537. The Court in *Nebbia* also abandoned its practice of strictly scrutinizing laws that interfere with liberty to contract. In a thinly veiled repudiation of *Lochner*, the Court warned:

> With the wisdom of the policy adopted, with the adequacy or practicability of the law enacted to forward it, the courts are both incompetent and unauthorized to deal. . . . [T]hough the court may hold views inconsistent with the wisdom of the law, it may not be annulled unless palpably in excess of legislative power.

Id. at 537-538. In determining whether or not a law violates the Due Process Clause, said the Court, "every possible presumption is in favor of its validity. . . ." Id. at 538.

Three years later in *West Coast Hotel Co. v. Parrish*, 300 U.S. 379 (1937), the Court upheld a state law setting minimum wages for women and children. In doing so, it overruled *Adkins v. Children's Hospital*, 261 U.S. 525 (1923), a *Lochner*-era decision that had invalidated a similar law for the District of Columbia. The Court in *West Coast Hotel* rejected *Lochner*'s elevation of freedom of contract to what had amounted to fundamental liberty status. While freedom to contract was still a protected aspect of liberty, it was no longer entitled to special protection. As Chief Justice Hughes wrote for the Court:

> The Constitution does not speak of freedom of contract. It speaks of liberty and prohibits the deprivation of liberty without due process of law. . . . [A] regulation which is reasonable in relation to its subject and is adopted in the interests of the community is due process. *This essential limitation of liberty in general governs freedom of contract in particular.*

300 U.S. at 391-392 (emphasis supplied). The Court reiterated that in such cases great deference must be shown to the legislature. "Even if the wisdom of the policy be regarded as debatable and its effect uncertain, still the legislature is entitled to its judgment." Id. at 399.

West Coast Hotel rejected another critical aspect of *Lochner* as well, namely, its conclusion that laws seeking to redress inequality in bargaining power violate due process because they do not promote the *public* good.

Citing the nation's "recent economic experience" in the Great Depression, the Chief Justice explained:

> The exploitation of a class of workers who are in an unequal position with respect to bargaining power and are thus relatively defenceless against the denial of a living wage is not only detrimental to their health and well being but casts a direct burden for their support upon the community. What these workers lose in wages the taxpayers are called upon to pay.

Id. While the Court would still insist that laws advance the public good, the vision of what was in the public interest had expanded greatly since the time of *Lochner.*

West Coast Hotel's enlarged view of the public good was actually consistent with one of the principles recognized by the *Lochner* Court. In this respect, *Lochner* contained the seeds of its own destruction. The *Lochner* doctrine acknowledged that governmental intervention was permissible if it was on behalf of those who, *as a group,* were especially vulnerable and unable to protect themselves in the struggle for existence. For assuming that the group performed a socially useful function, the public as a whole would be harmed if the entire group were allowed to perish. During the *Lochner* era, this exception was applied sparingly. It was extended to underground coal miners (*Holden v. Hardy,* 169 U.S. 366 (1898)) and women (*Muller v. Oregon,* 208 U.S. 412 (1908)), but not to bakers. For as the Court noted in *Lochner,* "There is no contention that *bakers as a class* . . . are not able to assert their rights and care for themselves without the protecting arm of the State. . . . They are in no sense wards of the State." 198 U.S. at 57 (emphasis supplied). Yet within *Lochner*'s framework, if changing economic and social conditions were to render most groups of workers unable to defend themselves in the competitive marketplace, governmental intervention would then be justified on a far more sweeping basis. This is exactly what had occurred during the Great Depression.

By 1937, the Supreme Court had rejected all three of the features that had characterized its approach to economic due process during the *Lochner* era. First, though liberty to contract was still protected by the Due Process Clause, it no longer amounted to a fundamental liberty, whose infringement would trigger strict scrutiny. Second, since freedom to contract was now just an ordinary liberty, the Court in reviewing a law that impaired this liberty interest would cease to substitute its own judgment for that of the legislature and would instead treat the measure as being presumptively valid. Finally, laws that sought to redress inequalities of wealth or bargaining power on behalf of certain groups would no longer be overturned on the ground that they did not further the public good.

The extreme deference to the legislature that the Court displayed in

West Coast Hotel has continued to the present time. As a result, substantive due process challenges that are brought on the basis of an alleged interference with property or with economic liberty are almost certain to fail. We turn now to consider the Court's contemporary approach to such economic due process cases.

§2.2.3   *Property and Economic Liberty Today*

The Court today uses the rational basis test to decide whether a governmental deprivation of property or economic liberty is so arbitrary or unreasonable as to violate substantive due process. The rational basis test was first articulated in *United States v. Carolene Products Co.*, 304 U.S. 144 (1938), where the Court rejected a substantive due process challenge to a federal law excluding nondairy milk products from interstate commerce. The producers of these goods complained that the law impaired the value of their property and interfered with their freedom to contract with buyers in other states. However, the Court rejected their claims, holding that a law "affecting ordinary commercial transactions" is valid as a matter of substantive due process if it "rests upon some rational basis within the knowledge and experience of the legislators." Id. at 152. To satisfy this test, it is unnecessary that the legislature have made findings identifying either the purpose of the law or the basis on which it might further its goal. "Even in the absence of such aids the existence of facts supporting the legislative judgment is to be presumed. . . ." Id. Thus, "where the legislative judgment is drawn in question . . . the issue [is] whether any state of facts either known *or which could reasonably be assumed* affords support for it." Id. at 154 (emphasis supplied).

Under the rational basis test, courts may engage in the purely speculative exercise of hypothesizing a legitimate goal that the challenged law might have been designed to further. Whether this was the law's actual goal and whether the law in fact furthers it are both irrelevant. The only question is whether there is some legitimate end that a rational legislature might have thought the law would further. In *Williamson v. Lee Optical Inc.*, 348 U.S. 483, 488 (1955), the Court thus upheld an Oklahoma statute that drastically curtailed the ability of opticians to practice their profession: "It is enough that there is an evil at hand for correction, and that it might be thought that the particular legislative measure was a rational way to correct it." The statute's ban on advertising eyeglass frames, for example, was found not to violate substantive due process on the ground that "[i]f the advertisement of lenses is to be abolished or controlled, the advertising of frames must come under the same restraints; *or so the legislature might think.*" Id. at 490 (emphasis supplied).

The rhetoric and the result in *Lee Optical* made clear that the Court's approach to economic due process had returned to the noninterventionist model that prevailed in the late nineteenth century before the appearance of *Lochner.* With respect to rhetoric, *Lee Optical* chose to "emphasize again" what the Court said in *Munn v. Illinois,* 94 U.S. 113, 134 (1877), one of the leading pre-*Lochner* substantive due process cases: "'For protection against abuses by legislatures the people must resort to the polls, not to the courts.'" 348 U.S. at 488. And in terms of result, *Lee Optical* bore a striking resemblance to another pre-*Lochner* economic due process decision, i.e., the *Slaughter-House Cases,* 83 U.S. (16 Wall.) 36 (1872), which upheld Louisiana's butcher monopoly law. In both instances, the Court rejected substantive due process challenges to laws that severely limited the right of individuals to practice their chosen occupation.

The rational basis test employed in economic due process cases today is so deferential as to be virtually toothless. It is always possible to hypothesize a conceivable purpose for a challenged law. In some instances, the Court has not even bothered to go through this ritual. See, e.g., *Ferguson v. Skrupa,* 372 U.S. 726, 731 (1963) (law restricting business of debt adjusting to attorneys did not violate due process because the "Kansas Legislature was free to decide for itself that legislation was needed to deal with the business of debt adjusting"). While other clauses of the Constitution, such as the dormant Commerce Clause, the Takings Clause, and the Equal Protection Clause, may afford meaningful protection against governmental interference with property or economic liberties, challenges based on *substantive* due process are virtually certain to fail. As we will see in Chapter 5, however, property and economic liberties do receive protection as a matter of *procedural* due process.

EXAMPLE 2-B

The City of Oakville has an ordinance that makes it illegal for anyone who owns a pet to work as a bus driver. Mary recently received a yellow canary as a birthday present. Shortly after she mentioned this to a co-worker, Mary was fired from her job as a bus driver for the Oakville School District. Mary has challenged her dismissal, claiming that it violated the Fourteenth Amendment Due Process Clause. Is Mary likely to win?

EXPLANATION

To the extent that Mary is raising a procedural due process claim, she might succeed if the city failed to give her notice and an opportunity to be heard before it fired her. See Chapter 5. However, Mary is likely to lose a substantive due process challenge. While the ordinance impairs her liberties to pursue an occupation and to contract for employment, all that a defender of the law or the court must do is suggest some hypothetical goal that the city might rationally have thought the law would further. Almost any story will do. The city may have believed that bus drivers who own pets will be tempted to bring their animals to work with them, interfering with their ability to drive safely. Or the city might have thought that pet owners will get animal hair, bird feathers, or snake scales in their eyes, impairing their ability to see the road clearly. Either scenario would more than likely suffice to sustain the ordinance as a rational safety measure. That the ordinance is both foolish and unnecessary to further these hypothetical safety goals does not matter. In the area of economic due process, the remedy for foolish or oppressive laws is, as the Court declared in *Munn* and *Lee Optical,* to complain to the legislature rather than to the courts.

———————————

Some have been critical of the sharp distinction that the Court has drawn in the substantive due process area between property and economic liberties on the one hand and civil and personal liberties on the other. While the former receive only rational basis review, which ordinarily means no protection at all, the latter often trigger strict scrutiny. Yet certain economic freedoms, such as the liberty to pursue one's livelihood, and certain types of property, such as one's home and basic earnings, are as vital to an individual as the most coveted of personal liberties. As Justice Stewart observed:

> [T]he dichotomy between personal liberties and property rights is a false one. Property does not have rights. People have rights. The right to enjoy property without unlawful deprivation, no less than the right to speak or the right to travel, is in truth a "personal" right, whether the "property" in question be a welfare check, a home, or a savings account. In fact, a fundamental interdependence exists between the personal right to liberty and the personal right to property. Neither could have meaning without the other.

Lynch v. Household Fin. Corp., 405 U.S. 538, 552 (1972). Moreover, the line between economic liberty and personal liberty is not always an easy one to draw. In the *Lochner* case, for example, while liberty to contract from the employer's standpoint may have been simply a matter of economics, to the individual baker what was at stake was personal health and survival. Yet the Court has shown no inclination to give heightened scrutiny even to those economic liberties and species of property that are central to a person's existence.

Punitive Damages

The one notable exception to the rule that substantive due process claims are generally unavailing in cases involving deprivations of property or economic liberty involves the award of punitive damages. In *BMW of North*

America, Inc. v. Gore, 517 U.S. 559 (1996), which involved a seller's failure to disclose that a new car had been partly repainted, the Court held that Alabama had denied defendant BMW substantive due process by awarding $2 million in punitive damages when the plaintiff's actual damages amounted to only $4,000. The Court declined to "draw a bright line marking the limits of a constitutionally acceptable punitive damage award," but concluded that "the grossly excessive award imposed in this case transcends the constitutional limit" and, therefore, deprived BMW of property without due process of law. Id. at 585-586. See also *TXO Production Corp. v. Alliance Resources Corp.*, 509 U.S. 443, 458 (1993) (punitive damages award may be "so 'grossly excessive' as to violate the substantive component of the Due Process Clause"). However, it is unlikely that the five-member majority's willingness to review the reasonableness of this Alabama punitive damages award signals a general retreat by the Court from its usual hands-off approach to economic due process cases. The facts of the *BMW* case appear to have been so egregious that the Court felt compelled to momentarily abandon its noninterventionist stance.

§2.3   Noneconomic Liberty from *Lochner* to *Carolene Products*

§2.3.1   *The* Lochner *Era and Noneconomic Liberties*

When the Court in *Allgeyer v. Louisiana*, 165 U.S. 578 (1897), set out to define the meaning of the word "liberty" in the Due Process Clause, its list included more than just nontextual economic freedoms such as liberty to contract and the freedom to pursue an occupation. In addition, the Court recognized that the Clause protects such unenumerated personal liberties as freedom from physical restraint, freedom to enjoy all of one's faculties, and freedom to reside (and work) where one wishes. Id. at 589.

The Court added further to the list of unenumerated personal liberties that are protected by the Due Process Clause in a number of cases decided at the height of the *Lochner* era. In *Meyer v. Nebraska*, 262 U.S. 390 (1923), the Justices struck down a Nebraska law that criminalized the teaching of German and other foreign languages in the schools. The Court held that the statute arbitrarily and unreasonably interfered with several liberties protected by the Due Process Clause, including the right of parents to have their children learn German. Id. at 399-401. The *Meyer* Court took a broad view of the nontextual personal liberties that are protected by the Due Process Clause. While it cited *Allgeyer* and *Lochner, Meyer* went well beyond those cases, declaring that among the liberties protected by the Fourteenth Amendment are "the right . . . to acquire useful knowledge, to marry, establish a home and bring up children, . . . and generally to enjoy those privileges long recognized at common law as essential to the orderly pursuit of happiness by free men." Id. at 399. Two years later in *Pierce v. Society of Sisters,* 268 U.S. 510 (1925), the Court relied on *Meyer* to overturn an Oregon law that compelled parents to send their children to public rather than private school; the statute violated due process, said the Court, because it "unreasonably interfere[d] with the liberty of parents and guardians to direct the upbringing and education of children under their control." Id. at 534-535.

The process that the Court applied in *Meyer* and *Pierce* with respect to certain personal liberties was indistinguishable from that which it had employed in *Lochner* concerning liberty to contract. In each case, the Court first defined an unenumerated liberty as being protected by the Due Process Clause. It then elevated that nontextual liberty interest to what amounted to "fundamental" status and accorded it a strict level of judicial protection. During the *Lochner* era, the Court thus used substantive due process as a means of invalidating statutes that interfered with judicially created liberties of both an economic and a noneconomic nature.

§2.3.2   Carolene Products' *Footnote Four*

In the late 1930s, when the Supreme Court abandoned its interventionist approach to substantive due process in the economic sphere, it indicated that a similar retreat was called for in other areas as well. In *United States v. Carolene Products Co.,* 304 U.S. 144 (1938), the Court had held that laws impairing liberty to contract were subject merely to rational basis review. But in dicta contained in footnote four, Justice Stone's opinion for the Court suggested that the rational basis standard should govern other unenumerated liberty interests as well. Stone wrote that more rigorous judicial scrutiny is called for only in three exceptional situations: (1) if "legislation appears on its face to be within a *specific prohibition* of the Constitution, such as those of the first ten amendments"; (2) if legislation "restricts those *political processes* which can ordinarily be expected to bring about repeal of undesirable legislation," such as impairments of the right to vote; and (3) if legislation is aimed at "*discrete and insular minorities*" who, because of prejudice against them, are unable to protect themselves through the ordinary political processes. Id. at 152-153 n.4 (emphasis supplied). The first of these exceptions involves the Due Process Clause. The other two primarily concern the Equal Protection Clause and will be discussed in Chapters 6 and 7.

According to the first exception of footnote four, if an unenumerated liberty interest is at stake, such as the liberty to contract at issue in *Carolene Products* itself, a mere rational basis standard of review should be employed.

The only liberties that will trigger more demanding scrutiny are those *specifically enumerated* in the Bill of Rights. For these purposes, if a Bill of Rights provision has been incorporated into the Fourteenth Amendment so that it applies against the states, it will be deemed to be "equally specific" as to the states even though the text of the Fourteenth Amendment does not mention it. Id. at 152 n.4.

The intended effect of footnote four on the Due Process Clause was to divide the universe of constitutionally protected liberties into two categories: those such as freedom of speech that are mentioned in the Bill of Rights and those such as liberty to contract that are unenumerated, but that the Court has nonetheless deemed to be protected. In Justice Stone's view, while the textual liberties of the first category should be entitled to heightened protection, those in the second category should receive only minimal protection under a rational basis test.

Carolene Products thus implicitly rejected the substantive due process approach taken in *Meyer v. Nebraska* and *Pierce v. Society of Sisters,* the two leading *Lochner*-era cases that dealt with personal liberties. In both of those cases, the Court had applied a strict standard of review to overturn state laws that infringed on unenumerated liberty interests in acquiring knowledge and raising children. According to footnote four, since only nontextual liberties were involved, the state laws should have received rational basis review under the Due Process Clause. The *Carolene Products* Court mentioned *Meyer* and *Pierce* as cases where strict scrutiny may have been justified under the Equal Protection Clause, 304 U.S. at 153 n.4, for both involved statutes that targeted minority groups who at the time were victims of extreme prejudice —i.e., German Americans in *Meyer* and Roman Catholics in *Pierce*. While *Meyer* and *Pierce* were thus perhaps defensible in equal protection terms, as substantive due process cases they had been discredited.

Not surprisingly, in the decades following *Carolene Products,* the Supreme Court very seldom overturned laws that interfered with unenumerated liberty interests. The collapse of substantive due process in the late 1930s affected all nontextual liberties. Liberty interests that were not specifically enumerated in the text of the Constitution, whether they were economic or personal in nature, were thus generally denied any substantive due process protection. There were a few exceptions. In *Aptheker v. Secretary of State,* 378 U.S. 500 (1964), the Court invalidated a federal law barring certain Communist Party members from obtaining passports, ruling that the law violated the Due Process Clause by impairing the nontextual "right to travel abroad." Id. at 505. In *Skinner v. Oklahoma,* 316 U.S. 535, 541-542 (1942), involving a state law that allowed mandatory sterilization of repeat felons, the Court applied strict scrutiny to protect the unenumerated right to procreate, though it did so under the Equal Protection rather than the Due Process Clause.

§2.4   *Griswold* and the Reemergence of Unenumerated Liberties

The collapse of substantive due process in the late 1930s has been permanent with respect to property and economic liberty. However, in the area of personal liberty there was a revival that began in the mid-1960s with *Griswold v. Connecticut*, 381 U.S. 479 (1965). That revival has persisted to the present day.

Griswold struck down a Connecticut law that made it illegal to use or counsel others to use contraceptives. The Court held that as applied to advice given to married couples, the statute violated the Due Process Clause by interfering with the "right of privacy" in marriage and by in effect allowing the government to invade "the sacred precincts of marital bedrooms. . . ." Id. at 485-486. The newly recognized right of marital privacy, though nowhere mentioned in the Constitution's text, was found to lie "within the zone of privacy created by several fundamental constitutional guarantees." Id. at 485. The Court applied an extremely strict standard of review and invalidated the statute without any consideration of the state's possible justifications for it.

Griswold made it clear that the rebirth of substantive due process was limited to the sphere of personal liberties. The Court expressly declined to revive *Lochner v. New York* and said that it would not "sit as a super-legislature to determine the wisdom, need, and propriety of laws that touch economic problems, business affairs, or social conditions." Id. at 482. Justice Douglas explained that in contrast to *Lochner*, the statute at issue in *Griswold* "operates directly on an intimate relation of husband and wife and their physician's role in one aspect of that relation." Id. Yet he did not explain the significance of the distinction between economic and personal affairs, or how this critical distinction was to be made. Nor did he explain why, if the *Lochner* Court had acted as a "super-legislature," the *Griswold* Court was not so acting as well.

§2.4.1   *Penumbras and Emanations*

The *Griswold* Court offered an unusual explanation as to the source of the newly discovered constitutional right of marital privacy. In earlier cases, such as *Allgeyer v. Louisiana* (1897) and *Meyer v. Nebraska* (1923), the Court announced that certain liberties were included in the "liberty" protected by the Due Process Clause. Justice Douglas, writing for the Court in *Griswold*, chose not to follow this route. Instead, he carefully sought to link the right of privacy in marriage to specific guarantees of the Bill of Rights. The First, Third, Fourth, and Fifth Amendments, said Douglas, "have penumbras, formed by emanations from those guarantees that help give them life and substance." 381 U.S. at 484. The right of marital privacy lies within these penumbras, hidden in the shadows of the First Amendment's right of association, the Third and Fourth Amendments' protection of the home, and the Fifth Amendment's guarantee against self-incrimination.

There are several reasons why Justice Douglas may have insisted on tying the right of marital privacy to specific provisions of the Bill of Rights rather than simply declaring it a protected aspect of "liberty" under the Due Process Clause. First, he may have hoped to distinguish his approach from that taken by the Court during the *Lochner* era; rather than inventing a new constitutional right, the Court in *Griswold* was exercising judicial restraint by merely protecting a right that was derivable from the Constitution's text. Yet the penumbras and emanations approach was hardly a means of imposing judicial self-restraint. Douglas's discovery of marital privacy within the penumbras of the Bill of Rights was far from self-evident, requiring at least a small leap of judicial faith. Moreover, the penumbras and emanations approach is capable of justifying virtually any liberty interest the Court might wish to create. Indeed, *Lochner* could easily be reinterpreted and justified on this basis, for liberty to contract may be said to lie within the penumbras and emanations of several constitutional provisions — including the Due Process Clause's protection of "property" and the Contracts Clause of Article I, §10.

Douglas's penumbras and emanations approach may also have been designed to square *Griswold* with the framework of *Carolene Products*. There, as we saw, the Court in footnote four suggested that strict scrutiny should be applied under the Due Process Clause only if a law is contrary to a "specific prohibition" of the Constitution. Though footnote four was only dictum, Douglas agreed with this aspect of it. He also subscribed to Justice Black's position that under §1 of the Fourteenth Amendment, it is wrong for the Court to use a "natural-law-due-process" approach to create any additional rights against the states beyond those explicitly set forth in the Bill of Rights. *Adamson v. California*, 332 U.S. 46, 68-92 (1947) (Black & Douglas, JJ., dissenting); see also *Duncan v. Louisiana*, 391 U.S. 145, 162-171 (1968) (Black & Douglas, JJ., concurring). See §1.3.

However, use of the penumbras and emanations approach to determine the scope of the Bill of Rights drains the "specific prohibitions" of the Bill of Rights of any coherent meaning, as Justice Black complained in his *Griswold* dissent. This is evident from the fact that the *Griswold* Court used this rationale to rescue and revive two *Lochner*-era personal liberty cases — *Meyer v. Nebraska* (1923) and *Pierce v. Society of Sisters* (1925) — which had seemingly been discredited as due process precedents by *Carolene Products*. The decisions in *Meyer* and *Pierce* were now reinterpreted and reaffirmed as having been justified under the penumbras and emanations principle. According to *Griswold*, the liberty interests in learning German and in directing the education of one's children that were protected by those earlier rulings in fact lay within the shadows of the First Amendment. 381 U.S. at 482.

§2.4.2 Alternative Approaches: Liberty and the Ninth Amendment

The penumbras and emanations theory did not satisfy all members of the *Griswold* majority. Justice Harlan, in a separate concurring opinion, rejected the approach. Instead, he rested the right of marital privacy squarely on the word "liberty" in the Fourteenth Amendment Due Process Clause, without linking it to any provision of the Bill of Rights. Because the right of marital privacy is "implicit in the concept of ordered liberty," it was, therefore, constitutionally protected. 381 U.S. at 500. While this approach gives the Court considerable leeway, Harlan noted that any "judicial 'self restraint'" imposed by the penumbras and emanations theory "is more hollow than real." Id. at 501. In a separate concurrence, Justice White also declined to endorse the penumbras and emanations theory and, like Harlan, relied simply on the word "liberty" contained in the Due Process Clause.

Three other members of the *Griswold* majority also agreed with Justice Harlan that the right of marital privacy is an aspect of due process "liberty," but buttressed their conclusion with the Ninth Amendment. That Amendment states: "The enumeration in the Constitution of certain rights shall not be construed to deny or disparage *others retained by the people*" (emphasis supplied). While Douglas had referred to the Amendment in passing, Justice Goldberg, joined by Chief Justice Warren and Justice Brennan, relied on it as authority for construing the Fourteenth Amendment Due Process Clause to encompass rights not enumerated elsewhere in the Constitution. Justice Goldberg wrote that "[t]he language and history of the Ninth Amendment reveal that the Framers of the Constitution believed that there are additional fundamental rights, protected from governmental infringement, which exist alongside those fundamental rights specifically mentioned in the first eight constitutional amendments." Id. at 488. While not "an independent source of rights protected from infringement by either the States or the Federal Government," id. at 492, the Ninth Amendment provides a rule of construction for the courts in interpreting other provisions of the Constitution, such as the word "liberty" in the Due Process Clause. On this basis, Justice Goldberg concluded that the unenumerated "right of privacy in the marital relation is . . . a personal right 'retained by the people' within the meaning of the Ninth Amendment" and that it is, therefore, among the "fundamental" personal liberties that are "protected by the Fourteenth Amendment from infringement by the States." Id. at 499.

Justice Goldberg's reliance on the Ninth Amendment drew fire from Justices Stewart and Black, who believed that "[t]he Ninth Amendment, like its companion the Tenth, . . . was . . . adopted by the States simply to make clear that the adoption of the Bill of Rights did not alter the plan that the *Federal* Government was to be a government of express and limited powers, and that all rights and powers not delegated to it were retained by the people and the individual States." Id. at 529-530 (Stewart & Black, JJ., dissenting) (emphasis in original). It was intended as a means to "protect state powers against federal invasion," not as a basis for recognizing unenumerated rights that may be judicially enforced against the federal or state governments. Id. at 520 (Black & Stewart, JJ., dissenting). One difficulty with the Stewart-Black reading, however, is that it renders the Ninth Amendment synonymous with the Tenth and thus redundant. The Tenth Amendment does say that those powers not conferred on the federal government are reserved to the states or to the people. But the Ninth Amendment says something quite different, i.e., that the people have other rights against the government besides those enumerated in the Bill of Rights. If these other rights are not judicially enforceable, if there is no remedy for their violation, then they are not rights in a strong or meaningful sense, but mere norms or platitudes that government officials may ignore with impunity. It is difficult to believe that the Founders would have troubled themselves to include the Ninth Amendment if this is all that it was intended to accomplish.

§2.4.3 *The Risks in Protecting Unenumerated Rights*

While the seven members of the *Griswold* majority offered a variety of bases for finding a fundamental right of marital privacy, they all agreed that the Court may give protection to liberty interests that are nowhere specifically mentioned in the text of the Constitution. A clear majority, in other words, refused to give the Constitution a strictly literal reading that would protect only those specific liberties — such as the Third Amendment guarantee against having soldiers quartered in one's home during peacetime — that are spelled out in full by the text itself. To construe the document as Justices Black and Stewart proposed in their dissent would have given an extremely narrow reading to the "liberty" protected by the Due Process Clause. Moreover, it would have been contrary to the apparent intent of the Founders, who included the Ninth Amendment to guard against just such a crabbed reading of the Constitution's enumeration of rights.

In the years since *Griswold*, the Court has added to the personal liberties that are protected by the Due Process Clause. In doing so, the Court has disavowed Justice Douglas's penumbras and emanations explanation, *Whalen v. Roe*, 429 U.S. 589, 598 n.23 (1977), and candidly acknowledged that the task requires giving meaning to the "Fourteenth Amendment's concept of personal liberty," *Roe v. Wade*, 410 U.S. 113, 152-153 (1973). Even some of the Court's more conservative members have accepted the validity of this judicial undertaking. In *Thornburgh v. American College of Obstetricians &*

Gynecologists, 476 U.S. 747, 789 (1986), Justice White, joined by Justice Rehnquist, declared that

> this Court does not subscribe to the simplistic view that constitutional interpretation can possibly be limited to the "plain meaning" of the Constitution's text or to the subjective intention of the Framers. The Constitution is not a deed setting forth the precise metes and bounds of its subject matter; rather, it is a document announcing fundamental principles in value-laden terms that leave ample scope for the exercise of normative judgment by those charged with interpreting and applying it.

Similarly, in *Richmond Newspapers, Inc. v. Virginia,* 448 U.S. 555, 579 (1980), Chief Justice Burger, writing for the majority, noted that "[n]otwithstanding the appropriate caution against reading into the Constitution rights not explicitly defined, the Court has acknowledged that certain unarticulated rights are implicit in enumerated guaranties."

The issue that has continued to divide the Justices is not the question of whether the Court should give constitutional protection to unenumerated, nontextual liberty interests, but rather what sources it should look to in doing so and how those sources should be construed. For example, should the Court consider only the Founders' specific intent, or is it permissible to consider the more general concepts the Founders hoped to protect? Are history and tradition legitimate guides, and if so, at what point and at what level of generality are they to be measured? To what extent is the Court confined to past case law? And of what relevance are principles of philosophy, political theory, or sociology? These important questions are explored in Christopher N. May & Allan Ides, *Constitutional Law: National Power and Federalism,* ch. 1 (2001).

When the Court seeks to define and protect rights that are not specifically enumerated in the text of the Constitution, it takes some institutional risks. One is that the Court may lose credibility if it is perceived by the public as having simply enshrined the personal beliefs and prejudices of individual Justices. Another risk is that by operating without close textual moorings, the Court may seek to protect values that are so out of touch with those of the public that the people will refuse to accept the Court's judgment. Both of these dangers materialized during the *Lochner* era, when the Court, in the name of liberty to contract, continued to impose the doctrine of laissez faire on a nation prostrated by the Depression. As Justice Powell wrote in *Moore v. City of East Cleveland,* 431 U.S. 494, 502 (1977):

> Substantive due process has at times been a treacherous field for this Court. There *are* risks when the judicial branch gives enhanced protection to certain substantive liberties without the guidance of the more specific provisions of the Bill of Rights. As the history of the *Lochner* era demonstrates, there is reason for concern lest the only limits to such judicial intervention become the predilections of those

who happen at the time to be Members of this Court. That history counsels caution and restraint. But it does not counsel abandonment. . . .

(Emphasis in original) (footnote reference omitted).

§2.4.4 *The Fundamental Rights Model with Variations*

Since *Griswold,* the constitutional right of privacy has expanded well beyond a married couple's freedom to decide to use birth control. This fundamental right now extends to unmarried individuals and embraces other personal decisions, most of them having to do with procreation, marriage, or family. In analyzing claimed violations of these fundamental liberty interests, the Court has adopted what might be thought of as a basic due process model. In some cases, the Court applies a variation of this model. We will first examine the basic model and then consider a few variations to it.

The Basic Fundamental Rights Model

In contrast to *Griswold,* where Justice Douglas's opinion for the Court struck down a Connecticut law under what amounted to a per se rule of invalidity, the Court typically employs a more subtle approach in fundamental rights due process cases. That basic approach consists of five steps or inquiries:

1. Is the interest in question one that qualifies as a *protected liberty* under the Due Process Clause?
2. Is the protected liberty one that is deemed to be *fundamental?*
3. Does the challenged law interfere with the fundamental liberty in a serious enough way to *impinge on* or *unduly burden* that liberty, thereby triggering strict scrutiny?
4. If a fundamental liberty has been impinged on or unduly burdened, does the law substantially further a *compelling governmental interest?*
5. Has the government chosen the *least burdensome means* of achieving its compelling interest?

Step 1 of this basic model is usually noncontroversial, since virtually all forms of individual freedom qualify for at least minimal due process protection. See §5.2.1; but cf. *Paul v. Davis,* 424 U.S. 693 (1976) (interest in reputation not a liberty interest protected by Due Process Clause). Step 2 of the analysis, however, presents the more difficult question of determining whether any particular liberty interest is entitled to special protection as a fundamental right. In §§2.5 and 2.6, we will examine those liberty interests the Court has deemed fundamental (or nonfundamental) as well as the methods through which the Court has arrived at those conclusions. Of course, the various opinions in *Griswold* lay the foundation for that process. Step 3 requires an assessment of the degree to which the liberty interest is burdened, since de minimis infringements will not trigger strict scrutiny. Finally, steps 4 and 5 represent the application of strict scrutiny; i.e., the challenged law or practice will be held to violate the Due Process Clause unless it is shown that the measure is necessary to achieve a compelling governmental interest. These steps are not reached, however, unless we have obtained affirmative answers to inquiries 1, 2, and 3. If any of the first three inquiries is answered in the negative, the court will apply only the rational basis standard of review.

The Concept of Impingement

There are several important points to remember about the impingement or undue burden requirement. First, virtually all of the rights we enjoy under the Constitution are negative rather than positive rights. In other words, they operate as protections against governmental interference, not as guaranties of governmental assistance. As the Court has explained:

> The [Due Process] Clause is phrased as a limitation on the State's power to act. . . . It forbids the State itself to deprive individuals of life, liberty, or property without 'due process of law,' but its language cannot fairly be extended to impose an affirmative obligation on the State to ensure that those interests do not come to harm through other means.

DeShaney v. Winnebago County Dept. of Social Servs., 489 U.S. 189, 195 (1989). The government has no affirmative constitutional duty to assure that each of us is able to exercise, enjoy, or realize the benefits of a particular right. For example, the freedoms to marry, to use contraceptives, and to choose an abortion are all fundamental liberties under the Due Process Clause, yet the government is not constitutionally obligated to pay for the wedding, purchase the contraceptives, or provide a free abortion for someone who cannot otherwise afford it. See *Poelker v. Doe*, 432 U.S. 519 (1977) (city-owned hospital need not perform abortions). All that the Constitution usually requires is that the government not actively interfere — whether through criminal punishment or otherwise — with our ability to exercise our constitutional rights.

Second, even where the government does interfere with our ability to exercise a protected liberty interest, not all forms of governmental interference are serious enough to count as an impairment of a constitutional right. The purpose of the impingement or undue burden requirement is to separate insignificant governmental actions from those that are substantial enough to trigger strict scrutiny. For example, the application of a general sales tax to the purchase of contraceptives would probably not be deemed to impinge on the freedom to practice birth control, whereas a law that criminalized such sales would impose an undue burden and would be subject to strict scrutiny.

Variations on the Basic Strict Scrutiny Model

The Court does not always follow this basic five-step due process model in analyzing laws that allegedly interfere with a fundamental liberty interest. One variation involves eliminating the last two steps of the analysis and asking only the first three questions. Under this approach, if the law places an "undue burden" on a fundamental liberty interest, it is invalid; if it does not impose an undue burden, it will be upheld under a rational basis standard of review. As we will see in the next section, this variation is currently used by the Court to test laws that interfere with a woman's freedom to decide whether to have an abortion. See §2.5.4.

A second variation involves eliminating the last step of the basic analysis and ending with the fourth inquiry. If a law impinges on a fundamental liberty interest (thereby satisfying steps 1, 2, and 3), the only remaining issue is whether the measure furthers a compelling governmental interest; if it does, the law will be upheld whether or not it was the least burdensome means available to the state. This variation greatly relaxes the standard of review, for the government does not have to show that it was necessary to burden the fundamental liberty in question. This variation was used in *Youngberg v. Romeo,* 457 U.S. 307 (1982), to reject a suit brought against a state hospital by a mentally retarded inmate who claimed that the hospital had violated his liberty interests in safety and freedom from bodily restraint. See §2.6.1.

A third variation on the basic model involves skipping steps 2 and 3 of the analysis. Under this approach, the Court assumes arguendo that a fundamental liberty interest was impinged upon, but upholds the law on the ground that the government's action was justified. By taking this route, the Court avoids having to decide whether a claimed interest qualifies as a fundamental liberty under the Due Process Clause. The Court used this approach in *Cruzan v. Director, Missouri Department of Health,* 497 U.S. 261 (1990), in upholding a Missouri law that prevented a family from withdrawing artificial feeding equipment from their daughter, who was hospitalized in a persistent vegetative state. The Court refused to decide whether the state had abridged the daughter's claimed fundamental liberty to refuse life-sustaining food and hydration. Instead, it held that even if the state had unduly burdened such a liberty, the state had an adequate basis for doing so. See §2.5.7.

§2.5   The Right of Privacy and Personal Autonomy

The right of marital privacy recognized by the Court's path-breaking 1965 decision in *Griswold v. Connecticut* was soon extended to persons who were not married and to conduct that did not occur in the privacy of the home. The Court held that unmarried persons (*Eisenstadt v. Baird*, 405 U.S. 438 (1972)), including minors (*Carey v. Population Servs. Intl.*, 431 U.S. 678 (1977)), have the same fundamental liberty interest in using contraceptives as did the married couples protected by *Griswold*. The right of privacy was also held to protect a married or unmarried woman's liberty to choose an abortion even though this procedure usually takes place outside the home in a doctor's office, clinic, or hospital. *Roe v. Wade*, 410 U.S. 113 (1973). With this expansion of *Griswold*, it became increasingly difficult to speak of the right in question as being one of privacy, much less of marital privacy. The Court, therefore, reformulated the liberty interest recognized in *Griswold* as one that "protects *individual decisions* in matters of childbearing from unjustified intrusion by the State." *Carey v. Population Servs. Intl.*, 431 U.S. at 687 (emphasis supplied). What had begun as a right of privacy was thus transformed into a right of personal autonomy, "the interest in independence in making certain kinds of important decisions." *Whalen v. Roe*, 429 U.S. 589, 599-600 (1977). While courts continue to speak of the constitutional *right of privacy*, this phrase is normally used to mean the same thing as the *right of personal autonomy*. We will use these terms interchangeably in the balance of this section as we examine the different kinds of personal decisions that the Court has deemed to be protected by this right.

§2.5.1   Marriage

One of the fundamental liberties protected by the right of personal autonomy is the right to marry, i.e., the freedom to decide to enter into the marital relationship. In *Loving v. Virginia*, 388 U.S. 1, 12 (1967), the Court described marriage as "one of the 'basic civil rights of man,' fundamental to our very existence and survival." The Court later explained that "the right to marry is part of the fundamental 'right of privacy' implicit in the . . . Due Process Clause." *Zablocki v. Redhail*, 434 U.S. 374, 384 (1978). Laws that impinge on or unduly burden the freedom to marry are subject to strict scrutiny under the Due Process Clause. The Court has suggested that because marriage has traditionally been governed by the states, it may be more difficult than in other fundamental liberty cases to establish that a law has sufficiently burdened the right to marry to trigger strict scrutiny.

In trying to determine when a law that interferes with the marriage decision will receive strict scrutiny under the Due Process Clause, cases decided under the Equal Protection Clause may be instructive. This is because laws that impinge on the freedom to marry on a *discriminatory* basis are also subject to strict scrutiny under the Equal Protection Clause. See §7.2. Since these impingement requirements are similar, the equal protection cases shed light on what types of restrictions on the right to marry are likely to trigger strict scrutiny under the Due Process Clause.

Laws that directly and seriously interfere with the decision to marry, e.g., by prohibiting a person from exercising this fundamental liberty, impose an "undue burden" on the right to marry and trigger a generally fatal strict scrutiny. See *Zablocki v. Redhail*, 434 U.S 374 (1978) (law barring marriage by certain parents who have not complied with child support orders violates Equal Protection Clause); *Loving v. Virginia*, 388 U.S. 1 (1967) (ban on marriage between whites and nonwhites violates Due Process and Equal Protection Clauses).

On the other hand, "reasonable regulations that do not significantly interfere with decisions to enter into the marital relationship" will not be "subjected to rigorous scrutiny." *Zablocki*, 434 U.S. at 386. Traditional state requirements that merely delay exercise of this right — e.g., minimum age requirements for marriage and waiting periods for divorce (a legal prerequisite for remarriage) — are unlikely to be tested under strict scrutiny. Cf. *Sosna v. Iowa*, 419 U.S. 393 (1975) (applying less than strict scrutiny to uphold one-year waiting period for divorce under Equal Protection Clause, but without specifically addressing law's impact on right to marry). Even some traditional restrictions that permanently interfere with the marriage decision, such as laws against bigamy and incest, may not be regarded as unduly burdening the right to marry. See *Zablocki*, 434 U.S. at 392 (Stewart, J., concurring); id. at 398-399 (Powell, J., concurring). Yet other traditional restrictions that seriously interfere with the right to marry may be subjected to strict scrutiny despite their lineage. See *Loving v. Virginia*, 388 U.S. 1 (1967) (using strict scrutiny to overturn Virginia's anti-miscegenation laws that dated from seventeenth century and had counterparts in many other states).

Since it is often unclear whether a law will be found to impinge on the right to marry, it is a good idea in cases of doubt to employ a dual analysis, approaching the problem first on the assumption that the law imposes an undue burden and then on the assumption that it does not.

EXAMPLE 2-C

Alice is 16 years old and was recently married. Shortly after her marriage, the state terminated her $550/month welfare grant under a law that allows those who are under 21 to receive welfare benefits only if they are unmarried. Does this law violate Alice's rights under the Fourteenth Amendment Due Process Clause?

EXPLANATION

Alice will argue that the law interferes with her liberty interest in marriage. Since the right to marry is a protected and fundamental liberty interest, the first two steps of the basic due process analysis are satisfied. Alice will have a harder time meeting the undue burden requirement. The state has not directly interfered with the marriage decision by prohibiting her from getting married. On the other hand, it has indirectly punished her for deciding to marry by terminating her subsistence benefits as a result. In *Califano v. Jobst,* 434 U.S. 47 (1977), the Court held that the termination of Social Security benefits to a child who marries does not impinge on the liberty interest in marriage; there, however, the benefits were relatively low and were not intended to meet subsistence needs. Alice will claim that because of the critical nature of the benefits at stake, her case is distinguishable from *Jobst* and that the state has, therefore, impinged on her fundamental liberty to marry.

If the Court agrees, the law will receive strict scrutiny. Under step 4, the state may claim a compelling interest in encouraging children on welfare to work or educate themselves before starting their own families, thus reducing the chances that they will continue to be dependent on welfare. Alice would respond that the mere saving of money is not a compelling interest; if it were, the government could justify curtailing our most basic liberty interests such as freedom of speech and assembly on the ground that their exercise is too costly. Even if the interest in saving money were compelling, Alice will argue under step 5 that the state has less burdensome ways to achieve its goals, such as simply requiring children who are on welfare to work or attend school whether or not they are married. Thus, if the court applies strict scrutiny, the law might well be struck down on the basis that it was not necessary for the state to interfere with Alice's right to marry in order to achieve its goal of reducing welfare costs. If, on the other hand, the court were to apply the rational basis test, the law would be upheld, since a rational legislature could reasonably conclude that this law was a good way to reduce long-term dependence on welfare.

§2.5.2   *Family Integrity*

Family Living Arrangements

The right to marry was held to constitute a fundamental liberty partly because marriage establishes "the relationship that is the foundation of the family in our society." *Zablocki v. Redhail,* 434 U.S. at 386. The family constitutes a sphere of life that lies at the heart of what is private and personal. In order to shield this sphere from unwarranted governmental intrusion, the

Court has held that the interest in maintaining the integrity of the family is a protected aspect of the fundamental right of privacy under the Due Process Clause. This liberty interest usually comes into play in settings where the government has interfered with family living arrangements by making it difficult or impossible for family members to share a common household. See *Moore v. City of East Cleveland*, 431 U.S. 494 (1977) (invalidating ordinance that barred a grandmother, her son, and two grandsons from living together in the same home).

EXAMPLE 2-D

A city ordinance provides that no household may be occupied by more than two persons under the age of ten. As a result of the ordinance, the Sutro family, which contains three children under the age of ten, is being evicted from the apartment where they have lived for the past 12 years. Can the Sutros avoid being evicted on the ground that the ordinance violates their rights under the Fourteenth Amendment Due Process Clause?

EXPLANATION

The fundamental liberty interest recognized in *Moore* protects the right of persons who are related by blood or marriage to live together in a common household. The city's ordinance directly and substantially interferes with this right by barring the Sutros from preserving the integrity of their family unit. The only way they could avoid being evicted is by sending one of the children to live somewhere else or by giving the child up for adoption. The ordinance clearly impinges on the family's fundamental liberty interest. It is no answer that the Sutros could live together as a family in some other city. This option was available to the family in *Moore*, but did not suffice to avoid the application of strict scrutiny there.

Since the first three steps of the due process analysis have been satisfied, the ordinance will be struck down unless the city can show that it furthers a compelling governmental interest and that it is the least burdensome means of doing so. The city may argue that it has an interest in preserving the peace and tranquillity of residential areas and that households with many young children often disturb others, particularly senior citizens. It is far from clear that this interest is sufficiently compelling to justify a law that strikes so close to the heart of the family. Small children have always been part of the American landscape, and the noise that they make is an unavoidable fact of life.

Even if a court were to find this interest to be compelling, there are less burdensome ways of achieving the city's goals, such as by enforcing noise control ordinances, allowing landlords to limit the occupancy of certain buildings to senior citizens, or perhaps even zoning parts of the city exclusively for adults.

As is true with the liberty interest in marriage, however, not all laws that burden a family's interest in living together are necessarily subject to strict scrutiny.

EXAMPLE 2-E

A state welfare program provides assistance to needy families with children. The state pays $150/month for each child living in the home, with a maximum monthly grant of $450 per household. Mary and Joe Alt, who live with their six children, receive a welfare grant of $450/month. This is not enough to meet their basic needs. If Joe and three of the children were to move to a separate apartment, they would be eligible for a separate grant of $450/month, so that the family as a whole would receive $900/month. Does the state's "maximum grant" rule violate the Due Process Clause by forcing poor families to break up their shared living arrangements?

EXPLANATION

Probably not. In contrast to *Moore v. City of East Cleveland*, and to Example 2-D, the state has not made it illegal for family members to maintain a common household. While the structure of the welfare program may give needy families an incentive to split their household, the incentive is probably weak. While the Alts could double their welfare benefits by breaking up their household, the additional rent and utility costs associated with doing so might more than offset the additional income they would receive. Because the state has probably not impinged on the Alts' liberty interest in family integrity, the state's maximum grant rule would be upheld under the rational basis test. See *Lyng v. Castillo*, 477 U.S. 635 (1986) (no impingement on liberty interest in family integrity where government gave reduced food stamps to households with related persons even though family could increase its food stamp allowance by living apart); *Dandridge v. Williams*, 397 U.S. 471 (1970) (upholding state maximum grant in AFDC welfare program). In our hypothetical, strict scrutiny might be triggered if the state instead refused to pay *any* welfare benefits to households with more than three children, for then the incentive for a needy family to split into separate households might be irresistible.

The liberty interest in maintaining the integrity of the family does not protect all groups of people who wish to share a common household. While the Court in *Moore* was willing to extend the constitutional protections of family beyond the traditional nuclear family consisting of parents and their children, the Court has held that there are limits on how far the definition of family can be stretched for due process purposes. In *Village of Belle Terre v. Boraas*, 416 U.S. 1 (1974), the Court thus applied the rational basis test to uphold a zoning ordinance that barred six college students from occupying a house together. The key difference between *Moore* and *Belle Terre* was that in the latter case, the ordinance "affected only *unrelated* individuals. It expressly allowed all who were related by 'blood, adoption, or marriage' to live together. . . ." *Moore*, 431 U.S. at 498 (emphasis in original). However, even if unrelated individuals are not able to invoke the liberty interest in family integrity, they may be able to protect their right to live together through another fundamental liberty interest, namely, the freedom of intimate association. See §2.5.3.

The Parent-Child Relationship

The liberty interest in preserving the integrity of the family is closely related to the interest of parents in their children. Indeed, the parent-child relationship lies at the heart of our notion of family. When the Court in *Moore v. City of East Cleveland* held that there is a fundamental liberty interest in maintaining family living arrangements, it relied on earlier cases such as *Meyer v. Nebraska* and *Pierce v. Society of Sisters*, which recognized that parents have a liberty interest in raising their children. This same liberty interest is implicated when the state seeks to disrupt the parent-child relationship through such actions as removing a child from the custody of its parents or denying a parent visitation rights.

Not all parent-child relationships are protected by the liberty interest in family. While *Moore* seemed to suggest that ties of blood, adoption, or marriage are *necessary* for there to be a "family" that can invoke the liberty interest in preserving family relationships, the existence of these ties will not always be *sufficient* to create a constitutionally protected family unit. In *Michael H. v. Gerald D.*, 491 U.S. 110 (1989), Michael claimed a fundamental liberty in maintaining a parental relationship with his biological daughter, Victoria — a relationship that the state sought to terminate by denying him all visitation rights. Even though earlier cases had recognized that parents, including unwed fathers, have a fundamental liberty interest in the parent-child relationship, the Court rejected Michael's challenge. Justice Scalia, writing for the plurality, emphasized that Michael was an *adulterous* natural father, for the child's mother was married to and living with another man at the time the child was born. Because the relationship between an adulterous natural father and his child has not been traditionally protected by our society, Michael and Victoria were not deemed to be a "protected family unit" for purposes of the Due Process Clause. As a result, neither Michael nor his daughter could claim a constitutional liberty interest in the biological parent-child relationship that existed between them.

Michael H. exemplifies the sharply contrasting approaches individual Justices may take in construing the Constitution. While no member of the Court urged that the word "liberty" in the Due Process Clause be limited to those specific interests that the drafters of the Fifth and Fourteenth Amendments had in mind, the Justices disagreed as to what method of interpretation should be employed. Justice Scalia, joined by Chief Justice Rehnquist, asserted that the Due Process Clause protects only those liberties that are "rooted in history and tradition. . . ." Id. at 123. In determining whether this test is met, Scalia insisted that an asserted liberty interest be described narrowly in terms of "the most specific tradition available. . . ." Id. at 128 n.6. Thus, the relevant inquiry in *Michael H.* focused on "historical traditions *specifically relating to the rights of an adulterous natural father,* rather than inquiring more generally 'whether *parenthood* is an interest that historically has received our attention and protection.'" Id. at 127 n.6 (emphasis supplied). Since there was no tradition protecting adulterous fathers, Scalia and Rehnquist concluded that Michael had no liberty interest whatsoever in preserving his relationship with Victoria.

Other Justices adopted less restrictive methodologies in *Michael H.* Justices O'Connor and Kennedy agreed with Scalia that the Court was obligated to look to history and tradition but rejected his "imposition of a single mode of historical analysis"; instead, they believed that it might sometimes be proper to consider "relevant traditions protecting asserted rights at levels of generality that might not be 'the most specific level' available." Id. at 132 (O'Connor & Kennedy, JJ., concurring in part). Justices Brennan, Marshall, and Blackmun objected both to Scalia's narrow approach to history and tradition and to the plurality's focus on history and tradition to the exclusion of other possible sources of interpretation. While history and tradition are not irrelevant, said Brennan, the Court should not "requir[e] specific approval from history before protecting anything in the name of liberty." Id. at 141 (Brennan, Marshall, & Blackmun, JJ., dissenting). In Brennan's view, the Court may reason from earlier precedents by asking whether a claimed liberty interest is "close enough to the interests that we already have protected to be deemed an aspect of 'liberty' as well." Id. at 142. Justice White appeared to adopt an approach similar to Brennan's.

Nonparental Visitation Statutes

All fifty states have enacted statutes that allow persons who are not a child's parents to obtain a court order granting them visitation rights with the child. These statutes vary widely in terms of who may seek such visitation, the circumstances under which a petition seeking visitation may be filed, and the showing that is required before a court may grant visitation rights. If a child's custodial parents favor visitation by grandparents or other third parties, the matter will usually be handled amicably and informally, without judicial intervention. State nonparental visitation statutes are thus likely to come into play only when a child's parent or parents oppose the visitation sought by a third party. If a court orders visitation under such circumstances, it interferes with parents' fundamental liberty interest in directing the upbringing of their children. On the other hand, to allow parents unilaterally to block visitation by grandparents or others who have developed a close relationship with a child may interfere with the child's liberty interest in preserving familial or family-like bonds, and undermine the state's interest in protecting children from harm. Nonparental visitation statutes thus raise complex issues of substantive due process.

A sharply divided Supreme Court addressed these issues for the first time in *Troxel v. Granville*, 120 S. Ct. 2054 (2000). The case involved a Washington statute that allowed "any person" to petition for visitation rights "at any time," and authorized courts to order such visitation over a parent's objection if the judge decided that "visitation may serve the best interest of the child." Under this statute, a state trial court granted visitation rights to the Troxels, who were the paternal grandparents of two children whose father had committed suicide. The rights granted were more extensive than the children's mother, Tommie Granville, was willing to allow. On appeal, the Washington Supreme Court held that the statute was facially invalid because it unconstitutionally infringed on the fundamental right of parents to raise their children. The U.S. Supreme Court affirmed six to three, but none of the six opinions in the case commanded a majority of the Court. Though seven Justices agreed that nonparental visitation statutes may at times violate parents' fundamental liberty interest in directing the upbringing of their children, these Justices were unable to articulate any general principles governing this area. Instead, as Justice O'Connor wrote in a plurality opinion joined by three of her colleagues (id. at 2064):

> We do not, and need not, define today the precise scope of the parental due process right in the visitation context. In this respect, we agree with Justice Kennedy that the constitutionality of any standard for awarding visitation turns on the specific manner in which the standard is applied and that the constitutional protections in this area are best "elaborated with care." Because much state-court adjudication in this context occurs on a case-by-case basis, we would be hesitant to hold that specific nonparental visitation statutes violate the Due Process Clause as a *per se* matter.

The plurality concluded that the statute was unconstitutional as applied to this case. Rather than employing the Court's basic strict scrutiny model or any of its recognized variations (see §2.4.4), the plurality declared the law invalid due to the "combination of several factors" that made it too easy for the state to infringe on Granville's "fundamental right to make decisions concerning the rearing of her two daughters." Id. at 2061. First, there was no allegation that the children's mother was an unfit parent. Where "a parent adequately cares for his or her children (i.e., is fit), there will normally be no reason for the State to inject itself into the private realm of the family to further question the ability of that parent to make the best decisions concerning the rearing of that parent's children." Id. Second, in finding that visitation by the grandparents was in the children's best interest, the Washington trial court — unlike courts in many other states — was not required to give any deference or weight to the mother's opposition to the petition, thereby ignoring the "presumption that fit parents act in the best interests of their children." Id. Finally, rather than seeking to bar visitation entirely, Granville merely opposed the frequency and length of the visits sought by the grandparents. The plurality thus suggested that if a state accords more deference to a fit parent's wishes than Washington did — e.g., by employing a rebuttable presumption that third party visitation is not in a child's best interest — a nonparental visitation statute might be valid. The state's interest in intervention would be even more compelling if there were a showing of parental unfitness or if a parent sought to deny all visitation to those with whom the child had developed a close relationship.

Concurring separately, Justice Souter voted to affirm the Washington's Supreme Court's ruling that the statute was facially invalid because it allowed the state, at the behest of "any person" at "any time" to impair a parent's relationship with her child "merely because the judge might think himself more enlightened than the child's parent." Id. at 2067. In contrast to the plurality, Justice Souter did not discuss whether a narrower, more deferential statute might pass constitutional muster.

To the extent that the plurality and Justice Souter focused primarily on the liberty interests of parents, Justices Stevens and Kennedy, in separate opinions, suggested that children may have a countervailing liberty interest in preserving relationships with persons other than their parents. As Justice Stevens wrote, "Cases like this do not present a bipolar struggle between the parents and the State over who has final authority to determine what is in a child's best interests. There is at minimum a third individual, whose interests are implicated in every case to which the statute applies — the child." Id. at 2071. Children have "liberty interests in preserving established familial or family-like bonds," which may warrant state protection "against the arbitrary exercise of parental authority that is not in fact motivated by an interest in the welfare of the child." Id. at 2072. In a similar vein, Justice Kennedy noted that there are cases "in which a third party, by acting in a caregiving role over a significant period of time, has developed a relationship with a child which is not necessarily subject to absolute parental veto. . . . In the design and elaboration of their visitation laws, States may be entitled to consider that certain relationships are such that to avoid the risk of harm, a best interests standard can be employed by their domestic relations courts in some circumstances." Id. at 2077-2078. It seems likely that Justices Stevens and Kennedy, like the plurality, would uphold a nonparental visitation statute that was less sweeping than the "any person" at "any time" measure enacted by Washington.

Nor is there any doubt that Justice Scalia would sustain such a law, for he was the only Justice who found no constitutional difficulties with the Washington statute either on its face or as applied. In his view, nonparental visitation statutes do not trigger constitutional concern because the Due Process Clause does not protect the unenumerated right of a parent to raise children. Justice Thomas would probably agree. He concurred in the judgment on the basis that existing case law recognizes a fundamental right of parents to direct the upbringing of their children. However, Thomas pointedly added that since none of the parties had argued that the Court's "substantive due process cases were wrongly decided," he would leave for another day the question of whether "the original understanding of the Due Process Clause precludes judicial enforcement of unenumerated rights under that constitutional provision." Id. at 2067.

In sum, while *Troxel* affirmed that parents have a liberty interest that comes into play when a state grants visitation rights to third parties, the parent's right is far from absolute. Instead, it is likely to yield where, under a narrower statute aimed at protecting preexisting relationships, the state requires a stronger showing that nonparental visitation is necessary. How strong that showing must be, however, remains an open question. The Washington Supreme Court held that merely protecting a child's "best interests" is never enough to justify third party visitation; instead, such interference with a parent's liberty to raise her children is permissible, it said, only when necessary to prevent "harm or potential harm" to the child. Though Justices Stevens and Kennedy appear to have endorsed use of a "best interests" standard, the rest of the Court declined to address this critical issue.

§2.5.3   *Intimate Association*

The fundamental liberty interest in family integrity extends only to relationships that are based on ties of blood, adoption, or marriage. Other group relationships, such as those that existed among the would-be college roommates in *Village of Belle Terre*, are not protected by the liberty interest in family. However, some nonfamily groups may enjoy constitutional protection under another aspect of the right of privacy and personal autonomy, i.e., the freedom of intimate association. See also §8.6 (discussing the First Amendment right of association). Like the interest in family integrity, which it closely resembles, this fundamental liberty affords "certain kinds of highly personal relationships a substantial measure of sanctuary from unjustified interference by the State." *Roberts v. United States Jaycees,* 468 U.S. 609, 618 (1984). Such relationships promote personal autonomy, for they "act as critical buffers between the individual and the power of the State." Id. at 619. Moreover, since "individuals draw much of their emotional enrichment from close ties with others," the freedom of intimate association "safeguards the ability independently to define one's identity that is central to any concept of liberty." Id. When this liberty interest comes into play, it may enable a group to resist governmental actions that might force the group to disband or compel it to accept unwanted members.

For a group to qualify for protection under the right of intimate association, it must possess some of the attributes that characterize a family, such as "relative smallness, a high degree of selectivity in decisions to begin and maintain the affiliation, and seclusion from others in critical aspects of the relationship." Id. at 620. In addition, the Court will take into account the group's purpose and congeniality.

In *Roberts v. United States Jaycees,* the Jaycees argued that a state human rights law that required the Jaycees to admit women violated the group's freedom of intimate association under the Due Process Clause. However, the Court held that the Jaycees could not invoke this right because its local chapters were quite large and its membership policies essentially nonselective. See also *Board of Directors of Rotary Intl. v. Rotary Club of Duarte,* 481 U.S. 537 (1987) (rejecting claim that state-ordered admission of women violated group's right of intimate association).

EXAMPLE 2-F

Beverly owns a house with ten bedrooms. She lives there with eight adult boarders who are not related by blood, marriage, or adoption. Over the years, the group has developed strong social, economic, and psychological commitments to each other. They share expenses, rotate chores, and eat evening meals together. In addition, they often attend movies, go bowling, and take vacations together. A city zoning ordinance provides that no household may contain more than five people who are unrelated by blood, marriage, or adoption. The city has sued Beverly for an injunction, claiming that she is in violation of the ordinance. May Beverly oppose enforcement on the ground that the ordinance violates her rights under the Fourteenth Amendment Due Process Clause?

EXPLANATION

Beverly cannot invoke the fundamental liberty interest in protecting family living arrangements, since this right applies only to groups that are related by blood, adoption, or marriage. However, she may be able to invoke the privacy-based right of intimate association. In contrast to the students in *Belle Terre*, her household shares many attributes normally associated with a typical family. Beverly can argue that the group is relatively small and congenial, that she is very selective in whom she takes in as boarders, and that the group's purpose transcends mere convenience. She and her tenants have formed bonds that are intimate and similar to those developed in traditional family households.

If the court finds that Beverly and her tenants are protected by the right of intimate association, the city's effort to break up her household impinges on this right so as to trigger strict scrutiny. Even if the city has compelling interests in limiting density, controlling noise, and reducing the number of cars in residential areas, there are other ways to achieve these goals without burdening the right of intimate association. See *City of Santa Barbara v. Adamson*, 27 Cal. 3d 123, 610 P.2d 436 (1980) (state constitution barred use of zoning ordinance to force dissolution of household of 12 unrelated persons who shared many attributes of family).

§2.5.4 *Abortion*

Roe v. Wade and the Trimester Framework

The Court's first right of privacy decisions involved laws that, by barring the use of contraceptives, had the effect of forcing individuals to have children and create a family against their wishes. In striking down these laws, the Court held that one of the fundamental liberties protected by the Due Process Clause is the "decision whether to bear or beget a child." *Eisenstadt v. Baird*, 405 U.S. 438 (1972). This decision is as much impaired by laws outlawing abortion as by bans on the use of contraceptives. In 1973, the Court recognized this fact, holding that the right of privacy in matters concerning procreation and family "is broad enough to encompass a woman's decision whether or not to terminate her pregnancy." *Roe v. Wade*, 410 U.S. 113, 153 (1973).

Roe involved a Texas statute that made it illegal to have an abortion except where necessary to save the mother's life. By absolutely prohibiting most abortions, the statute impinged on a woman's fundamental liberty to choose an abortion, thus triggering strict scrutiny under the Due Process Clause. It was, therefore, necessary for Texas to show that its interference with this right of personal privacy "was necessary to support a compelling state interest. . . ." Id. at 156. The Court agreed that the state had two compelling interests in regulating the abortion decision, i.e., the interest in protecting *maternal health* and the interest in protecting *potential life*. In an opinion written by Justice Blackmun, the Court held that neither of these interests was compelling at the outset of pregnancy. Rather, the interest in protecting the mother's health becomes compelling at the end of the *first trimester* (i.e., after about three months of pregnancy); before then, it is safer for a woman to have an abortion than to proceed with childbirth. The state's interest in potential life, on the other hand, does not become compelling until roughly the end of the *second trimester* (i.e., after about six months of pregnancy); only then is the fetus *viable* in the sense that it is capable of surviving outside the mother's womb.

Under this trimester framework, the state's interest in regulating abortion becomes stronger as the period of pregnancy lengthens. During the first trimester, the state has no compelling reason to regulate abortion. In the second trimester, it acquires a compelling interest in protecting maternal health. This interest allows the state to impose restrictions that are necessary to ensure that the abortion procedure is safe, but it cannot justify a total prohibition on abortion. During the last trimester of pregnancy, the state acquires a compelling interest in protecting the fetus. At this point, the state may "regulate, and even proscribe, abortion except where it is necessary, in appropriate medical judgment, for the preservation of the life or health of the mother." Id. at 165. Once the fetus has become viable, the state may restrict or completely outlaw *nontherapeutic abortions,* i.e., those that are not medically necessary to protect the mother's health or life; however, the state may not prevent a woman from choosing to have a *therapeutic abortion.*

While *Roe* invalidated *prohibitions* on abortion during the first and second trimesters, the decision left room for states to *regulate* the procedures for obtaining abortions. Such regulations might be upheld under the trimester framework if they did not unduly burden the abortion decision (and thus did not trigger strict scrutiny), if they became applicable after the first trimester and were necessary to protect maternal health, or if they were limited exclusively to the third trimester.

In the years following *Roe,* state and local governments tested the limits of that decision by enacting scores of laws that restricted the ability of women to obtain abortions. These measures were invariably challenged, forcing lower courts and the Supreme Court to apply and clarify the ruling handed down in *Roe.* The Court upheld some first- and second-trimester restrictions on the abortion process, including requirements that women give written consent; that doctors keep certain records; that tissue samples be examined by a pathologist; and that immature minors obtain the consent of a parent, or that they wait 48 hours after notifying both parents, unless a judge allowed them to bypass these requirements. However, many other pre-viability restrictions were struck down, including so-called informed-consent provisions that required doctors to make specific statements to a woman concerning the fetus; 24-hour waiting periods for adults; laws limiting abortions exclusively to hospitals or licensed clinics; bans on certain inexpensive abortion methods; requirements that all minors, regardless of maturity, obtain the consent of a parent or a judge; and requirements that doctors report personal information about abortion patients to the state. The Court also struck down a number of third-trimester restrictions that, in order to protect the fetus, jeopardized maternal health.

The Court was sharply divided in many of these cases. The majority typically applied a low threshold for determining whether a restriction unduly burdened or impinged on a woman's fundamental liberty interest and was thus subject to strict scrutiny. As a rule, the Court's majority found the impingement requirement to be satisfied if a regulation had the effect of delaying, discouraging, or increasing the cost of an abortion. The dissenting Justices, on the other hand, employed a higher threshold of impingement, so that regulations that did not constitute an absolute barrier to abortion were tested and upheld under a rational basis standard. See, e.g., *City of Akron v. Akron Center for Reproductive Health, Inc.*, 462 U.S. 416, 461-475 (1983) (O'Connor, White, & Rehnquist, JJ., dissenting) (applying rational basis review to a law that imposed a 24-hour waiting period, required second-trimester abortions to be performed only in a hospital, and forced physicians to read a statement to pregnant women concerning the fetus).

By 1989, the split within the Court had reached the point where four Justices — Rehnquist, White, Scalia, and Kennedy — had gone on record urging that *Roe v. Wade* be either overruled or limited to statutes that outlawed abortions; laws that simply regulated the abortion procedure would then be reviewed under the rational basis standard. See *Webster v. Reproductive Health Servs.*, 492 U.S. 490, 517-522 (1989) (opinion of Rehnquist, White, & Kennedy); id. at 532 (opinion of Scalia, J.); *Thornburgh v. American College of Obstetricians & Gynecologists*, 476 U.S. 747, 786-797 (1986) (opinion of White & Rehnquist). It seemed that only one more vote was needed to overrule *Roe*. When Justices Brennan and Marshall, both staunch supporters of *Roe*, resigned from the Court in the early 1990s, President Bush replaced them with David Souter and Clarence Thomas. In light of Bush's campaign promises to appoint anti-abortion judges to the federal bench, it was widely expected that these new Justices would provide the necessary votes to finally overturn *Roe*. The vehicle for the anticipated *coup de grace* was *Planned Parenthood v. Casey*, 505 U.S. 833 (1992), a case challenging the Pennsylvania Abortion Control Act.

Planned Parenthood v. Casey and the End of the Trimester Approach

In *Planned Parenthood v. Casey*, the Court struck down that part of Pennsylvania's abortion law that required married women, except in certain limited circumstances, to notify their husbands before having an abortion. The Court upheld the rest of the Act, including an informed-consent provision that required physicians to give women specific information about the fetus; a 24-hour waiting period; a parental consent requirement for immature minors; and a recordkeeping and reporting requirement for facilities performing abortions. In order to uphold these provisions, the Court had to overrule several prior decisions that had declared similar regulations to be unconstitutional. And while *Casey* preserved what it viewed as the "essential holding" of *Roe v. Wade,* it rejected *Roe*'s trimester framework and replaced it with a new "undue burden" test for analyzing the validity of all abortion restrictions.

Casey was the product of a highly splintered Court. Four Justices — Rehnquist, White, Scalia, and Thomas—voted to overrule *Roe* in its entirety and to sustain all the challenged regulations. Justice Blackmun, on the other hand, adhered fully to *Roe* and believed that all of the Pennsylvania restrictions were invalid. Justice Stevens also endorsed *Roe* and voted to invalidate most of the state's restrictions. With the Court split four to two, the outcome lay in the hands of Justices O'Connor, Kennedy, and Souter. They issued a joint opinion that staked out a middle position between completely overruling *Roe* and preserving the decision intact. Because their opinion played such a pivotal role, it needs to be examined closely.

The authors of the joint opinion, some of whom had been quite critical of *Roe,* explained that the principle of stare decisis prevented them from abandoning *Roe* in its entirety. Justice Kennedy's vote was particularly surprising, since three years earlier he had joined Chief Justice Rehnquist's opinion in *Webster* suggesting that *Roe* be overruled. Justices O'Connor, Kennedy, and Souter now declared that "the essential holding of *Roe v. Wade* should be retained and once again reaffirmed." 505 U.S. at 846. This essential holding was that a woman has "the right . . . to choose an abortion before viability and to obtain it without undue interference from the State," and the right to elect an abortion even after viability where it is necessary to protect her health or her life. Id.

However, the joint authors "reject[ed] the trimester framework, which [they did] not consider to be part of the essential holding of *Roe.*" Id. at 873. That framework was flawed in their eyes because "it undervalues the State's interest in the potential life within the woman." Id. at 875. Whereas *Roe* had held that this interest becomes compelling only at viability, they believed that "there is a substantial state interest in potential life throughout pregnancy." Id. at 876. This upgrading of the interest in potential life gave the state a much stronger ground for regulating abortion during the first and second trimesters. It also eliminated any reason for distinguishing between the first and second trimesters, since the state now had a compelling reason for restricting abortion from the very beginning of pregnancy. On the other hand, the joint authors refused to abandon the "viability line" that divides the second and third trimesters. As they explained, part of "*Roe*'s central holding [was] that viability marks the earliest point at which the State's interest in fetal life is constitutionally adequate to justify a legislative ban on nontherapeutic abortions." Id. at 860. Thus, prior to viability, a woman still has a fundamental right to choose an abortion — even if it is not necessary to protect her life or her health. After viability, the state may outlaw abortion except where it is necessary to preserve the health or life of the mother.

The Undue Burden Test

Besides abandoning the trimester framework of *Roe,* Justices O'Connor, Kennedy, and Souter refused to apply the strict scrutiny approach normally used in fundamental rights due process cases. Under the standard approach, a law that impinges on or unduly burdens a fundamental liberty will be upheld if it is the least burdensome means of achieving a compelling governmental interest; the fact that the government has unduly burdened the right is not itself necessarily fatal. See §2.4.4. However, the joint opinion formulated a new undue burden test for judging the constitutionality of abortion regulations. Under this test, a law or practice that unduly burdens a woman's liberty interest in the abortion decision is automatically invalid. In other words, "an undue burden is an unconstitutional burden." 505 U.S. at 877. At first blush, the undue burden test appears to increase the level of protection afforded the abortion decision, for the state seemingly has no opportunity to justify a regulation that imposes an undue burden. In reality, however, the new standard makes it easier for the government to regulate abortion than it was under *Roe.*

According to the undue burden test, a law will be found to impose an undue burden "if its *purpose* or *effect* is to place a *substantial obstacle* in the path of a woman seeking an abortion before the fetus attains viability." Id. at 878 (emphasis supplied). As far as the purpose element is concerned, a law imposes an undue burden if it is "calculated to . . . hinder" a woman's freedom of choice. Id. at 877. This element is not violated if the state's purpose is "to persuade the woman to choose childbirth over abortion." Id. at 878. The state, therefore, is allowed to "enact persuasive measures which favor childbirth over abortion, even if those measures do not further a health interest." Id. at 886. Since a state can almost always claim that its purpose was "to persuade" rather than "to hinder," it is hard to imagine any law being held to constitute an undue burden because of its purpose.

With respect to the effect element of the undue burden test, it is more difficult to establish that a law unduly burdens the right to choose an abortion than it was under *Roe* and its progeny. According to the joint opinion, the government may adopt measures that interfere with a woman's ability to obtain an abortion as long as they do not actually prevent or "prohibit any woman from making the ultimate decision to terminate her pregnancy before viability." Id. at 879. "The fact that a law . . . has the incidental effect of making it more difficult or more expensive to procure an abortion cannot be enough to invalidate it." Id. at 874. Previously, regulations that added to the difficulty or expense of obtaining an abortion were routinely deemed to impinge on a woman's freedom of choice and were usually overturned. See, e.g., *City of Akron v. Akron Center for Reproductive Health, Inc.*, 462 U.S. 416 (1983) (invalidating waiting period, requirement that certain abortions be performed in hospitals, and other restrictions that increased the expense of abortions or reduced access to them). *Casey* overruled those parts of *Akron* and *Thornburgh* that had invalidated waiting-period and informed-consent requirements that were indistinguishable from those contained in the Pennsylvania statute.

Though the undue burden test was subscribed to by only three Justices in *Casey*, it represented the holding of the Court in that case. "When a fragmented Court decides a case and no single rationale explaining the result enjoys the assent of five Justices, 'the holding of the Court may be viewed as that position taken by those Members who concurred in the judgments on the narrowest grounds. . . .'" *Marks v. United States*, 430 U.S. 188, 193 (1977). Since Justices Blackmun and Stevens concurred on the rationale that *Roe* should be reaffirmed in its entirety, the undue burden test was the narrowest ground for the judgment invalidating the spousal consent provision. Any doubt as to the status of the undue burden test was eliminated in *Stenberg v. Carhart*, 120 S. Ct. 2597 (2000), where for the first time a majority of the Court (Justices Breyer, Stevens, O'Connor, Souter, Ginsburg, and Kennedy) endorsed use of the test to evaluate the constitutionality of laws that regulate abortion.

EXAMPLE 2-G

A state law provides that before an abortion may be performed, a woman must have two in-person consultations with a physician, at least 48 hours apart; another 48 hours must elapse between the second consultation and the abortion. At each consultation, the physician must seek to persuade the woman not to have an abortion. Does this law violate a woman's rights under the Due Process Clause?

EXPLANATION

The law may well be valid. Under the undue burden standard, the state may enact laws whose explicit purpose is to discourage women from having abortions. While a challenger might claim that the state's goal here is to prevent a woman from exercising free choice, the state would successfully reply that it is seeking to persuade rather than hinder and that it is also trying to assure that a woman's decision to have an abortion is deliberate and well informed.

Since the purpose of the law does not violate the undue burden test, the measure will be found invalid only if its effect is to place a substantial obstacle in a woman's path by preventing her from having an abortion. The consultation and waiting-period requirements will surely increase the cost and difficulty of having an abortion, for a woman must make three separate trips to a clinic, hospital, or doctor's office. Yet increased cost or increased difficulty alone does not constitute an undue burden. Without proof that the effect of this law is to actually prevent abortions, the measure would be upheld under the undue burden test.

EXAMPLE 2-H

A Nebraska law prohibits the performance of a "partial birth abortion" unless the procedure is necessary to save the life of the mother. A partial birth abortion is defined as "an abortion procedure in which the person performing the abortion partially delivers vaginally a living unborn child before killing the unborn child and completing the delivery." A physician who violates the statute may be sentenced to 20 years in prison, fined up to $25,000, and automatically loses his or her medical license. Partial birth abortions, also known as the D&X (intact dilation and extraction) procedure, are performed during the second trimester. The D&X procedure is not used with great frequency, but for some women it is safer than any other method of abortion. Nebraska's statutory definition of "partial birth abortion" also covers the intact D&E (dilation and evacuation) procedure, the most common method of abortion during the second trimester. Does the Nebraska statute violate a woman's right to choose to terminate her pregnancy?

EXPLANATION

The statute is vulnerable for two reasons. First, under both *Roe* and *Casey*, even after the point of viability the government may not outlaw an abortion "where it is necessary, in appropriate medical judgment, for the preservation of the life *or health* of the mother." (Emphasis added.) While the Nebraska statute allows partial birth abortion where it is necessary to save a woman's life, it makes no exception for those cases in which a physician concludes that this is the safest method for performing the abortion. By failing to include the health exception required by *Roe* and *Casey*, Nebraska's statute unconstitutionally forces some women to use riskier methods.

Second, the Nebraska statute places an "undue burden" on a woman's decision to obtain a pre-viability abortion. Because the statute's definition of partial birth abortion is so broad, it outlaws the D&X procedure as well as the D&E procedure, the most commonly used method for performing pre-viability second trimester abortions. As such, the statute has the *effect* of placing a substantial obstacle in the path of a woman's decision have an abortion. Had Nebraska, like some states (e.g., Kansas and Utah), carefully limited its ban to the D&X procedure, the statute would probably have passed the undue burden test since women could still easily obtain pre-viability second trimester abortions through the D&E procedure. Even a more narrowly crafted statute, however, would have to contain a health exception allowing use of the D&X procedure in those cases where it is the safest procedure available. See *Stenberg v. Carhart*, 120 S. Ct. 2597 (2000) (employing this reasoning to invalidate Nebraska law banning partial birth abortions).

Facial versus As-Applied Challenges

Whether or not an abortion regulation violates the undue burden standard may depend on whether the regulation is attacked on its face or as applied. In a *facial challenge*, a law will normally be set aside only if it is shown "that no set of circumstances exists under which [the law] would be valid." *United States v. Salerno*, 481 U.S. 739, 745 (1987). But see *City of Chicago v. Morales*, 527 U.S. 41, 55 n.22 (1999) (stating that the *Salerno* standard was mere dictum and has not been consistently used by the Court as the standard for facial challenges) (opinion of Justice Stevens, joined by Justices Souter and Ginsburg). A law that is found to be facially invalid is, for practical purposes, removed from the books and can no longer be enforced against anyone. By contrast, a law that operates unconstitutionally in only some settings will not usually be facially invalidated; it must instead be challenged *as applied*, by those against whom its enforcement is unconstitutional. If the law is struck down as applied, it may still be enforced in other settings unless other as-applied challenges further limit its enforcement.

The Court in *Casey* eased the rules for mounting facial challenges to laws that regulate abortion. Five Justices (the three joint authors plus Stevens and Blackmun) agreed that Pennsylvania's spousal notification requirement was facially unconstitutional because it was "likely to prevent a *significant number* of women from obtaining an abortion." 505 U.S. at 893 (emphasis supplied). The requirement was facially invalid even though its application would not be unconstitutional in all circumstances; it was enough that "in a *large fraction* of the cases in which [the provision] is relevant, it will operate as a substantial obstacle to a woman's choice to undergo an abortion." Id. at 895 (emphasis supplied).

EXAMPLE 2-I

If the multiple-consultation and waiting-period requirements in Example 2-G were challenged facially, they would be invalidated only if the plaintiffs proved that the requirements prevent a significant number of women from obtaining abortions. If the factual evidence shows that the requirements operate as a substantial obstacle for only a relatively small percentage of women, a facial challenge would fail. Is there any other way the law might be successfully challenged?

EXPLANATION

An as-applied challenge might still be filed on behalf of those women for whom the law poses a substantial obstacle. For example, suit might be brought by or on behalf of those women who are poor, or who live a great distance from the nearest clinic or hospital, or who require secrecy and risk being discovered if they must make three separate trips. As applied to these groups of women, the multiple consultation and waiting-period requirements might be shown to be so burdensome as to be prohibitive. See *Casey,* 505 U.S. at 886-887 (suggesting that such proof might support a finding of invalidity if a 24-hour waiting period were challenged on an as-applied basis).

We have assumed that under the undue burden test, the state is denied the opportunity to justify an otherwise burdensome abortion restriction by showing that it is necessary to achieve a compelling interest. However, this might not always be true. The joint authors in *Casey* suggested that a state might be able to invoke the least burdensome alternative defense if an abortion restriction was adopted to protect the "health or safety of a woman seeking an abortion"; in that case, the measure would be struck down only if it were found to be "[u]nnecessary." Id. at 878. Otherwise, the measure might be upheld regardless of how substantial an obstacle it poses to women seeking abortions.

EXAMPLE 2-J

State X law requires that abortions be performed by a licensed physician. There is only one licensed physician in the state who performs abortions. For many women, the time and expense of traveling to this physician or to the nearest abortion provider in another state are prohibitive. Is the licensed-physician requirement invalid under the undue burden test?

EXPLANATION

The state would defend the restriction as being one that protects a mother's health and safety. *Roe v. Wade* held that states could for health and safety reasons insist that abortions be performed solely by licensed physicians. 410 U.S. at 165. Since the *purpose* of this law is valid, the question is whether its *effect* is to impose an undue burden. In a facial challenge, it might be possible to show that the law poses a substantial obstacle for "a large fraction" of women in the state who seek abortions. Otherwise, it could no doubt be shown that the requirement poses a substantial obstacle as applied to women who are poor and/or who live far from the nearest abortion provider.

Yet even if the law seems to impose an undue burden, it may still be upheld if it is proved that it is a *necessary health or safety measure*. A challenger might try to show that the licensed-physician requirement is more burdensome than necessary to protect women's health because, for example, registered nurses are as capable as doctors of safely performing certain types of abortions. However, if the law is found to be no more restrictive than necessary to protect health or safety, it might be upheld despite the substantial obstacle that it poses for women who seek abortions.

———————————

By making it easier for the government to regulate and restrict abortions, the Supreme Court in *Casey* significantly weakened its 1973 decision in *Roe v. Wade*. After almost two decades of highly divisive involvement in the abortion area, during which the judiciary invalidated dozens of state and local abortion laws, the Supreme Court signaled a retreat. *Roe* had generated deep and continuing opposition, both on and off the Court. The undue burden test represented a compromise between Justices White, Rehnquist, and Scalia, who wished to completely overrule *Roe*, and Justices Blackmun, Brennan, and Marshall, who continued to support *Roe* in full.

The authors of the joint opinion went to lengths to deny that the Court was surrendering to political or popular pressure. *Casey*, 505 U.S. at 864-869. Yet politics and public pressure appear to have contributed greatly to the decision. Presidents Reagan and Bush both campaigned for the White House by promising to use their power of judicial appointment to secure a reversal of *Roe v. Wade*. The Court that decided *Casey* was composed of five Reagan-Bush appointees, all of whom contributed to *Roe*'s undoing. Two of these Justices — Scalia and Thomas — voted to completely overrule *Roe*. The other three — O'Connor, Kennedy, and Souter — adopted the undue burden test as a means of diluting the protections of *Roe*.

Though the Supreme Court is an unelected body, it is, nevertheless, subject to various forms of majoritarian control. If the people strongly disagree with the Court, one thing that they can do is "pack the Court" by electing Presidents and senators who will use the appointment process to change the Court's ideological make-up. *Casey* may have partly reflected this type of "courtpacking," but only to a degree. The decision did bring the Court more closely into line with the views held by a majority of Americans. See *Gallup Poll Monthly*, Jan. 1992, at 5-9 (64 percent of the public opposes overruling *Roe*, but even larger majorities favor abortion restrictions of the type contained in the Pennsylvania law). On the other hand, the decision was a disappointment to *Roe*'s most ardent opponents, for it left in place the "essential holding" of *Roe* and the principle that the Constitution protects the right of personal privacy.

§2.5.5 *Sexual Intimacy:* Bowers v. Hardwick

In addition to having narrowed the right of privacy in the abortion setting, the Court has proved reluctant to expand the right of privacy to include other highly personal and intimate decisions. While the Court has described the right of privacy in sweeping and majestic terms — e.g., as covering "choices central to personal dignity and autonomy" and "the right to define one's own concept of existence, of meaning, of the universe, and of the mystery of human life" (*Casey,* 505 U.S. at 851) — the Court's decisions have not matched its rhetoric. A good example is *Bowers v. Hardwick,* 478 U.S. 186 (1986).

In *Bowers,* the Court upheld Georgia's criminal sodomy law as applied to sexual conduct engaged in by two adult men in the privacy of their home. Justice White, writing for the majority, framed the issue as "whether the Federal Constitution confers a fundamental right upon homosexuals to engage in sodomy. . . ." Id. at 190. The Court held that because no such right exists, the statute was subject to mere rational basis review. This standard was satisfied by the fact that the law reflected the "belief of a majority of the electorate in Georgia that homosexual sodomy is immoral and unacceptable." Id. at 196.

Quite apart from the result in the case, the *approach* taken by the Court in *Bowers* seemed inconsistent with its earlier privacy decisions. As Justice White observed for the Court in *Whalen v. Roe,* 429 U.S. 589, 599-600 (1977), the right of privacy shields a person's "interest in independence in making certain kinds of important decisions." It is the right to make these decisions without governmental interference, not the right to engage in any particular conduct, that is central to the right of personal autonomy. Had the *Bowers* majority followed this approach, it might have asked whether the right of privacy embraces a decision made by two consenting adults as to their private sexual conduct. Instead, the Court focused solely on the conduct that resulted from that decision, asking whether the right of "homosexuals to engage in acts of consensual sodomy" is "'deeply rooted in this Nation's history and tradition' or 'implicit in the concept of ordered liberty'" — questions that, of course, had to be answered in the negative. 478 U.S. at 192-194.

By contrast, in the abortion cases, the Court did not inquire whether the *right to abort a fetus* is a fundamental right rooted in history and tradition or implicit in the concept of ordered liberty. What was found to be fundamental was a woman's *right to make a highly personal decision* even though that decision might result in *conduct* that many would regard as being unfortunate, undesirable, or immoral. Indeed, Justice White had earlier acknowledged the critical distinction between a decision and the conduct that may flow from it. In *Thornburgh v. American College of Obstetricians & Gynecologists,* 476 U.S. 747 (1986), he thus explained that "*Roe v. Wade* is not premised on the notion that abortion is itself desirable (either as a matter of constitutional entitlement or of social policy)"; rather,

> the freedom recognized by the Court in *Roe v. Wade* and its progeny is essentially a negative one, based not on the notion that abortion is a good in itself, but only on the view that the legitimate goals that may be served by state coercion of private choices regarding abortion are . . . outweighed by the damage to individual autonomy and privacy that such coercion entails. In other words, the evil of abortion does not justify the evil of forbidding it.

Id. at 797 (White, J., dissenting).

The same thing might have been said about the choice made by two consenting adults in Georgia concerning their private sexual conduct. Thus, while the state could attempt to regulate or prohibit conduct that results from this protected decision, it could do so only if—as in the abortion cases —it was able to satisfy a strict scrutiny standard of review. And as in *Roe,* the mere fact that a majority believes the conduct to be immoral would not suffice to meet this test. By contrast, a state might be able to justify a law criminalizing private consensual sexual conduct that results in the infliction of severe physical harm to one of the participants. But as the dissenters in *Bowers* noted, Georgia failed to offer any compelling interests to which its criminal sodomy statute was narrowly tailored. 478 U.S. at 208-213. Thus, had the Court there recognized that the case involved a choice that is protected by the right of privacy and personal autonomy, the Georgia law would have been held unconstitutional under a straightforward application of strict scrutiny. Justice Powell, who provided the critical fifth vote to uphold the statute in *Bowers,* later regretted his vote, believing that "it was inconsistent in a general way with *Roe.*" *National Law Journal,* Nov. 5, 1990, at 3.

§2.5.6   *Medical Treatment*

A Right to Choose Certain Medical Treatment?

The privacy right to "independence in making certain kinds of important decisions," *Whalen v. Roe,* 429 U.S. 589, 599-600 (1977), extends to some decisions concerning what medical treatment one wishes to receive. In *Roe v. Wade,* 410 U.S. 113, 164-165 (1973), the Court held that even after a fetus has become viable, a woman retains the right to choose an abortion if this medical procedure is necessary to protect her health or her life. This holding was reaffirmed in *Stenberg v. Carhart,* 120 S. Ct. 2597 (2000). This suggests that the liberty interest recognized in *Roe* is composed of two distinct strands: first, the general right to choose an abortion for whatever reason a woman wishes; and second, the right of a woman to make choices concerning her health, such as the decision to have a therapeutic abortion. After the point of viability, the first of these liberties is outweighed by the state's interest in protecting the fetus; however, that state interest is not strong enough to trump the second liberty interest, i.e., a woman's freedom to choose medical procedures that are necessary to protect her health or her life.

Though *Roe* and its progeny implicitly recognized a fundamental liberty to choose medical procedures that are necessary to protect one's health, courts have been reluctant to extend this right beyond the abortion setting to include other treatments or drugs whose use the government has outlawed. While courts may acknowledge that a fundamental liberty interest is implicated, they usually quickly conclude that the government was justified in barring use of the desired drug or treatment. See, e.g., *United States v. LeBeau,* 985 F.2d 563 (table), 1993 WL 21970 (7th Cir. 1993); *United States v. Burzynksi Cancer Research Inst.,* 819 F.2d 1301, 1314 (5th Cir. 1987), *cert. denied,* 484 U.S. 1065 (1988) (rejecting privacy-based claims with respect to unlicensed drugs); but see *Rutherford v. United States,* 438 F. Supp. 1287, 1298-1301 (W.D. Okla. 1977), *aff'd,* 582 F.2d 1234 (10th Cir. 1978), *rev'd on other grounds,* 442 U.S. 544 (1979) (government violated cancer patient's fundamental right of privacy by prohibiting use of Laetrile). The liberty to choose drugs or medical procedures that the government has outlawed appears for the time at least to be largely confined to the area of abortion.

EXAMPLE 2-K

Robert is suffering from a form of cancer for which there is no proven cure. For the past few months, he has been using a new drug for treating cancer that was developed by a French company, but that has not been approved by the U.S. Food and Drug Administration (FDA). Robert has been indicted under a state law that makes it a crime to use any medication that has not been approved by the FDA. May Robert defend the action on the ground that the state, by barring him from using the drug, is violating his Fourteenth Amendment due process right to privacy and personal autonomy?

EXPLANATION

If the court is willing to recognize that the fundamental right of privacy extends to decisions concerning what medical treatment a person wishes to receive, the court must still decide whether the state has adequate grounds for interfering with this right. The state will claim that it has a compelling interest in protecting public health and safety and that until a drug is approved by the FDA, there is no way to be sure that the drug will not cause serious harm or even death to those who use it. If the court uses a variation on the basic strict scrutiny model and asks only whether the state has a compelling interest (see §2.4.4), Robert will probably lose, since the state's interest in public health will probably be found to outweigh an individual's liberty interest in choosing his or her own medical treatment.

On the other hand, if the court applies the basic strict scrutiny due process test and insists (under the fifth step) that the state use the least burdensome means of achieving a compelling interest, the law may be unconstitutional as applied to Robert. Since he suffers from an otherwise fatal disease, to apply the law to him is arguably more burdensome than necessary, for it does little, if anything, to advance the state's goals. A less burdensome approach would be for the state to make sure that Robert is aware of the risks entailed, but once his decision is fully informed, it should prevail over the state's interest in protecting public health and safety.

The Right to Reject Unwanted Medical Treatment

In the abortion cases, the liberty interest in making decisions about one's health involved the right to receive or undergo certain medical procedures. This liberty interest may also come into play in the context of decisions to refuse medical treatment. In *Jacobson v. Massachusetts,* 197 U.S. 11, 24-30 (1905), decided at the height of the *Lochner* era, the Court recognized that there is a liberty interest in rejecting unwanted medical care. The modern Court has reaffirmed this liberty interest. See, e.g., *Washington v. Harper,* 494 U.S. 210 (1990) (prisoner has fundamental liberty interest in avoiding forced administration of antipsychotic drugs); *Vitek v. Jones,* 445 U.S. 480 (1980) (prisoner has liberty interest in avoiding mandatory behavior modification treatment); *Parham v. J.R.,* 442 U.S. 584 (1979) (person has liberty interest in not being confined unnecessarily for medical treatment). This liberty was initially viewed as part of the right of bodily integrity, i.e., the right to be free from state interference with one's physical person. In more recent years, it has been treated as an aspect of the liberty interest in privacy and personal autonomy.

Like other liberty interests, the right to refuse unwanted medical treatment is not absolute. The Court in *Jacobson* found that the state's goal of preventing smallpox was sufficient to outweigh an individual's interest in refusing a smallpox vaccination. In *Washington v. Harper,* the Court ruled that in the prison setting, where constitutional rights are of diminished stature, the state did not violate substantive due process by forcibly administering antipsychotic drugs to prisoners diagnosed as suffering from a mental disorder that made them likely to cause harm to themselves or to others. In *Harper*, the state did not need to show that the forced administration of drugs was necessary to achieve its goals; it was enough that the policy was reasonably related to legitimate penological interests. However, the *Harper* Court noted that in another setting not involving prisoners, "the State . . . would have been required to satisfy a more rigorous standard of review." 494 U.S. at 223.

§2.5.7 The Right to Refuse Lifesaving Hydration and Nutrition

The liberty to refuse unwanted medical treatment may sometimes be equivalent to choosing the time and manner of one's death. For example, if a person suffering from a life-threatening disease is told that unless she takes a certain drug she will die, a decision to refuse that drug is in effect a decision to die. The same is true of the more tenuous liberty to choose to receive a particular drug or medical procedure. A decision to take what one knows to be a lethal dose of morphine in order to relieve excruciating pain has the same *effect* as a decision to die even though one's *intent* may be very different. In our previous discussion of the liberty to receive or reject a particular drug or medical treatment, the individual's choice did not pose a direct threat to life or raise a certainty of death. Does the liberty interest in medical treatment reach far enough to encompass a right to die?

This question was presented in a narrow form in *Cruzan v. Director, Missouri Department of Health*, 497 U.S. 261 (1990). There, the Missouri Supreme Court refused to allow the withdrawal of artificial food and hydration procedures from a patient who was in a persistent vegetative state because there was no "clear and convincing evidence" that the withdrawal accorded with the patient's wishes. The patient's parents challenged the state court's ruling on the ground that it violated their daughter's fundamental liberty to refuse unwanted medical treatment. Their position was supported by decisions from a number of state courts, which had found such a right as a matter of common law, and in some cases as part of the constitutional right of privacy.

In an opinion by Chief Justice Rehnquist, the Supreme Court came close to but stopped short of recognizing such a liberty interest. Rehnquist conceded that "[t]he principle that a competent person has a constitutionally protected liberty interest in refusing unwanted medical treatment may be inferred from our prior decisions." Id. at 278. Moreover, he agreed that "the logic of these cases" would cover "the forced administration of life-sustaining medical treatment, and even of artificially-delivered food and water essential to life." Id. at 279. Yet even then a state might be justified in barring exercise of such a liberty in situations where death would result, for "the dramatic consequences involved in refusal of such treatment would inform the inquiry as to whether the deprivation of that interest is constitutionally permissible." Id. Having toyed with the idea, the Court declined to hold that the liberty to refuse unwanted medical treatment includes a right to refuse life-sustaining treatment. Rather, said the Court, "*for purposes of this case, we assume* that the United States Constitution would grant a competent person a constitutionally protected right to refuse lifesaving hydration and nutrition." Id. (emphasis supplied). While five Justices in *Cruzan* expressed the view that such a right does exist (id. at 287 (O'Connor, J., concurring); id. at 304-314 (Brennan, Marshall, & Blackmun, JJ., dissenting); id. at 330-344 (Stevens, J., dissenting)), their views were not necessary to the decision and thus do not constitute a holding of the case. As the Court has subsequently noted, *Cruzan* "assumed, and strongly suggested" — but did not hold — "that the Due Process Clause protects the traditional right to refuse unwanted lifesaving medical treatment." *Washington v. Glucksberg*, 521 U.S. 702, 720 (1997).

Once the *Cruzan* Court assumed that a *competent person* has a fundamental liberty to reject life-sustaining medical treatment and that this will trump any countervailing state interests, the case presented the additional difficulty that the decision to withdraw food and hydration was made not by the patient, but by her parents and guardians. This being so, Missouri claimed an interest in protecting (rather than thwarting) the patient by making sure her surrogates' decision to withdraw life-sustaining treatment in fact reflected her true desires. Though the facts left no doubt that the parents were acting with the purest of motives, the state had a valid interest in assuring that its right-to-die procedures would not be abused by those purporting to act on behalf of an incompetent. The Missouri Supreme Court ruled that withdrawal of life-sustaining treatment from an incompetent person is permitted only if the patient has previously executed a formal "living will" or if there is other "clear and convincing, inherently reliable evidence" that the decision conforms to wishes the patient had expressed while competent. The state court found that neither of these requirements was satisfied in the case before it.

The U.S. Supreme Court affirmed, ruling that the state's strict procedural requirements did not violate the Due Process Clause. The Court applied a modified strict scrutiny test under which it simply balanced the state's interests against the liberty interests of the patient. See §2.4.4. The Court found that the state's interests in preserving life and assuring the authenticity of a person's decision to die were sufficient to outweigh any possible frustration of a patient's liberty interest. The dissent objected that less rigorous procedural requirements would protect the state's interests equally well, 497 U.S. at 321-326 (Brennan, J., dissenting), but the Court did not require the state to show that these less burdensome alternatives were for some reason inadequate.

Having found that any state interference with the *patient's* liberty was justified, the Court rejected the argument that the state had violated the liberty interests of the patient's family. Any liberty to reject life-sustaining medical treatment belongs exclusively to the individual, not to his or her family, friends, or legal guardians. The state is under no obligation "to repose a right of 'substituted judgment'" with others; "we do not think the Due Process Clause requires the State to repose judgment on these matters with anyone but the patient herself." Id. at 286. Accordingly, "the State may choose to defer only to those wishes, rather than confide the decision to close family members." Id. at 286-287. The Court left open the possibility that a state might be required to defer to the decision of a surrogate where a patient had expressed a clear desire that the decision to withdraw life-sustaining treatment be made for her by that individual. Id. at 287 n.12.

EXAMPLE 2-L

As a result of an automobile accident, James lost use of both legs and must breathe with a respirator. He is 36 years old, is married, and has two young children. This past year James on several occasions removed his respirator, but each time his nurse promptly reconnected it, citing a state law that requires that all reasonable steps be taken to keep a patient alive. James has brought suit, asking that the state law be declared unconstitutional and that he be allowed to disconnect his respirator and die. How should the court rule in his case?

EXPLANATION

Unlike *Cruzan,* there is no doubt here concerning the patient's wishes. James is fully competent and has expressed his desires in unmistakably clear terms. The only issue is one that the *Cruzan* Court did not have to address, i.e., whether the state may thwart a competent individual's decision to reject life-sustaining medical treatment.

Assuming the court recognizes a *fundamental* liberty to refuse lifesaving medical treatment, *Cruzan* suggested that this interest must be balanced against the interests of the state. The state here is likely to assert several interests, i.e., preserving life, preventing suicide, and protecting innocent third parties such as family members and loved ones. The Court in *Cruzan* suggested that the strength of these interests may vary, depending on a person's condition and prognosis.

The quality of James's life is certainly impaired by the fact that he is a paraplegic and dependent on a respirator. Yet in contrast to more typical right-to-die cases, he is neither comatose nor suffering from a painful and incurable degenerative disease. Thus, the state's interests in preserving life and preventing suicide would seem to be quite strong. Moreover, since James has a wife and two small children, the state's interest in protecting innocent third parties is more compelling than it would be in a case involving someone who was single and/or elderly.

James will respond that his fundamental liberty to make "choices central to personal dignity and autonomy," *Casey*, 505 U.S. at 851, should allow him, not the state, to decide how long he will be kept alive by artificial means. However, for the reasons noted, there is a good chance the state's interests will be found to outweigh James's liberty to reject life-sustaining medical procedures.

§2.5.8   *Suicide and Physician-Assisted Suicide*

Closely related to the issue raised in *Cruzan* is whether those who are terminally ill have a constitutional right to obtain medication from their doctors in order to hasten their deaths. Persons in this situation, rather than seeking to *reject lifesaving* treatment, as was the case in *Cruzan*, wish to *receive life-ending* medication. Yet both cases could be said to involve the same liberty interest, i.e., the "right to die."

Any thought that *Cruzan* had implicitly recognized a constitutional open-ended "right to die" was put to rest by *Washington v. Glucksberg*, 521 U.S. 702 (1997), and *Vacco v. Quill*, 521 U.S. 793 (1997). *Glucksberg* unanimously rejected a due process challenge to a Washington law that made it a crime for anyone, including physicians, to assist another in committing suicide. *Vacco* held that a similar New York law did not violate the Equal Protection Clause.

The Court in *Glucksberg* noted that "we have required in substantive-due-process cases a 'careful description' of the asserted fundamental liberty interest." 521 U.S. at 721. Because the Washington law prohibited "aid[ing] another person to attempt suicide," the issue was not, as the Ninth Circuit had put it, whether there is an all-embracing "right to die" or "a liberty interest in determining the time and manner of one's death." Id. at 722-723. Instead, said the Court, "the question before us is whether the 'liberty' specially protected by the Due Process Clause includes a *right to commit suicide* which itself includes a right to assistance in doing so." Id. at 723 (emphasis supplied).

Having thus framed the issue, the Court ruled "that the asserted 'right' to assistance in committing suicide is not a fundamental liberty interest protected by the Due Process Clause." Id. at 728. The nation's history and tradition rejected such a right, for assisted suicide had long been banned and continued to be illegal in nearly every state. Nor could such a liberty be distilled from the Court's prior substantive due process cases. While many of those cases, including *Roe* and *Cruzan*, had recognized constitutional liberties that involve "personal autonomy," this did "not warrant the sweeping conclusion that any and all important, intimate, and personal decisions are so protected. . . ." Id. at 727. Those cases had turned on a finding that the specific activities or decisions at stake were "so deeply rooted in our history and traditions, or so fundamental to our concept of constitutionally ordered liberty, that they are protected by the Fourteenth Amendment." Id. The fact that suicide entails an exercise of personal autonomy was, therefore, not enough to elevate this nontraditional interest to fundamental liberty status.

The Court's reluctance to find a fundamental liberty in *Glucksberg* was heightened by the fact that such a ruling would come in the midst of a vigorous national debate about assisted suicide and related issues concerning the protection of personal dignity and independence at the end of life. For the Court to have stepped in and declared that there is a constitutional right to assistance in committing suicide would have preempted that debate. By contrast, as the Court observed in the concluding paragraph of its opinion, "Our holding permits this debate to continue, as it should in a democratic society." Id. at 735.

Once the Court in *Glucksberg* held that no fundamental liberty interest was present, it easily sustained Washington's assisted suicide ban under the rational basis test. The ban was found to be reasonably related to a number of legitimate state interests, including saving human life, assuring proper treatment for those suffering from depression or mental illness, preserving trust in the doctor-patient relationship, protecting vulnerable groups (such as the poor, the elderly, and persons with disabilities) from those who might seek to bring about their premature death, and guarding against euthanasia. Id. at 728-735. The Court thus upheld Washington's assisted suicide ban on its face and "'as applied to competent, terminally ill adults who wish to hasten their deaths by obtaining medication prescribed by their doctors.'" Id. at 735.

Glucksberg left open the possibility that future challengers of an assisted suicide ban might be able to claim a fundamental liberty interest, but the Court warned that any such claim would have to be "quite different" from the "asserted liberty interest in ending one's life with a physician's assistance" rejected in that case. Id. at 735 n.24. If there is such a right, the Court did not describe it. However, several Justices suggested they might look favorably on a claim that "a mentally competent person who is experiencing great suffering has a constitutionally cognizable interest in controlling the circumstances of his or her imminent death." Id. at 736 (O'Connor, Ginsburg, & Breyer, JJ., concurring); see also id. at 791 (Breyer, J., concurring) (noting that there may be a fundamental liberty interest in the "avoidance of severe physical pain (connected with death)"). Such a liberty interest in avoiding pain was not implicated by these Washington and New York statutes, since both states allowed doctors to provide patients with drugs sufficient to control pain even where this would hasten death. Id. Justice Stevens, though agreeing that there is no "open-ended constitutional right to commit suicide," likewise believed that "there are situations in which an interest in hastening death is legitimate" and "entitled to constitutional protection." Id. at 741-742 (Stevens, J., concurring). It is thus conceivable that a terminally ill individual might be able to establish a protected liberty interest in physician-assisted suicide, but as the Court noted in *Vacco,* he or she "would need to present different and considerably stronger arguments than those advanced" in the Washington and New York cases. 521 U.S. at 809 n.13.

In *Vacco,* the Court found that New York's assisted suicide ban did not violate the Equal Protection Clause. Because no fundamental right and no suspect classification were involved, only a rational basis standard of review was called for. See §6.3. The plaintiffs argued that New York's law could not meet this test because the state, consistent with *Cruzan,* allowed competent individuals to choose to die by refusing lifesaving medical treatment, but denied competent individuals the right to achieve the same end by taking lethal medication. The Court disagreed, concluding that "the distinction between assisting suicide and withdrawing life-sustaining treatment, a distinction widely recognized and endorsed in the medical profession and in our legal traditions, is both important and logical; it is certainly rational." Id. at 800-801.

The two situations differ, said the Court, in terms of both the cause of death and the actors' intent. When life-sustaining treatment is withdrawn from a terminally ill patient, death is caused by the underlying disease; when an individual is given lethal medication, however, death is caused by the medication. With respect to intent, when life-sustaining treatment is withdrawn, the intent of the patient and her physician is not necessarily to cause death, but perhaps to live without unwanted medical technology, surgery, or drugs. In the case of assisted suicide, on the other hand, the intent of the patient and her physician must at least in part be to cause the patient's death. As the Court observed, "The law has long used actors' intent or purpose to distinguish between two acts that may have the same result." Id. at 802. In addition, the very fact that many other states drew a similar distinction between the withdrawal of life-support systems and physician-assisted suicide itself supported the reasonableness of the New York law.

§2.6   Other Protected Liberty Interests

§2.6.1   *Freedom of Movement*

Freedom from Physical Restraint

The liberty protected by the Due Process Clause has been held to include freedom of movement. This fundamental liberty interest may be impaired by government in a number of ways. One involves subjecting someone to "physical restraint of his person." *Allgeyer v. Louisiana,* 165 U.S. 578, 589 (1897). "'Liberty from bodily restraint always has been recognized as the core of the liberty protected by the Due Process Clause from arbitrary governmental action.'" *Youngberg v. Romeo,* 457 U.S. 307, 316 (1982) (quoting *Greenholtz v. Nebraska Penal Inmates,* 442 U.S. 1, 18 (1979) (Powell, J., concurring)). This liberty interest has usually been asserted in institutional settings, such as hospitals or prisons, where inmates allege that the government has placed excessive restrictions on their freedom of physical movement. The Court has not been especially sympathetic to such claims.

In the prison context, the Court has held that a criminal conviction and a sentence of imprisonment extinguish the right to be free from confinement and any constitutional liberty interest in not being transferred within the prison system or subjected to more severe conditions of confinement. See, e.g., *Hewitt v. Helms,* 459 U.S. 460 (1983) (prisoner has no due process liberty interest in avoiding solitary confinement); *Meachum v. Fano,* 427 U.S. 215 (1976) (prisoner has no due process liberty interest in avoiding transfer to maximum security prison with more burdensome conditions). Though no *constitutionally based* liberty interests are implicated in these situations, prisoners may occasionally be able to invoke procedural due process protections by showing that a liberty interest was created by *statute or regulation.* See §5.2.1. Prisoners may also be able to invoke other constitutional provisions, such as the Cruel and Unusual Punishment Clause of the Eighth Amendment, to challenge the conditions of their confinement. And as the Court recognized in *Young v. Harper,* 520 U.S. 143 (1997), inmates who have been conditionally released from prison under parole or other similar programs normally have a statutorily created liberty interest in their continued freedom that will entitle them to procedural due process if their parole is to be revoked or terminated.

The liberty interests of those confined in public mental hospitals have received only slightly greater protection from the Court. In *Youngberg v. Romeo,* 457 U.S. 307, 324 (1982), the Court recognized that, unlike prisoners, those in state mental institutions retain constitutional liberty interests in freedom of bodily movement and in "reasonably nonrestrictive confinement conditions." However, the Court refused to employ its normal strict scrutiny test, which would have required the state to show that any such restrictions are necessary to achieving a compelling interest. Instead, the Court applied a balancing test and concluded that the state's interest in operating such institutions in accord with professional standards outweighs any interest an inmate has in preserving physical liberty. Such restrictions are, therefore, automatically valid as long as "professional judgment deems [them] necessary to assure . . . safety or to provide needed training." Id. See §2.4.4.

Freedom to Move About

The due process liberty of physical movement may also be implicated by governmental interference with a person's freedom to move about. The liberty to move about in the sense of being able to travel freely from one state to another has been linked to a number of constitutional provisions, including the Commerce Clause of Article I, the Privileges and Immunities Clause of Article IV, the First Amendment right to petition government, and both the Equal Protection and Privileges or Immunities Clauses of the Fourteenth Amendment.

The freedom to move about is protected as well by the Due Process Clause. This due process liberty has been invoked to strike down limitations on international travel. *Aptheker v. Secretary of State,* 378 U.S. 500, 505-514 (1964) (statute denying passports to Communists invalid partly because it impaired the Fifth Amendment liberty to travel abroad). This liberty interest is also implicated by laws that interfere with a person's freedom simply to walk or move about. See *Papachristou v. City of Jacksonville,* 405 U.S. 156, 164 (1972) (invalidating vagrancy ordinance on vagueness grounds, but suggesting that Due Process Clause protects the liberty to wander and stroll around). In *City of Chicago v. Morales,* 527 U.S. 41 (1999), the Court struck down a Chicago anti-gang loitering ordinance. Three members of the Court noted that "the 'liberty' protected by the Due Process Clause" includes "the freedom to loiter for innocent purposes," the "right to remove from one place to another according to inclination," and "an individual's decision to remain in a public place of his choice. . . ." Id. at 53-54 (Justices Stevens, Souter, and Ginsburg). However, rather than striking the ordinance because of its impact on this substantive due process liberty interest, the Court ruled that the measure was unconstitutionally vague.

The due process freedom of movement may be relevant in a number of other contemporary settings as well. These include juvenile curfew ordinances, and anti-stalking laws, which make it illegal to follow another person in public. However, even if the freedom to move about is infringed by a law, it does not necessarily mean that the law is unconstitutional; as with all other liberty interests, the law's validity will depend on whether it can survive strict scrutiny.

EXAMPLE 2-M

The City of Glenwood adopted a curfew making it illegal for anyone under the age of 18 to be on the streets between the hours of 11 P.M. and 6 A.M. The purpose of the curfew is to protect children from becoming victims or perpetrators of crimes. Does the curfew violate the Fourteenth Amendment Due Process Clause?

EXPLANATION

Applying a basic strict scrutiny analysis, since this law impinges on children's freedom to move about, the city would have to prove that the curfew is necessary to achieve a compelling governmental interest. This of course assumes that the Court would treat this as being a "fundamental" liberty. While protecting children from becoming victims of crime is a legitimate goal, it may not be compelling enough to justify such a serious impairment of a basic liberty. For if this goal is compelling as to children, it would likewise justify imposing curfews on other groups thought to be particularly vulnerable, such as the elderly, women, and persons with disabilities. Indeed, if valid, a protection rationale might justify imposing a general curfew, since everyone is potentially a victim of street crime. There are similar difficulties with the city's goal of preventing children from becoming perpetrators of crime. If this is deemed sufficient to justify such a severe curtailment of children's freedom of movement, it would seemingly allow a curfew to be imposed on everyone since it is impossible to know who might otherwise perpetrate a crime.

Even if these goals are found to be compelling, the city must show that the law is no more restrictive than necessary to achieve its ends. There would appear to be many alternative approaches that would not as heavily burden the freedom of movement and which might be as effective in attaining the city's goals. These would include enhanced policing; better street lighting; increased educational, employment, and recreational opportunities for youths; and requiring minors on the street at night to be accompanied by or have the written permission of a parent. For the ordinance to pass strict scrutiny, the city would have to show that these less intrusive alternatives would not be as effective in achieving its goals.

The city might urge that a rational basis standard should be applied here because the law impairs only the constitutional rights of children. The Court has recognized that children may have fewer constitutional rights than adults, due to the "peculiar vulnerability of children"; "their inability to make critical decisions in an informed, mature manner"; and the need to respect the "parental role in childrearing." *Bellotti v. Baird*, 443 U.S. 622, 633-639 (1979) (plurality opinion). However, arguably none of these reasons for diluting the rights of minors is present here. First, there is probably no evidence that children are peculiarly vulnerable to street crime. Second, with the exception of very young children, the decision to leave the house at night is not one that a mature adult is likely to make any differently than a child; most people who have someplace to go at night will do so even though they are aware of the potential dangers. Third, the curfew interferes with rather than respects the parental role in childrearing, for it usurps a parent's right to decide when a child should be allowed out of the house after 11 P.M.

Compare *Nunez v. City of San Diego*, 114 F.3d 935 (9th Cir. 1997) and *Waters v. Barry*, 711 F. Supp. 1125 (D.D.C. 1989) (invalidating juvenile curfew laws partly based on liberty interest in free movement), with *Hutchins v. District of Columbia*, 188 F.3d 531 (D.C. Cir. 1999) (en banc) and *Schleifer v. City of Charlottesville*, 159 F.3d 843 (4th Cir. 1998), *cert. denied*, 526 U.S. 1018 (1999) (upholding constitutionality of juvenile curfew laws).

§2.6.2   *The Rights to Protection and Care*

As we noted earlier, the liberties guaranteed by the Due Process Clause are *negative* liberties in the sense that they usually confer merely a right to be free from governmental interference with one's ability to exercise certain freedoms. The Due Process Clause normally places the government under no affirmative duty to assure that people are able to enjoy their liberties if for some reason they cannot fully do so on their own. See §2.4.4.

There is, however, one exception to this rule. If the government assumes or enters into a "special relationship" with an individual by "restraining the individual's freedom to act on his own behalf — through incarceration, institutionalization, or other similar restraint of personal liberty," the government may have "affirmative duties of care and protection" so as to assure that the individual's liberty interests are satisfied. *DeShaney v. Winnebago County Dept. of Social Servs.*, 489 U.S. 189, 197-200 (1989). The right to protection and care exists only where the government has limited an individual's "freedom to act on his own behalf," thereby rendering the individual "more vulnerable" than he or she would otherwise have been. Id. at 200-201.

In *Youngberg v. Romeo*, 457 U.S. 307 (1982), this principle was invoked to find that the state owed a duty of protection and care toward those involuntarily confined in a state mental hospital. These inmates had both a *negative liberty* interest in being free from state interference with their physical safety and bodily freedom and an *affirmative liberty* to be provided with "such training as an appropriate professional would consider reasonable to ensure [their] safety and to facilitate [their] ability to function free from bodily restraints." Id. at 324. In addition to affirmative duties of protection and training, the state owed these individuals a general affirmative duty of care. Since the demise of *Lochner*, the interest in acquiring the necessities of life is normally a negative liberty that receives only minimal protection as part of the liberty in earning a livelihood. However, the hospital inmates in *Youngberg* had an affirmative due process right to have their subsistence needs met by the state. Id. As the Court later explained, "[W]hen the State by the affirmative exercise of its power so restrains an individual's liberty that it renders him unable to care for himself, and at the same time fails to provide for his basic human needs — e.g., food, clothing, shelter, medical care, and reasonable safety — it transgresses the substantive limits on state action set by . . . the Due Process Clause." *DeShaney*, 489 U.S. at 200.

In *DeShaney*, the Court distinguished *Youngberg* and held that a state had no affirmative constitutional duty to protect a child from being beaten by its father. Since the child was living at home rather than in the care or custody of the state, the Court found there was no "special relationship" comparable to that which existed in *Youngberg*. And though the state knew of the dangers the child faced living at home with his father, the state still had no affirmative duty to protect the child because the dangers were not of the state's "creation, nor did it do anything to render [the child] any more vulnerable to them." Id. at 201.

Even if it can be shown that a setting is one in which the government has an affirmative constitutional duty to protect and care for an individual's well-being, the government will not be found to have violated this duty on the basis of mere negligence by its employees or agents. For the government to "deprive" a person of life, liberty, or property within the meaning of the Due Process Clause, it must be shown that the impairment was caused either by a deliberate decision on the part of governmental officials — or possibly by recklessness or gross negligence. See *Davidson v. Cannon*, 474 U.S. 344 (1986) (negligence by prison officials that resulted in an inmate being assaulted by another inmate did not implicate the affirmative liberty to protection while in state custody). See also §2.1.

EXAMPLE 2-N

Lucy is a freshman at Central State University, where she lives on campus in a school dormitory. She was recently attacked in the middle of the night by an intruder who forced his way into her locked dormitory room. The only lock on the door consists of a push button in the doorknob. As a result, the door may be opened from the outside by sliding a credit card between the latch and the door frame. Several months before the attack, a group of students asked the school to either install better locks or permit the students to do so at their own expense. The school denied both requests on the ground that it did not wish to turn the dormitories into fortresses. Can Lucy sue the state-owned school on the ground that it violated her rights under the Fourteenth Amendment Due Process Clause?

EXPLANATION

Lucy will argue that because she was living in the school's dormitory, a special relationship existed that placed the state under an affirmative constitutional duty to protect her due process liberty interest in bodily safety. The school will reply that Lucy freely chose to attend the university, thus distinguishing her case from *Youngberg*, where the state hospital inmates were involuntarily committed. Lucy will respond that despite the voluntary nature of her decision to attend the university, once there, she was in the state's care and custody; unlike the child in *DeShaney*, she was not living at home with her parents. And as a freshman, she may have been required to live in the dormitory. Moreover, the school restrained Lucy's freedom to protect herself by prohibiting her from installing a better lock on her door and, in doing so, increased her vulnerability to danger.

If the court agrees that the school had an affirmative constitutional duty to protect Lucy's personal safety, the school's refusal to install adequate locks is the kind of deliberate conduct that is sufficient to implicate the Due Process Clause: The school was specifically advised of the problem and consciously chose not to do anything about it. Contrast the situation if Lucy's door had been equipped with a proper lock that, due to the school's negligence, was not in working order; such negligence would not trigger the Due Process Clause. Once Lucy establishes a deprivation of her liberty interest in protection, the school has to show that its refusal to install proper locks served a compelling interest, a showing it would be hard pressed to make. Cf. *D.R. by L.R. v. Middle Bucks Area Vocational Technical School*, 972 F.2d 1364, 1368-1373 (3d Cir. 1992) (state has no affirmative duty to protect students attending public high school from molestation by other students).

§2.7   What Happened to Life?

We have examined the extent to which liberty and property are protected as a matter of substantive due process. Yet the first interest mentioned in the Due Process Clause — ahead of both liberty and property — is life. Strangely enough, there have been almost no cases in which the Court has considered the application of substantive due process to governmental conduct that impairs a person's fundamental interest in life.

Abortion

This issue did not play a direct role in the abortion cases because the Court held that the human fetus is not a "person" within the meaning of the Due Process Clause. Therefore, state laws allowing abortion did not cause a deprivation of a "life" within the meaning of the Fourteenth Amendment. See *Roe v. Wade*, 410 U.S. 113, 156-158 (1973). The interest in life was peripherally involved in the abortion cases, however, for the Court did note that a state may not outlaw abortion where it is necessary to preserve a woman's life. See §2.5.4.

Subsistence Benefits

The interest in life played no role in the cases dealing with federal and state welfare, medical care, housing, and food assistance programs. Governmental decisions denying, terminating, or reducing these benefits do not impinge on (and thus do not trigger) the *constitutional* interest in life, no matter how severe their actual impact on a person's life. The Court has held that "even where such aid may be necessary to secure life, liberty, or property interests of which the government itself may not deprive the individual," the Due Process Clause "generally confer[s] no affirmative right to governmental aid. . . ." *DeShaney v. Winnebago County Dept. of Social Servs.*, 489 U.S. at 196. The government is thus under no more of an obligation to assure the basic necessities of life than it is to assure that people are able to exercise their constitutional liberty interests. See, e.g., *Harris v. McRae*, 448 U.S. 297 (1980) (government has no constitutional duty to provide funds to indigent women who otherwise cannot afford to have abortions); *Lindsey v. Normet*, 405 U.S. 56, 74 (1972) (government has no constitutional duty to provide adequate housing). While governmental decisions affecting a person's benefits under these programs may give rise to statutory claims or implicate other constitutional principles—such as equal protection or procedural due process protection of property—the due process interest in life is simply not implicated. The only exception would be in those cases where there is a special relationship that places the government under an affirmative duty to protect a person's life, liberty, and property. See §2.6.2.

In contrast to our Constitution, which generally places the government under no affirmative duty to assure the necessities of life, Article 25(1) of the Universal Declaration of Human Rights provides:

> Everyone has the right to a standard of living adequate for the health and well-being of himself and of his family, including food, clothing, housing and medical care and necessary social services, and the right to security in the event of unemployment, sickness, disability, widowhood, old age or other lack of livelihood in circumstances beyond his control.

Similar affirmative rights to the necessities of life are found in the constitutions of many other countries, although as a practical matter, they may often be unenforceable.

The Death Penalty

One area in which the substantive due process interest in life would be expected to have played a prominent role—but where it has played no role whatsoever—is the death penalty. The function that the Due Process Clause might have served in this area is quite different from that performed by the Eighth Amendment's Cruel and Unusual Punishment Clause. The latter Clause has been construed to impose certain procedural limitations on the use of the death penalty. See, e.g., *Woodson v. North Carolina*, 428 U.S. 280 (1976) (requiring heightened degree of reliability); *Gregg v. Georgia*, 428 U.S. 153 (1976) (requiring channeling of jury discretion). Even when these procedural safeguards have been honored, however, substantive due process would play the much more fundamental role of requiring the government to defend its decision to take a person's life rather than impose a lesser punishment.

Life is expressly mentioned in the Due Process Clause. It is surely as fundamental as any conceivable liberty interest, for without life, there can be no liberty. Since the death penalty impinges on the interest in life in the most direct and severe manner possible, the government should seemingly have the burden of proving not only that the death penalty furthers a compelling state interest, but also that no less life-threatening form of punishment would serve its goals equally well. Even if the interests in retribution, general deterrence, and/or incapacitation (specific deterrence) were deemed to be compelling, the government would have the additional burden of showing that the death penalty furthers these goals and does so more effectively than life imprisonment without possibility of parole, or any other form of punishment. Given the highly inconclusive nature of most of the studies and statistics concerning the death penalty, it seems unlikely that the government could carry this burden. Yet for reasons that remain unexplained, the Supreme Court has not employed a substantive due process analysis to test the constitutionality of the death penalty. Cf. *Commonwealth v. O'Neal*, 339 N.E.2d 676, 677-688 (Mass. 1975) (Tauro, C.J., concurring) (applying substantive due process analysis under Massachusetts Constitution to invalidate imposition of death penalty).

Death Caused by Government Officials

In *County of Sacramento v. Lewis*, 523 U.S. 833 (1998), a police car engaged in a high-speed pursuit ran over and killed Lewis, a passenger on the motorcycle the police were chasing. Plaintiff's complaint alleged that "Lewis was deprived of his right to life in violation of substantive due process. . . ." Id. at 840. The Court disposed of the case on the basis that mere "reckless disregard" of life by executive officials is not in this context sufficiently egregious or conscience-shocking to state a due process claim. See §2.1. Because the majority treated egregiousness as a "threshold" and "antecedent" issue, it did not address whether there is "a substantive due process right to be free of such executive action. . . ." Id. at 847 n.8. Nor did Justice Stevens, who declared that "the question is both difficult and unresolved."

Id. at 859. Only Justices Kennedy and O'Connor were willing to concede that "an interest protected by the text of the Constitution is implicated: The actions of the State were part of a causal chain resulting in the undoubted loss of life. We have no definitional problem, then, in determining whether there is an interest sufficient to invoke due process." Id. at 856. On the other hand, Justices Scalia and Thomas, citing the lack of textual, historical, and precedential support, rejected the alleged substantive due process "right to be free from 'deliberate or reckless indifference to life in a high-speed automobile chase aimed at apprehending a suspected offender.'" Id. at 862. The fact that only two members of the Court agreed that cases like this potentially raise due process "life" issues reveals just how peripheral this term in the Due Process Clause has become.

3

The Takings Clause

§3.1   Introduction and Overview

The Takings Clause of the Fifth Amendment, also referred to as the Just Compensation Clause, provides that the federal government may not take private property for public use without paying just compensation. The Clause also applies to the states through the Fourteenth Amendment. See §1.3. This chapter explores the question of when the government will be deemed to have taken a person's property. The separate issue of what constitutes just compensation is not usually part of the basic Constitutional Law course. Suffice it to say that just compensation is ordinarily measured in terms of the fair market value of the property that the owner has lost through the taking.

§3.2   Condemnation and Inverse Condemnation

The most obvious setting in which the Takings Clause comes into play is when the government invokes its power of eminent domain to seize or confiscate private property. The power of eminent domain allows the sovereign to take private property for public use. While the state and federal governments may acquire property through purchase, there may be instances where a private owner either is unwilling to sell or demands an exorbitant price. The power of eminent domain permits the government to take property against the owner's wishes. If it does so, however, the Fifth and Fourteenth Amendments command that the owner be paid just compensation, calculated on the basis of the property's fair market value.

The several states possess the power of eminent domain as a complement to their police power to promote the general welfare. The federal government has no enumerated power of eminent domain, but may nevertheless exercise this authority to the extent it falls within the Necessary and Proper Clause.

Thus, the United States could use the power of eminent domain to acquire land on which to build a post office, this being necessary and proper for the government to establish post offices under Article I, §8.

If the federal government or a state wishes to exercise the power of eminent domain, it normally brings a condemnation action against the property in question. When the government institutes a condemnation proceeding, it acknowledges that property is being taken; the only issue is usually how much compensation is due. This straightforward exercise of eminent domain is studied in Real Property and Eminent Domain classes and is not a part of the course in Constitutional Law.

Constitutional Law focuses on a second and more subtle way in which property may be taken within the meaning of the Takings Clause. This involves situations where the government, without invoking its power of eminent domain by filing a condemnation action, acts in such a way as to *in effect* take private property, but without admitting that it is doing so or offering to pay just compensation. In these so-called de facto or constructive takings cases, the property owner may be forced to bring an inverse condemnation action, asking a court to order the payment of just compensation on the ground that the government has in fact taken the plaintiff's property. In contrast to eminent domain proceedings, where the government concedes that it is taking the property, the key issue in an inverse condemnation action is whether or not a taking has occurred.

For example, suppose that Tom owns four acres of undeveloped land on the outskirts of Elm City. If the city wishes to use the land as a municipal park, it could attempt to buy the land from Tom at whatever price he is willing to accept. If Tom refuses to sell or demands an unreasonable price, the city can invoke its power of eminent domain by bringing a condemnation action and asking a court to determine what compensation is due. Under either of these scenarios, however, the city will have to pay Tom for the land, i.e., either his asking price or just compensation determined on the basis of the property's fair market value.

What if the city instead passes a zoning ordinance that permits Tom's land to be used only for recreational purposes? Or it adopts a law allowing the public to use the property as a place of recreation on weekends? Or the city bars Tom from erecting any structures on the land? While each of these options may further the city's goal of setting aside land for public recreational use, in none of them has the city sought to exercise its power of eminent domain by condemning the land, nor has the city agreed to pay Tom any compensation. The city has regulated the extent to which Tom or the public may use the land, but without acknowledging that a taking may have occurred. In these circumstances, Tom might bring an inverse condemnation action against the city, requesting the court to find that the city has worked a de facto taking of his land and that just compensation is due.

In this chapter, we explore the question of when governmental regulation or treatment of private property will be deemed to constitute a taking, so as to require the government to pay just compensation. Even though most of the examples used here involve real property, the Takings Clause applies as well to personal property, including tangible personal property, such as horses and automobiles, and intangible property, such as bank accounts and trade secrets. It is also important to note that "a State may not sidestep the Takings Clause by disavowing traditional property interests long recognized under state law." *Phillips v. Washington Legal Foundation,* 524 U.S. 156, 167 (1998) (holding that Texas could not avoid a takings issue with respect to the interest earned on lawyers' trust accounts by deeming such interest to no longer be "private property").

§3.3   An Approach to Analyzing Takings Problems

To determine whether or not a compensable taking of private property has occurred, it is helpful to approach the problem through a series of inquiries. This approach is unnecessary when the government has chosen to exercise its power of eminent domain, for it has then acknowledged that property is being taken and that compensation must be paid. The inquiries suggested here are designed rather for cases involving de facto takings where the government has not admitted that a taking has occurred or that just compensation is due.

The inquiries are framed so as to recognize the fact that the government may effect a taking in three different ways:

- by physically invading, occupying, or seizing private property;
- by regulating the use of private property; or
- by imposing conditions on the development of private property.

The inquiries are as follows:

A. Has the government caused a physical invasion of private property? If so,
   1. Was there a permanent physical invasion and, therefore, a taking per se? Or,
   2. Was there a temporary physical invasion in which the harm to the owner outweighs any public benefit conferred? Or was the government's action either arbitrary or destructive of basic expectations?
B. Has the government regulated the use of private property? If so,
   1. Is there a taking because the regulation is inherently arbitrary?

2. Is there a taking because the regulation violated basic expectations?
3. Is there a taking because the regulation stripped the property of all use or value?
4. If the regulation caused a taking, does the nuisance exception apply?

C. Has the government attached to a building permit a condition that would have effected a taking had the condition been imposed outright? If so, the condition amounts to a taking unless the following two inquiries are both answered in the affirmative:

1. Does the condition bear an essential nexus to a legitimate government purpose?
2. Are the nature and extent of the condition roughly proportional to the impact of the proposed development?

We will discuss each of these steps or inquiries in the balance of this chapter.

§3.4   The Difference between Physical Occupation and Regulation

The first step in deciding whether there has been a taking of property is to determine the character of the governmental action. For these purposes, the government may act in either of two distinct capacities. In some cases, it causes a physical occupation or invasion of the property by public officials or third parties. In other instances, the government merely regulates the use to which the property may be put by its owner.

There is an easy way to distinguish a physical occupation or invasion of property from a mere regulation of use. In cases of physical invasion, private property is seized or used by the government or by third parties acting with the government's permission. By contrast, in cases of regulation, an owner is not forced to let others use the property, but is simply restricted in the uses to which he or she may put the property.

EXAMPLE 3-A

State X is considering two alternative means of improving the public's ability to view the ocean while traveling along the coast. The first would involve requiring owners of beachfront property to provide a viewing spot on their land so that travelers may stop and look at the ocean. The second approach would require owners of beachfront land to leave a 15-foot visual corridor on each side of their property in which nothing may be built. How would each of these requirements be characterized for purposes of a takings analysis?

EXPLANATION

The first requirement would involve a physical occupation or invasion, for it authorizes use of private property by third parties, i.e., members of the public. The second requirement would entail a mere regulation of use, for while the owner's use of the property is restricted, neither the government nor any third party has been authorized to invade or occupy the land.

In the context of personal property, the government's seizure or confiscation of the property is the equivalent of a physical invasion. Thus, in *Webb's Fabulous Pharmacies, Inc. v. Beckwith*, 449 U.S. 155 (1980), a taking occurred when a county appropriated all interest that accrued on an interpleader fund while it was deposited with the court clerk.

The Supreme Court has said that a taking may more readily be found when there is a physical invasion than when the government is merely regulating use. This is due partly to the fact that physical invasions by the government or by third parties are more likely to seriously interfere with the use and enjoyment of property than are laws that merely restrict use. In addition, physical invasions are arguably more disruptive of an owner's basic expectations. While we can readily anticipate limitations being placed on how we may use our property, we are less prepared for situations in which "a *stranger* directly invades and occupies [our] property." *Loretto v. Teleprompter Manhattan CATV Corp.*, 458 U.S. 419, 436 (1982).

§3.5 Physical Occupations and Invasions

The Court's greater willingness to find a taking when there has been a physical invasion of property, as opposed to a mere restriction on use, is reflected in the rule that a *permanent* physical occupation constitutes a per se taking. This per se rule applies regardless of the extent of loss inflicted or the importance of the public benefit that may result.

A permanent physical occupation occurs, for example, if the government, or third parties acting pursuant to its authority, is given a right to use private property on an indefinite and continuous basis. In *Loretto v. Teleprompter Manhattan CATV Corp.*, 458 U.S. 419 (1982), the Court found a per se taking when New York required owners of apartment buildings to allow cable television companies to install cables in their buildings. The fact that the cables occupied less than two cubic feet of space and that the harm to the owners was minimal had no bearing on whether a taking had occurred; these factors were relevant only to the amount of just compensation New York would have to pay. Permanent invasions are not limited to the placement of fixed structures on land. A permanent invasion would likewise occur if a state gives the public an easement to cross a private beach at any hour of the day or night even though there will be times when no one is exercising the right to be there. See *Nollan v. California Coastal Commn.*, 483 U.S. 825, 831-832 (1987).

The per se rule for permanent physical occupations probably applies as well where the public is given the right to use private property only at specific times of the day or year, i.e., where the government permanently authorizes third parties to use private property on a *regular, but interrupted* basis.

EXAMPLE 3-B

Elm City gives the public a right to use Tom's four acres of land every weekend for recreational purposes. Is this a per se taking?

EXPLANATION

While the public does not have the right to use Tom's land at all times, it has been given an indefinite right to use the property on a regular and recurring basis. That the occupation is broken and discontinuous should not defeat application of the per se rule. Otherwise, the government could avoid the per se rule by giving the public access to private land for 11 months a year or 20 hours a day rather than on a full-time basis. The fact that the public may use Tom's property solely on weekends is relevant to determining what compensation is due, but should not alter the conclusion that a per se taking has occurred.

The Court has strongly suggested that the regular use of private property by the government or the public is equivalent to a permanent physical occupation for purposes of the per se taking rule. "'The one incontestable case for compensation (short of formal expropriation) seems to occur when the government deliberately brings it about that its agents, or the public at large, "regularly" use, or "permanently" occupy, space or a thing which theretofore was understood to be under private ownership.'" *Loretto v. Teleprompter Manhattan CATV Corp.*, 458 U.S. at 427 n.5 (quoting Professor Frank Michelman with approval). As long as the regular use is of permanent or indefinite duration, it should qualify as a form of permanent physical occupation and a per se taking for which just compensation must be paid.

If a physical invasion is temporary rather than permanent, the Court has not employed the per se rule. Instead, it may use a more flexible balancing approach, which compares the importance of the public benefit with the economic impact on the owner. The Court may also evaluate temporary physical invasions under an approach similar to that used in cases involving regulation of use. See §3.6. While the Court has hinted that it may extend the per se rule to all physical invasions, temporary as well as permanent, see *Lucas v. South Carolina Coastal Council*, 505 U.S. 1003, 1015 (1992), the rule presently applies only to invasions or occupations that are permanent.

Not every law that gives persons a right to enter or remain on private property constitutes a physical invasion for purposes of the Takings Clause. If an owner has invited members of the public to use property for certain purposes, the government may regulate the owner's ability to exclude specific individuals without being deemed to have caused a physical invasion. States may thus bar landlords from evicting tenants who have complied with their leases, just as civil rights statutes may prohibit owners of hotels, restaurants, and other businesses from ejecting patrons because of their race. While such laws have the effect of allowing private property to be occupied by particular individuals whom an owner might prefer to evict, for takings purposes they are mere regulations of use, not state-mandated physical invasions. It was the owner rather than the government that decided to open the property to others. The owner retains the right to close the property to the public at any time by dedicating it to another use. See *Yee v. City of Escondido*, 503 U.S. 519 (1992).

EXAMPLE 3-C

Elm City advised Tom that he must allow the public to use his land every summer for camping purposes and that no one may be denied access on account of their race. Does this amount to a taking?

EXPLANATION

The city's action constitutes a per se taking, as a permanent physical invasion, for Tom had not invited the public to use his property. But if Tom had decided to use the land as a public campground, the city's requirement that he not discriminate would have amounted to a mere regulation, even though it means that Tom will have to admit some people whom he might prefer to exclude.

§3.6   Regulatory Takings

The other capacity in which the government may act for purposes of Takings Clause analysis is as a regulator. Rather than itself occupying or authorizing others to invade private property, the government imposes restrictions on what a person may do with his or her own property. In some situations, a court may find that the nature or extent of the interference caused by the regulation of use is such as to constitute a regulatory taking for which just compensation must be paid.

The Court is more tolerant of regulatory interference with property than it is of interference caused by physical invasion. This stems from the fact that in an organized society, regulation of private activity for the common good is unavoidable. At the same time, virtually all state and federal regulations have a negative impact on some property interests. If every government-induced reduction in property value were deemed to constitute a taking for which compensation had to be paid, government at all levels would come to a standstill. The Court has refused to read the Takings Clause to produce such an outcome.

While the Court has accepted that government must be able to regulate without being hamstrung by the Takings Clause, it has also emphasized that "if regulation goes too far it will be recognized as a taking." *Pennsylvania Coal Co. v. Mahon*, 260 U.S. 393, 415 (1922). The difficulty is that the Court has been unable to come up with "any 'set formula' for determining how far is too far, preferring to 'engage in . . . essentially ad hoc, factual inquiries.'" *Lucas v. South Carolina Coastal Council*, 505 U.S. at 1015.

Despite the lack of a "set formula," it appears that regulation may be found to have worked a taking in at least three situations: (1) The regulation arbitrarily singles out some persons for adverse treatment; (2) the regulation destroys well-founded investment-backed expectations; or (3) the regulation strips property of virtually all use or value. If any of these tests is met, the regulation will probably be deemed to constitute a prima facie taking. The government may then be able to rebut the conclusion that a taking has occurred by showing that the so-called nuisance exception applies. Otherwise, it will have to pay just compensation. We will address each of these factors and the nuisance exception in the sections that follow.

§3.6.1   Arbitrary Action

From what we know of the origins of the Takings Clause, it was designed not to protect property owners against the mere fact of loss, but rather to safeguard against loss by potentially arbitrary or unjust means. The Court has thus suggested that if a property owner is arbitrarily singled out to bear a burden that is not imposed on other similarly situated owners, this will suffice to establish a prima facie taking.

EXAMPLE 3-D

City X's Historic Preservation Act prohibits owners of officially designated historic landmarks from tearing down or fundamentally altering those structures. Because officially designated landmarks are exempt from local taxation, city X can afford to give designated status to only 100 of the nearly 1000 historic landmarks located within its boundaries. Sara owns a two-story office building that has been officially designated as a historic landmark by city X.

As a result, Sara has suffered a considerable economic loss because she cannot replace the structure with a modern 25-story office building. How might she establish a prima facie taking of her property?

EXPLANATION

If Sara can show that the selection of her building from among the city's landmarks was arbitrary because the choice was purely a matter of subjective taste or because the designated structures were chosen by lot, the city's action would constitute a prima facie taking. On the other hand, if the city can prove that the selection was not arbitrary because the designated landmarks were the 100 oldest in the city, this basis for establishing a taking would fail. See *Penn Central Transp. Co. v. City of New York*, 438 U.S. 104, 131-133 (1978).

Similarly, in *City of Monterey v. Del Monte Dunes at Monterey, Ltd.*, 526 U.S. 687 (1999), the Court upheld a lower court ruling that a taking had occurred partly on the basis that the city, which had a longstanding interest in acquiring the tract of coastal property for public use, refused to approve any of 19 different plans for developing the land, and in doing so subjected the owner to "treatment inconsistent with zoning decisions made in favor of owners of similar properties. . . ." Id. at 705. Though the Court did not couch its analysis in terms of arbitrariness, this appears to have been at the heart of its conclusion that the city's action was not "reasonably related to the city's proffered justifications." Id. at 706.

§3.6.2   Defeating Investment-Backed Expectations

The Court will occasionally find a taking on the ground that a regulation interferes with those investment-backed expectations of a property owner that are so well founded as to warrant the protection of law. While it is often said that interference with investment-backed expectations may suffice to require payment of just compensation, this ground for finding a prima facie taking is usually invoked only where the government has given specific assurances to a property owner on which the owner then relied. In these instances, while the government will not be estopped from reneging on its promise, it may be forced to compensate the aggrieved property owner for any losses inflicted.

EXAMPLE 3-E

Tom decided to build a rifle range on the land he owns in Elm City. Before doing so, he contacted Elm City officials, who advised him that the project had the city's approval. Tom proceeded with construction. At several points during construction, city officials reassured him that the project was fine. When the range was completed, the city refused to give Tom a business license on the ground that it had now decided to ban rifle ranges. Can Tom establish a prima facie taking of his land?

EXPLANATION

Tom has a good argument that the city's refusal to let him operate a rifle range constitutes a prima facie taking. The city gave Tom explicit assurances that the project was permissible, thereby creating well-founded investment-backed expectations on which the city then reneged. While the city cannot be estopped from outlawing the rifle range, the Takings Clause may require it to pay Tom just compensation for the loss he suffered. See *Kaiser Aetna v. United States,* 444 U.S. 164 (1979).

In the preceding example, if the city had not given Tom any specific assurances that he could build a rifle range and he had instead simply relied on a zoning ordinance that permitted such uses, a subsequent change in the ordinance would not interfere with his expectations in a way that would give rise to a takings claim. Tom would be in no different position than any other owner whose land is subject to zoning regulations. As the Court has noted, takings challenges to zoning laws "have . . . been held to be without merit in a wide variety of situations when the challenged governmental actions prohibited a beneficial use to which individual parcels had previously been devoted. . . ." *Penn Central Transp. Co. v. City of New York,* 438 U.S. at 125. In short, it is not enough to show that a property owner's expectations have been disappointed. To establish a taking on this basis, it must be shown that the expectations stemmed from explicit governmental assurances.

§3.6.3 Destroying All Use or Value

The third situation in which a court may find a prima facie regulatory taking is when a use restriction effectively deprives property of all use or value. The extent of loss that must be inflicted to create such a taking depends on whether the regulation affects real property or personal property.

Real Property

In the case of real property, the Court will automatically find a prima facie taking if a regulation deprives land of all economically beneficial or productive use, so that it must be left economically idle. Use restrictions that have this effect are sometimes referred to as "confiscatory regulations" or "total regulatory takings." *Lucas v. South Carolina Coastal Council*, 505 U.S. at 1026, 1029. The Court has said that it will be "extraordinary" and "relatively rare" that a regulation will deprive real property of all economically beneficial uses so as to trigger this categorical rule. Id. at 1017, 1018.

EXAMPLE 3-F

Tom had planned to build 12 homes on the four acres he owns in Elm City. The city recently passed a zoning ordinance that bars Tom from erecting any permanent structures on his land. As a result, his property has declined in value by 80 percent and is now usable only for agricultural purposes. Can Tom establish a prima facie taking?

EXPLANATION

Despite the severe impact of this law, Tom cannot automatically establish a prima facie taking on the basis of loss in value, since his land retains market value. However, as we will see, even though Tom cannot invoke the categorical rule for total regulatory takings, he may be able to establish a partial taking due to the substantial loss in value that his property has suffered. See §3.6.4.

If it can be shown that the impact of a use restriction is to deprive real property of virtually all economic value, a prima facie taking is established under the Court's categorical rule even if the property retains some non-economic use. Thus, in Example 3-F, if Tom had been able to demonstrate that the zoning ordinance stripped his property of virtually all market value, the fact that he could still use the property for his own purposes, such as camping, hunting, or kite flying, would not alter the conclusion that a prima facie taking had occurred.

Moreover, a prima facie taking would still have been established if, after passage of the ordinance that precluded Tom from making any economically viable use of the property, the city had bought the land from him for $50,000. Once a regulation strips property of all economically viable use, the state cannot avoid a finding that it effected a taking simply by buying or offering to buy the property for use as open space. Where the effect of a regulation is to deprive real property of all economically viable use, with the result that its only remaining value is to the state as open space, a taking has occurred. If, as is presumably the case, the price paid by the state was less than the property's fair market value before the confiscatory regulation was adopted, the government must pay the difference as just compensation. Were the rule otherwise, the government could avoid a total regulatory taking by simply buying or offering to buy the property for a nominal or sub-market-value price. See *City of Monterey v. Del Monte Dunes at Monterey, Ltd.*, 526 U.S. 687 (1999) (affirming finding of total regulatory taking where the government, after repeatedly denying permission to develop the land, bought the land from the property owner for $4.5 million).

Personal Property

In the case of *personal property*, it is more difficult to establish a prima facie taking on the basis of a regulation's impact on use and value. In contrast to real property, it must be shown that the use restriction has stripped personal property of all worth, both *economic and noneconomic*. The mere fact that personal property no longer has any market value is not enough. The Court has justified this disparate treatment on the ground that it is more foreseeable that the regulation of commercial dealings may render personal property economically worthless. In *Andrus v. Allard*, 444 U.S. 51 (1979), the Court thus ruled that there was no taking when a federal statute banning the sale of eagle feathers reduced their market value to zero, for the feathers still had noneconomic value to their owners, who remained free to possess, exhibit, donate, or bequeath them.

The Court's insistence that personal property be stripped of all economic and noneconomic value makes this basis for finding a regulatory taking almost meaningless as far as personal property is concerned. About the only time the test would be met is if the government seized or confiscated the property. If the seizure were permanent, there would probably be a taking on the basis of a physical invasion or occupation, and there would then be no need to establish a taking based on loss of use or value. However, if the confiscation were only temporary, this regulatory taking argument might be of help in establishing a "temporary taking." See §3.6.6.

Measuring Loss in Value: The Denominator Problem

To decide whether a regulation has deprived real or personal property of all market value, it is necessary to define the scope of the property whose value has been reduced. If a governmental regulation destroys the market value of a 40-acre section of an owner's 160-acre parcel of land, does this represent a 100 percent loss of 40 acres, or only a 25 percent loss of 160 acres? Because this test for a regulatory taking requires courts "to compare the value that has been taken from the property with the value that remains in the property, one of the critical questions is determining how to define the unit of property 'whose value is to furnish the denominator of the fraction.'" *Keystone Bituminous Coal Assn. v. DeBenedictis*, 480 U.S. 470, 497 (1987).

The Court has expressed conflicting views as to how this so-called denominator problem should be resolved. It has sometimes insisted on looking at the parcel as a whole, including those parts of the parcel that may not have been affected by the use restriction in question. On other occasions, however, the Court has suggested that it may be proper to focus solely on that part of the property that is subject to the use restriction.

The parcel-as-a-whole approach was employed in *Penn Central Transp. Co. v. City of New York*, 438 U.S. 104 (1978), where the Court rejected an argument that New York's historic preservation law would have effected a taking had the measure stripped the airspace above Grand Central Station of all market value. "'Taking' jurisprudence does not divide a single parcel into discrete segments and attempt to determine whether rights in a particular segment have been entirely abrogated. . . . [T]his Court focuses rather . . . on the nature and extent of the interference with rights in the parcel as a whole — here, the city tax block designated as the 'landmark site.'" Id. at 130-131. Under this approach, if a use restriction deprives 40 acres in a 160-acre parcel of essentially all economic value, the loss will be measured as 25 percent of the whole parcel, not as 100 percent of the 40-acre section.

EXAMPLE 3-G

Tom sold all rights to the coal beneath his land to the Ajax Mining Company. Ajax would like to remove the entire coal deposit, but state law requires that enough pillars of coal be left in place to prevent the land surface from collapsing. As a consequence, Ajax is unable to remove 2 percent of the coal from under Tom's land. Can Ajax establish a prima facie taking on the basis that the coal that must be left in place has been stripped of 100 percent of its market value?

EXPLANATION

Under the *Penn Central* approach, to decide whether Ajax has suffered a total loss of its property, we must determine what value, if any, remains in the parcel as a whole. Since Ajax owns all the coal under Tom's land, the parcel as a whole for these purposes consists of the entire coal deposit; the coal pillars that must be left in the ground do not constitute a separate parcel for takings purposes. Ajax has thus suffered only a 2 percent loss in the market value of its property and, therefore, cannot establish a prima facie taking on this basis.

———————————

Example 3-G is based on *Keystone Bituminous Coal Assn. v. DeBenedictis*, 480 U.S. 470, 497 (1987). While the majority there ruled that no taking had occurred, Chief Justice Rehnquist and three of his colleagues dissented. The dissenters rejected the *Penn Central* approach and treated the coal that had to be left in place as a separable property interest; on this basis, they concluded that there had been a taking, for the state regulation "extinguishes the whole bundle of rights in an identifiable segment of property. . . ." Id. at 517-518.

The position of the *Keystone* dissenters resurfaced in *Lucas v. South Carolina Coastal Council,* 505 U.S. at 1016 n.7, where Justice Scalia, writing for five members of the Court, stated that if

> a regulation requires a developer to leave 90 percent of a rural tract in its natural state, it is unclear whether we would analyze the situation as one in which the owner has been deprived of all economically beneficial use of the burdened portion of the tract, or as one in which the owner has suffered a mere diminution in value of the tract as a whole.

This suggests that Example 3-G (and the *Keystone* case) might be decided differently today; i.e., the Court might well find a taking on the basis that the state had deprived Ajax of all economically viable use of the pillars of coal that had to be left in place.

Regardless of how one resolves the denominator problem, the smaller a property owner's holdings, the better the chance of establishing a prima facie taking on the basis of total loss in value. Thus, in *Penn Central,* if the owners of Grand Central Station had sold the airspace over the station to a developer who planned to erect a skyscraper there, the developer could allege a prima facie taking on the basis of a total loss in market value if the city's historic preservation law subsequently barred all economic use of the airspace. Even under the parcel-as-a-whole approach, the parcel against which the loss in value is measured would no longer consist of the entire station, but would be the airspace alone, for this is all that the developer owned. Similarly, in our example involving the destruction of a 40-acre section of land, if the rest of the 160-acre parcel were owned by someone else, the owner of the 40-acre section could claim a prima facie taking by having suffered a 100 percent loss in the economic value of his or her land.

§3.6.4 *Partial Deprivations*

Even if a regulation does not strip real property of all economic value, it is still possible that a court will find that there has been a partial regulatory taking if the loss in value is substantial. A mere diminution in value will not automatically establish a taking; i.e., no categorical rule applies. Instead, courts will examine such partial diminutions on a case-by-case basis. Thus, in *Lucas v. South Carolina Coastal Council,* 505 U.S. at 1019 n.8, the Court agreed that "in at least *some* cases the landowner with 95 percent loss will get nothing, while the landowner with total loss will recover in full." Yet, said the Court, it was error to assume that simply because an owner who has suffered a less-than-total loss could not "claim the benefit of our categorical formulation," just compensation was necessarily foreclosed. In some instances, "the landowner whose deprivation is one step short of complete" may be entitled to compensation, depending on the circumstances of the case. Id. See *Florida Rock Indus., Inc. v. United States,* 18 F.3d 1560 (Fed. Cir. 1994), *cert. denied,* 513 U.S. 1109 (1995) (holding that where a use restriction reduced the value of petitioner's wetlands by nearly 40 percent, just compensation might have to be paid on the basis that there had been a partial regulatory taking).

One context in which this issue may be important is where the government, in stripping a piece of property of all economic value, gives the owner certain "transferable development rights," or TDRs. Since TDRs can be sold to others who may then use them to develop their own property, TDRs have market value. Should the government be able to defeat a finding that there has been a regulatory taking simply by giving the owner some TDRs and then claiming that the land has not been deprived of all market value? Or should the award of TDRs be irrelevant to the question of whether there has been a taking, and instead affect only the additional compensation the owner is entitled to, over and above the value of any TDRs received? To the extent courts allow a regulatory taking to be established by a partial diminution in market value, how TDRs are treated will make no difference; the property owner will in any event receive just compensation for the net loss in market value inflicted by government. On the other hand, if a total deprivation is necessary to establish a regulatory taking, the use of TDRs could be extremely beneficial to government. For example, by giving a property owner TDRs worth $1,000, the government might avoid a finding that it has taken a parcel of land worth $250,000. The Supreme Court has yet to resolve this issue of how TDRs should be treated in regulatory takings cases. See *Suitum v. Tahoe Regional Planning Agency,* 520 U.S. 725, 728 (1997); but see id. at 747-750 (Scalia, O'Connor, & Thomas, JJ., concurring) (arguing that TDRs should not be put "on the taking rather than the just compensation side of the equation" and are thus irrelevant in deciding whether there was a taking).

§3.6.5   The Nuisance Exception

If a regulation is shown to have worked a prima facie taking because it is arbitrary, because it defeats basic expectations, or because it has stripped property of all use and value, the government may nonetheless avoid the conclusion that a taking has occurred by showing that the regulation falls within the nuisance exception.

At one time, the nuisance exception was read broadly to allow the government to prohibit virtually any use of property that it deemed to be "noxious" or "akin to" to a nuisance, whether or not it was a nuisance at common law. In recent years, the Court has limited the exception to regulations that do no more than make explicit those "restrictions that background principles of the State's law of property and nuisance already place upon land ownership." The nuisance exception does not apply to regulations that outlaw "a productive use that was previously permissible under relevant property and nuisance principles." The prohibited use must rather be one that "was *always* unlawful" according to principles of the common law, in which case the forbidden use was not part of the owner's "bundle of rights" to begin with. *Lucas v. South Carolina Coastal Council*, 505 U.S. at 1026-1031. While the government is free to impose new restrictions on the use of property in order to prevent harms that were accepted at common law, the nuisance exception cannot be invoked to avoid the payment of just compensation if such restrictions have the effect of causing a taking.

EXAMPLE 3-H

Tom received permission from Elm City to build a nuclear power plant on his land. A year after the plant went into operation, the city ordered it shut down when it was discovered that the plant sits on an earthquake fault. Tom claims a prima facie taking because the city's action has stripped his property of all market value and because the city has interfered with Tom's expectations that stemmed from the city's prior assurances that he could build the plant there. May the city invoke the nuisance exception to prevent a court from finding that a compensable taking has occurred?

EXPLANATION

The use that the city has prohibited is one that would qualify as a public nuisance under principles of the common law, since it poses a grave threat to public health and safety. Even though nuclear power plants were unknown to the common law, the threatened harm — the loss of human life — is one that the common law of public nuisance was designed to prevent. The city may, therefore, invoke the nuisance exception to defeat Tom's claim that his property has been taken.

_____

If, after a state outlaws a particular use of property, the state courts rule that no taking occurred because the prohibited use was a common law nuisance, the state's ruling on the nuisance issue is not necessarily controlling for purposes of the Takings Clause. The U.S. Supreme Court may review the state judiciary's determination to make sure that it rests on "an *objectively reasonable application* of relevant precedents." *Lucas v. South Carolina Coastal Council*, 505 U.S. at 1032 n.18. If the Supreme Court concludes that the state has attempted to recast the background principles of the common law, the nuisance exception will not apply, and the state may have to pay just compensation.

EXAMPLE 3-I

Tom's four acres of land in Elm City consist of undeveloped swamp and marshland. Many surrounding owners of such wetlands previously filled or drained their property in order to build on it. However, in 1980, the state supreme court held that the filling or draining of wetlands is a common law nuisance. Relying on this decision, the state recently passed a law that prohibits any further alteration of local wetlands. As a result, Tom's property has been deprived of all economic value. May the state avoid paying just compensation by invoking the nuisance exception?

EXPLANATION

Though state courts have the last word as to what their common law of nuisance is, the U.S. Supreme Court may decide whether a state-declared nuisance qualifies under the nuisance exception to the Takings Clause. Here, the fact that the prohibited use was long tolerated by the state strongly suggests that it was not "*always* unlawful" under "background principles of the State's law of property and nuisance." As the Court said in *Lucas,* "[T]hat a particular use has long been engaged in by similarly situated owners ordinarily imports a lack of any common-law prohibition. . . ." 505 U.S. at 1031. In our example, while the state is free to adapt its law of nuisance to contemporary needs, it may have to pay just compensation for having deprived Tom's land of all economically beneficial use.

§3.6.6   *Remedies for Temporary Regulatory Takings*

As we have seen, if a regulation goes too far, it will be found to constitute a taking. When the regulation was originally enacted, the government may not have realized that it would be held to work a taking for which just compensation must be paid. Once the true costs of the measure become known, the state may decide to repeal or abandon it. However, the government must still pay just compensation for any temporary taking of property that occurred during the period the regulation was in effect.

EXAMPLE 3-J

An Elm City zoning ordinance prohibited Tom from erecting any permanent structures on his land. Tom brought an inverse condemnation action against the city, claiming that the ordinance works a taking because it has denied him all economically beneficial use of his land. After three years of litigation, the court found in Tom's favor. The city immediately repealed the ordinance and advised Tom that he may now build on the property. Does the city owe Tom any just compensation?

EXPLANATION

By repealing the ordinance, the city has assured that there will be no further taking of property. However, the temporary taking that occurred between the time the ordinance was first applied to Tom's land and the time it was repealed is compensable under the Takings Clause. The city cannot avoid the just compensation requirement by simply abandoning a regulation the moment a court finds that it has effected a taking. See *Lucas v. South Carolina Coastal Council*, 505 U.S. at 1011-1012; *First English Evangelical Lutheran Church of Glendale v. County of Los Angeles*, 482 U.S. 304 (1987).

The result would have been the same if, instead of repealing the ordinance, the city later bought the land from Tom at less than its pre-ordinance fair market value. While any taking due to loss of all economically beneficial use of the land was temporary, ending when Tom sold the land to the city, he could still seek just compensation for the period between the adoption of the ordinance and his sale of the property. See *City of Monterey v. Del Monte Dunes at Monterey, Ltd.*, 526 U.S. 687 (1999) (affirming finding of a "temporary regulatory taking," based on city's refusal over ten-year period to approve any of 19 site development plans, where landowner ultimately sold the property to the state).

§3.7   The Requirement of Public Use

If, under any of the approaches we have discussed above, a litigant demonstrates that a taking has occurred, the only remedy usually available is payment of just compensation. A litigant ordinarily cannot obtain an injunction to prevent the government from continuing with the challenged action. Thus, in Example 3-E above, if Tom had shown that Elm City took his property by reneging on its assurances that he could operate a rifle range there, he would have to settle for just compensation even though he might prefer to enjoin the city from interfering with his using the land as a rifle range.

However, because the Fifth Amendment requires that even a compensated taking be for a public use, if it is demonstrated that a taking is not for a public use or a public purpose, the government's action may be enjoined. The Court has "many times warned that one person's property may not be taken for the benefit of another private person . . . even though compensation be paid." *Thompson v. Consolidated Gas Utilities Corp.*, 300 U.S. 55, 80 (1937).

While the public use requirement would appear to limit the government's ability to take property, as a practical matter it is virtually impossible to defeat a taking on this ground. This is because "the scope of the 'public use' requirement of the Taking Clause is 'coterminous with the scope of a sovereign's police powers.'" *Ruckelshaus v. Monsanto Co.*, 467 U.S. 986, 1014 (1984). The requirement has been found satisfied even when the direct beneficiaries of a taking are other private parties rather than the general public. Such a redistribution of property will be upheld as long as it "is rationally related to a conceivable public purpose." *Hawaii Hous. Auth. v. Midkiff*, 467 U.S. 229, 241 (1984).

EXAMPLE 3-K

Elm City authorizes an exclusive ten-member hunting club to use Tom's property every Tuesday afternoon. What remedies might Tom have against the city?

EXPLANATION

Tom can probably show that this is a per se taking for which just compensation must be paid, since the city has authorized a permanent physical invasion of his land. See §3.5. However, Tom probably cannot enjoin the city's action by arguing that the taking is not for a public use. Even though the property is being used for the immediate benefit of other private individuals, the city could argue that this rationally furthers the legitimate goal of reducing violence by providing a safe recreational outlet for those who like to use guns.

§3.8   Conditions Attached to Building Permits

The state may sometimes cause a taking if, as a condition for granting a building or development permit, it insists that the owner dedicate property for public use or submit to certain use restrictions. In contrast to other forms of takings, in these so-called exactions or dedications cases the government does not *absolutely insist* that property be opened to public use or that specific uses be prohibited. Instead, it gives the property owner a choice: either agree to the state's condition or forgo the right to develop the land. Since a permit is usually necessary before property can be developed, the state may attempt to employ the permit process as a means of exacting from the owner something for which it would otherwise have to pay just compensation.

EXAMPLE 3-L

Elm City wishes to build a park, but the only suitable land is Tom's four-acre parcel on the edge of town. How might the city seek to achieve this objective?

EXPLANATION

The city would normally have to buy Tom's land or use its power of eminent domain and pay him just compensation. However, if by chance Tom needs a building permit because he wants to erect a house on his land, the city might condition the permit on Tom's agreeing to dedicate an acre of his property for a public park. If this scheme were allowed, Elm City could acquire a public park without having to pay for it.

This manipulation of the permit process is invalid because it involves an unconstitutional condition. The government is hinging the receipt of a discretionary benefit (i.e., a building permit) on the recipient's surrender of a constitutional right (i.e., the right to just compensation). If the condition were imposed outright, it would be a per se taking entitling Tom to just compensation, for it works a permanent physical invasion. By instead insisting that Tom give up an acre of his land if he wants a permit, the city is using its control over a governmental benefit to in effect buy up Tom's constitutional right to just compensation.

To prevent the state from using the permit process as a means of evading the just compensation requirement, the Court has created a special test that must be met whenever a building permit condition is such that, *if it were imposed outright,* it would constitute a taking. Under this two-part exactions test,

1. There must be an essential nexus between a legitimate state interest and the permit conditions exacted by the state, and
2. The permit conditions must be related in both nature and extent to the impact of the proposed development.

If either part of this test is not met, the condition or exaction will be found to constitute a taking for which just compensation must be paid. *Dolan v. City of Tigard,* 512 U.S. 374 (1994).

§3.8.1   *Only Certain Types of Conditions Qualify*

The Court's exactions test does not apply to all types of building permit conditions. It may be used to establish a taking only where the exaction is one that would have amounted to a taking had the state imposed it outright. If the condition would not have caused a taking were it imposed as a flat requirement, there is obviously no danger that the state is using its control over the permit process to avoid paying just compensation, and the two-part exactions test does not come into play. Application of the test is typically limited to "land-use decisions conditioning approval of development on the dedication of property to public use." *City of Monterey v. Del Monte Dunes at Monterey, Ltd.*, 526 U.S. at 702.

EXAMPLE 3-M

Tom applied for a permit to construct a 300,000-square-foot warehouse on his land in Elm City. The city conditioned the permit on Tom's agreeing to plant 45 trees on the property and to limit the building's height to 70 feet. The city has imposed similar conditions on other property owners. The effect of the conditions is to reduce the value of the property, but not to prevent it from being used for warehouse purposes. Will the imposition of these conditions trigger the exactions test?

EXPLANATION

These conditions are not the type that will trigger the Court's exactions test. If they had been imposed as mandatory requirements rather than as conditions on granting a building permit, the exactions would not have worked a taking under our regular takings analysis; i.e., none involves a physical invasion by government or the public; none is arbitrary, since similar conditions were imposed on others; there is no indication that Tom relied on assurances that the conditions would not be imposed; and the conditions do not render the property economically worthless. There is thus no risk that the city is using the permit process to evade its obligation to pay just compensation. The exactions test, therefore, does not apply.

By contrast, had the city conditioned Tom's permit on his not developing a vacant lot he owned in the center of town, this might have triggered the exactions test if the result was to strip the lot of all market value, for this limitation would have constituted a prima facie taking had it been imposed outright rather than as a permit condition.

§3.8.2   *The Essential Nexus Requirement*

If a building permit condition would have amounted to a taking had it been imposed outright, then it will be deemed to constitute a taking unless the Court's exactions test is met. The first part of this test insists that there be an essential nexus between a legitimate governmental interest and the permit condition.

This requirement was not satisfied in *Nollan v. California Coastal Commission*, 483 U.S. 825 (1987), where California exacted a lateral public easement across a beachfront lot in return for permitting the owners to build a larger house on their property. If this condition had been imposed outright, it would have involved a permanent physical invasion and a per se taking. The state said that it imposed the condition because the proposed development would reduce the public's view of the sea from the roadway behind the house. While the Court assumed that the state's goal of protecting visual access to the ocean was legitimate, there was no essential nexus between that goal and the condition that the public be granted an easement to cross the property at the shoreline. Allowing people to walk along the beach in no way furthers the goal of assuring visual access from the highway. The Court noted that had the state instead exacted the condition that the owners provide a public viewing spot on their property, it would then have met the essential nexus requirement, since such a condition would have furthered the goal of improving visual access to the ocean.

EXAMPLE 3-N

Tom applied for a permit to build a small shopping mall on his property in Elm City. The city conditioned the permit on Tom's building a 1000-space public garage on his land. Does the exactions test apply here, and if so, is the essential nexus requirement satisfied?

EXPLANATION

The exactions test applies because the condition, had it been imposed outright, would have amounted to a permanent physical invasion and hence a per se taking. The first part of the exactions test, the essential nexus requirement, is met because the city's legitimate goal of assuring adequate parking space is clearly promoted by a condition that Tom build a public parking garage.

§3.8.3   The Rough Proportionality Requirement

If the essential nexus requirement is met, the government must also show that both the *nature* and the *extent* of the permit condition bear a rough proportionality to the projected impact of the development. In other words, if the state is to avoid having to pay just compensation, it must demonstrate that it is not exacting more than is appropriate to compensate for the negative effects caused by the proposed use.

The Nature of the Condition

The conditions attached to a building permit must, by their nature, relate to the anticipated impact of the development in question. Otherwise, even if a condition meets the essential nexus test because it furthers a legitimate state interest, it will constitute a compensable taking.

For example, in the *Nollan* case discussed above, California might have defended its permit condition that the Nollans give the public a lateral easement across their beach, not on the ground that it promoted *visual* access from the highway (which it did not), but on the basis that it enhanced the public's *physical* access to the sea. While this condition would meet the essential nexus requirement, since it clearly advances a legitimate state goal, it would have failed the second part of the exactions test because there was no evidence that the proposed development would reduce the public's physical access to the sea. There would have been no logical relationship between the nature of the condition and any negative impact caused by building a new house.

The same problem was posed in *Dolan v. City of Tigard*, 512 U.S. 374 (1994). There, among the conditions imposed by the city in granting a permit to enlarge a hardware store and paved parking lot were that the landowner not build on part of the property lying within a floodplain, and that she dedicate this land to the city for recreational purposes. The condition that Dolan not build in the floodplain met the rough proportionality requirement, for this restriction would reduce the danger of flooding created by the enlarged store and lot. However, the additional requirement that she deed this land to the city was not, by its nature, related to any negative impact of the proposed development; it did not tend to mitigate or offset any identifiable burdens that would be caused by the new store. The city was instead using the permit process to acquire public recreational land without having to pay for it.

EXAMPLE 3-O

In Example 3-N above, Elm City conditioned Tom's permit to build a shopping mall on his constructing a public parking garage. This condition is, by its nature, reasonably related to the impact of the proposed development, since the new mall will increase the demand for public parking. Suppose that the city instead, in order to enhance recreational opportunities for people living in the area, had conditioned the permit on Tom's building a public swimming pool next to the mall. Would the city's action pass muster under the exactions test?

EXPLANATION

This exaction would meet the essential nexus test, for a pool would further the city's recreational goal. However, it would fail the first part of the rough proportionality requirement, since the pool, by its nature, does not relate to or tend to offset any negative impact of the proposed shopping development.

The Extent of the Condition

Even if the *nature* of the condition is such that it relates to public needs created by the proposed use, the *degree or extent* of the condition must also bear a rough proportionality to the anticipated impact of the development. Otherwise, by exacting more than is reasonably necessary to correct problems created by the project, the government is using the permit scheme as a means of taking property without paying just compensation for it.

In *Dolan v. City of Tigard,* this requirement was not met by one of the permit conditions imposed on the landowner, i.e., that in order to enlarge her hardware store, she must dedicate a 15-foot strip of land to the city for a pedestrian/bicycle pathway. Unlike the condition that she deed land within the floodplain to the city, the *nature* of this exaction was reasonably related to the negative impact of the development, for the pathway would tend to offset some of the traffic created by the new store. However, the city failed to show that the *extent or degree* of the exaction was roughly proportional to the impact of the development, for it did not prove to what extent the estimated 435 additional daily car trips generated by the project would be reduced if customers could reach the store by a pedestrian/bicycle pathway. The Court explained that while "[n]o precise mathematical calculation is required . . . the city must make some effort to quantify its findings in support of the dedication for the pedestrian/bicycle pathway beyond the conclusory statement that it could offset some of the traffic demand generated." *Dolan,* 512 U.S. at 395-396.

EXAMPLE 3-P

In our earlier example involving Tom's desire to build a shopping mall, we saw that the condition that he construct a 1000-space parking garage was reasonably related by its *nature* to the negative impact of the mall. Might the condition, nonetheless, constitute a compensable taking?

EXPLANATION

Yes. The condition will still amount to a compensable taking unless the city proves that the *extent and degree* of the exaction are roughly proportional to the increased parking demand caused by the project. The city will have to estimate the number of new parking spaces likely to be needed as a result of the customers visiting Tom's mall. Unless that number is fairly close to 1000, the permit condition would fail the rough proportionality requirement.

It is important to remember that the exactions test for finding a taking does not apply to all governmental regulations of land use. Rather, it may be used only with respect to conditions that are attached to a building or development permit, and then only if the conditions would have constituted a taking had they been imposed as mandatory requirements. Thus, in *City of Monterey v. Del Monte Dunes at Monterey, Ltd.*, 526 U.S. at 702-703, the Court explained that "we have not extended the rough-proportionality test of *Dolan* beyond the special context of exactions. . . . The rule applied in *Dolan* considers whether dedications demanded as conditions of development are proportional to the development's anticipated impacts. It was not designed to address, and is not readily applicable to, the much different questions arising where, as here, the landowner's challenge is based not on excessive exactions but on denial of development. We believe, accordingly, that the rough-proportionality test of *Dolan* is inapposite to a case such as this one."

4

The Contracts Clause

§4.1   Introduction and Overview

The Contracts Clause limits the power of a state to alter the legal obligations created by preexisting contractual relationships. Specifically, Article I, §10, of the Constitution provides, "No State shall . . . pass any . . . Law impairing the Obligation of Contracts." The apparent absolute proscription, however, has been tempered to accommodate the "inherent police power of the State 'to safeguard the vital interests of its people.'" *Energy Reserves Group, Inc. v. Kansas Power & Light Co.,* 459 U.S. 400, 410 (1983). In other words, the Contracts Clause is subject to the reserved powers of the states to protect the health, safety, and welfare of their citizens. Thus, not all state laws that alter contractual obligations are void under the Contracts Clause. In general, the test is one of reasonableness, in which a court must examine the expectations of the contracting parties, the severity of the impairment, and the public interest at stake.

From an analytical perspective, the examination of every Contracts Clause problem begins with three questions, each of which must be answered affirmatively in order to establish a potential violation of the Clause:

- Is there a contractual obligation?
- Does a change in state law impair the contractual obligation?
- Is the impairment substantial?

See *General Motors, Inc. v. Romein,* 503 U.S. 181, 186 (1992). If each of these questions is answered affirmatively, the next step is to determine whether the state has acted reasonably under the circumstances. *Energy Reserves Group,* 459 U.S. at 411-413. Here, the substantiality of the state's interest is measured against the extent of the impairment. Id. The specific elements of this analysis will be examined below.

By its terms, the Contracts Clause does not apply to the federal government. The Due Process Clause of the Fifth Amendment, however, may be triggered by federal legislation that has a substantial retroactive effect on a preexisting contractual relationship. The test for such retroactive legislation is a modestly heightened rational basis. See *United States v. Carlton*, 512 U.S. 26 (1994) (upholding the retroactive application of a federal tax law under the rational basis test, but noting that rationality in the context of retroactivity requires a somewhat stronger showing than rationality in the context of prospective applications).

Be careful not to confuse the due process concept, liberty of contract, with the interest that is protected by the Contracts Clause. The liberty of contract that comes into play under the Due Process Clause involves the freedom to enter into contracts, while the Contracts Clause protects one's freedom from unreasonable state interference with the terms of a contract previously entered into. In other words, the Contracts Clause in no manner limits the ability of a state to legislate *prospectively* with respect to the substantive terms that may be included in future contracts or with respect to the conditions under which future contracts may be formed. The essence of a Contracts Clause violation is a change in state law that alters the obligations established by a preexisting contract.

§4.2   The Preliminary Questions

§4.2.1   *Is There a Contractual Obligation?*

For purposes of the Contracts Clause, the question of whether a contractual obligation exists is ultimately a question of federal law. *General Motors, Inc. v. Romein*, 503 U.S. at 187. Yet despite this often-stated rule, one should not expect to discover a large body of federal contract law elucidating such matters as offer, acceptance, and consideration. In reality, the focus of this preliminary inquiry is most often on general principles of contract law, including any state and local variations on those principles. After all, these are the principles relied on by the parties in creating what purports to be a contractual relationship. The term *contract*, therefore, is used in the ordinary sense of the word as connoting an agreement for consideration between two or more persons under which the parties obligate themselves to one another. See *Louisiana v. New Orleans*, 109 U.S. 285, 288 (1883).

The "federal" aspect of this initial question serves more as a potential trump on state law principles that may be used to eviscerate what otherwise seem to be contractual rights. In other words, although state law provides guidance in determining whether a contract exists, state law may not be used to circumvent the protections afforded by the Contracts Clause by *retroactively* defining the law of contracts in a manner that obliterates the legitimate contractual expectations of the parties.

Implied Contractual Obligations

Quite often in a Contracts Clause dispute, it is clear from the express provisions of the contract that a contractual obligation or right exists, and the critical question is whether that obligation has been substantially impaired. At times, however, the issue is whether an unstated obligation or right should be deemed to be implied into the contract. The *Romein* case, for example, involved a Contracts Clause challenge to a 1987 Michigan statute that required General Motors (GM) and the Ford Motor Company (Ford) to pay workers' compensation benefits that they had previously withheld under the terms of a 1981 statute. As construed by the Michigan Supreme Court, the 1981 statute permitted employers to coordinate benefits by paying reduced workers' compensation to workers who received benefits from other sources, including workers who were injured before the effective date of the 1981 statute. In 1987, the state legislature amended the 1981 statute to require that full rather than reduced benefits be paid to workers whose injuries predated the 1981 law. The result was that GM and Ford were ordered to pay an additional $25 million in withheld benefits. The auto makers claimed that the 1987 statute's "retroactive" imposition of this refund violated the Contracts Clause.

The essence of the auto makers' argument was that the existing contracts with their employees included an implied term that gave the employer the right to rely on past disability payment periods as closed and that the 1987 statute impaired this contractual obligation. In ruling against the auto makers, the U.S. Supreme Court explained that while the terms of a contract may be implied, no such implication was proper under these facts: "Michigan law does not explicitly imply a contractual term allowing an employer to depend on the closure of past disability compensation periods. Moreover, such right does not appear to be so central to the bargained-for exchange between the parties, or to the enforceability of the contract as a whole, that it must be deemed to be a term of the contract." 503 U.S. at 188-189. In arriving at its conclusion, the Court accorded "respectful consideration and great weight to the views" of the Michigan Supreme Court, which had also found that the employment contracts at issue did not contain the implied provision asserted by GM and Ford. Id. at 187. Thus, the Court's resolution of this "federal" question was strongly informed by state law.

State Law as an Implied Contractual Obligation

On occasion, a party asserting a Contracts Clause claim will argue that a repealed provision of state law was an implied term of a contract and that by repealing that law, the state impaired a contractual obligation. Typically, however, state laws are treated as implied contractual terms "only when those laws affect the validity, construction, and enforcement of contracts" or when those laws are part of the bargained-for exchange between the parties. 503 U.S. at 189. For example, the remedy of specific performance is a legal device used to enforce certain types of contracts. The right to obtain specific performance would, therefore, be an implied term in those contracts if it was part of a state's law at the time the contract was made. A repeal of the remedy might well run afoul of the Contracts Clause if the repeal made preexisting contracts unenforceable. On the other hand, a provision of state law that allows employers to coordinate benefits for injured employees has no bearing on the validity, construction, or enforceability of a contract. Rather, it provides a substantive right that may or may not have been negotiated between the parties. Therefore, this provision of state law would be an implied term of an employment contract *only if* benefit coordination was part of the bargained-for exchange between the parties.

EXAMPLE 4-A

On July 1, 1985, Bill and Ted entered into a real estate financing agreement under which Bill lent Ted $100,000 for the purchase of a new home. The loan, which was secured by the purchased property, was amortized over 30 years, during which time Ted was to make monthly payments. At the time the agreement was reached, the state law of foreclosure permitted a defaulting debtor to redeem the secured property within one year of a foreclosure sale as long as the debtor had not abandoned the property. In the case of abandonment, however, the state law provided no period of redemption, and the purchaser at foreclosure was granted immediate possession. Several years later and while the agreement was still in effect, state law was amended to create a one-year redemption period even for abandoned property. Was the original state law on redemption an implied term of Bill and Ted's agreement?

EXPLANATION

Probably. Because foreclosure is an important remedy for the enforcement of contracts between creditors and debtors, the state's law of foreclosure as it stood on July 1, 1985, might well be an implied term of the contract between Bill and Ted. Under that law, if Ted had defaulted on the loan and abandoned the property, Bill would have had a right of foreclosure and immediate sale, with no obligation to give Ted an opportunity to redeem the property. Under the law as amended, Ted would retain a right to redeem the property within one year of foreclosure, thereby altering the immediate enforceability of Bill's rights under the contract.

§4.2.2 Does a Change in State Law Impair a Contractual Obligation?

Once a contractual obligation has been identified, the next step to consider is whether that obligation has been impaired by a change in state law. This inquiry should create little difficulty. Simply compare the terms of the obligation created by the contract with the provisions of the state law being challenged. If the change in state law *increases, diminishes,* or *extinguishes* an obligation created by the contract, the state law has impaired the obligation. As illustrated by Example 4-A, a change in the state law of foreclosure that created a redemption period for abandoned property diminished Bill's implied right of foreclosure and, therefore, impaired an obligation created in the original agreement. One could also view the change in state law as increasing Ted's rights of redemption. In either case, the contractual obligation has been altered and thus impaired.

EXAMPLE 4-B

Allied operates a factory within the State of Minnesota. Its 40 employees are covered under a company-sponsored pension plan. Under the plan, employees are eligible for a pension at age 65. The amount of the pension is computed by a formula that takes into account the employee's length of service and annual compensation. An employee who leaves the company before reaching age 65 loses all pension benefits unless that employee has worked for the company a total of 15 years and is at least 60 years old at the time of separation. Due to a business slowdown, Allied has announced its intention to close its Minnesota plant. As a consequence, a large number of Allied's employees will lose their pension eligibility. In response, the state has adopted legislation that requires Allied and other like-situated businesses that terminate their operations in Minnesota to treat pensions as vested for all employees with ten or more years of seniority. The net result is that Allied must pay a $185,000 pension funding charge to cover these newly vested pensions. Does this legislation impair a contractual obligation between Allied and its employees?

EXPLANATION

Yes. By retroactively increasing the pension obligations of the employer, the state has impaired contractual obligations between the parties. Presumably the employer and the employee bargained for a particular benefit package under which the employer was obligated to pay a pension if the employee satisfied certain specified terms. To revise that package retroactively is, in essence, to rewrite the terms of that bargained-for exchange. Under the revised contract, the employer's obligations are increased, while the employee's are diminished. Regardless of the perspective from which one views this impairment, the critical factor is that the state has interfered with the terms of a preexisting contract. Consistent with the Contracts Clause, a state is free to regulate the vesting of pensions prospectively as long as it does not alter the contractual expectations of the parties by rewriting the terms of the contract that already exists between them. See *Allied Structural Steel Co. v. Spannaus*, 438 U.S. 234 (1978).

§4.2.3   Is the Impairment Substantial?

Only substantial impairments of contractual obligations trigger further Contracts Clause scrutiny. *Allied Structural Steel*, 438 U.S. at 244-245. Stated somewhat differently, a finding that an alteration of a contractual obligation is minor or de minimis may end the inquiry. Id. As a practical matter, however, courts rarely find that a clear impairment of a contractual obligation is so insubstantial as to warrant no further scrutiny. Rather, the tendency is to measure the "substantiality" or "severity" of the impairment and to gear the level of judicial scrutiny to the perceived harm. Thus, a truly substantial impairment will generate a close examination of the state's justification, while a minor or less substantial impairment will generate a more deferential scrutiny.

Under what circumstances will an impairment be deemed substantial enough to warrant close judicial scrutiny? The answer to this question remains somewhat elusive. We can say with certainty that a substantial impairment does not require a total destruction of contract rights, but that it does require something more than a technical alteration of those rights. The critical issue in determining substantiality is the extent to which the state has upset the *reasonable expectations of the contracting parties*.

In determining the reasonableness of the parties' expectations, the Court looks to at least four factors. One factor concerns what the parties actually intended or expected to create through their contractual relationship. *Energy Reserves Group*, 459 U.S. at 411. Second, the more central a particular contractual expectation is to the bargained-for exchange, the more likely it is that an impairment of that expectation will be deemed substantial. Another factor is the economic consequence of the change in state law. *Allied Structural Steel*, 438 U.S. at 246-247. The greater that consequence is, the more likely it is that a court may find a substantial impairment; this is particularly so if the contract was designed to avoid the particular economic burden imposed by the change in state law. Finally, if the subject of the contract relates to an area that has been heavily regulated by the state in the past, a court is extremely unlikely to find a substantial impairment regardless of the size of the economic burden. A party who has been subject to regulation cannot *reasonably* expect to rely on contractual rights to avoid the consequences of continued state regulation.

EXAMPLE 4-C

Returning to the facts of Example 4-B, was the state's imposition of a retroactive pension obligation a *substantial impairment* of the contractual obligation between the employer and its employees?

EXPLANATION

We must try to ascertain the extent to which the state has interfered with the reasonable expectations of the parties. First, there is little doubt that the employer expected or intended that pensions would be funded only in accord with the specific terms of the employment agreement. And it is quite likely that the employer made pension investments on the basis of those expectations. Moreover, nothing in the facts indicates that the employees had any other expectation. Even though the employees may have hoped or assumed that the company would remain in business a sufficient length of time for their pensions to vest, nothing in the contract seems to directly support that expectation. Second, although the pension plan may not have been the key ingredient in the employment contract, the plan was probably of more than marginal significance to both parties, since it was certainly part of the compensation package. Third, the economic consequences of the change in state law are severe, namely, an unanticipated $185,000 penalty imposed on a relatively small company. Finally, in the absence of information to the contrary, there is no suggestion that the state had previously regulated pensions in a manner that would have alerted the employer to anticipate changes in state law. Considering these factors together, the impairment is likely to be found substantial. See *Allied Structural Steel*, 438 U.S. at 245-247.

EXAMPLE 4-D

In order to finance its system of public education, the State of Texas sold millions of acres of public land under contracts in which the purchasers were required to make a down payment of 1/40 of the value of the land plus annual payments of interest and principal. The contracts provided for termination of the contract and forfeiture of the land for failure to pay interest. However, the defaulting purchaser was given an open-ended right to reinstate his or her claim at any time by filing a request, accompanied by the payment of delinquent interest, as long as rights of a third party had not intervened. On the other hand, state policy required that any forfeited property be placed for sale immediately, thus increasing the likelihood that third party rights would intervene prior to any request for reinstatement. Thirty years after entering into these contracts, Texas adopted legislation that limited the potential reinstatement period to five years from the date of forfeiture. Does this measure substantially impair an obligation established in the purchase contracts?

EXPLANATION

Probably not. The potentially impaired obligation is the contractual term that grants purchasers an open-ended right to reinstate ownership upon the payment of delinquent interest. By diminishing that right, the five-year limitation impairs a contractual obligation. Whether this impairment is substantial turns largely on the contractual expectations of the parties. If the purchasers entered into these contracts under the reasonable expectation that they would retain forever an irrevocable right to redeem forfeited property, then the newly imposed limitation could be seen as a substantial impairment of that expectation. Yet given the very real possibility that the rights of third parties would intervene due to the state's policy of immediately placing the property for sale, any expectation of permanent redemption rights would seem almost fanciful. Moreover, the purchasers would have a difficult time establishing that the supposed unlimited right of redemption was central to these contracts when first entered. Presumably the contracts were entered into with an intent to abide by the terms and thereby avoid forfeiture. Yet despite these conclusions of "insubstantiality," a court would still be likely to consider the state's justification, albeit under a very deferential standard of review. See *El Paso v. Simmons,* 379 U.S. 497, 509-517 (1965) (so ruling on similar facts).

§4.3   The Balancing Test and the Reserved Powers Doctrine

If the impairment is deemed sufficiently substantial to warrant further judicial review, a court will balance the severity of the impairment against the public's interest in abrogating the contractual obligation at issue. However, there is a strong presumption that the states retain their reserved powers to promote and to protect the health, safety, and welfare of their citizens. Stated somewhat differently, "One whose rights, such as they are, are subject to state restriction, cannot remove them from the power of the State by making a contract about them." *Hudson Water Co. v. McCarter,* 209 U.S. 349, 357 (1908). As a result of this presumption in favor of the state's right to exercise its police powers, it is difficult, though not impossible, to establish a violation of the Contracts Clause.

The balancing test focuses on the reasonableness of the challenged action. In the Court's words, "Legislation adjusting the rights and responsibilities of contracting parties must be upon reasonable conditions and of a character appropriate to the public purpose justifying its adoption. . . . As is customary in reviewing economic and social regulation, however, courts properly defer to legislative judgment as to the necessity and reasonableness of a particular measure." *United States Trust Co. v. New Jersey,* 431 U.S. 1, 22-23 (1977). This is simply another way of saying that the state action must be reasonable under the circumstances, a classic due-process-type formula.

Although the general standard is one of reasonableness, the level of judicial scrutiny is somewhat variable. "The severity of the impairment measures the height of the hurdle the state [law] must clear. . . . Severe impairment . . . will push the inquiry to a careful examination of the nature and purpose of the state legislation." *Allied Structural Steel,* 438 U.S. at 245. The opposite is true as well. A less severe impairment will "push the inquiry" toward a posture of almost complete deference. In addition, as discussed further below, if a state attempts to diminish its own contractual obligations, the principle of deference is obviated, and the level of judicial scrutiny is somewhat more intense. *United States Trust Co.,* 431 U.S. at 26.

EXAMPLE 4-E

During the Great Depression, communities throughout the United States were faced with massive unemployment, a crash in the real estate market, and a virtual epidemic of home foreclosures and evictions. In response to this crisis, the State of Minnesota adopted the Mortgage Moratorium Act (MMA), which granted county courts the authority to extend the period during which a homeowner could redeem his or her home from foreclosure. The practical effect of the MMA was to prevent banks from effectively exercising their contractual rights of foreclosure during the extension period. The homeowner was, however, required to pay the mortgagee reasonable rental value during any judicially granted extension, and the homeowner also remained liable for any accrued interest or deficiency. The MMA was to remain in effect "only during the continuance of the emergency," but no more than two years in any event. By impairing the contractual rights of foreclosure, did the MMA violate the Contracts Clause? Or, stated in terms of the judicial inquiry, was the adjustment of contract rights effected by the MMA "upon reasonable conditions and of a character appropriate to the public purpose justifying its adoption"?

EXPLANATION

First, we must consider the severity of the impairment. Unquestionably the MMA alters the contractual rights of the mortgagee, for the mortgagee cannot obtain or convey title during the extension period. In this sense, the rights of the mortgagee are clearly diminished. On the other hand, the MMA does not alter any other obligations under the mortgage contracts, and it provides a compensating protection to the mortgagee by requiring the homeowner to pay reasonable rental value during the extension period. Thus, in one sense, the impairment is severe in that it clearly alters the contractual expectations of the parties; in another sense, however, the impairment is relatively minor, since it merely extends the period of redemption and during this time the mortgagee's interests are otherwise protected. Yet regardless of which perspective one takes, the degree of impairment is certainly substantial enough to warrant further judicial scrutiny.

Having discovered a sufficiently substantial impairment of contractual rights, the next step is to determine if the impairment is reasonable under the circumstances. A state has a legitimate and even substantial interest in preventing widespread dislocation caused by an epidemic of foreclosures and evictions. Moreover, the means adopted by the state seem appropriate to the public purpose, since they intrude on contractual expectations only to the extent necessary to advance that purpose for the duration of the emergency. Specifically, the impairment is temporary, is geared to addressing the precise crisis confronted by the state, and is designed so as to otherwise protect the economic interests of the mortgagee. Thus, given the deference normally accorded a state in this realm and the relatively limited nature of the impairment, the MMA did not violate the Contracts Clause. See *Home Building & Loan Assn. v. Blaisdell,* 290 U.S. 398, 444-447 (1934).

EXAMPLE 4-F

In Examples 4-B and 4-C, we considered a state law that retroactively imposed pension obligations on an employer about to close its business within the state. We concluded that the impairment of the employment contract was substantial given the expectations of the parties and the relatively large economic impact of the increased obligations. Assume, for purposes of this example, that the state's interest in imposing that retroactive pension obligation was to protect employees with "unvested" pensions who are working for companies about to terminate operations within the state. Is this contractual impairment "upon reasonable conditions and of a character appropriate to the public purpose justifying its adoption"?

EXPLANATION

The public purpose asserted by the state, namely, the protection of employees whose pension rights may be foreclosed by businesses that terminate operations within the state, is certainly legitimate and, from the perspective of the affected employees, even quite important. The public interest is not, however, commensurate with the interest at issue in Example 4-E, where the state was confronted with severe economic problems generated by the Great Depression. Nothing in the facts indicates that Minnesota was faced with an epidemic of such closures. Moreover, the intrusion on the contractual expectations of the parties here is much more severe than was the case with the mortgage moratorium described in Example 4-E. The mortgage moratorium was temporary and was designed to minimize the economic impact on the mortgagee. In this example, on the other hand, the impact on the employer is immediate, drastic, and permanent. Thus, given the severity of the impairment and the relatively discrete problem being addressed by the state, a court could well find that the state had exceeded the scope of its reserved powers. In other words, the contractual impairment was not "upon reasonable conditions and of a character appropriate to the public purpose justifying its adoption." See *Allied Structural Steel,* 438 U.S. at 244-251.

The discussion in Examples 4-E and 4-F could lead one to conclude that the Contracts Clause is a relatively potent weapon for assessing the constitutionality of state legislation that retroactively impairs contractual obligations. However, the decision on which those examples were constructed, *Allied Structural Steel Co. v. Spannaus,* has not led to a resurgence of Contracts Clause jurisprudence. The Court's overall approach to the Contracts Clause remains one of general deference marked by occasional and fact-bound instances of increased judicial scrutiny.

§4.4 The Special Problems of Contracts to Which a State Is a Party

All the examples we have considered so far have involved state interference with *private contracts,* i.e., contracts entered into between private parties. When a state interferes with a *public contract,* i.e., a contract to which the state itself is a party, the Contracts Clause analysis is different in two respects from that applied in the case of private contracts. First, the reserved powers doctrine may render the Clause wholly inapplicable to certain public contracts. Second, if the Contracts Clause does apply, the standard of review will be less deferential than that for private contracts.

The reserved powers doctrine takes on a special importance when applied to public contracts. Under this aspect of the reserved powers doctrine, a state will not be bound by any contractual obligation that purports to "surrender an essential attribute of its sovereignty." *United States Trust Co.,* 431 U.S. at 23. Stated somewhat differently, "the legislature cannot bargain away the police power of a State." *Stone v. Mississippi,* 101 U.S. 814, 817 (1880). The net result is that "one legislature cannot abridge the powers of a succeeding legislature" by binding the latter in a manner that limits its authority to protect the health, safety, and welfare of the community. *Fletcher v. Peck*, 10 U.S. (6 Cranch) 87, 135-139 (1810). Thus, a contract under which a state agreed not to regulate safety conditions in the workplace would be void ab initio. A subsequent legislature would, therefore, be free to ignore the provision without further consideration of the Contracts Clause. See also *West River Bridge Co. v. Dix*, 47 U.S. (6 How.) 507 (1848) (power of eminent domain may not be contracted away).

The exact contours of this aspect of the reserved powers doctrine have not been fully defined by the Court. The Court has made it clear, however, that the doctrine will not insulate a state's "purely" financial obligations from Contracts Clause review. *United States Trust Co.*, 431 U.S. at 25. A state may, therefore, contractually bind itself to grant a tax exemption or to desist from exercising its power to spend money under certain defined circumstances. And the Contracts Clause will stand as a substantial barrier to any effort by the state to relieve itself of these obligations. This, of course, assumes that the financial obligation does not prevent or prohibit the state from exercising its police powers. If it does, the obligation is invalid and not entitled to Contracts Clause protection. For example, suppose that a state agrees to operate a nuclear reactor for a specified number of years as security for a revenue bond through which the reactor was financed. The agreement is financial in the sense that the pledge functions as a security for the bondholders. But if the state later discovers that the plant is on an active earthquake fault, the contractual obligation, although ostensibly financial, will not prevent the state from shutting down the reactor.

EXAMPLE 4-G

The Port Authority of New Jersey, a state entity, issued bonds under which it agreed that the revenues pledged as security for the bonds would not be used to subsidize mass transit operations. Subsequently, the State of New Jersey passed legislation that retroactively repealed this security provision. The purpose of the repeal was to free up much-needed funds to improve mass transit facilities in order to encourage private automobile users to shift to public transit. Essentially, the repeal was one step in an effort to alleviate serious problems of traffic congestion. Bondholders brought suit, challenging the repeal as a violation of the Contracts Clause. Does the reserved powers doctrine insulate the repeal from Contracts Clause analysis?

EXPLANATION

Since the state is, in essence, a party to the contract, the first question must be whether this contractual obligation runs afoul of the reserved powers doctrine. In other words, did the contract between the Port Authority and the bondholders contract away the police powers of the state? Certainly the promotion of public transportation is well within the police powers of a state. This would be especially true in states, such as New Jersey, where highway congestion is a particularly acute problem. One could argue, therefore, that the bond provision limits the state's authority to exercise its police powers in the context of mass transit. But the bond provision does not *prevent* or *prohibit* the state from improving its mass transit facilities or from promoting public transit; it precludes the state from using certain specified revenues to do so. Thus, in order to accomplish its goals, the state will simply have to dip into some other financial resource. The state has not contracted away its authority to exercise its police powers in the context of mass transit. The obligation, therefore, is purely financial and is not void under the reserved powers doctrine. See *United States Trust Co.,* 431 U.S. at 23-25.

If the reserved powers doctrine does not render a public contract void ab initio, then the Contracts Clause will be applied with a greater rigor than it would be if the state had interfered with a private contract. When a state attempts to relieve itself of its own contractual obligations, the Court is understandably more suspicious of the state's motivations. This suspicion does not alter the factors considered by the Court, but it does lead to a significantly less deferential treatment of the state's justifications for its actions. Thus, in *United States Trust Co.,* the Court explained that while the same constitutional standard governs private and public contracts, "[i]n applying this standard [to public contracts], complete deference to a legislative assessment of reasonableness and necessity is not appropriate because the State's self-interest is at stake." 431 U.S. at 25-26. The result is a heightened, although not necessarily fatal, scrutiny. Essentially, the state must prove that its action was both *reasonable* and *necessary* to effect an important public purpose. Id.

EXAMPLE 4-H

In Example 4-G, we concluded that the contractual provision was not void ab initio under the reserved powers doctrine. Continuing with the same facts, was the state's repeal reasonable?

EXPLANATION

In assessing the reasonableness of the state's repeal, since the state is a party to the contract the normal deference due the state will not be afforded. Instead, the state must demonstrate that the repeal was both reasonable and necessary to effect some important public purpose. This standard is unlikely to be met unless the state can show that the problem of traffic congestion can be solved by no means short of the repeal. If there are reasonable alternatives, such as the encouragement of car pooling or the use of other resources, then the Contracts Clause will not allow the state to relieve itself of its contractual obligation. See *United States Trust Co.*, 431 U.S. at 25-32.

5

Procedural Due Process and Irrebuttable Presumptions

§5.1   Introduction and Overview

The Due Process Clauses of the Fifth and the Fourteenth Amendments prohibit the federal government and the states from depriving a person of "life, liberty, or property, without due process of law." A law that impairs a liberty or property interest may be struck down under the Due Process Clause either because of the law's substantive content or because of the process by which it is enforced. The first of these bases for invalidation involves substantive due process, while the second involves procedural due process. As we saw in Chapter 2, a *substantive* due process claim asserts that a law is invalid because the government lacks a sufficient reason or justification to warrant interfering with liberty or property. A *procedural* due process argument, on the other hand, assumes that a law is otherwise valid, but asserts that the manner employed in enforcing or applying it is unfair.

Procedural due process usually requires that before the state may impair a person's life, liberty, or property interests, it must give him or her notice and a reasonable opportunity to be heard. By forcing the government to use a "fair process of decision-making" when it implements a law, procedural due process seeks "to ensure abstract fair play to the individual" and to minimize "unfair or mistaken deprivations" that may result from the government's having acted on the basis of erroneous information. *Fuentes v. Shevin,* 407 U.S. 67, 81 (1972).

The difference between substantive and procedural due process may be seen more clearly through an example.

EXAMPLE 5-A

A State X law prohibits doctors from performing more than one abortion per month; any doctor who violates this statute is barred from the further practice of medicine. Dr. Mary Jones was recently notified by State X that her medical license has been revoked because she performed two abortions last March. How might Dr. Jones challenge the validity of the state's action?

EXPLANATION

Dr. Jones might first argue that the law is substantively invalid because it interferes with her liberty interest in practicing her profession or because it burdens her patients' liberty interest in the abortion decision. If either of these arguments is successful, the law will be struck down as a matter of substantive due process, and Dr. Jones will be allowed to keep her license.

However, if these challenges to the substantive validity of the law fail, Dr. Jones might argue that her procedural due process rights were violated because the state, in applying this otherwise valid law to her, did not use a fair decision-making process. She would assert that State X should not be allowed to revoke her license without first giving her notice and an opportunity to be heard. If Dr. Jones were to prevail on this procedural due process argument, the state could not revoke her license until after it granted her a hearing. This would allow Dr. Jones to show that the state was mistaken in believing she had violated the law or that it was unfair under the circumstances to enforce this law against her.

———————

As a lawyer representing Dr. Jones, you would obviously prefer to win on substantive as opposed to procedural due process grounds. A substantive due process victory will preclude the state from revoking your client's license even if she violated the statute. By contrast, a procedural due process argument will simply afford your client a chance to be heard and to show that the state was mistaken concerning her conduct. Nevertheless, a procedural due process challenge is still of value, for if your client is given an opportunity to present her side of the story, she may be able to persuade the government to change its mind.

Procedural due process is not triggered when the government acts in a legislative capacity, i.e., when it enacts or adopts a particular rule or policy. Rather, procedural due process comes into play only when the government acts in an adjudicatory capacity, i.e., when it applies that rule or policy to specific individuals. Thus, if a state welfare department issues a regulation providing that no one may receive welfare benefits for more than two years, procedural due process does not give welfare recipients or anyone else a constitutional right to be heard in connection with the *adoption* of the regulation. At this legislative or rulemaking stage, fairness and due process are protected in other ways, such as through the right to vote, the right to petition government, and the freedoms of speech and press. However, if the state later seeks to *enforce* the two-year rule by terminating those who have been on the rolls for the maximum allowable time, those threatened with termination have a procedural due process right to notice and an opportunity to be heard in order to prevent unfair or mistaken deprivations of benefits.

There are three major steps in analyzing a procedural due process problem:

1. The right to procedural due process is triggered only if a protected interest in life, liberty, or property is threatened by governmental action.
2. The impairment of the protected interest in life, liberty, or property must be sufficient to trigger the application of procedural due process.
3. If the constraints of procedural due process apply, both the timing and the nature of the required hearing will depend on the circumstances of the particular case.

In the balance of this chapter, we will explore each of these steps of the procedural due process analysis. We will also look at the related doctrine of irrebuttable presumptions. However, we will not focus on the procedural due process protections that attach to life, as this subject is covered in courses dealing with criminal procedure.

§5.2   A Protected Liberty or Property Interest?

§5.2.1   *What Constitutes Liberty?*

Liberty interests that are entitled to procedural due process protection may stem from a variety of sources, including the Constitution, statutes, regulations, and simply official custom and practice.

All the constitutional liberty interests that qualify as liberties for purposes of substantive due process are likewise protected as a matter of procedural due process. See Chapter 2. These include fundamental liberty interests, such as freedom of speech and the right of privacy, as well as "garden variety" liberty interests, such as the liberty to contract and the freedom to pursue a trade. While fundamental liberties and "garden variety" liberties are treated quite differently under substantive due process, they stand on equal footing when it comes to triggering the right to procedural due process. Thus, in Example 5-A above, when the state revoked Dr. Mary Jones's license to practice medicine, this impaired her liberty interest to practice her profession; though this interest receives little meaningful protection as a matter of substantive due process, its impairment is sufficient to trigger Dr. Jones's procedural due process right to notice and an opportunity for a hearing.

For purposes of procedural due process, liberty interests may also derive from non-constitutional sources, such as federal or state statutes, regulations, and policies. If, through any of these means, the government creates or recognizes certain liberty interests *and provides that they may be impaired only for cause,* these non-constitutional liberty interests may be entitled to full procedural due process protection. If, on the other hand, the government creates a liberty interest and does not limit the grounds on which it may be withdrawn, the interest can be impaired without triggering any procedural due process protection.

EXAMPLE 5-B

Smith was convicted of burglary and sentenced to ten years in prison. A state law authorizes mandatory sentence reduction on the basis of prisoners' good behavior. Under this law, prisoners may earn good-time credits, which can be revoked only for "flagrant or serious misconduct." Prison officials revoked Smith's good-time credits on the ground that he had smuggled a knife into his cell; the revoked credits would have allowed Smith to leave prison six months early. Did Smith have a procedural due process right to notice and an opportunity to be heard before the state revoked his good-time credits?

EXPLANATION

Smith has no *constitutionally based* liberty interest in receiving credit for good behavior. The Constitution does not compel prison officials to reward good behavior in this manner. Yet Smith may be able to show that he has a *non-constitutional* liberty interest in a shortened prison sentence, for state law seems to allow good-time credits to be revoked *only* for specified reasons, i.e., for "flagrant or serious misconduct." If Smith can show that these grounds are exclusive in the sense that they constitute a mandatory limitation on the discretion of prison officials, he will have a state-created liberty interest protected by the Due Process Clause. See *Wolff v. McDonnell,* 418 U.S. 539 (1974) (finding protected state-created liberty interest based on similar facts). In that event, Smith's due process rights would have been violated by the state's revocation of his good-time credits without notice and an opportunity to be heard.

The Court has similarly found that a statutorily created liberty interest usually exists when inmates are conditionally released on parole or under a similar early-release program. As long as the state explicitly or implicitly promised that the individual would be reincarcerated only if the conditions of release were violated, a protected liberty interest exists. See *Young v. Harper*, 520 U.S. 143 (1997) (state must afford procedural due process when terminating pre-parole release); *Morrissey v. Brewer*, 408 U.S. 471 (1972) (state must afford procedural due process when revoking parole).

The Court has been much less hospitable to procedural due process complaints by prisoners concerning changes in the circumstances or degree of their confinement. In these cases, a state-created liberty interest will receive constitutional protection only if the nature of the deprivation is such that it "imposes atypical and significant hardship on the inmate in relation to the ordinary incidents of prison life." *Sandin v. Conner*, 515 U.S. 472, 484 (1995). Changes in an inmate's treatment that do not "present a dramatic departure from the basic conditions" of prison life will not trigger procedural due process protection—even if state law allows those changes to occur only for cause. Id. at 485. In *Sandin*, the Court held that the transfer of a prisoner to solitary confinement "did not present the type of atypical, significant deprivation in which a state might conceivably create a liberty interest." Id. at 486. However, the Court emphasized that a significant change in the "duration" of an inmate's confinement — such as that suffered by Smith in Example 5-B — could qualify for procedural due process protection as a state-created liberty interest. Id. at 486-487.

§5.2.2   What Constitutes Property?

Property interests are not created by the Constitution, but stem from other sources, such as state or sometimes federal law. Property within the meaning of the Due Process Clause embraces all the traditional forms of real and personal property. Thus, procedural due process protections apply if the government seeks to enforce a lien against real property, garnish a person's wages, or attach a bank account because all of these are types of property long recognized under state law.

For procedural due process purposes, the term property also embraces many public benefits and statutory entitlements that were once regarded as mere privileges or gratuities not deserving of constitutional protection. Welfare benefits, unemployment compensation, tax exemptions, Social Security pensions, public employment, licenses to engage in a trade or profession, and a myriad of other governmental benefits today may all qualify as property for procedural due process purposes. The Court has rejected the "rights/privileges distinction" under which government was once free to ignore the Constitution in dealing with mere privileges or public benefits.

A governmental benefit qualifies as property for procedural due process purposes if it may be denied or withdrawn only for cause. This test for determining whether public benefits are a protected form of property is the same as that used in deciding whether government-created liberties are entitled to procedural due process protection: That is, has the state agreed that it will not deny or impair the interest except under certain conditions? If the government by statute, regulation, contract, or otherwise has so provided, an individual is normally entitled to notice and an opportunity to be heard in connection with an impairment of that interest.

EXAMPLE 5-C

In Example 5-A above, if the state seeks to revoke Dr. Jones's medical license, would she be entitled to procedural due process?

EXPLANATION

Yes. The state has threatened to impair both liberty and property interests. We noted earlier that revocation would infringe on Dr. Jones's constitutional liberty interest in pursuing a profession. In addition, because the state grants medical licenses only to those who meet certain eligibility criteria and revokes such licenses only for cause (e.g., performing too many abortions), a medical license is a statutory entitlement that qualifies as a form of property protected by procedural due process.

By contrast, if the government has not tied its hands by limiting the grounds on which it may deny or withdraw a benefit, no *property* interest is involved, and procedural due process will be triggered only if a *liberty* interest happens to be impaired.

EXAMPLE 5-D

Chuck was hired as a summer law clerk in the State Attorney General's Office. He expected to work during June, July, and August, but on July 2, Chuck was fired. When he asked why, his boss told him that he could not divulge the reason. Was Chuck entitled to notice of the reasons for his firing and an opportunity to be heard?

EXPLANATION

To establish that he had a property interest in the summer clerkship, Chuck would have to show that there was some basis on which he could legitimately and objectively expect not to be fired without cause. If there was no statute, regulation, written office policy, or formal contract to this effect, Chuck might be able to rely on correspondence or on advertisements announcing the position. If, for example, there was a letter offering him a three-month clerkship or the Attorney General's Office announced the position as being for a three-month period, a court might find an implicit assurance that the job would not be terminated within that period unless good cause existed. This would be enough to create a property interest in the position.

If Chuck cannot establish a property interest in the position, he is unlikely to trigger procedural due process protection on the basis that a liberty interest was impaired. While he does have a liberty interest in pursuing employment, he remains free to seek other work. Nor was his liberty interest in his good name directly impaired, since no reasons were given for his termination. See *Board of Regents of State Colleges v. Roth*, 408 U.S. 564 (1972).

Many government benefits are provided under statutes or regulations that entitle people to receive those benefits if they meet certain specified eligibility conditions. This is true of drivers' licenses, welfare benefits, unemployment insurance, homestead exemptions, Social Security, workers' compensation, and medical licenses. An individual may therefore be said to have a property interest in his or her *claim* to these benefits, in the sense that the government by law cannot deny the claim or application of someone who meets the eligibility criteria. On the other hand, a person does not have a property interest in the *benefits* themselves until such time as they have been found eligible. Once benefits are awarded to an eligible individual, the same statutes and regulations that define eligibility now provide the recipient with assurance that the benefits will not be withdrawn or terminated except for cause. The recipient thus has a property interest in the benefits themselves. In short, one may have a property interest in a *claim* to certain benefits and yet not have a property interest in the *benefits themselves*.

If one has only a property interest in a claim, i.e., a legitimate expectation that the claim will not be denied except for cause, the due process right to a prior or pre-deprivation hearing simply means that before the claim is *finally denied* and the case closed, the applicant must be given an opportunity to be heard. Yet since a mere *applicant* does not have a property interest in the benefits themselves, the right to a pre-deprivation hearing does not mean that the government must pay the applicant benefits pending the hearing. Instead, the right to receive benefits or aid pending the hearing exists only for a *recipient* who, having been found eligible, has a property interest in the benefits themselves.

EXAMPLE 5-E

Delores was found eligible to receive workers' compensation benefits based on her having suffered a work-related injury. A state statute provides those found eligible to receive workers' compensation benefits are also eligible to have their employer or the employer's workers' compensation insurance carrier pay for all of the worker's "reasonable and necessary" medical treatments. If a worker's doctor submits a bill, the insurer may challenge the expense and withhold payment until a "utilization review" hearing is held to determine whether the expense was "reasonable and necessary." Delores has challenged this procedure claiming that by withholding medical payments without a pre-deprivation notice and opportunity to be heard, the state has violated her right to procedural due process. How should the court rule on this constitutional claim?

EXPLANATION

The state has not violated Delores's procedural due process rights. Although she has been found eligible to receive workers' compensation benefits, eligibility for medical payments exists only if a particular expense was "reasonable and necessary." While Delores clearly has a property interest in her *claim* for medical payments since her claim cannot be denied without cause, she does not have a property interest in any *medical payment* until it has first been determined that the treatment in question was reasonable and necessary. Only then does a property interest in the payment attach. Therefore, the right to hearing before she is deprived of her property does not require that medical payments be withheld only after a hearing has occurred. See *American Manufacturers Mutual Ins. Co. v. Sullivan*, 526 U.S. 40 (1999).

If, on the other hand, Delores had been found eligible to receive payment for a series of medical treatments that were deemed to be reasonable and necessary, she would probably be entitled to notice and hearing *before* the carrier could withhold further payments for those treatments. In this case, Delores would have a property interest in the payments themselves, not just in her claim for payment. See id. at 63 (Justices Breyer and Souter, concurring).

§5.2.3   *The Relevance of Custom and Practice*

It may be possible to prove the existence of a protected liberty or property interest even if there is no express statute, regulation, or contract provision stating that the interest will not be denied or terminated except for cause. Even without a formal provision establishing a liberty or property interest, the protections of procedural due process may be called into play if it can be shown that there is an "unwritten 'common law'" custom or practice under which a particular privilege or benefit will be withdrawn only for certain reasons. *Perry v. Sindermann*, 408 U.S. 593, 599-603 (1972).

Were custom and practice irrelevant, a state could avoid the strictures of procedural due process by the formalistic device of including in every law dealing with governmental benefits or jobs a clause stating: "The benefits or employment provided for by this law may be terminated at any time, with or without cause." If a program is in fact administered so as to create a legitimate expectation that its benefits will not be denied or withdrawn without cause, procedural due process guaranties attach.

The Court thus relied on custom and practice as a separate basis for finding that Nebraska state prisoners had a protected liberty interest in not being sent to a mental hospital. The Court noted that "in practice prisoners are transferred to a mental hospital only if it is determined that they suffer from a mental disease or defect. . . . This 'objective expectation, firmly fixed in state law and official Penal Complex practice,'" created a liberty interest and triggered the protections of procedural due process. *Vitek v. Jones,* 445 U.S. 480, 489-490 (1980).

EXAMPLE 5-F

In Example 5-D above, how might Chuck have shown that he had a protected property interest in his clerkship position on the basis of custom and practice?

EXPLANATION

Even if there was no explicit statutory, regulatory, or contractual provision limiting the bases on which he could be fired, Chuck might have been able to prove that the well-established practice of the Attorney General's Office was to retain summer clerks for the entire three-month summer period unless their work was unsatisfactory. If Chuck had made such a showing, procedural due process would protect him to the same extent as if state law expressly provided that summer law clerks may be fired during the period of their clerkship only for cause.

§5.3   What Constitutes a Deprivation?

Not every governmental action that impairs a liberty or property interest will necessarily trigger the protections of procedural due process. First, if the deprivation resulted from a mere lack of due care by governmental officials, the Due Process Clause does not come into play. As the Court said in *Daniels v. Williams,* 474 U.S. 327, 328 (1986), "[T]he Due Process Clause is simply not implicated by a *negligent* act of an official causing unintended loss of or injury to life, liberty, or property." In such cases, the Constitution affords a litigant no redress. Relief, if any, will depend on the extent to which the government has allowed itself to be sued in tort. The Court has left open the issue of whether "something less than intentional conduct, such as recklessness or 'gross negligence,' is enough to trigger the protections of the Due Process Clause." Id. at 334 n.3. See *County of Sacramento v. Lewis,* 523 U.S. 833 (1998); and see §2.1.

Second, even an intentional act that impairs a liberty or property interest will trigger the protections of procedural due process only if the impairment exceeds a certain threshold; if the impact is one that the Court regards as "de minimis" or "insubstantial," *Goss v. Lopez,* 419 U.S. 565, 576 (1975), the Due Process Clause is not applicable. This is closely analogous to the principle sometimes applied in substantive due process cases, i.e., that a law will not receive strict scrutiny unless it impinges on or unduly burdens a fundamental liberty. See §2.4.4.

The Court relied on the notion of a de minimis impairment to avoid triggering procedural due process in *Board of Regents of State Colleges v. Roth,* 408 U.S. 564 (1972). There, the Justices rejected a college professor's argument that the state's refusal to renew his one-year contract impaired his liberty interests in his good name and in securing future employment. While the Court later acknowledged that the state's failure to rehire Roth "might make him somewhat less attractive to other employers . . . it would stretch the concept too far 'to suggest that a person is deprived of "liberty" when he simply is not rehired in one job but remains as free as before to seek another.'" *Bishop v. Wood,* 426 U.S. 341, 348 (1976). In the Court's eyes, the impairment of Roth's liberty interests was too insignificant for procedural due process to come into play.

EXAMPLE 5-G

In Example 5-A involving the state's revocation of Dr. Jones's license to practice medicine, we saw that this action may have impaired Dr. Jones's liberty interest in practicing her profession and her property interest in the license itself. However, suppose that a few weeks after Dr. Jones was notified of the revocation, the state advised her that the action had been a mistake and had resulted from a secretary's having accidentally pulled the wrong file. May Dr. Jones still assert that the state violated her procedural due process rights?

EXPLANATION

If the state proves that the revocation was a result of mere negligence, the Due Process Clause would simply not apply. However, if the secretary's conduct rose to the level of gross negligence or reckless disregard for Jones's rights, Dr. Jones might be able to claim a procedural due process violation, since she was given no notice or opportunity to be heard. The state might then argue that any harm to Dr. Jones's liberty and property interests was de minimis if the revocation was in effect for such a brief period that it did not really interfere with Dr. Jones's ability to practice medicine.

§5.4   The Content of Notice

Once we have cleared the first two hurdles by demonstrating that a threatened governmental action will cause a deprivation of a protected liberty or property interest, procedural due process is triggered. The questions that remain focus on what type of notice and what kind of hearing must be afforded.

The due process aspects of notice are treated in some detail in the course in Civil Procedure. You may recall from that course, the Court's classic statement concerning notice, as set forth in *Mullane v. Central Hanover Bank and Trust Co.,* 339 U.S. 306, 314-315 (1950):

> An elementary and fundamental requirement of due process in any proceeding which is to be accorded finality is notice reasonably calculated, under all the circumstances, to apprise interested parties of the pendency of the action and afford them an opportunity to present their objections. . . . The notice must be of such nature as reasonably to convey the required information, . . . and it must afford a reasonable time for those interested to make their appearance. . . . But if with due regard for the practicalities and peculiarities of the case these conditions are reasonably met the constitutional requirements are satisfied.

In the Civil Procedure class, the principal questions concerned the *type* of notice an individual was entitled to, e.g., whether personal service was always required, whether service by mail was adequate, and whether notice by publication would ever suffice. On this score, *Mullane* stated that, "The means employed must be such as one desirous of actually informing the absentee might reasonably adopt to accomplish it." Id. at 657.

Our concern here is with the content of notice. Where the government seeks to terminate or withdraw benefits or services, the Court has sometimes required that the notice provide a recipient with specific information concerning the remedies and procedures available for challenging the threatened governmental action so that the individual can fully protect his interests. In *Memphis Light, Gas & Water Division v. Craft,* 436 U.S. 1 (1978), the Court held that the Due Process Clause required a municipal utility company to give customers advance notice and an opportunity to be heard before terminating their utility services. The notice, said the Court, must be "'reasonably calculated' to inform them of the availability of 'an opportunity to present their objections' to their bills," and must "advise the customer of the availability of a procedure for protesting a proposed termination of utility service as unjustified." Id. at 14-15.

Memphis Light's requirement that notice must inform an individual of the remedies available for challenging the government's action, and how those remedies may be invoked, is the exception rather than the rule. In *City of West Covina v. Perkins*, 525 U.S. 234 (1999), the Court recently held that a police department that had seized goods from a home pursuant to a warrant did not have to notify the homeowner — who was absent at the time of the search — as to the legal remedies and procedures available for obtaining a return of the goods. All that was necessary, said the Court, was that the owner be given notice that the property had been taken by the police. In rejecting the argument that procedural due process also required notice of existing legal remedies, the Court distinguished *Memphis Light* on the ground that there, "the administrative procedures at issue were not described in any publicly available document. . . . While *Memphis Light* demonstrates that notice of the procedures for protecting one's property interests may be required when those procedures are arcane and are not set forth in documents accessible to the public, it does not support a general rule that notice of remedies and procedures is required." Id. at 242. Where "state law remedies . . . are established by published, generally available state statutes and case law," it is up to the individual himself to consult "these public sources to learn about the remedial procedures available to him. The City need not take other steps to inform him of his options." Id. at 241.

§5.5   What Kind of Hearing Must Be Afforded?

Assuming notice is adequate, the remaining due process question concerns the kind of hearing that is required. This involves two separate considerations. First, as to timing, must an opportunity to be heard be afforded before the deprivation occurs, or will a postdeprivation hearing suffice? Second, how formal or informal may the hearing be? We will briefly consider both of these questions.

§5.5.1   The "Bitter with the Sweet" Approach

In answering the question of what kind of hearing must be afforded, a few members of the Court have taken the position that if a *government-created* liberty or property interest is involved, the government may decide for itself what procedures, if any, will accompany a decision affecting that interest. As Justice Rehnquist wrote in *Arnett v. Kennedy*, 416 U.S. 134, 153-154 (1974), a case involving the dismissal of a federal employee, "[W]here the grant of a substantive right is inextricably intertwined with the limitations on the procedures which are to be employed in determining that right, a litigant . . . must take the bitter with the sweet."

However, the Court's majority has consistently rejected the "bitter with the sweet" approach, for "[t]he right to due process 'is conferred, not by legislative grace, but by constitutional guarantee. While the legislature may elect not to confer a property [or liberty] interest . . . it may not constitutionally authorize the deprivation of such an interest, once conferred, without appropriate procedural safeguards.'" *Cleveland Bd. of Educ. v. Loudermill,* 470 U.S. 532, 541 (1985). Thus, regardless of the type of liberty or property interest, if procedural due process protections are triggered, the timing and the nature of the required hearing are determined according to constitutional standards and not by reference to federal or state law.

EXAMPLE 5-H

Helen was hired as a public school teacher by the City of Plainville. According to her contract, Helen may be fired only if the superintendent determines that her dismissal is in the best interests of the city. The contract provides that if Helen is fired, she is entitled to prompt post-termination notice of the reasons for her firing and an opportunity to respond in writing. If Helen is fired by the city and is afforded only the procedures specified by her contract, can she claim that the city has violated her rights to procedural due process?

EXPLANATION

The city chose to give Helen a property interest in her job by stating in her contract that she may be fired only for cause; moreover, termination clearly deprives her of this interest. The requirements of procedural due process, therefore, apply here. While the city did not have to give Helen a property interest in her job, having done so it is the Due Process Clause, not the terms of her contract, that will determine whether the procedures she was given are adequate. Helen is thus free to argue that the city's action was unconstitutional on the ground that she was not given notice or an opportunity to be heard prior to her dismissal. We will discuss this prior hearing requirement in §5.5.3.

§5.5.2   *The* Mathews v. Eldridge *Test*

In resolving the issues of when a hearing must occur and how elaborate the hearing must be, the Court often uses a balancing test that takes into account three factors: (1) the significance of the private interest that will be affected by the governmental action; (2) the extent to which additional procedural safeguards would reduce the risk of error; and (3) the public interest in resolving the matter quickly and efficiently. This test, which derives from

Mathews v. Eldridge, 424 U.S. 319, 335 (1976), involves a cost-benefit analysis in which the Court evaluates the need for a particular procedure by balancing the added benefits it might afford an aggrieved individual against burdens it will impose on the government and the public. As the Court said in *Mathews*, "At some point the benefit of an additional safeguard to the individual affected by the administrative action and to society in terms of increased assurance that the action is just, may be outweighed by the cost." Id. at 348. Moreover, the Court cautioned that in applying the *Mathews* test, "substantial weight must be given to the good-faith judgments" of those who determined that the challenged procedures were adequate. Id. at 349.

EXAMPLE 5-I

For the past five years, Dorothy has received state disability benefits due to a back condition that prevents her from working. The state recently terminated Dorothy's benefits after concluding that the condition no longer prevents her from engaging in employment. Prior to the termination, the state gave Dorothy a statement of the reasons for the proposed termination, an opportunity to review the state's evidence, a chance to respond to the state's case in writing, and the right to submit further evidence. She was also advised that she could later seek a full trial-type hearing before the State Disability Appeals Board, which had the authority to restore her benefits retroactively if it determined that an error had been made. Can Dorothy successfully claim that her procedural due process rights were violated because the state did not give her a trial-type hearing before cutting off her benefits?

EXPLANATION

Since state law presumably provides that disability benefits may be terminated only for cause, Dorothy has a protected property interest in the continued receipt of those benefits, thereby triggering the protections of procedural due process. Whether the procedures afforded her were sufficient must be determined by applying the *Mathews* test.

First, the private interest affected here is clearly very important. Disability benefits may represent the principal or sole source of income for those entitled to receive them. However, since there is a right to an elaborate post-termination hearing that could result in benefits being retroactively restored, the individual interest is not as strong as it would be if there were no right to a subsequent hearing.

Second, the court will look to the "fairness and reliability of the existing pretermination procedures, and the probable value, if any, of additional procedural safeguards." *Mathews*, 424 U.S. at 343. Here, since the termination decision turns largely on standard medical reports from physicians and specialists, the state's existing procedures are likely to pose a low risk of error. A trial-type hearing at which witnesses testify in person and are subject to cross-examination by counsel would no doubt improve the truth-finding process, but probably not by a great deal. By contrast, the added benefit of an evidentiary hearing would be greater if issues of witness credibility and veracity were more directly involved; this would be the case, for example, if benefits were being terminated because a recipient had allegedly concealed outside income that would render him or her ineligible for state assistance.

Finally, *Mathews* requires courts to consider the public interest in avoiding the expense, delay, and other societal costs of affording more elaborate procedures. Here, the burden of conducting in-person trial-type hearings is obviously greater than under a scheme that permits only written submissions. Moreover, the delay entailed in holding pretermination evidentiary hearings would mean that benefits might be continued for a longer period of time to those who were in fact ineligible. While the state might seek to recover these payments, the recipients might well be judgment proof.

On balance and in light of the deference the court shows toward a government's chosen procedural scheme, Dorothy's procedural due process challenge is likely to fail here. See *Mathews v. Eldridge,* 424 U.S. 319, 335 (1976) (finding no procedural due process violation on similar facts).

§5.5.3 *The Requirement of a Prior Hearing*

With respect to timing, the Court has held that "'the root requirement' of the Due Process Clause" is "'that an individual be given an opportunity for a hearing *before* he is deprived of any significant [liberty or] property interest.'" *Cleveland Bd. of Educ. v. Loudermill,* 470 U.S. at 542. The prior hearing requirement makes good sense given that procedural due process is intended as a safeguard to help minimize the occasions when government mistakenly impairs liberty or property interests. While postdeprivation remedies in the form of damages or injunctive relief may help compensate for the harms that result from erroneous governmental action, it is obviously preferable that such injuries be avoided in the first place.

EXAMPLE 5-J

Ollie was employed as a highway patrol officer by State Z. After the state received an anonymous tip that Ollie had accepted bribes from motorists in exchange for not giving them speeding tickets, the state fired him. Under State Z law, highway patrol officers may be fired only for cause. A fired officer may appeal to the State Civil Service Board, which can order reinstatement with backpay. Did State Z violate Ollie's procedural due process rights by dismissing him without a prior hearing?

EXPLANATION

Procedural due process is triggered here. Ollie had a property interest in his job, since he could be fired only for cause and the dismissal totally deprived him of this property interest. State Z might argue that Ollie had no right to a prior hearing because any benefit he would derive from this is outweighed by the burdens such a requirement would impose on the state. Under the *Mathews v. Eldridge* balancing test, however, Ollie was probably entitled to a prior hearing.

First, the private interest at stake is the vital one of retaining employment and earning a livelihood; that interest was seriously impaired when Ollie was fired. Second, the risk of the state's erroneously impairing this interest would be greatly reduced by a prior hearing, for the decision turns entirely on issues of fact; here, the state acted solely on the basis of an anonymous report; unless the decisionmaker is more fully informed, the chance of error is high. Third, the benefit that Ollie would derive from a prior hearing is probably not outweighed by the burden such a hearing would place on the state. The cost to the state of the hearing itself is low, since the hearing need not be elaborate. See §5.5.5. Nor is this a case where a delay in keeping Ollie on the job would endanger public health or safety, for Ollie's alleged misconduct harms the state only in a financial way. And even if a more serious danger existed, the state could suspend Ollie, with or without pay, rather than summarily firing him. It is thus likely that State Z violated Ollie's procedural due process rights by not affording him a prior hearing. See *Cleveland Bd. of Educ. v. Loudermill,* 470 U.S. 532 (1985).

§5.5.4   Exceptions to the Prior Hearing Requirement

Despite the general principle that an opportunity for a hearing must be afforded *before* there is a deprivation of liberty or property, the Court sometimes allows a hearing to be held only after the deprivation has occurred. These exceptions have involved situations where it would be impossible or impracticable to conduct a prior hearing or where a court believes that any risk of an erroneous, serious deprivation is low.

In rare instances, it is virtually impossible for the government to hold a prior hearing. An example of this was presented in *Hudson v. Palmer,* 468 U.S. 517 (1984), where prison guards intentionally destroyed an inmate's personal property during a search. Since the guards' conduct was "random and unauthorized," there was no way the state could have conducted a hearing before the property was destroyed. The Court held that procedural due process was satisfied by the postdeprivation tort remedy available to the inmate under state law.

Most exceptions to the prior hearing requirement involve situations where it would be *possible* to hold a hearing before the deprivation occurs, but where doing so would for one reason or another be *impracticable*. In considering whether to make an exception on grounds of impracticability, the Court often weighs the benefits that would flow from affording a prior hearing against the burdens that this requirement would place on the government and the public, sometimes expressly invoking the *Mathews v. Eldridge* three-factor balancing test.

The classic case where impracticability may allow the government to dispense with a prior hearing in favor of postdeprivation remedies is an emergency, when swift action is necessary to avert serious public harm. Thus, if the Food and Drug Administration believes that there is a mislabeled drug on the market that could be fatal if consumed, it may order the drug seized without first affording the drug's manufacturer an opportunity to be heard. See *Ewing v. Mytinger & Casselberry, Inc.,* 339 U.S. 594 (1950). While a prior hearing would clearly reduce the risk of a mistaken governmental seizure, the benefit this would afford the company in terms of protecting its profits is outweighed by the harm that could result to the public if a prior hearing had to be conducted.

The Court has also allowed the government to ignore the prior hearing rule in some non-emergency situations. In *Ingraham v. Wright,* 430 U.S. 651 (1977), the Court upheld a Florida statute that authorized the infliction of corporal punishment on schoolchildren without giving them an opportunity to be heard before punishment was imposed. The Court agreed that procedural due process was triggered, for paddling impairs a child's liberty interest in bodily security. But using the *Mathews v. Eldridge* balancing test, the Court found that it would be impracticable to require a prior hearing in this setting. It concluded that the danger of excessive or erroneous paddlings was sufficiently low that any benefit from a prior hearing was outweighed by the burden such a requirement would place on teachers and school officials. Accordingly, the postdeprivation common law remedies available to students under state law were deemed sufficient to satisfy the demands of procedural due process.

EXAMPLE 5-K

Homer was suspended without pay from his job as a police officer with the state university after the district attorney informed the university that Homer had been arrested and charged with possession of marijuana. The university gave Homer no notice or opportunity to be heard before suspending him. A week after the suspension, the criminal charges were dismissed. Two weeks later Homer was given a hearing by university officials at which it was found that he had possessed marijuana; as a result, he was demoted to a position as groundskeeper. Were Homer's procedural due process rights violated by the timing of the hearing?

EXPLANATION

The university took two actions that may have impaired Homer's procedural due process rights: the suspension, and the demotion three weeks later. Because Homer was given notice and an opportunity to be heard before he was demoted, the timing of the hearing presents no problem as to that action. However, the lack of notice and opportunity to be heard prior to the three-week suspension raises a distinct procedural due process issue.

Assuming that under the university's rules Homer could be suspended only for cause, he had a property interest that was infringed by the suspension. Since the suspension was without pay and lasted three weeks, the infringement was not de minimis. The suspension action, therefore, triggered the requirements of procedural due process.

Whether a predeprivation hearing was required must be determined by applying the *Mathews* test. First, the private interest at stake, Homer's means of livelihood, is an important one. Yet in contrast to Ollie in the previous example, Homer was suspended temporarily rather than fired. While he received no pay in the interim, other job benefits may have continued. Second, the failure to offer a prior hearing carried a much lower risk of error here than was true in Ollie's case. The university acted not on an anonymous tip, but on information from the district attorney, an independent outside party that had probable cause to believe Homer had committed a serious crime. Whether or not Homer was actually guilty of that crime, the arrest and charge were themselves objective facts that gave the university valid grounds to suspend an employee. Since the university acted on the basis of reliable information, any added benefit of a prior hearing in terms of preventing an erroneous deprivation was relatively low. Finally, on the state's side of the balance, the university had a strong interest in maintaining public confidence in the integrity of its police by not having accused felons on the force. Under these circumstances, the university was probably justified in dispensing with a presuspension hearing. See *Gilbert v. Homar*, 520 U.S. 924 (1997) (upholding summary suspension on similar facts, but remanding case for a determination of whether delaying the postsuspension hearing for two weeks after charges had been dropped violated procedural due process).

§5.5.5   *The Formality of the Prior Hearing*

If a prior hearing is required by due process, "[t]he formality and procedural requisites for the hearing can vary, depending upon the importance of the interests involved and the nature of the subsequent proceedings." *Boddie v. Connecticut*, 401 U.S. 371, 378 (1971). The Court has normally not required a full trial-type hearing prior to adverse action taken by an administrative body or agency, as opposed to action taken by a court of law. When administrative action is involved, the Court has tended to uphold relatively informal prior hearing procedures, often justifying them under the *Mathews v. Eldridge* balancing test. It is ordinarily enough if the government gives a person notice of the proposed action and the reasons for it, as well as an opportunity to respond either in person or in writing. These rudimentary procedures are especially likely to suffice if, as is usually true, more elaborate postdeprivation remedies are available in the form of a full administrative hearing, judicial review, or an independent tort action.

EXAMPLE 5-L

In Example 5-J, suppose that under State Z law, before Ollie can be fired as a highway patrol officer, he must be told the reasons for his dismissal and given a chance to explain why he thinks the action should not be taken. In accord with this procedure, Ollie's boss called Ollie into his office and told him that he was being fired because he had taken bribes. Ollie said that this was not true and that there must have been a mistake. He was then fired. His boss advised Ollie that he could appeal his dismissal to the State Civil Service Board and thereafter, if necessary, obtain judicial review. Were Ollie's procedural due process rights violated?

EXPLANATION

Ollie's rights were probably not violated here. He has a right to procedural due process, since, as noted earlier, state law gives him a property interest in his position and the dismissal deprives him of that interest. This is not a situation where it is either impossible or impracticable to afford a prior hearing. But since postdeprivation administrative and judicial remedies are available, all that Ollie was entitled to prior to his dismissal was notice and an opportunity to tell his side of the story, both of which he was given. See *Cleveland Bd. of Educ. v. Loudermill*, 470 U.S. 532 (1985).

However, if postdeprivation remedies do not exist or if they would be of little utility because the harm caused by an erroneous deprivation is irreparable, the prior hearing must afford much more complete procedural safeguards. Thus, in *Goldberg v. Kelly*, 397 U.S. 254 (1970), the Court held that before welfare benefits may be terminated, a recipient must be given a trial-type hearing; even though the state provided recipients with full post-deprivation remedies, the injury caused by a mistaken cutoff of subsistence benefits is likely to be grave and irreparable.

Similarly, in *Vitek v. Jones*, 445 U.S. 480 (1980), the Court held that before a prisoner may be transferred to a mental hospital for treatment, due process requires an opportunity for a hearing that includes the right to introduce evidence, the right to present and cross-examine witnesses, the assistance of counsel or other competent help, an independent decision-maker, and a written decision. The nature of the harm caused if a prisoner were mistakenly subjected to such treatment, coupled with the fact that the state apparently provided inmates with no post-transfer remedies, made it essential to afford a trial-type hearing before a transfer could occur.

The issue of what specific procedures must be afforded at administrative hearings is covered more fully in Administrative Law courses.

§5.6   Possible Postdeprivation Remedies Where No Liberty or Property Interest Exists

We saw earlier that the government may create liberty or property interests that are entitled to procedural due process protection even if there was initially no constitutional right to the benefit in question. It is on this basis that there is often a right to a hearing if a state seeks to revoke a prisoner's parole, terminate welfare benefits, dismiss a public employee, or cancel a student's scholarship. The key to whether procedural due process attaches to these non-constitutional interests is whether they may be denied or withdrawn only for cause. If the government has reserved the right to withhold or terminate the interest on any basis it chooses, no liberty or property is involved, and the Due Process Clause does not come into play.

Yet under the doctrine of unconstitutional conditions, even if the government has reserved the authority to deny or terminate a particular benefit without cause, there are still some grounds of decision that the Constitution bars the state from employing. If a person can show that a purely discretionary benefit was withheld on a constitutionally forbidden ground, the government may be forced to grant or restore the benefit unless it can prove that it had a legitimate reason for its action.

EXAMPLE 5-M

Frannie was a nontenured public school teacher whose contract was not renewed. She believes that she was not rehired because she had criticized the city mayor during a radio interview. No statutory or contractual provision assures nontenured teachers that they will be rehired in the absence of cause, nor is there a custom or practice to this effect. Were any of Frannie's constitutional rights violated by her nonrenewal?

EXPLANATION

Frannie had no procedural due process right to a hearing prior to her dismissal; she lacked a property interest in her job, since she could be dismissed for no reason whatsoever. Nor will nonrenewal impair her liberty to seek future employment. See §5.3. However, if Frannie can show that a motivating factor in her nonrenewal was her exercise of First Amendment rights by speaking on the radio, the city will have to rehire her unless it proves that Frannie would have been let go even had she not engaged in this constitutionally protected activity. Otherwise, the city will have been permitted to impose an unconstitutional condition on rehiring nontenured teachers; i.e., to be rehired, they must surrender their First Amendment rights. See *Mount Healthy School Dist. v. Doyle*, 429 U.S. 274 (1977).

§5.7   The Irrebuttable Presumption Doctrine

As we have seen, procedural due process is designed as a safeguard against possibly erroneous deprivations of liberty or property. Persons whose liberty or property interests are threatened by governmental enforcement of a law are entitled to a hearing at which they may show that the government is wrong about the facts and that they do not fall within the purview of the law in question. However, an individual may also seek a hearing not to correct the government's version of the facts, but to rebut an express or implied presumption contained in a law.

§5.7.1   *Rebuttable and Irrebuttable Presumptions*

Suppose that a city ordinance provides that any police officer whose weight exceeds 300 pounds will be fired unless the officer can prove that he or she is still capable of functioning effectively. This law contains an express *rebuttable* presumption that police officers weighing over 300 pounds cannot perform their duties. If Max is notified by the city that he is being fired from his job as a police officer because he weighs 310 pounds, Max might seek a hearing for two very different purposes. First, as a matter of procedural due process, Max has a property interest in his job, since he can be fired only for cause; he is, therefore, entitled to a prior hearing to show that the city is mistaken about his weight and that the ordinance does not apply to him. Second, if Max falls within this law because he does weigh more than 300 pounds, he may still seek a hearing to rebut the presumption that he is too heavy to be a police officer.

The city might have instead drafted this ordinance so that it contained an *irrebuttable* presumption. The law might have said: "A police officer who weighs more than 300 pounds is unfit for duty and will be fired." If Max were notified that he was being fired under this law, he again might want a hearing in order to prove that though he weighs 310 pounds, he is physically fit. However, because the city has not afforded him a chance to be heard on this issue, the presumption is irrebuttable. While Max is still entitled to a hearing to contest the city's claim that he weighs more than 300 pounds, this would be of little use to him if the city's information is correct.

In contrast to the two preceding examples, which contained express presumptions, the city might have written the ordinance so that the irrebuttable presumption on which it is based is merely implicit in the measure, but does not appear on its face. Such a law might read: "Any police officer who weighs more than 300 pounds will be fired." We can discern the presumption underlying this law once we identify its purpose. If the City Council minutes or the city attorney defending the ordinance indicates that its goal is to assure that police officers are physically fit, it is clear that the measure rests on the implicit irrebuttable presumption that any officer weighing over 300 pounds is unfit for duty.

If the city were to use such an irrebuttable presumption, whether express or implied, Max might claim that he is entitled to a hearing to challenge the presumption by showing that however true it may be of others, it is not true of him. He might argue, in other words, that the city must convert the presumption from an irrebuttable to a rebuttable one, thereby affording him a chance to show that the generalization on which the law is based does not apply in his case, i.e., that despite his weight, he is physically fit.

§5.7.2   *The Doctrine in Its Prime*

Under the holding in *Vlandis v. Kline,* 412 U.S. 441 (1973), Max would probably prevail on this claim. *Vlandis* prohibited the government from using a permanent irrebuttable presumption "when that presumption is not necessarily or universally true in fact, and when the State has reasonable alternative means of making the crucial determination." Id. at 452. Max, on this basis, would be entitled to the opportunity to prove that he can perform the duties of a police officer, notwithstanding his weight. First, not everyone who weighs over 300 pounds is unfit for the position; nor would it be impractical to give him a hearing, for the city no doubt already gives periodic exams to make sure that officers and applicants are qualified for the job.

As a practical matter, however, the effect of allowing Max to challenge this ordinance on the ground that it contains an irrebuttable presumption is to require that the law not be at all overinclusive in terms of its goal. Normally an overinclusive classification will be struck down only if it is one that calls for heightened scrutiny under the Equal Protection Clause, either because it burdens a fundamental right or because it involves a suspect or quasi-suspect classification. See Chapters 6 and 7. Neither of these factors is present in Max's case, as there is no fundamental liberty interest in employment and weight is not a suspect or quasi-suspect basis of classification.

From a litigant's standpoint, the irrebuttable presumption doctrine articulated in *Vlandis* was a boon. It had the beauty of allowing successful challenges to be brought against a vast array of statutory classifications even though there was no basis for invoking heightened scrutiny under the Equal Protection Clause. For virtually every law rests on an irrebuttable presumption. If the presumption does not appear on the face of the statute, it is discernible as soon as the purpose of the measure is identified. For example, a speed limit law irrebuttably presumes that anyone going over the speed limit is driving unsafely. A law requiring that one pass a bar exam in order to practice law irrebuttably presumes that everyone who cannot pass the exam is unqualified for the profession. A law setting a mandatory retirement age irrebuttably presumes that anyone over that age can no longer perform effectively. And so on. Since all these measures employ generalizations that are not universally true in fact, and since it is possible to give individualized hearings to those who claim that the underlying presumption does not hold in their case, all of these measures would be vulnerable to challenge under the irrebuttable presumption doctrine as set forth in *Vlandis*.

§5.7.3   *The Doctrine Today*

The Supreme Court drastically narrowed this avenue of attack in *Weinberger v. Salfi*, 422 U.S. 749 (1975), a case involving a Social Security Act provision that denied survivors' benefits to widows and stepchildren whose relationships to the deceased wage earner had existed for less than nine months prior to his death. The legislative history revealed that this eligibility provision was adopted to discourage marriages entered into for the purpose of collecting Social Security benefits. The district court held that the Act contained an implicit irrebuttable presumption, i.e., that every marriage occurring less than nine months before a wage earner's death was a sham. Since this presumption is not universally true in fact, the trial court held that the applicant was entitled to a hearing to show that the law was overinclusive as to her, i.e., that her marriage was bona fide and that she was, therefore, entitled to widow's benefits.

The Supreme Court reversed. It narrowed the use of the irrebuttable presumption doctrine to cases where heightened scrutiny would be called for under the Equal Protection Clause. Otherwise, the government is free to legislate on the basis of generalizations that involve irrebuttable presumptions. Such presumptions—whether implied or express—are constitutional if the government "can rationally conclude . . . that generalized rules are appropriate to its purposes and concerns. . . ." Id. at 785; see *Usery v. Turner Elkhorn Mining Co.*, 428 U.S. 1 (1976).

The irrebuttable presumption doctrine is still of value in situations where intermediate or strict scrutiny is warranted under the Equal Protection Clause. In these cases, rather than invalidating a law entirely, a court may permit the government to continue using the classification in question, but require that it give each individual an opportunity to rebut the presumption on which the classification rests.

EXAMPLE 5-N

A State X law provides that anyone who has been convicted of spousal abuse is barred from marrying again. On what grounds might the statute be invalidated?

EXPLANATION

If the statute were challenged under the Equal Protection Clause, it would receive strict scrutiny, since the measure prohibits a class of persons from exercising the fundamental liberty to marry. See §7.2. A court could invalidate this law under the Equal Protection Clause by finding that the state's interest in guarding against spousal abuse is not compelling enough to justify a total ban on marriage, or that a less discriminatory way to achieve this goal would be to require that the new spouse be given notice of the prior conviction before the marriage takes place.

However, a court might instead use the irrebuttable presumption doctrine. Under this approach, the state law would be analyzed as containing the implied irrebuttable presumption that all persons convicted of spousal abuse are sufficiently likely to repeat this behavior that they must be barred from remarrying. A court might agree with the state that while such a prior conviction warrants concern, it cannot justify the use of a blanket prohibition against remarriage. The court could, therefore, insist that if the state wishes to use the presumption, it must be made rebuttable, thereby affording convicted spouse abusers a chance to prove that there is no danger they will again engage in such behavior.

The irrebuttable presumption doctrine thus allows a court to invoke a less intrusive remedy as far as the state is concerned. Rather than barring the state from making any use whatsoever of a particular classificatory scheme, the state may continue to use the classification if it does so in a nonconclusive way. Where the doctrine comes into play, it has the effect of giving a person a right to a hearing that would not otherwise exist.

6

Equal Protection: Ordinary, "Suspect," and "Quasi-Suspect" Classifications

§6.1 Introduction and Overview

The Constitution prohibits the state and federal governments from denying people the equal protection of the laws. Section 1 of the Fourteenth Amendment provides: "No State shall . . . deny to any person within its jurisdiction the equal protection of the laws." Though nothing in the Constitution's text imposes a similar restriction on the federal government, the Court has construed the Fifth Amendment Due Process Clause as "contain[ing] an equal protection component prohibiting the United States from invidiously discriminating between individuals or groups." *Washington v. Davis,* 426 U.S. 229, 239 (1976). Under most circumstances, the protections afforded by these Amendments are coextensive. But see *Hampton v. Mow Sun Wong,* 426 U.S. 88, 100 (1976) (variable standards in the context of discrimination against aliens). In this chapter, the term Equal Protection Clause will be used to include the equal protection guaranties of both the Fifth and the Fourteenth Amendments unless otherwise indicated.

The Equal Protection Clause might seem to bar the government from engaging in any type of discriminatory conduct. Yet if this were literally true, virtually no laws would be constitutional. Every law classifies by imposing burdens or conferring benefits on a selective basis, singling out some people or activities for treatment different from that accorded to others. A police officer who enforces a speed limit law pulls fast drivers out of the stream of traffic and allows other drivers to proceed unimpeded. A law regulating child labor treats employers who hire 10-year-olds differently from those who hire 25-year-olds. Each of these laws would be unconstitutional if the equal protection guarantee prohibited all discrimination on the part of government.

The Equal Protection Clause has never been interpreted as outlawing all forms of discrimination. Instead, the Clause prohibits government from engaging in arbitrary or invidious discrimination, i.e., from employing classifications that cannot be justified on the basis of any legitimate governmental interest and that are adopted merely for the sake of harming a particular group. For the government to treat people differently who are similarly situated, or to treat people the same who are not similarly situated, offends fundamental standards of fairness. Such arbitrary action on the part of government officials suggests that they are either acting capriciously or misusing their authority to reward friends and/or punish enemies. Whichever the case, governmental conduct that draws arbitrary distinctions between people violates the democratic principle that all persons stand equal before the law.

The question that the courts face in seeking to implement the Equal Protection Clause is how to determine whether a classification is so arbitrary as to be unconstitutional. How convincing an explanation must the defender of a discriminatory law offer in order to persuade a judge that the classification is relevant to a legitimate governmental interest?

EXAMPLE 6-A

A state law provides that in order to work as a carpenter, one must have a high school diploma and weigh at least 160 pounds. By classifying on the basis of education and weight, this law discriminates against those who lack a high school education and those who weigh less than 160 pounds. Shortly after the law took effect, Sheila, who is black, was fired from her carpenter's job because she weighs only 125 pounds and never graduated from high school. Can Sheila successfully challenge the law on the ground that it violates the Equal Protection Clause?

EXPLANATION

The answer depends on how closely a court will examine the explanation offered by the law's defender. The defender may argue that the weight minimum assures that carpenters are able to carry lumber safely on the job. The high school diploma requirement helps assure that carpenters can read blueprints and make the calculations necessary to build structures that are safe. If a court accepts this explanation, the classifications drawn by the law are not arbitrary or invidious since they further the state's legitimate interests in safety.

However, a judge who is prepared to scrutinize the measure more closely might find this explanation unconvincing. If strength is really a concern, why did the state adopt a weight requirement rather than insisting that carpenters be able to lift a certain number of pounds? And if the ability to read blueprints and make calculations is so critical, why require a high school diploma, which does not necessarily guarantee these abilities, when the state could instead give a test to see if a person has these skills? Like a suit that was made for someone else, this law fits the alleged safety goal so poorly as to suggest that it was enacted for some other purpose. If a court applies this more exacting standard of review, it might reject the safety explanation and, in the absence of any other plausible justification, conclude that the measure discriminates arbitrarily in violation of the Equal Protection Clause.

As this example suggests, whether or not a law will be invalidated under the Equal Protection Clause depends heavily on how rigorous a standard of review a court will apply. The Supreme Court analyzes most equal protection problems according to a three-tier model, which consists of three possible standards of review. If a law or practice discriminates on the basis of race, alienage, or national origin, or if it selectively burdens the exercise of a fundamental right, the Court will apply strict scrutiny. If the measure discriminates on the basis of gender or legitimacy, it will be examined under somewhat less exacting intermediate scrutiny. Finally, most other classifications are tested under a highly deferential rational basis standard of review. The first two standards of review are sometimes referred to as involving "heightened scrutiny," a term that may refer to either strict or intermediate scrutiny.

The key to approaching an equal protection problem is to first determine what type of discrimination is involved. If the law discriminates on any of the bases that trigger strict or intermediate scrutiny, there is a very good chance it will be found to violate the Equal Protection Clause. On the other hand, if the discrimination is such that it will be reviewed only under the rational basis standard, almost any explanation offered in support of the classification will usually suffice. Thus, in Example 6-A, if Sheila could show that the effect of the high school diploma requirement is to exclude a disproportionate number of racial minorities and that this was the purpose of the law, a court would apply strict scrutiny and probably invalidate the requirement. Similarly, if Sheila could prove that the weight requirement bars most women from carpentry jobs and that this was one of the reasons behind the measure, this aspect of the law would be examined under intermediate scrutiny and would probably be struck down. However, if Sheila is unable to show that the law discriminates on either of these bases, the court would probably apply a mere rational basis standard of review and uphold the measure.

To analyze an equal protection problem, it is necessary to answer three basic questions:

1. What type of discrimination is involved?
2. If the type of discrimination is one that calls for heightened scrutiny, has the plaintiff established a prima facie case that the defendant has been unable to rebut?
3. Has the defender of the law justified the discrimination under the applicable standard of review?

The first two questions will be explored in the following section. The remaining sections of this and the next chapter will consider the third question by examining application of the three-tier model to various forms of discrimination. We will see that the Court's approach to equal protection has been somewhat more subtle and varied than the three-tier model might suggest. Even though the Court still formally adheres to this model, the Court has also incorporated refinements that allow the model to be employed with some degree of flexibility.

§6.2   Equal Protection: General Principles

§6.2.1   Detecting Discrimination: Facial, Design, and Applied

To determine the standard of review that will be applied in an equal protection case, we must first figure out what type of discrimination is involved. Is it a type that calls for strict scrutiny or intermediate scrutiny, or is it a type that triggers only a rational basis standard of review? To determine what kind of discrimination may be effected by a law, we can look at the measure from several different angles. First, we can examine the face of the law to see what classifications are drawn by its text (facial discrimination). Second, we can probe behind the law to see what kind of discrimination it may have been designed to accomplish (discrimination by design). Finally, we can look to how the law is enforced or applied (discriminatory application).

Facial Discrimination

The most obvious place to look to determine the bases on which a law classifies is the face of the law itself, i.e., its text. In Example 6-A, the law regulating carpentry facially discriminates against those who lack a high school diploma and against those who weigh less than 160 pounds. A law does not need to use any specific words to facially discriminate on the basis of a particular trait as long as it is obvious from the text that the law discriminates in a particular way. A law that said "No descendents of slaves may own land" discriminates on the basis of race just as though it had read "No blacks may own land." Moreover, a law will be deemed to facially discriminate against a particular group even if it does not burden every member of that group. A law that states "Aliens may attend the university only after they have lived in this state for ten years" discriminates facially on the basis of alienage. The fact that the law also discriminates within the class of aliens by classifying on the basis of length of residence does not alter the fact that the measure, on its face, singles out aliens for adverse treatment. Thus, in *Rice v. Cayetano*, 120 S. Ct. 1044 (2000), the Court held that a state constitutional provision limiting the right to vote to certain "descendants" of specified "peoples" constituted racial discrimination, even though not all descendants of those peoples were given the right to vote. "Simply because a class defined by ancestry does not include all members of the race does not suffice to make the classification race neutral." Id. at 1056.

Discrimination by Design

Laws may classify in ways that are not apparent from reading their text. A law that is facially neutral may, nonetheless, have been designed to cause discrimination of a certain type. If a law disproportionately burdens a particular group and it can be shown that such discrimination was part of the law's purpose or design, the law will be deemed to involve discrimination against that group despite its facial neutrality. In Example 6-A, the statute requiring that carpenters weigh at least 160 pounds may have been adopted as a subtle means of excluding most women from the trade of carpentry, just as the high school diploma requirement may have been intended to exclude racial minorities. If Sheila could prove that the law had those effects and that they were part of the law's design, the measure would be tested for equal protection purposes under heightened scrutiny as involving both gender discrimination and racial discrimination.

Discriminatory Application

A law that is facially neutral and that was not adopted for the purpose of discriminating in a particular way may still be discriminatory as applied. As the Court recently reiterated, "the purpose of the equal protection clause of the Fourteenth Amendment is to secure every person within the State's jurisdiction against intentional and arbitrary discrimination, whether occasioned by express terms of a statute or by its improper execution through duly constituted agents." *Village of Willowbrook v. Olech*, 120 S. Ct. 1073, 1074 (2000) (quoting *Sunday Lake Iron Co. v. Township of Wakefield*, 247 U.S. 350, 352 (1918)). A statute making it illegal to drive over 55 mph does not discriminate on its face or by design against any group of speeding motorists. Yet the law could be challenged under the Equal Protection Clause as involving gender discrimination if it were shown that the police who enforce the measure give tickets only to female drivers. Similarly, in Example 6-A, even if the high school graduation requirement was not designed to discriminate against racial minorities, the statute would be deemed to involve racial discrimination if it were shown that the state routinely waives this requirement for white applicants.

§6.2.2   The Prima Facie Case

A plaintiff mounting an equal protection challenge must establish a prima facie case of discrimination. To establish a prima facie case, the plaintiff must prove two elements, impact and purpose; i.e., the plaintiff must show that (1) the law has a disproportionate or disparate impact on a particular group and (2) the impact on this particular group is intentional in the sense that it results from a discriminatory purpose or design. Think of these elements as serving to disclose the criterion on which a discriminatory line has been drawn. Thus, a law that disproportionately harms more women than men and that was designed to have this effect is a law that discriminates on the basis of the criterion of gender.

If a plaintiff seeks heightened scrutiny, then the impact and purpose elements must each focus on a criterion that triggers heightened review. For example, if a plaintiff can show that a law has a disproportionate impact on a racial group and that the law was purposefully designed to have that impact, strict scrutiny will apply. If either one of these elements is missing, however, the classification will probably fall into a "nonsuspect" category to which the rational basis standard applies.

Where a law is facially discriminatory against a particular group, the prima facie case of discrimination against that group is established by the text of the law itself. A law providing that "elementary school teachers must be citizens of the United States" obviously has a disproportionate impact on aliens, since it burdens them and no one else. Nor is there any question as to whether this discrimination was purposeful as to aliens, since aliens are singled out for special treatment by the very text of the statute.

If a law is not facially discriminatory, however, the prima facie case may be far more difficult to establish. The plaintiff must prove both disparate impact and discriminatory purpose by looking beyond the text of the law. And again, in order to trigger heightened review, both the impact and the purpose must be directed toward a specially protected classification, such as race or gender.

Disproportionate Impact

To establish that a law has a disproportionate impact, the plaintiff must prove that the law's practical effect is to burden one group of persons more heavily than it does others.

EXAMPLE 6-B

In Example 6-A, Sheila lost her job as a carpenter because she did not meet either the education or the weight requirement set by state law. If she wishes to challenge the law under the Equal Protection Clause, she may be able to have it reviewed under heightened scrutiny by establishing a prima facie case of racial discrimination, gender discrimination, or both. Leaving aside the element of purpose, how might Sheila satisfy the disproportionate impact element of the prima facie case?

EXPLANATION

With respect to the education requirement, Sheila might consult census data showing the educational levels for members of the work force in her state. If this data shows that a significantly higher percentage of whites than blacks completes high school, she will arguably have made a prima facie showing that the law will have a disparate impact on blacks by disqualifying a larger proportion of blacks than whites.

Similarly, Sheila could satisfy the impact element for a prima facie case of gender discrimination if she can show that the percentage of working-age men weighing more than 160 pounds is substantially higher than the percentage of working-age women who exceed this weight.

While most equal protection cases involve discrimination against a group or class of persons, equal protection claims may be brought "by a 'class of one,' where the plaintiff alleges that she has been intentionally treated differently from others similarly situated and that there is no rational basis for the difference in treatment." *Village of Willowbrook v. Olech*, 120 S. Ct. 1073, 1074 (2000). In *Olech*, the Court held that the plaintiff had stated a claim for relief under the Equal Protection Clause by alleging that the village demanded a 33-foot easement to connect her property to the municipal water supply while requiring only 15-foot easements from other property owners. Plaintiff asserted that she was intentionally singled out for this "irrational and wholly arbitrary" treatment because she had previously brought an unrelated, successful lawsuit against the village. The Court held that "the number of individuals in a class is immaterial for equal protection analysis." Id. at 1074 n.*. On this basis, in Example 6-B, Sheila could state a valid equal protection claim by alleging that though others also failed to meet the education and weight requirements, she was the only person to lose her job as a carpenter.

Discriminatory Purpose

The second element of the prima facie case is discriminatory purpose. This element was first explicitly recognized in *Washington v. Davis*, 426 U.S. 229 (1976), a case in which it was alleged that the District of Columbia police department was discriminating on the basis of race in recruiting new officers. The Court held that even if the disproportionate impact element of the plaintiffs' prima facie case was established, the plaintiffs failed to prove any discriminatory purpose on the part of the defendant police department. It is a "basic equal protection principle," said the Court, "that the invidious quality of a law claimed to be racially discriminatory must ultimately be traced to a racially discriminatory purpose." Id. at 240. The same principle applies with respect to other types of discrimination. Heightened scrutiny will be triggered under the Equal Protection Clause only if there is de jure, as opposed to de facto, discrimination. As the Court has stressed, the critical "differentiating factor" between the two is "*purpose* or *intent*" to discriminate. *Keyes v. School Dist. No. 1*, 413 U.S. 189, 208 (1973) (emphasis in original).

In order to satisfy the purpose requirement of the prima facie case, a plaintiff need not show "that the challenged action rested solely on . . . discriminatory purposes. Rarely can it be said that a legislature or administrative body operating under a broad mandate made a decision motivated solely by a single concern, or even that a particular purpose was the 'dominant' or 'primary' one." Instead, it is normally enough "that a discriminatory purpose has been *a motivating factor* in the decision. . . ." *Village of Arlington Heights v. Metropolitan Hous. Dev. Corp.*, 429 U.S. 252, 265-266 (1977) (emphasis supplied). The only exception to this requirement involves race-based electoral districting, where the prima facie case requires proof "that race was *the predominant factor* motivating the legislature's decision. . . ." *Miller v. Johnson*, 515 U.S. 900, 916 (1995) (emphasis supplied). See §7.3.5.

Proving that a challenged law or practice was motivated by a discriminatory purpose is automatic where a statute or policy is discriminatory on its face, for there is then no doubt as to the presence of a discriminatory intent. If the measure is facially neutral, however, satisfying the purpose element may be a major stumbling block. It is not enough to show merely that those who adopted the law or practice did so with the knowledge that it would have foreseeable discriminatory effects. "'Discriminatory purpose' . . . implies more than intent as volition or intent as awareness of consequences." The plaintiff must prove that the measure was adopted "at least in part 'because of,' not merely 'in spite of,' its adverse effects upon an identifiable group." *Personnel Administrator of Mass. v. Feeney*, 442 U.S. 256, 279 (1979).

EXAMPLE 6-C

In Example 6-B, suppose that after establishing the discriminatory impact element of her prima facie case for racial and gender discrimination, Sheila proved that when the law was pending before the legislature, a number of groups testifying against the measure pointed out that it would heavily impact racial minorities and women. Would this suffice to establish discriminatory purpose?

EXPLANATION

This evidence is not by itself enough to prove the element of purpose, for it is possible the legislators adopted the law in spite of, not because of, its adverse effects on these groups. Sheila will need to come up with other evidence of discriminatory purpose.

———————————

While mere awareness of "foreseeable and anticipated disparate impact" will not by itself support a finding of discriminatory purpose, the Court has held that "foreseeable consequences" may be "utilized as one of the several kinds of proofs" from which an inference of discriminatory purpose may be drawn. *Columbus Bd. of Educ. v. Penick*, 443 U.S. 449, 464-465 (1979).

Legislative History

There are a number of ways in which a plaintiff may be able to prove the element of purpose where a law is facially neutral. It is possible that the legislative history pertaining to the measure's adoption will reveal a discriminatory intent. This is fairly uncommon, since those who are motivated by an evil purpose rarely leave a public record to document their wrongdoing. Nevertheless, such evidence is sometimes available. In *Hunter v. Underwood*, 471 U.S. 222 (1985), the Court invalidated a 1901 Alabama constitutional provision that disenfranchised anyone convicted of a crime involving moral turpitude after finding that the provision was racially discriminatory. The impact element of the plaintiffs' prima facie case was established by showing that the provision had disenfranchised ten times as many blacks as whites. The purpose element was met by evidence from historians and from speeches made at the convention showing that "zeal for white supremacy ran rampant" in the constitutional convention that had adopted the provision. Id. at 229.

The Manner of Adoption

Discriminatory purpose may sometimes be inferred from the way in which the challenged measure was adopted. If the process that led to its adoption did not follow the normal procedures or if it involved a departure from the substantive criteria that normally govern such matters, the irregularity may suggest the presence of a discriminatory intent.

EXAMPLE 6-D

In Example 6-A, suppose that the state adopted the law requiring that carpenters have a high school diploma and weigh at least 160 pounds as an emergency measure two days after a local newspaper reported that 150 women and minorities were about to graduate from a federally funded training program for carpenters. The bill was drafted by the Brotherhood of Carpenters and was not reviewed by any of the state legislative committees that normally have jurisdiction over such matters. Would this evidence establish the element of discriminatory purpose?

EXPLANATION

The unusual timing and procedure that led to enactment of this law might allow the inference that it was motivated by a desire to exclude minorities and women from the carpentry trade.

Inferring Purpose from Impact and Other Circumstantial Evidence

Although a disproportionate impact alone will not suffice to establish discriminatory purpose, proof of impact along with other circumstantial evidence may satisfy the plaintiff's burden. Even if there is no direct evidence revealing the subjective state of mind of those who adopted the challenged measure, "an invidious discriminatory purpose may often be inferred from the totality of the relevant facts. . . ." *Washington v. Davis*, 426 U.S. 229, 242 (1976).

This principle was applied in *Rogers v. Lodge*, 458 U.S. 613 (1982). At issue there was an equal protection challenge to an "at-large" county election system under which a five-member board of commissioners was selected. The county was not divided into districts; instead, every registered voter could vote for all five seats on the board. The net effect of this system was that blacks, who comprised a minority of the registered voters countywide, were never elected to office. This disparate impact on the black community did not establish purposeful discrimination. However, coupling this impact with other evidence, the Supreme Court affirmed a lower court's ruling that the at-large system was being maintained for discriminatory purposes. That evidence was all circumstantial—e.g., blacks comprised a substantial majority of the population but made up a distinct minority of the registered voters; there was also overwhelming evidence of racial block voting, a history of past racial discrimination in voter registration and in education, continuing segregation in the public schools, various examples of discrimination in the political process, a failure of the political process to address the needs of the black community, and discriminatory use of public monies. Viewed as a whole, these facts provided a sufficient basis for the district court to conclude that the county's at-large system was being maintained for racially discriminatory purposes.

Thus, in Example 6-B, Sheila probably could not meet the discriminatory purpose element merely by showing that the law had a heavily disproportionate impact on racial minorities and women who wish to become carpenters. To fall within *Rogers,* she would have to present circumstantial evidence sufficient to convince a court that the law was adopted or being maintained for purposes of racial or gender discrimination.

Inferring Intent from Application

Proof that a facially neutral statute is being applied in a discriminatory fashion will also satisfy the purpose element of the plaintiff's burden. For example, in *Yick Wo v. Hopkins,* 118 U.S. 356 (1886), the Court struck down a San Francisco city ordinance that required a permit to operate a laundry in a wooden building. This ordinance, though facially neutral, was enforced in such a way that applications from all 201 Chinese applicants were denied, while virtually every non-Chinese application was approved. The disproportionate impact was so extreme as to allow an inference "that no reason for it exists except hostility to the race and nationality to which the petitioners belong. . . ." Id. at 374. To fall within *Yick Wo,* a plaintiff must prove that the law is being administered in a discriminatory manner. This would be the case in Example 6-B if Sheila could show that the state followed a practice of regularly waiving the education and weight requirements for whites and for males, while strictly enforcing them against minority and female applicants.

The *Keyes* Presumption

Discriminatory purpose may also be established if the actor whose conduct is in question has been guilty of the same type of intentional discrimination in another, but closely related, area. Under these circumstances, the *Keyes* presumption may allow a court to infer that the actor's currently challenged conduct was motivated by the same evil intent. The presumption takes its name from *Keyes v. School District No. 1,* 413 U.S. 189 (1973), a school desegregation case in which the plaintiffs were able to prove that the defendant school board had intentionally segregated schools in one part of the district, but could not prove a similar purpose with respect to other segregated schools in the same district. The Court held that the plaintiffs could satisfy the purpose element of their prima facie case as to the latter schools by in effect transferring the board's evil intent from one part of the district to another. "[A] finding of intentionally segregative school board actions in a meaningful portion of a school system, as in this case, creates a presumption that other segregated schooling within the system is not adventitious. It establishes, in other words, a prima facie case of unlawful segregative design on the part of school authorities. . . ." Id. at 208.

In *Keyes,* the presumption of discriminatory intent was applied with respect to actions taken at roughly the same time, though in different parts of the city. The *Keyes* presumption has also been employed in a historical or temporal sense to transfer the element of intent from one time period to another. Where a school board has been guilty of purposeful discrimination at some point in the past, this may allow a presumption that the actor's "subsequent" or "current" conduct was similarly motivated. Id. at 210-211 & n.17. And see *Dayton Bd. of Educ. v. Brinkman,* 443 U.S. 526, 535-538 (1979) (employing *Keyes* presumption to supply element of intent where school board had purposefully segregated schools several decades earlier).

Though the Court has applied the *Keyes* presumption in an expansive manner in school segregation cases, the Court does not appear to have employed the presumption either in other types of race discrimination cases or in cases involving discrimination on grounds other than race, such as alienage and gender. Thus, it is questionable whether the *Keyes* presumption has any role to play outside the school desegregation context.

EXAMPLE 6-E

In Example 6-B, suppose that Sheila challenged the carpenter qualifications law partly on the ground that it was being enforced in a racially discriminatory manner by the State Licensing Board. According to Sheila, all whites who apply are granted a license regardless of their weight or level of education, whereas racial minorities who do not meet these requirements are rejected. Assuming that the element of disparate impact can be proved by statistics from the board's files, how might Sheila prove the element of racially discriminatory purpose?

EXPLANATION

In addition to perhaps asking the court to infer intent from discriminatory application as in *Yick Wo,* Sheila might determine whether the board was ever found by a court to have engaged in purposeful racial discrimination in the past. If such a finding exists, Sheila might ask the court to invoke the *Keyes* presumption, in effect transferring the element of evil intent from that prior incident to the present case. However, since this is not a school desegregation case, it is possible, but unlikely, that the court would allow use of *Keyes.*

If courts were to permit broad use of the *Keyes* presumption, the distinction between de jure and de facto discrimination would all but collapse. There are probably few governmental entities that have not, at some time in their history, been guilty of purposeful racial discrimination. If *Keyes* could be used routinely to challenge current laws and practices that have a racially disparate impact, plaintiffs could almost always satisfy their prima facie case by borrowing the element of intent from the past. It is perhaps for this reason that the Court has employed the *Keyes* presumption only in the context of school desegregation cases. Even in this setting, the Court is likely to limit the presumption to actions that are very similar in nature. Thus, for example, the mere fact that a school board may have been guilty of past racial discrimination in hiring teachers would probably not permit use of the *Keyes* presumption in a later case charging the board with racial discrimination in assigning pupils to schools.

Difficulties with the Purpose Element

Even though a plaintiff might in theory meet the purpose element of the prima facie case in a number of different ways, this element is frequently impossible to satisfy in the context of suspect or quasi-suspect criteria, such as race or gender. As a result, the plaintiff's equal protection challenge is often reviewed and rejected under a rational basis standard of review. In essence, the failure to establish discriminatory purpose alters the nature of the classification. Thus, a job test that disproportionately disqualifies more blacks than whites is not racially discriminatory within the meaning of the Equal Protection Clause unless the purpose of using that test is to discriminate on the basis of race. Without proof of a racially discriminatory purpose, the classification—those who pass the test and those who fail—is nonsuspect and subject only to rational basis review.

Yet forcing plaintiffs to prove the existence of evil intent means that governmental actions that were undertaken with a discriminatory purpose will be upheld by courts applying the rational basis standard of review whenever plaintiffs lack the resources or the ability to uncover proof of the defendants' improper motivation. This is especially troubling in the area of racial discrimination, for as Justice Powell observed, "[I]f one goes back far enough, it is probable that all racial segregation, wherever occurring and whether or not confined to the schools, has at some time been supported or maintained by government action." *Keyes v. School Dist. No. 1,* 413 U.S. at 228 n.12 (Powell, J., concurring and dissenting). For this reason, Justices Powell and Douglas urged the Court to abandon the de jure/de facto distinction, at least in the context of school desegregation cases. Id. at 219-236.

It has also been objected that to demand proof of conscious or deliberate intent to discriminate is often to demand the impossible — not because the challenged action was free of discriminatory bias, but because that bias was unconscious. To focus, as the Supreme Court has, on proof of discriminatory purpose is to create "an imaginary world where," in a constitutional sense, "discrimination does not exist unless it was consciously intended." Charles Lawrence, "The Id, the Ego, and Equal Protection: Reckoning with Unconscious Racism," 39 *Stan. L. Rev.* 317, 325 (1987).

The Court has, nevertheless, adhered to the requirement that to trigger heightened scrutiny under the Equal Protection Clause, a plaintiff must prove discriminatory purpose as part of the prima facie case. The Court has defended this approach by noting that if disproportionate impact alone were enough to elevate the standard of judicial review, this "would raise serious questions about, and perhaps invalidate, a whole range of tax, welfare, public service, regulatory, and licensing statutes that may be more burdensome to the poor and to the average black than to the more affluent white." *Washington v. Davis,* 426 U.S. at 248 & n.14. In addition, judges would be transformed into a set of racial bookkeepers, forced to measure the gains and losses of each racial and ethnic group affected by a challenged law. Finally, a disparate impact approach would destroy our ideal of a colorblind society, for in order to avoid a potential violation of the Equal Protection Clause, governmental entities would be compelled to evaluate every proposed action in terms of its likely racial impact—a frightening, if not impossible, task.

§6.2.3 *Rebutting the Prima Facie Case*

Once the plaintiff has established a prima facie case, whether it be of racial discrimination, gender discrimination, or some other type of discrimination that triggers heightened scrutiny, the court will give the defendant an opportunity to rebut the prima facie case. If the defendant is able to do so, then the court will evaluate the statute under the rational basis standard of review rather than under either strict or intermediate scrutiny. On the other hand, if the defendant is unable to rebut, the court will proceed to apply the appropriate level of heightened scrutiny.

A defendant can attempt to rebut the plaintiff's prima facie case of discrimination in three possible ways: (1) by disproving the element of impact; (2) by disproving the element of purpose; or (3) by showing that the discriminatory impact was not caused by the defendant's purposefully discriminatory acts.

The first way a defendant can rebut the prima facie case is by showing that those allegedly discriminated against by the challenged law or practice have not in fact been harmed or burdened any more heavily than others. This typically involves proving that the data on which the plaintiff relied to show disparate impact is outdated, was obtained by faulty methods, or is for some other reason inaccurate.

EXAMPLE 6-F

In Example 6-B, Sheila established a prima facie case of racial and gender discrimination with statistics showing that a smaller percentage of blacks than whites graduates from high school and that a lower percentage of women than men weighs over 160 pounds. How might the defendant rebut this element of the prima facie case?

EXPLANATION

The defendant could rebut the showing of disparate impact by proving that despite Sheila's statistics concerning the working-age population in general, the law's education and weight requirements have not resulted in the exclusion of blacks or women at higher rates than whites or males. For example, the defendant's figures might show that under the high school graduation requirement, 23 percent of white applicants were rejected, as compared with 20 percent of black applicants, and that the weight restriction led to the rejection of 9 percent of males, but only 5 percent of females. If the defendant could make these showings, the law would not be discriminatory against racial minorities or women. Instead, the measure would be one that discriminates on the bases of education and weight, classifications that are subject only to a rational basis equal protection review.

The second means of rebutting the prima facie case is to show that those responsible for the challenged action were not moved by a discriminatory purpose. In a case where this element of the plaintiff's prima facie case was satisfied through use of the *Keyes* presumption, the defendant may be able to prove that despite its discriminatory intent in other situations, the actions at issue in this case were not so motivated. To rebut this element of the prima facie case, however, a defendant must show that its actions were not "to any degree motivated" by a discriminatory purpose, i.e., that such a purpose "was not among the factors" that prompted its conduct. *Keyes v. School Dist. No. 1,* 413 U.S. at 210. In *Hunter v. Underwood,* 471 U.S. 222, 230 (1985), for example, the state sought to rebut the prima facie case of race discrimination by arguing that "the real purpose" behind its disenfranchisement of those convicted of crimes involving moral turpitude "was to disenfranchise poor whites as well as blacks." This argument failed, said the Court, for it "concedes . . . that discrimination against blacks . . . was a motivating factor for the provision. . . ." Id. at 231.

Finally, a defendant may rebut the prima facie case by showing that there is no link between the discriminatory purpose and the disproportionate impact complained of. In other words, the defendant can seek to demonstrate that its deliberate efforts to discriminate were gratuitous and unnecessary because the same results would have occurred anyway due to other factors.

EXAMPLE 6-G

The Village of Avondale denied a request from Metro, Inc., to rezone a parcel of land on which Metro wished to build a ten-story low-income housing project. Metro sued the village, alleging that its refusal to rezone was racially discriminatory. Metro established a prima facie case by proving that the village's decision would have a racially disparate impact, since most tenants in the proposed project would be racial minorities, and by showing that the refusal was prompted by a desire to keep minorities from moving into the village. How might the village rebut Metro's prima facie case of racial discrimination?

EXPLANATION

Even if the village cannot disprove the elements of impact or purpose, it can rebut Metro's prima facie case by showing that for other reasons the project never would have been built. The village might, for example, prove that even in the absence of any racially discriminatory purpose, the rezoning request would have been denied under a uniformly applied ordinance that limits buildings to six stories in height. Or the village might show that if the rezoning request had been approved, the project would still not have been built because Metro lacked the necessary funding. In either of these ways, the village would have shown that the injury complained of is not attributable to the village's improper discriminatory purpose. The village's action would then be evaluated under a mere rational basis standard of review. See *Village of Arlington Heights v. Metropolitan Hous. Dev. Corp.*, 429 U.S. 252, 270 n.21 (1977).

———————————

In some instances, a defendant may be able to rebut only a portion of the plaintiff's prima facie case, in which event the court would apply heightened scrutiny to those aspects of the plaintiff's case that have not been rebutted. Thus, in a school desegregation case where the plaintiff made a prima facie showing that the school board had purposefully segregated the elementary and secondary schools in the district, the defendant might be able to show that the secondary schools would have become segregated in any event due to factors for which the board was not responsible, with the result that no prima facie case of race discrimination would exist as to the secondary schools.

In the balance of this chapter, we will examine the Court's application of the equal protection guarantee of the Fifth and Fourteenth Amendments, first under the rational basis standard of review and then where the plaintiff has established a prima facie case that triggers heightened scrutiny on the basis of a suspect or quasi-suspect classification. In Chapter 7, we will consider the application of strict scrutiny where there has been discrimination with respect to a fundamental right.

§6.3   The Rational Basis Equal Protection Test

If a law does not involve a suspect or quasi-suspect classification and does not discriminate with respect to a fundamental right, the courts will apply a rational basis test to decide whether the law violates the equal protection provisions of the Fifth or the Fourteenth Amendment. Over the years, the rational basis equal protection standard has been applied with varying degrees of rigor. From the late 1890s until the late 1930s, the Court often used the test to invalidate state and local laws on the ground that they discriminated arbitrarily. Yet during the same period, the Court also applied the test leniently to uphold challenged classifications. This oscillation between strict and relaxed applications of the rational basis test came to an end in the 1940s. Since then, in applying what is now sometimes referred to as the traditional rational basis test, the Court evaluates most classifications with such extraordinary deference that the test has frequently been described as "toothless."

The traditional rational basis standard of review requires only that there be some *conceivable* reason for the challenged classification, whether or not this was the actual purpose that motivated the legislature. A classification subject to mere rational basis review comes before a court "bearing a strong presumption of validity," and its challenger must "negative every conceivable basis which might support it. . . ." *FCC v. Beach Communications, Inc.*, 508 U.S. 307, 314-315 (1993). The asserted rationale may rest entirely on "rational speculation unsupported by evidence or empirical data." Id. at 315. The classification need not fit its supposed end "with mathematical nicety." *Dandridge v. Williams*, 397 U.S. 471, 485 (1970). It can be overinclusive, underinclusive, illogical, and unscientific, *Metropolis Theatre Co. v. Chicago*, 228 U.S. 61, 69-70 (1913), and may involve approaching an issue incrementally, "one step at a time, addressing itself to the phase of the problem which seems most acute to the legislative mind," *Williamson v. Lee Optical, Inc.*, 348 U.S. 483, 489 (1955). And if, as is often the case, the classification involves "a process of line-drawing," the fact that the legislature had to draw the line somewhere "renders the precise coordinates of the resulting legislative judgment virtually unreviewable. . . ." *FCC v. Beach Communications, Inc.*, 508 U.S. at 315-316.

EXAMPLE 6-H

The city council adopted an ordinance outlawing door-to-door sales in residential neighborhoods. The law contains an exemption for agents of the Bigelow Insurance Co., who are permitted to sell door to door in all parts of the city. Sherry, an agent for the Miller Insurance Co., was arrested and criminally charged with violating the ordinance. She has asked the court to dismiss the criminal action on the ground that the ordinance violates the Equal Protection Clause of the Fourteenth Amendment. How should the court rule?

EXPLANATION

The ordinance is probably constitutional. Even if we have no idea why the city council adopted the measure and even if we suspect that the council may have been bribed by Bigelow, the classification will be upheld if there is any conceivable legitimate reason for treating Bigelow more favorably than other door-to-door sellers. The council may have believed that Bigelow agents are more polite than other door-to-door sellers. Or the council may have thought that Bigelow had been operating in the city longer than any other door-to-door company, giving it an equitable claim to favored treatment. Even if none of these hypothetical rationales was in fact what moved the city council, it is enough that the classification might have been adopted for one or more of these reasons. See *New Orleans v. Dukes*, 427 U.S. 297 (1976) (upholding exemption to ordinance barring vendors from parts of city).

As the previous example suggests, it is almost impossible for a legislatively drawn classification to be found unconstitutional under the traditional rational basis standard of review. As we will see later, there are occasions when the modern Court has struck down classifications ostensibly using the rational basis test. In these cases, however, the Court has at times applied a standard that is in fact more demanding than the traditional rational basis test. See §§6.7.2-6.7.4.

One of the few times a law may fail the mere rational basis test is if the legislature has clearly identified a specific purpose for a classification, leaving no room for a reviewing court to hypothesize or speculate about other conceivable bases that might have sufficed to uphold the measure. If the classification does not rationally advance the given or stated purpose, the law will be struck down. See *Nordlinger v. Hahn,* 505 U.S. 1, 16 (1992) (upholding California property tax scheme and distinguishing it from nearly identical scheme invalidated in *Allegheny Pittsburgh Coal Co. v. Webster County,* 488 U.S. 336 (1989), on basis that in the latter case, the purpose identified by state law precluded reliance on other conceivable purposes). A classification may also be invalidated under the rational basis test if it is clear that its actual purpose was illegitimate. See *United States Dept. of Agric. v. Moreno,* 413 U.S. 528, 534 (1973) (invalidating federal food stamp law where legislative history revealed that law's purpose was to "prevent so-called 'hippies' and 'hippie communes' from participating in the food stamp program").

EXAMPLE 6-1

A city fire ordinance prohibits the operation of fraternity or sorority houses in residential areas of the city, on the stated ground that the occupants of such houses may have difficulty evacuating the building in the event of a fire. The city allows other types of group housing in residential areas, including regular student dormitories, boarding houses, senior citizen housing, and nursing homes. Is the city's discrimination against fraternity and sorority houses rationally related to a legitimate governmental purpose?

EXPLANATION

Perhaps not. Unless the city can demonstrate that there is something about fraternity and sorority houses that exposes their occupants to special risk in time of fire, the discrimination is literally irrational. To meet its burden, the city would have to explain why, in terms of fire safety, it allows student dormitories, boarding houses, and senior citizen and nursing homes, while prohibiting fraternity and sorority houses. All would seem to be equally safe and equally risky in the event of a fire. In terms of equal protection, in the absence of any relevant distinction between the permitted uses and the prohibited use, the classification would not rationally advance the city's avowed interest in fire safety.

If the ordinance had not identified fire safety as the purpose of the ban, the city could more easily defend the ordinance against an equal protection attack by arguing that the discrimination against fraternity and sorority houses is rationally related to another legitimate governmental purpose, i.e., preserving residential tranquillity. Since the occupants of fraternity and sorority houses are often particularly loud and boisterous, the ordinance's distinction between them and other types of group housing would rationally further the goal of maintaining peace and quiet in residential areas. However, the fact that the ordinance specifically identified fire safety as the purpose of the ban precludes any plausible inference that the reason for the discrimination was that of residential tranquillity.

We now leave the rational basis test and turn to those classifications that trigger some form of heightened scrutiny under the equal protection provisions of the Fifth and Fourteenth Amendments. We will visit the rational basis test again, however, for the Court in certain circumstances has been willing to apply the test with somewhat greater rigor. See §§6.7.2-6.7.4.

§6.4   Classifications on the Basis of Race or National Origin

§6.4.1   *Race as a Suspect Classification*

The Court's Early Treatment of Race

The driving force behind adoption of the Fourteenth Amendment was a determination to prevent states from continuing to discriminate against the recently emancipated slaves. Under the Black Codes adopted at the end of the Civil War throughout most of the former Confederacy, ex-slaves were typically "forbidden to appear in the towns in any other character than menial servants. They were required to reside on and cultivate the soil without the right to purchase or own it. They were excluded from many occupations of gain, and were not permitted to give testimony in the courts in any case where a white man was a party." *Slaughter-House Cases,* 83 U.S. (16 Wall.) 36, 70 (1872). While the Reconstruction-era Congress enacted a series of civil rights laws prohibiting mistreatment of the former slaves, Congress realized the importance of making these protections permanent and unrepealable by enshrining them in the Constitution. To this end, Congress approved the Fourteenth Amendment and sent it to the states for ratification. States that had joined the Confederacy were required to approve the Amendment as a condition for readmission to the Union.

The history of the Fourteenth Amendment makes clear that the "evil to be remedied" by its adoption was "[t]he existence of laws in the States where the newly emancipated negroes resided, which discriminated with gross injustice and hardship against them as a class. . . ." Id. at 81. Indeed, when the Supreme Court first construed the Equal Protection Clause of the Fourteenth Amendment in 1872, it expressed "doubt . . . whether any action of a State not directed by way of discrimination against the negroes as a class, or on account of their race, will ever be held to come within the purview of this provision." Id. It is not surprising that the Court in a number of early cases invoked the Equal Protection Clause to strike down state and local laws that discriminated against blacks. In *Strauder v. West Virginia*, 100 U.S. (10 Otto) 303 (1880), the Court thus used the Clause to reverse the conviction of a black defendant because state law excluded blacks from the jury. Six years later the Court extended the Clause to protect the Chinese, holding that the Fourteenth Amendment requires equality of treatment "without regard to any differences of race, of color, or of nationality." *Yick Wo v. Hopkins*, 118 U.S. 356, 369 (1886).

Despite its early promise as a shield against discrimination on the basis of race or national origin, the Equal Protection Clause was dealt a near-crippling blow in *Plessy v. Ferguson*, 163 U.S. 537 (1896). There, the Supreme Court upheld a "Jim Crow" law enacted in 1890 by Louisiana that required railroads to "provide equal but separate accommodations for the white, and colored races. . . ." *Plessy* explained that state laws forcibly segregating the races — whether in railroad cars, public schools, or marriage — do not offend the Equal Protection Clause because they are "reasonable regulation[s]" aimed at "preservation of the public peace and good order." Id. at 550. If such state-mandated segregation "stamps the colored race with a badge of inferiority," said the Court, "it is not by reason of anything found in the act, but solely because the colored race chooses to put that construction upon it." Id. at 551. The "separate but equal" doctrine created by *Plessy* in effect treated laws imposing racial segregation as having no disproportionate impact on racial minorities and hence as not being subject to heightened scrutiny under the Equal Protection Clause. In the wake of *Plessy*, laws imposing racial segregation were typically upheld under a rational basis standard of review as long as the state provided some sort of separate facilities for blacks.

The tide began to turn during the 1940s. In *Korematsu v. United States*, 323 U.S. 214, 216 (1944), while the Court upheld the government's wartime evacuation of Japanese Americans from the West Coast, it observed that "all legal restrictions which curtail the civil rights of a single racial group are immediately suspect" and subject "to the most rigid scrutiny." Four years later in *Shelley v. Kraemer*, 334 U.S. 1 (1948), the Court invoked the Equal Protection Clause to overturn a state court's enforcement of a racially restrictive covenant. With *Brown v. Board of Education*, 347 U.S. 483 (1954), the Equal Protection Clause finally recovered from the blow sustained in

Plessy. In *Brown* and its progeny, the Court emphatically rejected the doctrine of separate but equal. Instead, said the Court, laws that classify on the basis of race or national origin are "odious to a free people," and if "they are ever to be upheld, they must be shown to be necessary to the accomplishment of some permissible state objective, independent of the racial discrimination which it was the object of the Fourteenth Amendment to eliminate." *Loving v. Virginia,* 388 U.S. 1, 11 (1967).

The Rationale for Strict Scrutiny

The Court's determination to strictly scrutinize laws that discriminate against racial minorities is not only consistent with the goals of the Fourteenth Amendment, but is also justified by principles of democratic theory. In a democratic society, most decisions are made through the give-and-take of the majoritarian political process. Individuals and groups debate and decide issues under a principle of majority rule. Even groups that are themselves too small to command a majority may prevail on a particular issue by forming alliances with other groups, whom they may in turn agree to support on other issues. It is inevitable in such a process that some will win and some will lose. It would be utterly destructive of democratic principles if the losers in this process could routinely turn to the courts to reverse the defeat they suffered in the political arena. For this reason, federal courts normally apply a strong presumption in favor of the constitutionality of state and federal laws.

There may be times, however, when the political process cannot be trusted to produce outcomes that are fair to all concerned. In footnote four of *United States v. Carolene Products Co.,* 304 U.S. 144, 152-153 n.4 (1938), Justice Stone identified a number of circumstances under which "more exacting judicial scrutiny" might be warranted. One of these involves legislation "directed at particular religious . . . or national . . . or racial minorities." As Stone observed, "[P]rejudice against discrete and insular minorities may be a special condition, which tends seriously to curtail the operation of those political processes ordinarily to be relied upon to protect minorities, and which may call for a correspondingly more searching judicial inquiry." Where the political process has been skewed by prejudice against those who are targeted by a law, judicial deference is no longer warranted by the assumption that those who lost out in that process were given equal justice. Instead, because the political process may have malfunctioned, closer judicial review is warranted in order to assure that the law in question was not based on mere animus or a desire to harm.

In the years since Justice Stone wrote footnote four, the Court and commentators have noted that several types of "prejudice" and related factors may distort the legislative process in ways that call for heightened scrutiny.

In *Democracy and Distrust: A Theory of Judicial Review* (1980), Professor John Ely suggested a distinction between first-degree prejudice and second-degree prejudice. First-degree prejudice involves outright hostility, dislike, or a simple desire to harm a particular group. Second-degree prejudice refers to exaggerated negative generalizations or stereotypes about a certain group, such as the belief that all or most members of the group are stupid, dishonest, dangerous, or silly—when in fact these traits are shared by only a normal or relatively small portion of the group. If legislators share either of these forms of prejudice toward those burdened by a law, there is a good chance that the group's interests were undervalued or entirely ignored in the legislative process. Ely observed that the legislative process may also be distorted if the trait that defines the targeted group involves an immutable characteristic. In such cases, a legislator's ability to empathize with the burdened class may be curtailed by the fact that unless the trait is widely shared, most legislators will never have been in the group's shoes and they never need fear being there. Like first- and second-degree prejudice, the factor of immutability may sometimes cause the interests of the targeted group to receive minimal, if any, consideration in the legislative process. Moreover, if the immutable trait is one that is generally irrelevant to a person's ability, use of that trait as a classifying factor may suggest the presence of either first- or second-degree prejudice. Finally, some groups may simply have been excluded from the political process by laws that deny them the right to vote or that effectively undermine their ability to be heard within the political arena.

All of these suggested rationales for heightened scrutiny apply with respect to laws that disadvantage racial minorities. In terms of first-degree prejudice, this nation's history of black slavery and racial discrimination leaves no doubt that racial minorities have been and are often still the objects of hatred and vilification. Second-degree prejudice is likewise present in the form of widespread and exaggerated negative stereotypes about the intelligence, morality, industry, and honesty of racial minority groups. Next, race is an immutable characteristic; and since most legislators are white, there is a danger that laws singling out racial minorities for adverse treatment may have been adopted because of the legislature's inability to empathize with those targeted by the measure. In addition, race is generally, if not always, irrelevant to a person's abilities. Finally, racial minorities have historically been excluded from the political process, initially by outright denial of the right to vote and later through such devices as literacy tests, poll taxes, and physical intimidation.

§6.4.2 Strict Scrutiny as a Measure of Constitutionality

Laws or practices that draw distinctions on the basis of race or national origin are inherently suspect and subject to strict scrutiny under the equal protection provisions of the Fifth and Fourteenth Amendments. As we will see later, strict scrutiny is also applied to many classifications drawn on the basis of alienage and to classifications that bear on the exercise of a fundamental right. While the method of analysis is the same in all these areas, the strict scrutiny standard is applied with special rigor in cases that involve race or national origin discrimination.

A law or practice that is subjected to strict scrutiny under the Equal Protection Clause will pass constitutional muster only if it can be demonstrated that the challenged classification is (1) justified by a compelling governmental interest and (2) narrowly tailored to furthering that interest. Unless both of these requirements are met, the classification will be struck down because of the danger that its real purpose is to harm those burdened by the law or to discourage them from exercising a fundamental constitutional right.

Compelling Interest

The first step in testing a classification under strict scrutiny is to determine whether it is justified by a compelling governmental interest. The notion of a *compelling* governmental interest implies that not all legitimate governmental interests are important enough to justify a classification that is subject to strict scrutiny. The Court has not developed any formula for distinguishing among legitimate, important, and compelling governmental interests. Yet it has at times held that a governmental interest, while legitimate, is not weighty enough to satisfy this part of the strict scrutiny test. For example, the Court has held that administrative convenience, although clearly a legitimate state interest, is not sufficiently important to warrant the "compelling" label. *Frontiero v. Richardson*, 411 U.S. 677, 690 (1973).

In some cases, the Court may doubt the intrinsic importance of the asserted state interest. In such instances, the Court may insist that the law's defender "advance a factual showing" that the classification addresses "a real, as opposed to a merely speculative, problem to the State." In the absence of such a showing, the Court may reject the alleged goal as "lack[ing] the weight we have required of interests properly denominated as compelling." *Bernal v. Fainter*, 467 U.S. 216, 227-228 (1984).

Even if an asserted governmental interest is important enough to qualify as compelling, the defender of the law "must show that the alleged objective was the legislature's 'actual purpose' for the discriminatory classification," as opposed to engaging in mere "speculation about what 'may have motivated' the legislature." *Shaw v. Hunt*, 517 U.S. 899, 908 n.4 (1996). Moreover, it is not enough to show that "some legislators" had the asserted purpose in mind; instead, it must be demonstrated that the purpose was one that motivated enough legislators to cause the legislation to be adopted. Id. at 910.

Finally, even if an asserted governmental interest might otherwise qualify as compelling, the Court may conclude that any harm to that interest is too minor to justify the classification in question. Thus, in *Nyquist v. Mauclet*, 432 U.S. 1 (1977), New York claimed that denying scholarships to aliens who did not intend to become citizens furthered the compelling interest of educating the electorate, since the money denied to these aliens was paid instead to persons eligible to vote. The Court rejected the state's argument, noting that because only a small number of aliens were disqualified under this law, including them would have only "an insubstantial impact" on the state's otherwise compelling goal. Id. at 11-12 n.15.

Narrowly Tailored

If, under the first part of the strict scrutiny test, a court accepts that a classification was designed to further a compelling governmental interest, the measure will be upheld only if it is also narrowly tailored to furthering that interest. Narrowly tailored means that "the classification at issue must 'fit'" the alleged compelling interest "with greater precision than any alternative means." *Wygant v. Jackson Bd. of Educ.*, 476 U.S. 267, 280 n.6 (1986). If there were other means available to the government that would have achieved the asserted goal better, it becomes doubtful that the classification was really designed to further that goal. Instead, the inadequacy of the "fit" confirms our initial suspicion that the measure was designed for the improper purpose of harming the affected group or discouraging the exercise of a fundamental constitutional right.

Consider this analogy. After a clothing store was robbed, the police stop a man who was running down the street carrying an expensive suit. They suspect that the suit was stolen from the store, but the man claims it is his. The officers ask the man to try the suit on. If, when he does so, the suit is narrowly tailored and fits him well, the officers are likely to accept the man's assertion that the suit belongs to him. If, on the other hand, the fit is poor, e.g., the cuffed pants are too long and the sleeves are too short, the fact that the suit is not narrowly tailored to its alleged owner tends to confirm the suspicion that it was designed for someone else.

The "fit" of a statutory classification is likewise described in terms of how well it is tailored to its asserted goal. If the measure covers persons or activities that are irrelevant in terms of the alleged goal, the classification is said to be overinclusive (i.e., too big). If, on the other hand, the statute does not apply to persons or activities one would expect it to cover, the classification is underinclusive in relation to its goal (i.e., too small). Some laws are both overinclusive and underinclusive in terms of their underlying goals. If it would have been relatively easy to draft the measure so that it was more closely tailored to the alleged goal, the fact that the fit is so poor strongly suggests that the measure was really designed with some other purpose in mind.

The Court sometimes describes the strict scrutiny equal protection test in terms of whether there is a less discriminatory alternative available for attaining the government's asserted purposes. By "less discriminatory," the Court means alternatives that are not as overinclusive or underinclusive as the means chosen by the government and that will, therefore, accomplish the state's goal with less of a disproportionate impact on the affected group. If such less discriminatory alternatives exist, then under strict scrutiny, the government must use them rather than the poorly tailored measure it has adopted.

EXAMPLE 6-J

A state law requires that hospital emergency room personnel have been born in the United States. This law creates a suspect classification on the basis of national origin. It was challenged by Carlos, a naturalized U.S. citizen who was born in Mexico and who, because of the law, was refused a job in a local emergency room. The state has defended the law on the ground that it furthers a compelling interest in health and safety by assuring that emergency room personnel speak and understand English well enough to communicate perfectly with patients and medical staff. If the court accepts this interest as being compelling, will the law survive Carlos's equal protection challenge?

EXPLANATION

Under the "narrowly tailored" prong of the strict scrutiny test, this law must "fit" its alleged health and safety purpose better than any feasible alternative. The law is overinclusive in relation to its goal, for it applies to persons of foreign origin who speak and understand English perfectly. The law is also underinclusive, since it apparently allows anyone born in the United States to work in an emergency room even if their English is poor. If the state was really concerned about English fluency in hospitals, it could have achieved its goal as well or better by requiring all prospective employees to pass an English proficiency exam before they can be hired to work in an emergency room. The facts that the law is so poorly tailored to its alleged goal and that a less discriminatory alternative is available strongly suggest that the asserted health goal is a sham and that the law's real purpose is simply to burden people of foreign origin on the basis of prejudice or dislike. This law would, therefore, be found to violate the Equal Protection Clause.

As this example suggests, the second prong of the strict scrutiny equal protection analysis ultimately serves the same purpose as the first prong. Both are designed to ascertain whether or not the government was discriminating for an illicit purpose. Speaking in the context of race-based classifications, the Court has thus observed that "the purpose of strict scrutiny is to 'smoke out' illegitimate uses of race by assuring that the legislative body is pursuing a goal important enough to warrant use of a highly suspect tool. The test also ensures that the means chosen 'fit' this compelling goal so closely that there is little or no possibility that the motive for the classification was illegitimate racial prejudice or stereotype." *City of Richmond v. J.A. Croson Co.,* 488 U.S. 469, 493 (1989).

We turn now to an examination of how the strict scrutiny standard has been applied to classifications that are suspect because they are based on race or alienage. In the next chapter, we will return to the strict scrutiny standard and look at its application in cases that involve discrimination tied to the exercise of a fundamental constitutional right.

§6.4.3   *Racial Segregation of Public Schools*

Brown v. Board of Education

In *Brown v. Board of Education,* 347 U.S. 483 (1954) (*Brown I*), the Court invoked the Fourteenth Amendment's Equal Protection Clause to strike down laws in Kansas, South Carolina, Virginia, and Delaware that required or permitted racial segregation of the public schools. Laws in each of these states provided for assignment of pupils to schools on the basis of race, with the result that most schools were largely all-black or all-white in composition.

Since *Brown I* is widely regarded as one of the first cases in which the modern Court applied strict scrutiny to a race-based classification, it is interesting that the Court did not actually apply the strict scrutiny test. There was no discussion of whether the states had a compelling interest in creating racially segregated schools or of whether the states' pupil assignment laws were narrowly tailored. These omissions are explained by the fact that the states never suggested that they had a legitimate, much less compelling, reason for segregating their public schools. Instead, the states in effect argued that the plaintiffs had failed to make out a prima facie case of racial discrimination. The intent element of the prima facie case was established by the fact that the statutes in each of the four states were racially discriminatory on their face. However, the states relied on the "separate but equal" doctrine of *Plessy v. Ferguson* (see §6.4.1) to deny the existence of any disproportionate impact on black children who were forced to attend all-black schools.

Though the Supreme Court in *Brown I* was asked to overrule *Plessy,* it stopped short of doing so. Instead, the Justices applied the "separate but equal" doctrine and concluded that "[s]eparate educational facilities are inherently unequal." 347 U.S. at 495. The Court agreed that "the Negro and white schools involved have been equalized . . . with respect to buildings, curricula, qualifications and salaries of teachers, and other 'tangible' factors." Id. at 492. Nevertheless, the education provided in segregated schools was inherently unequal to that offered in a racially integrated setting due to the negative psychological impact of forced segregation on black schoolchildren. "To separate them from others of similar age and qualifications solely because of their race generates a feeling of inferiority as to their status in the community that may affect their hearts and minds in a way unlikely ever to be undone." Id. at 494. This sense of inferiority, said the Court, impaired the quality of the educational experience by adversely affecting a black child's motivation to learn. For this reason, said the Court, "in the field of public education the doctrine of 'separate but equal' has no place." Id. at 495. Since the states did not attempt to justify their purposeful racial discrimination, the Court held that the discrimination violated the Equal Protection Clause of the Fourteenth Amendment. In *Bolling v. Sharpe*, 347 U.S. 497, 500 (1954), a companion case decided the same day as *Brown I*, the Court held that the Fifth Amendment likewise barred the federal government from segregating schools in the District of Columbia because this constituted "an arbitrary deprivation of . . . liberty in violation of the Due Process Clause."

The Court's opinion in *Brown I* at least implied that in settings other than public education, government-imposed racial segregation might not violate the Equal Protection Clause if it did not result in any measurable harm to racial minorities. Yet in a series of per curiam orders issued in the years following *Brown I*, the Court held that racial segregation of public facilities was unconstitutional even in settings where *Brown I*'s psychological impairment rationale was clearly inapplicable. These decisions — involving segregation of public beaches, bathhouses, golf courses, parks, municipal buses, athletics contests, and courtroom seating — made it clear that *Plessy*'s doctrine of separate but equal had been overruled sub silentio. Today, the Equal Protection Clause thus prohibits the government from mandating racial segregation of any public facilities.

Implementing *Brown*

It was initially unclear what duty *Brown I* imposed on school boards that had operated racially segregated schools. In a remedial decision handed down a year after *Brown I*, the Court suggested that the goal was "to achieve a system of determining admission to the public schools on a nonracial basis." *Brown v. Board of Educ.*, 349 U.S. 294, 300-301 (1955) (*Brown II*). Some states construed this command as one of "desegregation, not integration." Under this approach, it was enough for a state to cease forcing students to attend racially segregated schools; the state was under no duty to actually dismantle its dual system of schools and bring about a unitary, integrated school system. Under the "desegregation, not integration" approach, states adopted freedom-of-choice plans that let students decide which school they would attend. Not surprisingly, this scheme left many schools largely all-white or all-black. In *Green v. County School Board,* 391 U.S. 430, 436 (1968), decided 14 years after *Brown I,* the Court emphatically rejected the "desegregation, not integration" formula and held that "[t]he transition to a unitary, nonracial system of public education was and is the ultimate end to be brought about. . . ." School boards that had been guilty of operating racially segregated public schools were "charged with the affirmative duty to take whatever steps might be necessary to convert to a unitary system in which racial discrimination would be eliminated root and branch." Id. at 437-438.

Green identified six parts of a school system that a court must examine to determine whether a dual school system has been converted to unitary status. For a school district to be in full compliance with *Brown II,* each of these six aspects of the system must be free of racial discrimination. The first of the *Green* factors is the pattern of student attendance, i.e., the racial composition of each school. In *Swann v. Charlotte-Mecklenburg Board of Education,* 402 U.S. 1 (1971), the Court noted that the goal is to bring about a racial balance in every school that is roughly comparable to the racial composition of the school district as a whole. If, as in *Swann,* the district as a whole is 71 percent white and 29 percent black, each school in the district should ideally have a racial balance of 71 percent-29 percent; the Court warned, however, that such ratios should be used as targets, not as strict quotas. The five other *Green* factors are faculty allocation, staff allocation, student transportation, extracurricular activities, and physical facilities. Some courts have added an additional factor: the overall quality of education.

In order to implement the commands of *Brown I, Brown II,* and their progeny where a school district has been found to have engaged in de jure segregation, a federal court must fashion remedies that address all these components of a school system and assure that each component is no longer tainted by racial discrimination. The process of federal judicial supervision frequently lasts for decades and may encompass such court-ordered measures as redrawing school attendance zones, busing students to schools outside their neighborhoods, repairing buildings, reassigning and upgrading the quality of teachers and staff, equalizing extracurricular programs, closing schools, and constructing new schools. The Supreme Court has stressed that while the specific content of the desegregation remedy will necessarily vary from case to case, the "decree must be *remedial* in nature, that is, it must be designed as nearly as possible 'to restore the victims of discriminatory conduct to the position they would have occupied in the absence of such conduct.'" *Milliken v. Bradley,* 433 U.S. 267, 280 (1977).

It is important to remember that federal courts may intervene to redress violations of the Equal Protection Clause only if plaintiffs have first established a prima facie case by proving both intent and impact. These requirements were easily met in *Brown I* and many other early school desegregation cases because the intent to discriminate was clear from the face of state laws providing for racially segregated schools. It was more difficult for plaintiffs to make out a prima facie case in states outside the South, where there was often no statute requiring or authorizing segregation. In these cases, while discriminatory impact was established by showing that a district's schools were racially imbalanced, "the Constitution is not violated by racial imbalance in the schools, without more." Id. at 280 n.14. As was noted previously, proving purpose or intent to discriminate can be difficult. See §6.2.2.

§6.4.4   *Interdistrict Remedies*

Even where a de jure violation has been proved, there are limits on the remedies a federal court may impose. One of these limits concerns the geographic scope of a court's remedial order. The Supreme Court has repeatedly held that "the nature of the desegregation remedy is to be determined by the nature and scope of the constitutional violation." *Milliken v. Bradley*, 433 U.S. at 280. Metropolitan areas have frequently been divided by the state into dozens of independent school districts, each run by its own local school board. If an equal protection violation has been proved with respect to one district, this does not itself establish a violation on the part of adjacent or surrounding districts. In the absence of proof of an interdistrict violation, i.e., a violation that caused segregation in more than one district, a federal court's remedial orders must be limited to the district against which a constitutional violation has been proved. In other words, an intradistrict violation can be redressed only through an intradistrict remedy.

EXAMPLE 6-K

Adams County is divided into five school districts, each run by an independent school board. The public school population in the county as a whole is 80 percent white and 20 percent black. District 1 is 80 percent black and 20 percent white; Districts 2 through 5, located in the surrounding suburbs, are each 90 percent white and 10 percent black. A suit was filed in federal court against the District 1 board, alleging that as a result of the board's purposeful acts, most children in District 1 attend one-race schools. If the judge orders District 1's board to integrate the schools there, each school will still be 80 percent black. May the court add the other four school boards as defendants and then order an interdistrict remedy that will result in each school being approximately 80 percent white and 20 percent black?

EXPLANATION

Even if the other boards are added to the suit, the scope of the remedy is limited by the scope of the proven violation. Unless the plaintiffs show that a constitutional violation caused segregation between these adjoining districts, the court cannot order an interdistrict remedy and must confine its relief to District 1. See *Milliken v. Bradley*, 418 U.S. 717 (1974).

Proving an Interdistrict Violation

Plaintiffs may be able to prove an interdistrict violation in several ways. One approach is to show that the state, an adjacent school district, or some other governmental body was guilty of purposeful discriminatory acts that had interdistrict effects. However, in proving the element of discriminatory purpose, plaintiffs cannot use the *Keyes* presumption to transfer intent between different governmental actors. Just because one school board was guilty of purposeful racial discrimination does not make it reasonable to infer that the actions of other entities were also animated by segregative intent. Instead, plaintiffs must independently prove the element of intent as to each separate governmental body.

EXAMPLE 6-L

In Example 6-K, how else might the plaintiffs prove an interdistrict violation?

EXPLANATION

The plaintiffs might prove such a violation if they could show that the state drew or redrew the school district lines for Districts 1-5 with a purpose of segregating the schools. Or plaintiffs might be able to show that the state, for segregative reasons, allowed white children living in District 1 to attend schools in the surrounding suburbs even though students are usually required to enroll in their own district. An interdistrict violation might also exist if the state or an adjacent suburb adopted racially discriminatory housing policies that encouraged whites to move from District 1 to the suburbs, while at the same time making it difficult for racial minorities to do so. Proof of an interdistrict violation by any of these means would allow a federal court to fashion an interdistrict remedy that could require busing of students across district boundary lines.

In each of the prior examples, an interdistrict violation was established by showing that a governmental actor in addition to the targeted school district engaged in purposeful discriminatory conduct. An interdistrict violation may also be proved where the unconstitutional actions of the targeted district itself had segregative effects in other school districts. However, it must be shown that any such interdistrict effects were "significant" and "directly caused" by the constitutional violation.

EXAMPLE 6-M

In Example 6-L, suppose that the plaintiffs could show that the District 1 school board decided to reduce funding for all schools in the district on account of the fact that the district was heavily minority in composition. As a result, many white families fled to adjacent suburbs, where the schools were better funded. Might this suffice to prove an interdistrict violation?

EXPLANATION

Perhaps. The District 1 board's racially motivated funding decision arguably had significant and direct segregative effects between school districts, for the "white flight" caused by the board's action exacerbated the racial imbalance existing between District 1 and the surrounding suburban districts. This interdistrict violation would allow a federal court to impose an interdistrict remedy that might include busing students across district lines.

These examples of how plaintiffs may establish an interdistrict violation might make it appear simple for a federal court to order interdistrict relief. In reality, plaintiffs are seldom able to make the showing necessary for a court to impose desegregation remedies that cross school district lines.

Responding to White Flight

In the absence of proof of an interdistrict violation, a federal court may encounter severe difficulties in dealing with white flight. The term *white flight* refers to the process by which white families remove their children from a public school. Either the children are sent to a private school, or the family moves to a surrounding district where the public schools are predominately white. The Supreme Court has recognized that "implementation of a deseg-regation remedy may result in 'white flight.'" *Missouri v. Jenkins,* 515 U.S. 70, 95 n.8 (1995). White parents, who were content to have their children attend segregated neighborhood schools, may balk either at integration or at the forced busing that it often entails. Because of white flight, judicial efforts to integrate the public schools may be self-defeating, for the composition of the district may become so heavily minority that any significant degree of integration is impossible.

A dramatic example of white flight was documented by the Court in

Missouri v. Jenkins, involving the Kansas City, Missouri, School District (KCMSD). Until 1954, Missouri mandated racial segregation in its public schools; at that time, 18.9 percent of KCMSD's students were black. After *Brown I* was decided in 1954, the state stopped enforcing its school segregation laws; in 1977, the federal court initiated a plan to integrate KCMSD's schools. Between 1954 and 1985, the percentage of KCMSD's students who were black increased steadily, as follows: 1961-1962: 30 percent black; 1965: 40 percent black; 1975-1976: 60 percent black; 1985-1986: 68.3 percent black. While the overall enrollment in the district declined once the integration plan was adopted, white enrollment declined at a much faster rate than that for blacks. Id. at 76, 94 n.6. By 1985, even if every school in the KCMSD were fully integrated, blacks would comprise more than two-thirds of the students at each school.

Where white flight results from a court's attempt to integrate an urban school district, this does not create an interdistrict violation that would allow the court to include in its remedial decree the surrounding districts to which the white students have fled. The Supreme Court has held such white flight is a consequence of "desegregation, not de jure segregation." Id. at 95. In other words, the interdistrict segregative effects caused by such white flight cannot serve as the basis for an interdistrict remedy. This does not prevent plaintiffs from trying to prove a direct causal link in some other manner (see Example 6-M), but such proof will ordinarily be difficult.

In response to the threat of white flight, federal courts may be reluctant to push remedies like mandatory busing beyond a certain point even if this means settling for a less than optimal racial balance in some schools. Rather than impose remedies that are likely to be self-defeating, courts have increasingly ordered school districts to adopt programs that are designed both to keep white children from leaving the public schools and to draw them out of private schools back into the public system. One common program of this type involves the use of magnet schools, which offer high quality, distinctive curricula that are frequently superior to anything found even in the private sector.

Yet in ordering a school district to adopt programs that are designed to retain and attract white students, a federal court must be careful that its decree does not go beyond what is necessary to remedy the proven constitutional violation. If the court requires a district to adopt programs designed to attract nonminority students *from surrounding school districts* to which they may have fled, the court is in effect imposing an interdistrict remedy that is invalid unless there was a proven interdistrict violation.

EXAMPLE 6-N

The Central City School District is 32 percent white. Before integration efforts began five years ago, the district was 80 percent white. This decline was largely the result of white flight to the suburbs and enrollment in private schools within the city. The only constitutional violation proved was confined to the city itself. To remedy this intradistrict violation, the federal court has ordered the city to develop a program of magnet schools designed in part to attract white students from the suburban districts to the Central City public schools. Is the remedial decree valid?

EXPLANATION

To the extent that the program's purpose is to draw students back into the city from adjacent school districts, it involves the pursuit of an *interdistrict goal* that is beyond the scope of the *intradistrict violation* being remedied. Since the district court could not have directly mandated the interdistrict transfer of students, it may not accomplish the same goal indirectly. On the other hand, the magnet school program would be valid to the extent that it can be justified by the need to limit any further withdrawal of white students and/or by the desire to draw white students out of private schools located within the district. See *Missouri v. Jenkins*, 515 U.S. 70 (1995).

§6.4.5 *Remedying Segregation at the College Level*

If a state is found to have racially segregated its public colleges or universities, the remedies available to a court will differ from those usually applied to elementary and secondary schools. At the elementary and secondary level, one of the primary goals in remedying racial segregation is to achieve a racial balance in each school that roughly matches the makeup of the district as a whole. The objective, in other words, is to racially *integrate* a district's schools, not merely to cease segregating them. At the college level, such a goal is impracticable for several reasons. First, a state's colleges are usually geographically dispersed throughout the state. To insist that each college or university be racially balanced would mean that students might be forced to attend a school hundreds of miles—rather than just a few miles—from their homes, a requirement that would be economically prohibitive for many.

In addition, unlike most elementary and secondary schools, a state's colleges usually are not fungible or the functional equivalent of one another. Each college may have unique goals, programs, course offerings, and faculty expertise. To force a student to attend a college other than one of her choice would significantly interfere with an individual's ability to shape her education. While the latter problem might be solved by making the state's colleges and universities essentially identical, this could severely constrict the breadth of the state's educational offerings by forcing the state to jettison programs that could not feasibly be provided at every school.

For these reasons, if a federal court finds that a state has deliberately maintained a racially segregated system of colleges or universities, the court cannot simply order the state to integrate these schools, as it would require at the elementary or secondary level. However, the federal court may compel the state to abandon any policies, practices, or requirements that meet the following four conditions:

1. The policy was part of or is traceable to the prior de jure system;
2. The policy continues to have segregative effects, such as influencing student enrollment decisions in a racially discriminatory way;
3. The policy lacks a sound educational justification; and
4. The policy can practicably be eliminated.

If the plaintiff carries the burden of establishing that the first two conditions are met as to a particular policy, the policy must be eliminated unless the state demonstrates that the policy is supported by a sound educational justification or that it cannot practicably be eliminated.

EXAMPLE 6-O

A state operates four colleges—two in the north (N-1 and N-2) and two in the south (S-1 and S-2). The state was found to have purposefully segregated these colleges on the basis of race, so that N-1 and S-1 were primarily white institutions, while N-2 and S-2 were historically black colleges. To be admitted to N-1 or S-1, a student had to score at least 15 on the ACT college admission test; about 70 percent of white applicants met this requirement as compared with 30 percent of blacks. On the other hand, to be admitted to N-2 or S-2, a student needed an ACT score of only 13 or higher. N-1 and N-2 duplicate many courses and programs; the same is true of S-1 and S-2. The combined student population at all four colleges is 60 percent white and 40 percent black. What may a federal court do to remedy the state's racial discrimination?

EXPLANATION

While the court cannot order the state to achieve a 60 percent-40 percent racial balance at each college, it can insist on the elimination of many policies that support the present segregated scheme. For example, the use of a higher minimum ACT score for admission to N-1 and S-1 than for admission to N-2 and S-2 might have to be abandoned, for the policy has a clear segregative effect, may lack a sound educational justification, and could practicably be eliminated. Indeed, the state might have to abandon rigid adherence to even a uniform ACT minimum score if it were shown that a more flexible formula that takes into account a student's high school grades would serve the state's legitimate admissions goals.

The state might also have to end any unnecessary duplication of programs and courses between N-1 and N-2 and between S-1 and S-2.

Unnecessary duplication has a racially segregative effect, for if students in the northern part of the state could pursue a particular program only at N-1 or N-2, but not both, students of all races who wished to take that program would end up attending the same school. Therefore, unless the state can offer a sound educational justification for such duplication, the practice would have to be eliminated. See *United States v. Fordice*, 505 U.S. 717 (1992).

§6.4.6   *Other Limitations on Desegregation Orders*

Minimizing the Degree of Federal Interference

When federal courts use their equitable powers to impose remedies in desegregation cases, they "must take into account the interests of state and local authorities in managing their own affairs, consistent with the Constitution." *Milliken v. Bradley*, 433 U.S. at 280-281. This principle, which reflects notions of comity and federalism, dictates that federal courts exercise their authority in a manner that avoids unnecessary interference with or intrusion on state and local governmental functions.

EXAMPLE 6-P

In Example 6-N, assume that the federal district court ordered the Central City School District to develop a program of magnet schools aimed at keeping students in the city's public schools and at drawing students who live in the city into the public system from private schools. The cost of this program is estimated to be $10 million. The Central City School District receives most of its operating expenses from a property tax that it is authorized to impose under state law. However, the state constitution prohibits the district from raising this tax by an amount sufficient to pay for the desegregation program. May the federal court order an increase in the local property tax?

EXPLANATION

The court must use the least intrusive form of relief that will effectively achieve its remedial goal. For a federal court itself to impose a state tax is a drastic and, in this case, unnecessary interference with local governmental authority. The court can achieve the same end by ordering the school district to raise the property tax by the requisite amount and by enjoining operation of the state constitutional provision that would otherwise bar the district from exercising this power. See *Missouri v. Jenkins*, 495 U.S. 33 (1990).

The same principle applies to a federal court's exercise of its contempt power in enforcing desegregation orders against recalcitrant state or local officials. While the contempt power may be used for these purposes in the desegregation context, the court must proceed cautiously, exercising "[t]he least possible power adequate to the end proposed." *Anderson v. Dunn,* 19 U.S. (6 Wheat.) 204, 231 (1821).

EXAMPLE 6-Q

In the preceding example, assume that the Central City School Board, which runs the school district, refused to comply with the federal court's order that it increase the local property tax. After warning the district that failure to comply would result in the imposition of contempt sanctions, the court issued an order providing that if the school board did not vote to raise the property tax before September 1, individual board members would be imprisoned by the U.S. marshal and fined $500 a day for each day of noncompliance. Is this order valid?

EXPLANATION

The order is probably invalid because it is more intrusive than necessary to secure compliance with the desegregation order. Before threatening individual board members with imprisonment and fines, the court could first have tried imposing fines on the school district itself. If this failed to produce compliance within a reasonable time, it might then have been appropriate for the court to increase the pressure by proceeding against the board members individually. See *Spallone v. United States,* 493 U.S. 265 (1990).

Duration of Federal Desegregation Orders

The goal of federal judicial intervention in desegregation cases is to remedy the constitutional violation to the extent practicable and then to "restore state and local authorities to the control of a school system that is operating in compliance with the Constitution." *Freeman v. Pitts,* 503 U.S. 467, 489 (1992). Federal oversight is "intended as a temporary measure to remedy past discrimination." *Board of Educ. v. Dowell,* 498 U.S. 237, 247 (1991). The Court has stressed that "[r]eturning schools to the control of local authorities at the earliest practicable date is essential to restore their true accountability in our governmental system." *Freeman v. Pitts,* 503 U.S. at 490. As a practical matter, the period of federal judicial tutelage may last for decades as the court seeks to eliminate the vestiges of past discrimination in all aspects of the school system. Yet a district that has complied in good faith with the court's decree is eventually entitled to partial or complete relief from further federal supervision.

The proper duration of a federal desegregation decree is closely tied to the legitimate scope of that decree. A federal court may retain jurisdiction over a school district solely for the purpose of assuring that "the vestiges of past discrimination [have] been eliminated to the extent practicable." Id. at 492. The court may not continue to exercise supervisory authority in order to redress problems that are "not traceable, in a proximate way, to the prior violation." Id. at 494. For example, a federal court may not maintain control over a school district with the goal of bringing the quality of the educational program up to national norms in all grade levels unless these deficiencies are clearly attributable to a past constitutional violation. See *Missouri v. Jenkins,* 515 U.S. 70 (1995).

Even if a particular problem being addressed by a federal decree was at one time traceable to prior de jure segregation, the passage of time may have eliminated any causal link between current conditions and the constitutional violation, in which case the condition is no longer one the federal court can insist on rectifying. Instead, the court may well have to relinquish jurisdiction, at least with respect to that particular area of school operations.

EXAMPLE 6-R

Fifteen years ago a federal court ruled that the Dixon School Board had segregated the district's schools. In its desegregation decree, the court ordered the board to achieve an approximate racial balance of 65 percent white and 35 percent black at each school, matching the composition of the district as a whole. The board achieved compliance with this decree ten years ago by adjusting attendance zones, creating magnet schools, and adopting a busing plan. In the past few years, however, four schools in the southern part of the district have become more than 80 percent black, though the district as a whole remains 65 percent white and 35 percent black. The plaintiffs seek an order requiring the board to remedy the racial imbalance in these four schools. May the court order this relief?

EXPLANATION

The federal court may redress this condition only if it is in fact a vestige of the prior de jure system. If the board can show that the current racial imbalance in the four schools is not traceable to past segregation, but is instead a result of demographic shifts in population, the racial imbalance would be beyond the court's remedial powers. Not only would the court lack authority to redress this problem, but the board might also be entitled to have the court relinquish remedial control over the student assignment facet of the school system or even have the entire desegregation case finally dismissed. See *Freeman v. Pitts*, 503 U.S. 467 (1992); *Pasadena City Bd. of Educ. v. Spangler*, 427 U.S. 424 (1976).

In the previous example, if the federal court terminated its jurisdiction over the Dixon School Board, releasing the board from the desegregation plan, the board would be free to make any operational changes it wished without needing authorization from a federal court. Such changes might entail dismantling the busing program or closing the magnet schools, programs that had been critical to maintaining an integrated system. While these changes may well produce new racial imbalance in the district's schools, the board's action would violate the Constitution only if the plaintiffs could establish a new prima facie case of de jure segregation. In proving a prima facie case, the plaintiffs could invoke the *Keyes* presumption to establish discriminatory intent on the basis of the board's earlier de jure violation. However, the board might rebut this presumption by noting that it acted in good faith for many years since the past violation occurred, or by demonstrating that the program changes were made for budgetary or other reasons that had nothing to do with race. Thus, once a federal court relinquishes control over a school district, as it must at some point, there remains "the potential for discrimination and racial hostility . . . and its manifestations may emerge in new and subtle forms after the effects of de jure segregation have been eliminated." *Freeman v. Pitts*, 503 U.S. at 490. Yet this danger does not justify a federal court's retaining perpetual jurisdiction over a school district simply because the district once violated the Constitution.

A federal desegregation decree usually covers a number of different facets of a school system, as identified by the *Green* factors. The court may order a partial withdrawal of its supervision in those areas where a school district has achieved compliance with the court's desegregation plan, even though other areas have not yet been brought into compliance. In *Freeman v. Pitts*, 503 U.S. at 491, the Court held that such an incremental relinquishment of jurisdiction is permissible if three requirements are satisfied:

1. There has been full and satisfactory compliance with the desegregation decree in those aspects of the school system where supervision is to be withdrawn;
2. Retaining control is not necessary or practicable to achieve compliance in other facets of the school system; and
3. The school district has shown its good-faith commitment to the entire desegregation plan for a reasonable period of time.

EXAMPLE 6-S

In Example 6-R, assume that the Dixon School Board has moved the court to relinquish control over student assignment policies on the ground that the board has achieved full compliance with this component of the desegregation plan. Two other facets of the system — achieving racial balance in teacher allocation and upgrading athletic facilities at two formerly black schools — are not yet in full compliance, though considerable progress has been made in these areas. May the court grant the motion to partially withdraw supervision?

EXPLANATION

The court could probably grant the motion to relinquish control over the assignment of students to schools. First, if the current racial imbalance in the four schools in the south end of the district was caused by demographic shifts and is not traceable to the prior constitutional violation, the board remains in full compliance with the aspect of the court's decree requiring racial balance in student assignments. Second, it appears that withdrawing control over student assignment policies will not impair the court's ability to secure compliance in the two other areas dealing with teacher assignments and athletic facilities. Third, since the board reached compliance in the area of student assignments ten years ago, if the court is satisfied that the board has demonstrated a genuine commitment to the principle of racial equality in its efforts to comply with other aspects of the desegregation plan, partial withdrawal of control would be appropriate. On the other hand, if the board's efforts in the two remaining areas have been halting or lackluster, casting doubt on its good-faith commitment to integration, the court should not relinquish even partial control until the board has attained full compliance with all aspects of the court's decree for a reasonable period of time.

§6.4.7 *Affirmative Action*

In the school desegregation cases that we have been discussing, the defendant never seriously contended that its actions might pass muster under a strict scrutiny equal protection analysis. Rather, the only issues that typically arose were whether the plaintiffs had established a prima facie case of de jure discrimination and whether the remedy imposed for a de jure violation was appropriate. However, in cases involving affirmative action or benign discrimination, the government usually defends its use of a race-based classification on the ground that because it is seeking to assist rather than harm racial minorities, the discrimination should be upheld as constitutional. In examining the Court's approach to affirmative action, we will focus on three issues: (1) what is the appropriate standard of review; (2) what constitutes a compelling interest; and (3) when is a classification narrowly tailored.

Strict Scrutiny for Affirmative Action

In *City of Richmond v. J.A. Croson Co.*, 488 U.S. 469 (1989), the Supreme Court held that all laws that discriminate on the basis of race are subject to strict scrutiny under the Equal Protection Clause, including laws that discriminate against whites. *Croson* resolved a debate that had been simmering in the Court for more than a decade. In *Regents of the University of California v. Bakke*, 438 U.S. 265 (1978), Justice Brennan and three of his colleagues had urged that since whites are not a "discrete and insular minority" needing special protection from the majoritarian political process, only intermediate scrutiny should be applied to laws that discriminate against whites for benign purposes. Id. at 288. Justice Powell, on the other hand, had argued that strict scrutiny is required in all race discrimination cases, since the guarantee of equal protection is a personal right that "cannot mean one thing when applied to one individual and something else when applied to a person of another color." Id. at 289-290. In *Croson*, a majority of the Court adopted the position staked out by Justice Powell in *Bakke*. The *Croson* majority noted that strict scrutiny is necessary to assure that allegedly benign classifications are not "in fact motivated by illegitimate notions of racial inferiority or simple racial politics" and to assure that they do not inflict "stigmatic harm" on those they are intended to benefit. 488 U.S. at 493. Applying strict scrutiny, *Croson* struck down a Richmond, Virginia, plan that required prime contractors awarded city construction contracts to subcontract at least 30 percent of the work to minority business enterprises (MBEs).

Croson's strict scrutiny principle was limited to affirmative action undertaken by state and local governments. In an earlier case, *Fullilove v. Klutznick*, 448 U.S. 448 (1980), the Court had applied a more relaxed standard of review in upholding a similar MBE set-aside program adopted by Congress. In *Metro Broadcasting, Inc. v. FCC*, 497 U.S. 547 (1990), decided a year after *Croson*, the Court again rejected the use of strict scrutiny for "benign race-conscious measures mandated by Congress" and ruled that such measures should be tested under the less-searching intermediate standard of review employed for gender discrimination. The Court defended its use of different standards of review under the Fifth and Fourteenth Amendments on the ground that Congress, as a coequal branch, was deserving of special deference from the federal courts. Id. at 563-566.

Metro Broadcasting proved short-lived. The decision was overruled in *Adarand Constructors, Inc. v. Pena*, 515 U.S. 200 (1995), which held that principles of "skepticism," "consistency," and "congruence" were violated by relaxing the standard of review for race-based affirmative action programs adopted by Congress when all other racial classifications are subject to strict scrutiny. Instead, said the Court, all racial classifications must be viewed skeptically; there should be consistency in the standard of review regardless of which race is burdened; and there should be congruence between the equal protection analyses employed under the Fifth and Fourteenth Amendments. *Adarand* restored these principles by holding that "all racial classifications, imposed by whatever federal, state, or local governmental actor, must be analyzed by a reviewing court under strict scrutiny. In other words, such classifications are constitutional only if they are narrowly tailored measures that further compelling governmental interests." Id. at 227. However, the Court sought "to dispel the notion that strict scrutiny is 'strict in theory, but fatal in fact.' . . . When race-based action is necessary to further a compelling interest, such action is within constitutional constraints if it satisfies the 'narrow tailoring' test this Court has set out in previous cases." Id. at 237. Yet this is an extraordinarily difficult standard to meet, even in the context of affirmative action.

Compelling Interests

In most instances of affirmative action, the government's goal is compensatory in nature; i.e., the government is taking positive steps to remedy or make up for wrongs that were perpetrated against racial minorities in the past. In some affirmative action cases, however, the goal may be something other than remedial, such as achieving racial diversity in the schools or among the nation's radio broadcasters. Justice Powell, who in *Bakke* applied strict scrutiny to overturn a medical school's special admissions program, suggested that a variety of interests might suffice to justify affirmative action, including eliminating the effects of past discrimination or attaining a diverse student body. Powell did not seem to envision a closed universe of compelling interests; instead, whether or not a particular goal was compelling would depend on the facts of the specific case.

The Supreme Court in recent years has taken a narrower view of what interests are sufficient to justify affirmative action. The Court has acknowledged that remedying the present effects of identified past discrimination qualifies as a compelling interest. However, it may be that this is the only governmental interest that a majority of the Court will find adequate to uphold a race-based classification. See *City of Richmond v. J.A. Croson Co.*, 488 U.S. at 511 (Stevens, J., concurring). If this is true, the goal of attaining a diverse student body, recognized by Justice Powell as compelling in *Bakke*, would no longer suffice to allow schools to take race into account in their admissions process. See *Hopwood v. Texas*, 78 F.3d 932 (5th Cir.), *cert. denied*, 518 U.S. 1033 (1996) (invalidating the use of racial preferences in the University of Texas School of Law admissions process). The remainder of this section will focus on how the strict scrutiny standard is applied when the government claims that it has a compelling interest in remedying past discrimination. At the same time, bear in mind that other nonremedial governmental interests may possibly qualify as being compelling as well.

Two basic requirements must be met before the Court will accept the government's claim that a racial classification was adopted for a benign remedial purpose:

1. The classification must seek to rectify the effects of identified racial discrimination within the entity's regulatory jurisdiction. The discrimination may have been that of the entity itself or of private parties subject to its authority. Thus, a city council may be entitled under state law to adopt ordinances that bar racial discrimination both by city government and by individuals and businesses within the city. However, "an effort to alleviate the effects of [past] *societal* discrimination is not a compelling interest," as this is too amorphous a basis for employing a racial classification. *Shaw v. Hunt,* 517 U.S. 899, 909-910 (1996) (emphasis supplied).

2. The entity adopting the remedial scheme must have a "'strong basis in evidence' to conclude that remedial action was necessary, '*before* it embarks on an affirmative action program.'" Id. In other words, prior to adopting the remedial scheme, the entity must have gathered evidence that factually demonstrates "a prima facie case of a constitutional or statutory violation" that needs to be redressed. *City of Richmond v. J.A. Croson Co.,* 488 U.S. at 500.

Unless each of these requirements is satisfied, the Court will find that the government did not have a compelling interest in remedying the effects of past discrimination.

EXAMPLE 6-T

The faculty of Baxter State College adopted an affirmative action plan for faculty hiring after finding that racial minorities were severely underrepresented on the college staff. Under the plan, every other faculty member hired must be black or Latino until the percentages of blacks and Latinos on the Baxter faculty reach the percentages these groups occupy in the state's population. The faculty adopted the plan after a U.S. Justice Department study found that the nation's colleges and universities had a long history of racial discrimination in faculty recruitment. Mary was turned down for a job in Baxter's history department because she is white. She has sued the college, claiming a violation of the Equal Protection Clause. Can Baxter establish that its action was warranted by a compelling interest in remedying past discrimination?

EXPLANATION

The college probably cannot prove that it had a compelling interest in adopting the affirmative action plan. As to the first requirement, even if Baxter was guilty of past racial discrimination in faculty hiring, it is doubtful that state law gives the college faculty, as opposed to the college's board of trustees or other governing body, the legal authority to adopt such a hiring plan.

The second requirement might not be met for several reasons. The fact that there are few minority faculty at Baxter does not by itself establish a constitutional violation; proof of discriminatory intent would also be needed. In short, Baxter must make findings establishing a prima facie case that it had violated the Equal Protection Clause *before* adopting the plan. Instead, the faculty seems to have relied solely on a federal study that probably did not address the specific conduct of Baxter State College. Even if many or most of the nation's colleges engaged in illegal discrimination, this does not establish that Baxter did so. On the other hand, if the faculty had first gathered evidence of Baxter's past illegal discrimination in faculty hiring, the second requirement would presumably be met.

Narrowly Tailored

Even if the government demonstrates that its affirmative action plan is justified by a compelling interest in remedying the effects of past discrimination, the plan will be invalidated unless the government also shows that the racially discriminatory scheme is narrowly tailored and necessary to achieve the government's remedial goal. There are two aspects to the narrowly tailored requirement: (1) The government must demonstrate that the race-conscious remedy was adopted as a last resort after all race-neutral remedies were examined and found inadequate, and (2) the use of race must be no more extensive than necessary.

As to the first requirement, the Court has emphasized that the proper remedy for past racial discrimination is ordinarily to take appropriate measures against those guilty of discriminating and/or to provide relief to the specific victims of that discrimination. These steps and any other race-neutral remedies that may fit a particular case must have been explored and found wanting before the government may choose a remedy that classifies on the basis of race. Otherwise, the use of affirmative action has not been shown to be *necessary* to achieving the government's remedial goal.

EXAMPLE 6-U

In Example 6-T, suppose that Baxter College met the compelling interest part of the strict scrutiny test through evidentiary findings that it was guilty of past racial discrimination in faculty hiring. Will the college be able to satisfy the first part of the narrowly tailored requirement?

EXPLANATION

The college's use of a race-based affirmative action plan will be constitutional only if there is evidence that the college considered and for good reason rejected any seemingly viable race-neutral means of remedying the effects of its past misconduct.

There are several race-neutral remedies that might have achieved the state's remedial goal instead of the race-based affirmative action hiring plan adopted by the faculty. First, the state or the college might have punished or otherwise sanctioned those faculty and staff who engaged in acts of racial discrimination and warned that similar action will be taken in the future against anyone who engages in similar acts. Second, the state or the college might have sought to identify all applicants who were rejected because of their race and offered them jobs and/or paid them damages. Third, the college might have tried to hire more minority faculty by recruiting at universities that have a significant number of minority graduates. Unlike the faculty's affirmative action hiring plan, none of these alternatives employs a racial classification. The college would have to show that it had considered these and any other race-neutral options a court might think of and demonstrate why they were rejected as inadequate. This would be a difficult showing to make.

Even if a race-conscious remedy is justified by the lack of adequate race-neutral alternatives, the remedy must also be narrowly tailored in the way it employs race. In other words, the race-based remedy must not be overinclusive in terms of its duration or its scope. The scheme must be temporary, lasting no longer than the discriminatory effects it seeks to eliminate. In addition, any numerical set-asides or goals contained in the plan must be reasonable. The remedy must be confined to those racial groups that were victims of past discrimination, rather than randomly including all racial minority groups. The plan must be designed so that it does not stigmatize those it seeks to help. In addition, the remedy must be applied flexibly; this may require including a waiver for situations where rigid adherence to the plan would prove harsh or unreasonable. It may also be necessary to provide an opportunity for individualized determinations as to whether specific beneficiaries have suffered from the effects of past discrimination.

EXAMPLE 6-V

In Example 6-U, if Baxter College shows that there are no race-neutral means of adequately remedying the effects of its past discrimination in faculty hiring, will its race-conscious plan satisfy the second part of the narrowly tailored requirement?

EXPLANATION

For this requirement to be met, the college must demonstrate that the plan's use of race is narrowly tailored to the remedial goal. While the plan is temporary, it may still be excessive because it is tied to achieving percentages of blacks and Latinos equal to their representation in the state's total population. Where, as here, special qualifications are required for a job, the relevant statistical pool is those who are qualified to take the job — in this case, college graduates or perhaps those with Ph.D.s. The percentages of blacks and Latinos may be much lower in these two pools than in the state's population as a whole. Thus, the plan's duration and percentage goals may not be narrowly tailored because they are tied to achieving a higher representation of blacks and Latinos than is necessary to redress the effects of past discrimination.

The plan may also fail because it includes both blacks and Latinos; if the college previously discriminated against only one of these groups, the plan is overinclusive by including the other.

The plan may be too rigid to pass muster. It in effect sets aside 50 percent of all new teaching jobs for racial minorities. While this number may not be excessive since it is temporary, there appears to be no waiver provision for situations in which there are no qualified minority applicants. Nor does there seem to be a procedure for making individualized determinations that would weed out minority applicants who were in no way harmed by any past discrimination.

The program may also stigmatize minority teachers if it does not hold them to the same hiring qualifications required of nonminority applicants; if this is the case, a black or Latino teacher at Baxter State College may be judged by others to be inferior because he or she was hired under less rigorous standards. For any or all of these reasons, the college's affirmative action faculty hiring plan may not be narrowly tailored.

So far we have been considering the remedial use of race by governmental entities and actors other than courts. It appears, however, that the Supreme Court will be equally demanding in its scrutiny of race-based remedies that are imposed by state or lower federal courts. The compelling interest component of strict scrutiny is presumably satisfied in such a case by the court's evidentiary findings of a constitutional or federal statutory violation. The problem may arise as to whether the remedy is narrowly tailored, including the requirement that the lower court have first explored every potential race-neutral alternative before ordering the race-conscious remedy. Even prior to the 1995 decision in *Adarand,* the Court in a number of cases subjected lower federal court orders in race discrimination cases to very searching review. *Adarand,* in rejecting the notion that Congress as a coequal branch is entitled to special leeway when using race for remedial purposes, made it clear that "*all* racial classifications, *imposed by whatever federal, state, or local governmental actor,* must be analyzed by a reviewing court under strict scrutiny." *Adarand Constructors, Inc. v. Pena,* 515 U.S. at 227 (emphasis supplied). This language is so all-embracing as to seemingly cover the actions of state and lower federal court judges. Thus, outside of well-established settings such as school desegregation, it may become increasingly rare that federal courts are permitted to order race-conscious remedies even in cases of proven past racial discrimination.

§6.5   Classification on the Basis of Alienage

§6.5.1   *The Standard for State and Local Laws*

The Reason for Strict Scrutiny

State and local laws that discriminate on the basis of alienage are, like laws based on race or nationality, generally deemed to involve a suspect classification and are thus subject to strict scrutiny. The Court has long recognized that the Fourteenth Amendment protects all persons who are within the jurisdiction of the United States, citizens as well as aliens. Most classifications based on alienage are suspect for many of the same reasons that strict scrutiny applies to laws that discriminate on the basis of race or national origin (see §6.4.1). As "foreigners," aliens are often the objects of first- and second-degree prejudice. And though alienage is not an immutable condition since aliens may become naturalized citizens, the condition is mutable in only one direction; legislators will, therefore, not be restrained from placing special burdens on aliens by the possibility that they might one day find themselves in the same category. Moreover, aliens are totally excluded from the political process since they are not allowed to vote in either state or national elections.

There is a further reason for subjecting state laws that discriminate against aliens to strict judicial scrutiny, namely, to prevent states from interfering with the national government's exclusive authority to regulate the terms and conditions on which aliens are admitted to the United States. If states were free to discriminate against aliens subject only to rational basis review from the courts, states could make the lives of aliens so difficult as to in effect nullify the federal government's decision giving these individuals permission to live in the United States. The Court has thus recognized that aliens lawfully admitted to the United States "have a right to enter and abide in any State in the Union 'on an equality of legal privileges with all citizens under non-discriminatory state laws.'" *Graham v. Richardson*, 403 U.S. 365, 378 (1971).

EXAMPLE 6-W

Paul is a French citizen who was admitted to the United States on a student visa. He attends Baxter State College and plans to return to France after receiving his degree. A state law denies student financial aid to aliens unless they intend to become U.S. citizens. Because Paul has no such intention, the state denied him a scholarship. The state defended the measure on the grounds that it encourages aliens to become citizens, promotes the goal of educating those who are or will become members of the electorate, and limits scarce resources to citizens. Has the state violated Paul's constitutional right to equal protection?

EXPLANATION

The law is most likely unconstitutional. It discriminates on the basis of alienage even though it denies financial aid to some, but not all, aliens; what is critical is that the law is directed at aliens, and only aliens are harmed by it. The measure is, therefore, subject to strict scrutiny. The goal of encouraging aliens to become citizens is probably not a valid *state* goal, since the federal government possesses exclusive authority over immigration and naturalization. Moreover, if this were accepted as being a valid and compelling state goal, it would justify virtually all forms of state discrimination against aliens.

The goal of educating the electorate may in theory be compelling, but it will be implicated here only if the state can show that including aliens would significantly impair this goal; if the number of aliens excluded by the law is small, the impact may be too trivial for this goal to come into play. See §6.4.2. Yet even if this goal is accepted as compelling, the statute is probably not narrowly tailored. The law is overinclusive in that it denies aid to aliens who will remain in the community and who will thus help to shape its future other than at the ballot box. The law is also underinclusive, for it does not withhold aid from those who are or may become citizens, but who plan to move to another state or country.

Finally, the claimed interest in reserving scarce resources to citizens is not compelling. In *Graham v. Richardson*, 403 U.S. at 376, which struck down state laws that denied welfare benefits to aliens, the Court held that there is no "special public interest" in reserving to citizens "tax revenues to which aliens have contributed on an equal basis with the residents of the State." The same result is called for with respect to the distribution of scholarship funds. See *Nyquist v. Mauclet*, 432 U.S. 1 (1977).

Governmental or Political Functions

The principal reason that classifications based on race, national origin, and alienage are inherently suspect is that they tend to be irrelevant to any *legitimate* state goal. Strict scrutiny in such cases serves as a way of uncovering any hidden improper purposes. Yet there are two exceptional circumstances in which state laws that discriminate against aliens are much more likely to have been adopted for valid reasons. In these two areas, the Court, therefore, applies only a rational basis standard of review rather than strict scrutiny.

The first area involves the so-called governmental functions or political functions exception, which permits a state to reserve certain jobs or positions exclusively for those who are citizens. This exception applies to classifications that bar aliens from elective or nonelective "positions intimately related to the process of democratic self-government." *Bernal v. Fainter,* 467 U.S. 216, 220 (1984). This exception is justified on the theory that every government should be able to "limit the right to govern to those who are full-fledged members of the political community." Id. at 221.

The political function exception will apply if three requirements are satisfied:

1. The classification that excludes aliens must be fairly specific as to the positions that are involved rather than a disqualification aimed at a wide range of positions;
2. The position must involve broad discretionary authority in the formulation or the execution of public policies; and
3. The authority exercised must have an important impact on the citizen population.

Jobs that are essentially ministerial or clerical in nature and that call for little exercise of discretion do not meet the second requirement of this exception. Thus, the political function exception does not apply to notaries public. *Bernal v. Fainter,* 467 U.S. 216 (1984). A police officer's job, on the other hand, easily falls within the exception, since it entails broad discretion in the execution of public policies that significantly affect people's lives. *Foley v. Connelie,* 435 U.S. 291 (1978).

EXAMPLE 6-X

Pursuant to a law that bars aliens from taking any job with the State District Attorney's Office, Cheryl was denied a position as a prosecutor because she is not a U.S. citizen. Is the state's refusal to hire Cheryl subject to strict scrutiny, or does the political function exception lower the standard of review to rational basis?

EXPLANATION

The position of state prosecutor is almost surely one to which the political function exception applies. Prosecutors wield tremendous discretion in enforcing the criminal law, with grave consequences for people's lives. In *In re Griffiths*, 413 U.S. 717 (1973), the Court held that states may not bar aliens from becoming members of the bar, but due to the political function exception, the position of prosecutor would probably be treated differently.

Yet the political function exception might still not apply here because of the first requirement of the test. The statutory exclusion of aliens from *any* job in the State District Attorney's Office is arguably so overinclusive as to defeat the exception. The ban seems to cover paralegals, secretaries, mail clerks, and maintenance personnel — positions that do not involve any discretionary authority in formulating or executing public policy. On the other hand, if the state courts have construed the statute as excluding aliens only from serving as prosecutors, the political function exception would probably apply, and the exclusion would be upheld under a rational basis standard of review.

Undocumented Aliens

The second area in which state alienage discrimination is subject to only rational basis review rather than strict scrutiny involves laws that discriminate against undocumented aliens. The Court has held that "[u]ndocumented aliens cannot be treated as a suspect class because their presence in this country in violation of federal law is not a 'constitutional irrelevancy.'" *Plyler v. Doe*, 457 U.S. 202, 223 (1982). This exception is also defended on the basis that if a state discriminates against undocumented aliens, it is not encroaching as seriously on the federal domain, since those whom the state is burdening have, by definition, violated federal law.

These rationales for employing a mere rational basis standard of review for classifications aimed at undocumented aliens are not entirely satisfactory. Undocumented aliens as a class are often the objects of severe first- and second-degree prejudice. At the same time, they are totally unable to protect themselves in the political process, since they cannot vote. Moreover, despite their undocumented status, some aliens in this group in fact have a right to remain in the United States as a matter of federal immigration law, e.g., because they may qualify for political asylum. If the purpose of heightened scrutiny is to afford added judicial protection to those who face a risk of serious harm from the political process, state laws that target undocumented aliens should be subject to something more than rational basis review. As we will see in the next chapter, the Court has been willing to apply a standard of review that is more searching than rational basis to at least some state laws that discriminate against undocumented alien children. See §7.8.3. State laws that discriminate against undocumented aliens in general, however, are subject only to rational basis review.

EXAMPLE 6-Y

In Example 6-W, after a court held that the state may not constitutionally limit student financial aid to those aliens who intend to become U.S. citizens, the state amended its law to provide that "no financial aid shall be awarded for college study to any undocumented alien, i.e., an alien who is present in the United States in violation of federal immigration laws." Paul, a 22-year-old citizen of France, was admitted to this country on a student visa that expired two months ago. Baxter State College has denied him a scholarship on the basis of the new state law. Has the college violated Paul's Fourteenth Amendment right to equal protection of the laws?

EXPLANATION

The new state law discriminates solely against undocumented aliens. As such, the measure is subject to mere rational basis review. Since the law pertains only to college students, it is unlikely that Paul could obtain a more elevated standard of review on the theory that this is a law discriminating against undocumented alien children. Under the rational basis test, the law is virtually certain to be upheld as rationally related to the state's legitimate interest in discouraging an influx of undocumented aliens.

§6.5.2 The Standard for Federal Laws

As we have seen, state and local discrimination against lawfully admitted aliens is subject to strict judicial scrutiny. By contrast, federal laws that discriminate against aliens are reviewed under a rational basis standard. This relaxed scrutiny of federal alienage classifications stems from the fact that

> the responsibility for regulating the relationship between the United States and our alien visitors has been committed to the political branches of the Federal Government. . . . The reasons that preclude judicial review of political questions also dictate a narrow standard of review of decisions made by the Congress or the President in the area of immigration and naturalization.

Mathews v. Diaz, 426 U.S. 67, 81-82 (1976). This deferential approach to federal alienage classifications marks one of the few areas where there is a lack of congruence between the equal protection standards applied under the Fifth and Fourteenth Amendments.

While the Court generally accords great deference to federal alienage classifications, this applies only if the classification was adopted by Congress, by the President, or by a federal agency that is charged with responsibility for protecting the nation's interest in immigration and naturalization. Otherwise, there is less reason for "presuming that the rule was actually intended to serve that interest," and strict scrutiny will be applied. *Hampton v. Mow Sun Wong*, 426 U.S. 88, 103 (1976). In *Hampton*, the Court thus invalidated on equal protection grounds a federal Civil Service Commission rule that barred aliens from most federal government jobs. The Court strongly suggested that the rule would have been upheld had it been mandated by Congress or the President or had it been issued by a federal agency that, unlike the Civil Service Commission, has "direct responsibility" for immigration and naturalization matters.

§6.6   Classification on the Basis of Gender or Legitimacy

§6.6.1   *Gender as a Quasi-Suspect Classification*

Laws that classify on the basis of a person's gender are "quasi-suspect" and are subject to so-called intermediate or mid-level scrutiny under the equal protection provisions of both the Fifth and the Fourteenth Amendments. Such discrimination is unconstitutional unless it is shown to be supported by an "exceedingly persuasive justification." *Mississippi Univ. for Women v. Hogan*, 458 U.S. 718, 731 (1982). At one point, four members of the Court — one shy of a majority — urged that gender classifications be regarded as "inherently suspect" and subject to the same "strict judicial scrutiny" that is accorded to classifications based on race, national origin, or alienage. *Frontiero v. Richardson*, 411 U.S. 677, 688 (1973) (Brennan, Douglas, White, and Marshall, JJ.). In later years, however, the Court settled on an intermediate standard falling somewhere between the extremes of strict scrutiny and rational basis review.

Gender classifications are subject to heightened scrutiny for some of the same reasons that call for strict scrutiny of laws that discriminate on the basis of race, national origin, or alienage. While first-degree prejudice or animus has probably not been a significant factor in the legislative process, second-degree prejudice has played a major role in the history of discrimination against women. Male-dominated legislatures have frequently enacted laws that burden or limit the opportunities of women on the basis of exaggerated negative stereotypes concerning the talents, capacities, preferences, and proper role of women. In terms of their participation in the political process, women did not win the constitutional right to vote until the Nineteenth Amendment was ratified in 1920, half a century after the Fifteenth Amendment sought to bar disenfranchisement on the basis of race. Even though women today are not a "discrete and insular minority," since they comprise roughly half the electorate, many laws still on the books are relics of an era when women were totally excluded from the political process. In addition, like race and national origin, gender is an immutable trait, which may make it easy for male-controlled legislatures to enact measures that burden women, since such laws can never be applied against the males who voted for them. Finally, while gender is a characteristic that is frequently irrelevant to any legitimate legislative objective, because there are certain physical differences between men and women gender is somewhat more likely than race to be a legitimate basis of distinction. For these reasons, gender has been treated as a "quasi-suspect," rather than a fully "suspect," basis of classification.

Gender classifications are subject to mid-level scrutiny even if they appear to burden men rather than women. In 1982, the Court declared that the fact that a law "discriminates against males rather than against females does not exempt it from scrutiny or reduce the standard of review." *Mississippi University for Women v. Hogan*, 458 U.S. at 723. This pronouncement in effect repudiated the approach employed in several earlier cases where laws discriminating against males were subjected to less demanding scrutiny. See *Michael M. v. Superior Court*, 450 U.S. 464 (1981) (upholding California statutory rape law that punished only males); *Rostker v. Goldberg*, 453 U.S. 57 (1981) (upholding Military Selective Service Act requirement that males register for the draft).

It may seem odd to apply heightened scrutiny to classifications that discriminate against men. After all, male-dominated legislatures surely harbor no first- or second-degree prejudice against men, nor do they lack empathy for their own kind. Nor have males as a class ever been excluded from the political process. However, stereotypes about the proper role of men implicitly rely on stereotypes about the proper role of women. Moreover, the Court's insistence that the standard of review not be reduced for laws that discriminate against males stems from the difficulty of determining which sex is burdened by a particular gender-discriminatory law. In *Mississippi University for Women v. Hogan*, for example, Mississippi barred males from enrolling in a state-run school of nursing. On its face, this law discriminated against males, such as Joe Hogan, who wished to attend nursing school. Yet the law could also be viewed as discriminating against women, for it helped perpetuate the stereotypical view that nursing is "woman's work," with the result that nurses have long been underpaid. Similarly, in *Schlesinger v. Ballard*, 419 U.S. 498 (1975), a male Navy officer challenged a federal statute that required the discharge of male officers who had gone without a promotion for 9 years, while female officers were given 13 years to obtain a promotion. This statute discriminated against males who faced dismissal at the nine-year mark, but it also discriminated against women by making it easier for the Navy to delay their promotion. Even though it may not be correct "that all discriminations between the sexes ultimately redound to the detriment of females, because they tend to reinforce 'old notions' restricting the roles and opportunities of women," *Craig v. Boren*, 429 U.S. 190, 220 n.2 (1976) (Rehnquist, J., dissenting), there is enough truth in this that the Court today will apply intermediate scrutiny to all gender classifications.

A law that requires or permits *individuals* to be treated differently on account of their sex will be deemed to involve discrimination even if it happens that in the aggregate, men and women *as groups* are treated equally. In *J.E.B. v. Alabama*, 511 U.S. 127 (1994), a case involving the use of gender-based peremptory challenges, the state struck nine men and one woman from the jury panel, while the defendant struck nine women and one man. Even though men and women were treated equally as groups (each lost ten members), every individual juror who was removed because of gender was denied the right to be treated as an equal without regard to his or her sex. The Court, therefore, held that a prima facie case of gender discrimination had been established and proceeded to invalidate the government's use of gender-based peremptory challenges under the intermediate scrutiny test.

§6.6.2   Mid-Level Scrutiny as a Measure of Constitutionality

Once the plaintiff has established a prima facie case of gender discrimination, a court will evaluate the classification under an intermediate standard of review, which in recent years has become increasingly rigorous even though it may not yet be quite as strict as that employed in race and national origin cases.

A law that classifies on the basis of gender will be found to violate the Equal Protection Clause unless its defender can establish an "exceedingly persuasive justification" for the classification. As the Court explained in *United States v. Virginia*, 518 U.S. 515, 531-534 (1996), "The burden of justification is demanding" and requires the defender of the measure to convincingly demonstrate that

1. the classification serves "important governmental objectives" that do not rely on archaic or "overbroad generalizations about the different talents, capacities, or preferences of males and females";
2. these objectives are "genuine" in the sense that they "describe actual state purposes, not rationalizations for actions in fact differently grounded"; and
3. the discriminatory means employed are "substantially related" to the achievement of these objectives.

We will look at how the Court has applied each of these elements of the mid-level gender discrimination test.

Important and Legitimate Objectives

Gender discrimination will be upheld only if it furthers an important governmental objective. However, the Court has been reluctant to reject a proffered state goal as too intrinsically unimportant to support a gender classification. Thus, unlike race cases, which are examined under strict scrutiny, remedying past societal discrimination is an objective that may sometimes justify a classification that favors women. In short, this part of the test is likely to be met as long as the government's objective is a *legitimate* one. An exception is found in Chief Justice Rehnquist's concurring opinion in *United States v. Virginia,* where he rejected Virginia's claim that excluding women from the Virginia Military Institute (VMI) served the important interest of maintaining VMI's so-called adversative method. Without "evidence in the record that an adversative method is pedagogically beneficial," Rehnquist concluded that such a goal was not sufficiently important to satisfy this part of the test. 518 U.S. at 564.

However, the Court has at times rejected state objectives as not being legitimate because they relied on overly broad generalizations about differences in the talents, character, or roles of men and women. For example, in *Orr v. Orr,* 440 U.S. 268, 279-280 (1979), the Court struck down an Alabama law that imposed alimony obligations on husbands, but not on wives. The state defended this discrimination partly on the ground that it reinforced a family model "under which the wife plays a dependent role"; the Court rejected this asserted objective as reflecting the "old notion" that "it is the man's primary responsibility to provide a home and its essentials. . . ." See also *Michael M. v. Superior Court,* 450 U.S. at 472 n.7 (suggesting that a law subjecting only males to prosecution for statutory rape could not be defended on the ground that it protected the virtue and chastity of young women, since this goal reflected "archaic stereotypes" about women).

Proof of Actual Purpose

If the Court has not placed a great deal of stress on the "importance" of a proffered state objective, the same cannot be said of its insistence that the objective be a "genuine" and "actual state purpose" and not one "hypothesized or invented post hoc in response to litigation." *United States v. Virginia,* 518 U.S. at 533. In some cases, the legislature may have recorded its purpose in either the text or the legislative history of a law; if it has not, the classification's defender must produce other evidence demonstrating that the alleged goal was in fact the actual purpose for the challenged gender discrimination.

EXAMPLE 6-Z

Joe was denied admission to the State School of Nursing under a law providing that only women may attend the school. Joe challenged the state's refusal to admit him as violating the Equal Protection Clause. The state defended its admissions policy on the ground that it serves the important objective of remedying past societal discrimination against women in the workplace by offering professional training that will assure women a job. Will the court accept the state's argument?

EXPLANATION

Remedying past societal discrimination against women is an objective that may justify a gender classification. However, for this compensatory goal to suffice, several requirements must be met, including proof that this was the actual objective of the law. In the absence of any evidence to this effect in the state statute or its legislative history, a court would be skeptical of the state's benign goal. This skepticism would be compounded if Joe shows that the nursing school is part of a state university that has been limited to women since it was created a century ago. Moreover, the fact that nursing is one of the few professional fields from which women have not been excluded would cast further doubt on the state's alleged remedial goal. While women may need special assistance in gaining access to fields such as law, medicine, or engineering, there is no similar need in the field of nursing. It is thus doubtful a court would accept the state's proffered remedial goal as being the real objective of its discriminatory admissions plan. See *Mississippi University for Women v. Hogan,* 458 U.S. 718 (1982).

Means Substantially Related to Goal

Once it is shown that a gender classification was adopted to achieve an important and genuine governmental purpose, the defender must also demonstrate that the discriminatory means are substantially related to that objective. Under this part of the test, the Court has required the government to show that it was necessary to discriminate in order to achieve the goal, i.e., that there were no gender-neutral alternatives that might have accomplished the objective equally well. If nondiscriminatory alternatives were available, then the government gained nothing by discriminating. The gender classification, in other words, is gratuitous and unnecessary, in which case the discrimination is not substantially related to furthering the state's goals. As the Court said in *Orr v. Orr,* 440 U.S. at 283, "Where, as here, the State's . . . purposes are as well served by a gender-neutral classification as one that gender classifies and, therefore, carries with it the baggage of sexual stereo-types, the State cannot be permitted to classify on the basis of sex."

EXAMPLE 6-AA

A state law makes it a crime for a male to have sexual intercourse with a female who is under the age of 18 unless the couple is married. Only the male partner is criminally punishable for such conduct. The state defends this gender classification on the ground that it is substantially related to the important goal of preventing illegitimate teenage pregnancies. According to the state, female minors would be less likely to file a complaint if they could then be prosecuted. Assuming that the court accepts the state's claimed objective as being both important and genuine, what should the state have to show to meet the "substantially related" requirement?

EXPLANATION

The state should have to persuasively demonstrate that its gender-discrimi-natory law is more effective in achieving the state's goal than would be a gender-neutral law under which both partners are potentially subject to criminal prosecution. While it is no doubt true that there would be fewer complaints filed by female minors if they were subject to punishment, the state's goal was not to maximize the number of complaints filed, but to reduce the number of teenage pregnancies. A gender-neutral law might have a much stronger deterrent effect than a law that threatens only males with punishment. The state should have the burden of proving that its gender-discriminatory approach actually has a greater deterrent effect than would a gender-neutral law.

This example is taken from *Michael M. v. Superior Court*, 450 U.S. 464 (1981), where the Court upheld California's statutory rape law by applying what amounted to rational basis review. The plurality opinion by Justice Rehnquist did not require the state to prove that its gender-discriminatory law "is any more effective than a gender-neutral law would be in deterring minor females from engaging in sexual intercourse." Id. at 496 (Brennan, J., dissenting). *Michael M.* would probably be decided differently under the standard of review applied by the Court today.

EXAMPLE 6-BB

Under the Immigration and Nationality Act (INA), a child born overseas to unmarried parents, only one of whom is a U.S. citizen, will be deemed to be an American citizen at birth only if certain statutory requirements are satisfied. These requirements make it harder for a child to qualify as a citizen if its citizen parent is the father rather than the mother. In particular, for the child to be eligible for American citizenship, a citizen father (but not a citizen mother) must (a) agree in writing to support the child until it reaches age 18, and (b) legitimate the child or formally acknowledge the child while it is under 18. Charlie is the American citizen father of Lorelyn, who was born in the Philippines to a woman who is not an American citizen. Because Charlie failed to comply with either of these two requirements, his daughter who is now aged 22 has been denied U.S. citizenship and a U.S. passport that would allow her to reside in the United States. Lorelyn has filed suit in federal court seeking a judgment declaring that she is an American citizen and entitled to a U.S. passport. She claims that the INA provisions on which the government relied to deny her citizenship violate the Fifth Amendment because they discriminate on the basis of gender. The government defends these provisions as discouraging fraudulent claims by those claiming to be children of U.S. citizen fathers, and as helping to ensure that citizen fathers become aware of their foreign-born children at an early age, thereby fostering the parent-child relationship and the child's ties to the United States. Assume that Lorelyn has third party standing to assert the constitutional rights of her father. Are the INA provisions invalid as constituting forbidden gender discrimination?

EXPLANATION

On their face the provisions discriminate based on gender, for they make it more difficult for citizen fathers to transmit American citizenship to their children than for citizen mothers to do so. The government may argue that intermediate scrutiny should not apply because the Court traditionally shows deference to the political branches in cases involving immigration or naturalization. However, this case involves the acquisition of citizenship at birth and, as such, does not concern either immigration (the terms on which aliens may be admitted to or remain in the United States) or naturalization (the process by which persons may obtain citizenship after birth). Thus, the mid-level standard of review should not be relaxed.

The government must show that these gender-based classifications are substantially related to an important governmental interest, i.e., that gender-neutral laws would not achieve its goals as well as a gender discriminatory law. As to the goal of discouraging fraudulent claims, because another section of the INA already requires proof of a blood relationship by "clear and convincing evidence," the support and acknowledgment provisions are entirely gratuitous and unnecessary in terms of this goal. As to the goals of encouraging fathers to develop a caring and supportive relationship with their child, the statute rests on the stereotype that fathers are less likely than mothers to care for children born out of wedlock. Even if this generalization may be true in most cases, it is not true for all fathers or all mothers. The government's goals would be equally well served by a gender-neutral law requiring that during the child's early years, a citizen parent (whether father or mother) have developed at least minimal contact with the child, established a relationship with the child, supported the child, or been the child's caretaker. The INA thus probably violates the Fifth Amendment by imposing support and acknowledgment requirements solely on citizen fathers. See *Miller v. Albright*, 523 U.S. 420 (1998) (upholding INA provisions partly on basis that daughter lacked standing to assert father's rights; however, a different five-member majority agreed that provisions would be held unconstitutional if challenged by the father).

The "substantially related" requirement, by insisting that the government not resort to gender discrimination if gender-neutral alternatives are available, means that gender may not be used as a proxy for other factors that are gender neutral. For example, while it is statistically true that women on the average live longer than men, this gender stereotype is not true of all women or all men; some women live fewer years than the average man, while some men live longer than the average woman. Thus, to use gender as a predictor of longevity is to employ a classification that is both overinclusive and underinclusive. Instead of relying on gender stereotypes, the state must look beyond the surface to gender-neutral factors that may affect an individual's life span. The use of gender stereotypes will probably survive the "substantially related" requirement only if the government can prove "that gender alone is an accurate predictor" of the matter in question. *J.E.B. v. Alabama*, 511 U.S. at 139. Rarely, if ever, will such a showing be possible.

EXAMPLE 6-CC

A state law requires female workers to pay higher annual premiums to the state retirement fund on the theory that because they live longer, women will draw retirement benefits for a longer period of time than men. The state has justified this discrimination on the basis that it needs to maintain the fiscal integrity of its pension plan. Is this gender discrimination valid?

EXPLANATION

The goal of preserving the fiscal soundness of the state pension fund is no doubt an important state goal. Yet the means chosen are not substantially related to that objective, since the state could achieve its ends without engaging in gender discrimination. The state could maintain the fiscal integrity of its plan by charging men and women the same premium, with the total premiums collected being the same as they would have been under a gender-discriminatory plan.

If the state wishes to vary premiums based on an individual's projected life span, it may not use gender as a proxy for longevity. Instead, the state must look beyond gender to other factors that influence life span, such as smoking, drinking, diet, exercise habits, and the like. See *City of Los Angeles v. Manhart,* 435 U.S. 702 (1978) (invalidating similar pension scheme under Title VII of the 1964 Civil Rights Act).

The prohibition against using gender stereotypes is another way of saying that the government may not employ a presumption that all members of a sex share a characteristic that may have statistical validity for the group as a whole, but that is not true of each member of the group. Virtually every law is based on stereotypes and presumptions. A speed limit law stereotypes those driving over the speed limit as dangerous drivers even though this presumption is not true of all speeders. Similarly, a law setting a minimum driving age of eighteen presumes that those under eighteen are unfit to drive even though this stereotype is not true in all cases. Stereotypes or presumptions based on group characteristics are the stuff of the law. They are problematic and generally prohibited only when the stereotype involves a trait such as race, national origin, or gender that calls for heightened scrutiny. In these cases, there is a danger that the government is using a racial or gender stereotype — in lieu of other more accurate factors — as a subtle way of harming the group in question. In addition, reliance on such stereotypes usually reinforces negative perceptions about racial minorities or women. See §5.7.1 (discussing irrebuttable presumptions).

There is a difference between classifications that use gender itself as a stereotype and classifications that are based on traits disproportionately or exclusively associated with one gender. While the former practice is usually prohibited, the latter type of classification may survive the "substantially related" test if it is not a pretext for gender stereotyping.

EXAMPLE 6-DD

The prosecution in a paternity case used all its peremptory challenges to excuse from the jury ten men who had previously been defendants in paternity actions. Does the prosecutor's action violate the Equal Protection Clause?

EXPLANATION

In *J.E.B. v. Alabama,* 511 U.S. 127 (1994), the state in a paternity suit used all but one of its peremptory challenges to remove men from the jury out of fear that male jurors would sympathize with the defendant. The Court held that such use of gender as a proxy for bias was unconstitutional; instead of employing "stereotypical and pejorative notions about a particular gender," id. at 143, the state was required to look beyond the surface to discover possible bias based on gender-neutral factors. Id. at 139 n.11. However, the Court in *J.E.B.* noted that "strikes based on characteristics that are dispro-portionately associated with one gender could be appropriate, absent a showing of pretext." Id. at 143 & n.16.

In our example, the prosecutor has not employed a stereotype about men in general or presumed that men will be biased toward the defendant. Instead, the prosecutor excused only those potential jurors who had been sued for paternity. While this group by definition consists only of men, it was not a juror's sex that led to exclusion, but rather the fact that he had been sued for paternity. Such conduct by the prosecutor does not constitute gender discrimination if the jurors were excused in spite of, not because of, their sex. See §6.2.2. In other words, if the prosecutor had a good-faith concern about the jurors' prior involvement in paternity cases rather than about their being males, this would rebut any prima facie case of gender discrimination by defeating the purpose element. To be sure, the prosecutor relied on the stereotype that those sued for paternity will be biased toward the defendant in a paternity suit; but since this presumption rests on a trait or characteristic — prior involvement in a paternity suit — that does not call for heightened scrutiny, reliance on the presumption is constitutionally un-objectionable. The prosecutor's action would, therefore, not violate the Equal Protection Clause because it probably does not involve gender dis-crimination.

Comparing the Tests for Gender and Race Discrimination

As we have seen, the standard of review employed in gender discrimination cases today is extremely demanding and may approach the strict scrutiny test, which governs race, national origin, and many alienage discrimination cases. In *United States v. Virginia,* 518 U.S. 515 (1996), the Court stated that it was not "equating gender classifications, *for all purposes,* to classifications based on race or national origin," implying that at least in some cases the level of scrutiny is the same. Id. at 532 (emphasis supplied). However, assuming that this is true, the Court has noted several circumstances under which its approach to gender and racial discrimination might lead to different results. One involves laws that draw distinctions based on the "[p]hysical differences between men and women"; while "[s]upposed 'inherent differ-ences' are no longer accepted as a ground for race or national origin clas-sifications," id. at 533, they may suffice to allow, for example, separate restrooms and living facilities for men and women in state colleges.

A second possible difference between the Court's approaches to gender and race classifications involves affirmative action. In the race setting, as we have seen, such programs are subject to the strictest scrutiny, whereas in gender cases, they are more easily justified. Thus, whereas remedying past societal discrimination is not a sufficient interest to allow a race-conscious remedial scheme, this may be an adequate objective in the gender setting.

Finally, the Court has left open the possibility that the principle of "separate but equal" may allow a state to operate separate undergraduate institutions for men and women even though the maintenance of racially segregated schools and colleges is clearly unconstitutional. In *United States v. Virginia,* the state defended its exclusion of women from the Virginia Military Institute (VMI) on the basis that single-sex colleges further the goal of providing diversity in educational opportunities. The Court rejected this argument because offering diversity in educational approaches was not the actual goal of VMI's male-only admissions policy. The Court added that even if this had been the state's goal, since there were no separate — much less equal — facilities for women, the "separate but equal" doctrine would not have justified the exclusion of women from VMI. However, the Court went out of its way to emphasize that "[w]e do not question the State's prerogative evenhandedly to support diverse educational opportunities," id. at 533 n.7, suggesting that in a different factual setting states might provide single-sex colleges for men and women.

§6.6.3   *Legitimacy*

The intermediate or mid-level standard of review is also applied to laws that classify on the basis of legitimacy and that thus discriminate against children born to unmarried parents. The use of intermediate scrutiny for laws aimed at nonmarital children may be justified on several bases. At one time at least, illegitimate children were the objects of considerable scorn and moral censure, as is suggested by the word "bastard," the dictionary definition of which is "counterfeit, sham, or inferior." Even though such first-degree prejudice against nonmarital children is probably rare today, our basic sense of fairness suggests that it is wrong for the law to heap burdens on a person because of a relationship over which he or she had no control. Moreover, while the condition of illegitimacy is not completely immutable since a child can become legitimized, the condition — like that of alienage — is alterable in only one direction, thus reducing the extent to which empathy might otherwise temper the legislative process.

The Court has described the standard of review for laws that discriminate on the basis of legitimacy as requiring that the "statutory classification . . . be substantially related to an important governmental objective." *Clark v. Jeter,* 486 U.S. 456, 461 (1988). This is the same verbal formula that has long been used in gender cases. The Court has noted that "intermediate scrutiny . . . generally has been applied to discriminatory classifications based on sex or illegitimacy," id., suggesting that the standards are the same. However, with the recent strengthening of the gender discrimination standard to the point where it often approaches strict scrutiny, the standard of review applied in legitimacy cases is probably less rigorous than that now employed in gender cases.

The standard is, nevertheless, demanding. The requirement that the discrimination serve an important governmental objective bars the state from employing "classifications that burden illegitimate children for the sake of punishing the illicit relations of their parents, because 'visiting this condemnation on the head of an infant is illogical and unjust.'" Id. The government cannot categorically exclude illegitimate children from receiving benefits that would be paid to them if they were legitimate. On the other hand, the government has an important interest in minimizing the problems often associated with proving paternity. Time limits on an illegitimate child's attempt to prove paternity as a precondition to receiving various benefits will thus be upheld if they are substantially related to the state's interest in avoiding litigation of stale or fraudulent claims. However, the time limits must be reasonable and not appreciably shorter than necessary to achieve the state's goal.

EXAMPLE 6-EE

State law provides that a father need not pay support on behalf of an illegitimate child unless paternity is established in an action filed prior to the child's fifth birthday; if paternity is so established, the father's support obligation shall not exceed 50 percent of the amount that would be owed to a legitimate child. Is this statute constitutional?

EXPLANATION

Insofar as the statute limits the support that must be paid on behalf of an illegitimate child to 50 percent of what would be paid to a legitimate child, the statute is surely unconstitutional. It is difficult to imagine any reason for the 50 percent limitation other than a desire to punish the mother and her child for the child's having been born out of wedlock.

The five-year statute of limitations for filing a paternity action is also problematic. The state may argue that this rule bars stale or fraudulent paternity claims brought at a time when the putative father can no longer defend himself. The Court has recognized the importance of this state interest, but has held that to meet the "substantially related" test, the state must allow a reasonable time for those interested in the well-being of such children to sue on their behalf. Moreover, the time limit may be shorter than necessary to protect the state's interest. Given the fact that scientific evidence is now often able to prove and disprove claims of paternity, the harm to the putative father of allowing suit after the child's fifth birthday is likely to be minimal. Thus, the five-year limitations period is probably also unconstitutional. See Clark v. Jeter, 486 U.S. 456 (1988) (invalidating six-year limitation on paternity suits as condition for receiving child support).

§6.7 Other Possibly Disfavored Bases of Classification

§6.7.1 *The Rejection of New "Suspect" and "Quasi-Suspect" Classes*

The Supreme Court has been unwilling to recognize any new bases of classification as being "suspect" or "quasi-suspect" for equal protection purposes. As a result, the list of "suspect" classifications that will trigger strict scrutiny is limited to race, national origin, and alienage, while only gender and legitimacy are deemed to be "quasi-suspect" and subject to intermediate scrutiny.

The Court has expressly rejected claims that discrimination based on age, mental retardation, or poverty should receive some form of heightened scrutiny. See *Massachusetts Bd. of Retirement v. Murgia*, 427 U.S. 307 (1976) (age classifications receive rational basis review); *City of Cleburne v. Cleburne Living Center*, 473 U.S. 432 (1985) (rejecting mental retardation as a quasi-suspect classification); *Harris v. McRae*, 448 U.S. 297, 323 (1980) (poverty or wealth not a suspect classification). *Cleburne* strongly implied that no new "suspect" or "quasi-suspect" classes will be recognized. The Court stated that if mental retardation were granted "quasi-suspect" status,

> it would be difficult to find a principled way to distinguish a variety of other groups who have perhaps immutable disabilities setting them off from others, who cannot themselves mandate the desired legislative responses, and who can claim some degree of prejudice from at least part of the public at large. One need mention in this respect only the aging, the disabled, the mentally ill, and the infirm. We are reluctant to set out on that course, and we decline to do so.

473 U.S. at 445-446. Thus, the list of classifications that will be deemed to be "suspect" or "quasi-suspect" appears, for now at least, to be frozen.

While the Court has refused *formally* to recognize additional bases of classification that call for heightened scrutiny, it has not always applied the rational basis test in its customarily toothless manner. In certain situations, the rational basis standard seems to take on added rigor, with the result that the challenged classification is sometimes held to violate the Equal Protection Clause. Because the Court in these cases does not *acknowledge* that it is applying anything other than the traditional rational basis test, it is difficult to state with certainty that a more demanding standard was employed. Yet the fact that a law fails the rational basis test is itself a powerful indicator that something more than ordinary rational basis review was employed. We will examine several settings in which the Court appears to have elevated the standard of rational basis review. In each instance, the group discriminated against was politically powerless or politically unpopular.

§6.7.2   Discrimination against Out-of-Staters

State laws that discriminate against persons from other states are often subject to challenge under the Commerce Clause (see Christopher N. May & Allan Ides, *Constitutional Law: National Power and Federalism*, ch. 8 (2001)); under the Privileges and Immunities Clause of Article IV, §2 (see id., ch. 8); or as impairing the right to travel under the Equal Protection Clause or the Privileges or Immunities Clause of the Fourteenth Amendment (see §7.4). There are times, however, when none of these approaches will work to invalidate discrimination against out-of-staters. In these instances, a litigant may wish to challenge such laws as being arbitrary and unreasonable under the Equal Protection Clause.

There is a strong argument that for equal protection purposes, discrimination against people from other states should receive heightened scrutiny due to the fact that the group targeted is not represented in the political process that produced the measure in question. While the Court has not used strict or intermediate scrutiny in this setting, it has occasionally employed an enhanced rational basis test to review laws that discriminate against current or former out-of-staters. See, e.g., *Metropolitan Life Ins. Co. v. Ward*, 470 U.S. 869 (1985) (rational basis equal protection test barred Alabama from taxing out-of-state companies at higher rate than domestic companies); *Zobel v. Williams*, 457 U.S. 55 (1982) (rational basis equal protection test barred Alaska from paying new residents lower annual dividends than are paid to long-term residents). See §7.4.3.

EXAMPLE 6-FF

Norman moved from Illinois to Vermont shortly after buying a car in Illinois. Vermont requires its citizens to pay a use tax upon registering a car that was purchased in another state. However, Vermont grants an exemption from the use tax for any sales tax paid to another state if, at the time of purchase, the registrant was a Vermont citizen. When Norman registered the car in Vermont, the state charged him the full use tax, with no credit for the sales tax he had paid to Illinois, because at the time of purchase he was not a Vermont citizen. Did Vermont violate the Equal Protection Clause by discriminating against people, such as Norman, who were recently citizens of another state?

EXPLANATION

Under the traditional rational basis test, Vermont's tax would easily be upheld. The difference in treatment may have been based on the assumption that those who lived in another state when they bought a car benefited from that state's roads. Since they will derive benefits from the roads in two states, it is not unfair that they pay taxes to two states. By contrast, those who were Vermonters when they bought a car in another state may have derived little benefit from the other state's roads and thus should not have to pay taxes to two states. This sort of speculation clearly affords a rational basis for the Vermont law. However, in *Williams v. Vermont*, 472 U.S. 14, 22 (1985), the Court, ostensibly applying the traditional rational basis test, invalidated this Vermont tax scheme as creating "an arbitrary distinction that violates the Equal Protection Clause." One explanation for the result is that the Court applied an enhanced form of rational basis review.

§6.7.3 Discrimination against the Mentally Retarded

As we noted earlier, in *City of Cleburne v. Cleburne Living Center*, 473 U.S. 432 (1985), the Supreme Court expressly refused to treat mental retardation as a "quasi-suspect classification" that calls for "intermediate-level scrutiny," id. at 437-438, and held that "[i]n such cases, the Equal Protection Clause requires only a rational means to serve a legitimate end," id. at 442. Yet the Court then ruled that by denying permission to operate a group home for the mentally retarded, the City of Cleburne had violated the Equal Protection Clause "[b]ecause in our view the record does not reveal any rational basis" for the denial. Id. at 448. Instead, said the Court, the city's action "appears to us to rest on an irrational prejudice against the mentally retarded. . . ." Id. at 450. Under the ordinary rational basis test, however, there need not be anything in the record to support the classification in question; mere speculation will suffice. Justices Marshall, Brennan, and Blackmun objected to the majority's "refusal to acknowledge that something more than mini-mum rationality review is at work here." Id. at 459. As Justice Marshall wrote, "[P]erhaps the method employed must hereafter be called 'second order' rational-basis review rather than 'heightened scrutiny.' But however labeled, the rational-basis test invoked today is most assuredly not the [traditional] rational-basis test. . . ." Id. at 458.

The fact that the Court in *Cleburne* struck down the city's ordinance does not necessarily mean that all laws discriminating against the mentally retarded are invalid. In *Cleburne*, there was considerable evidence to bolster the Court's conclusion that the ban on group homes for the mentally retarded was a product of "irrational prejudice," including language in the ordinance itself that barred homes "'*for the* insane or *feeble-minded* or alco-holics or drug addicts.'" Id. at 436 n.3 (emphasis in original). In other words, there were strong indications that the *actual* goal of the ordinance was an illegitimate one, causing the Court to show less than usual deference to the *hypothetical* purposes offered by the measure's defenders. Where evidence of "irrational prejudice" or another illegitimate purpose is lacking, the Court has upheld classifications that burden the mentally retarded. See *Heller v. Doe*,

509 U.S. 312 (1993) (upholding Kentucky involuntary commitment procedures that made it easier to commit the mentally retarded than the mentally ill).

The *Cleburne* Court's willingness to more closely examine classifications that appear to be based on "irrational prejudice" against a disfavored group was not unique. In *United States Department of Agriculture v. Moreno*, 413 U.S. 528 (1973), the Court invoked the equal protection component of the Fifth Amendment to overturn a federal law that denied food stamps to households containing unrelated members. The Court concluded that the aim of the classification was "to prevent so-called 'hippies' and 'hippie communes' from participating in the food stamp program." Id. at 534. Though only rational basis review was called for, said the Court, "if the constitutional conception of 'equal protection of the laws' means anything, it must at the very least mean that a bare congressional desire to harm a politically unpopular group cannot constitute a *legitimate* governmental interest." Id.

§6.7.4 *Discrimination on the Basis of Sexual Orientation*

The Court in *Romer v. Evans*, 517 U.S. 620 (1996), showed a similar willingness to enhance the rational basis test where necessary to protect a politically unpopular group. *Romer* involved Colorado's Amendment 2, a constitutional provision that rescinded all state and local laws protecting gays and lesbians and that prohibited any legislative, executive, or judicial action designed to protect these groups in the future. The Colorado Supreme Court held the provision unconstitutional under the Equal Protection Clause, applying strict scrutiny on the ground that the measure infringed on the fundamental right of gays and lesbians to participate in the political process. The U.S. Supreme Court affirmed, but on the ground that the provision "lacks a rational relationship to legitimate state interests." Id. at 632.

The rational basis test relied on in *Romer* was not the usual toothless version of the standard. Instead, the Court invalidated Amendment 2 for two reasons, neither of which would normally cause a classification to fail under the traditional rational basis test: First, the measure imposed such an "unprecedented," "broad and undifferentiated disability on a single named group," i.e., gays and lesbians, as to render it "an invalid form of legislation"; second, the law lacked "a rational relationship to a legitimate governmental purpose" because it "inflict[ed] . . . immediate, continuing, and real injuries that outrun and belie any legitimate justifications that may be claimed for it," thus "rais[ing] the inevitable inference that the disadvantage imposed is born of animosity toward the class of persons affected." Id. at 632-635. Yet the fact that a classification is sweeping or unprecedented is usually not enough to doom it under the rational basis standard test. Nor, under that standard, does a court normally test a classification to see how well it fits the proffered goals. To the contrary, the Court's traditional rational basis standard of review tolerates measures that are imprecise, illogical, and ill-suited to their supposed purposes. Testing the closeness of the fit is the stuff of heightened — not rational basis — scrutiny.

One might conclude that *Romer* employed an enhanced version of the rational basis test. On the other hand, *Romer* could be seen as one of those rare cases in which a law fails the rational basis test because of overwhelming evidence that the measure was enacted for an illegitimate purpose. Whichever view one takes, the critical factor was the Court's conviction that Amendment 2 was "inexplicable by anything but animus toward the class that it affects." Id. at 632. In this respect, the case is quite similar to *Moreno,* a decision the Court cited with approval, which struck down a federal law aimed at "hippies."

It remains unclear to what extent other laws discriminating against homosexual persons will be subject to a similarly enhanced rational basis review. At this point, we can only pose questions rather than answer them. Is *Romer* limited to settings in which the government has imposed a "broad and undifferentiated disability" on gays and lesbians, or will the enhanced standard be triggered whenever a court believes that the discrimination was the product of anti-homosexual animus? If the latter is true, how is a court to ascertain the presence of animus? It is not a satisfactory response to say that enhanced scrutiny will be applied whenever the poorness of the fit casts doubt on a classification's asserted goals, for a court has no business testing the fit in this way unless it has first decided that some mode of enhanced scrutiny is called for. If, instead, mere suspicion of animus is enough to trigger enhanced scrutiny, what must the suspicion rest on? Is mere intuition enough? Unlike *Moreno,* where the Court cited specific legislative history in finding an animus against "hippies," *Romer* did not cite or rely on any background materials showing that Colorado's Amendment 2 was motivated by hostility toward gays and lesbians.

These uncertainties would be eliminated if the Court were explicitly to hold that due to widespread first- and second-degree prejudice against gays and lesbians, all laws that discriminate against these groups are subject to heightened scrutiny. However, as the Court has carefully avoided making such a determination, it is unclear what standard of review is to be applied in these cases. Where laws discriminate against homosexual persons, some courts have employed "active rational basis review" in order to ensure that the classification is not based on impermissible prejudice. Under this approach, the government must actually prove the existence of a legitimate rational basis rather than merely alleging such a purpose. See, e.g., *Pruitt v. Cheney,* 963 F.2d 1160 (9th Cir.), *cert. denied,* 506 U.S. 1020 (1992); *Dahl v. Secretary of Navy,* 830 F. Supp. 1319 (E.D. Cal. 1993).

7

Equal Protection: Fundamental Rights

§7.1 Introduction and Overview

In the previous chapter, we examined application of the Equal Protection Clause in situations that call for mere rational basis review and in situations where the basis of classification was "suspect," "quasi-suspect," or otherwise such as to call for some form of heightened scrutiny. We turn now to an examination of the Equal Protection Clause in settings where the basis of the classification is unproblematic, but where the law discriminates in such a way as to impinge on a fundamental constitutional right. After exploring this fundamental-rights branch of the equal protection doctrine, this chapter will conclude by looking briefly at an alternative approach to equal protection that Justice Thurgood Marshall advocated as a replacement for the Court's three-tier model that we have been discussing.

§7.2 Equal Protection and Fundamental Rights

Laws that classify in ways that infringe on the exercise of a fundamental constitutional right will be upheld only if they survive the same strict scrutiny test that is applied to suspect classifications. In other words, the defender of the law must demonstrate that the discrimination is narrowly tailored to serve a compelling governmental interest (see §6.4.2).

EXAMPLE 7-A

Roger is 18 years of age and the father of a 3-year-old girl who was born out of wedlock. Two years ago Roger was ordered to pay child support in

251

the amount of $200/month. Because he has been unemployed, Roger has not paid child support and owes an arrearage of almost $5,000. Roger recently applied for a marriage license. The license was denied under a state law that prohibits anyone from marrying who has not met his or her child-support obligations. Roger sued, alleging that the license denial violates his rights under the Equal Protection Clause. How should the court rule?

EXPLANATION

The right to marry is a fundamental constitutional liberty. *Loving v. Virginia,* 388 U.S. 1 (1967). In this case, the state has created a classification that allows some people to marry, while denying that right to others. The classifying trait—payment of child support—is not one that calls for heightened scrutiny. However, because the law severely impairs a person's fundamental constitutional right to marry, the law is subject to strict scrutiny.

The state might argue that its discrimination against those who fail to support their children serves the compelling interest of assuring that minor children are cared for. Even if this is a sufficiently compelling interest to justify interference with the right to marry, the state must show that the marriage ban is narrowly tailored to that goal in the sense that it is neither overinclusive nor underinclusive. Here, the ban is overinclusive because it applies even when preventing a marriage will in no way further the state's child-support goal. Whether or not Roger gets married, it is unlikely he can pay child support. The state thus gains nothing by impairing Roger's constitutional rights. The law, therefore, violates the Equal Protection Clause because it creates a classification that burdens the fundamental right to marry without being narrowly tailored to the state's interest in seeing that children are adequately supported. See *Zablocki v. Redhail,* 434 U.S. 374 (1978).

Rights that are considered fundamental for equal protection purposes are of two types. The first embraces *due process liberties,* i.e., interests that qualify as fundamental liberties under the Due Process Clauses of the Fifth and Fourteenth Amendments. These due process liberties include rights that are *enumerated* in the Constitution, such as freedom of speech and religion, as well as certain *nonenumerated* interests that the Court has deemed to be fundamental, such as the freedom to marry, the freedom to choose whether to bear or beget a child, and the right to determine one's family living arrangements. See Chapter 2. The second type of fundamental liberty that may trigger strict scrutiny under the Equal Protection Clause is what we might call *equal protection liberties.* These consist of certain implied liberty interests that are deemed to be fundamental for equal protection purposes even though they do not enjoy fundamental liberty status under the Due Process Clause. These so-called equal protection liberties include the right to vote, the freedom to travel, and perhaps the liberty to obtain a basic education.

For strict scrutiny to be triggered when a law discriminates with respect to a fundamental constitutional liberty, the Court sometimes insists that the impairment of that right exceed a minimum threshold; i.e., the classification must infringe or impinge on the right in question by substantially interfering with it. This requirement was easily satisfied in Example 7-A, since the state totally barred people such as Roger from getting married. Suppose, however, that the state instead required parents who had not met their child-support obligation to obtain financial counseling before they could marry. If the counseling requirement did not significantly delay the ability to marry, a court might conclude that the classification is not subject to strict scrutiny because the state has not infringed or impinged on the right to marry.

§7.3   The Right to Vote

§7.3.1   The Absolute versus the Equal Right to Vote

There are two distinct senses in which the Constitution protects the right to vote. First, in a few instances, the Constitution confers an *absolute right to vote* for a particular office by requiring that the office be filled through a popular election rather than by appointment or some other means. There are only two provisions in the Constitution that expressly guarantee the right to vote in this absolute sense: Article I, §2, cl. 1 requires that members of the House of Representatives be "chosen . . . by the People," and the Seventeenth Amendment commands that U.S. Senators be "elected by the People." While "the People" thus have a federal constitutional right to vote for members of the House and the Senate, both Article I, §2 and the Seventeenth Amendment leave it up to the states to decide *which people* shall enjoy this right. These constitutional provisions merely insist that the qualifications to vote for members of Congress be the same as the state establishes "for electors of the most numerous branch of the State legislature." As we shall see, however, other constitutional provisions limit the states' ability to determine voter qualifications.

One might argue that the Republican Form of Government Clause (Art. IV, §4) implicitly confers an absolute right to vote for key state government officials, but the Supreme Court has never construed the Clause in this way. It could also be argued that the references in Article I, §2 and the Seventeenth Amendment to "*electors* of the most numerous branch of the State legislature" implicitly require that this state body be popularly elected, but again the Court has never so held. Thus, while the Constitution guaranties the people a right to vote for members of Congress, it "does not confer the right to vote in state elections. . . ." *Harris v. McRae*, 448 U.S. 297, 322 n.25 (1980). For example, nothing in the Constitution would prevent the City of Los Angeles from abolishing its practice of popularly electing the mayor and providing that the mayor shall instead be appointed by the city council. See *Rodriguez v. Popular Democratic Party*, 457 U.S. 1 (1982) (upholding Puerto Rico law under which legislative vacancies were filled by the legislator's political party rather than by popular election); *Fortson v. Morris*, 385 U.S. 231 (1966) (upholding Georgia law allowing state legislature in certain circumstances to choose state governor).

The second sense in which the Constitution protects the franchise is by guaranteeing people an *equal right to vote* for those federal and state officials who are chosen by popular election. Four constitutional amendments expressly protect the right to vote in this way by prohibiting the federal and state governments from selectively denying the franchise on certain bases: i.e., the Fifteenth Amendment (race), the Nineteenth Amendment (sex), the Twenty-fourth Amendment (failure to pay a tax), and the Twenty-sixth Amendment (age). In *Rice v. Cayetano*, 120 S. Ct. 1044, 1047-1048 (2000), the Court thus struck down a Hawaii constitutional provision that limited the right to vote for trustees of a state agency to descendants of certain races, holding that the voting restriction was "a clear violation of the Fifteenth Amendment."

In addition, the Court has construed the Equal Protection Clause of the Fourteenth Amendment as implicitly protecting the equal right to vote. The Fourteenth Amendment right to vote is the "right to participate in the electoral process equally with other qualified voters." *Harris v. McRae*, 448 U.S. at 322 n.25. Because this is a fundamental right, state and local laws that distribute the franchise on a selective basis or in an unequal manner are usually subject to strict scrutiny. It makes sense for the courts to closely scrutinize laws that discriminate in this way, for those who are burdened by such laws are, by definition, harmed in terms of their access to "those political processes which can ordinarily be expected to bring about repeal of undesirable legislation." *United States v. Carolene Prod. Co.*, 304 U.S. 144, 152 n.4 (1938). See §2.3.2.

The Fourteenth Amendment confers only a "right to participate in elections on an equal basis with other citizens in the jurisdiction," *Dunn v. Blumstein*, 405 U.S. 330, 336 (1972); it does not confer the right to vote in an absolute sense. The Fourteenth Amendment right to vote, therefore, comes into play only when some *other* provision of law requires that a particular federal, state, or local office be filled by popular election. In such cases, laws that discriminate with respect to the franchise will generally be subject to strict scrutiny, requiring the state to show that the measure is narrowly tailored to serve a compelling state interest. The Fourteenth Amendment right to vote is thus a fundamental right for *equal protection* purposes, but not for *due process* purposes.

EXAMPLE 7-B

The state has passed a law providing that from now on, the state attorney general shall be appointed by the governor rather than elected by the people. May state citizens successfully challenge the statute on the ground that it violates the Fourteenth Amendment Due Process Clause by impairing their fundamental liberty interest in voting?

EXPLANATION

The suit should be dismissed. There is no such fundamental liberty under the Due Process Clause. The Fourteenth Amendment protects only the right to vote on an equal basis with other citizens. This right is not violated when all citizens are deprived of the right to choose the attorney general.

Five types of laws or practices may potentially infringe on the equal right to vote so as to trigger strict scrutiny: (1) selective denial of the franchise; (2) individual vote dilution; (3) group vote dilution; (4) assignment of voters to districts predominantly on the basis of their race; and (5) denial of access to the ballot. We will consider each of these in turn.

§7.3.2   Selective Denial of the Franchise

The most obvious way that a state might infringe on the Fourteenth Amendment's fundamental right to vote is by imposing conditions whose effect is to completely deny the vote to selected people. The Court has held that "any classification restricting the franchise on grounds *other than residence, age, and citizenship* cannot stand unless the . . . State can demonstrate that the classification serves a compelling state interest." *Hill v. Stone*, 421 U.S. 289 (1975) (emphasis supplied). Let us first consider these exceptions to the strict scrutiny requirement.

Denial of the franchise to nonresidents and noncitizens of the state is subject only to rational basis review. This follows from the fact that state and local governments have a legitimate interest in limiting the vote to those with a stake in the community. Otherwise, the fate of a state or a town could be decided by busloads of outsiders who swarm in on election day just to cast a ballot. States and cities may restrict the vote to those who are citizens and bona fide residents of the jurisdiction. Such denials are subject only to rational basis review. While a citizenship restriction involves discrimination against aliens, the political function exception applies to the act of voting, and thus strict scrutiny would not be triggered. See §6.5.1.

It is one thing for a city or state to impose a bona fide residence requirement for voting. It is another matter to deny the vote to those bona fide residents who have not lived in the city or state for a prescribed period of time. Such durational residency requirements for voting are subject to strict scrutiny, since they temporarily deny the vote to persons who are in fact bona fide residents of the jurisdiction. See *Dunn v. Blumstein,* 405 U.S. 330 (1972) (invalidating Tennessee law that conditioned right to vote on residence in the state for one year and in the county for three months prior to the election). As we will see in §7.4, durational residency requirements may also trigger strict scrutiny due to their impact on the fundamental equal protection right to travel.

Age restrictions on voting, like bona fide residence requirements, are subject to mere rational basis review under the Equal Protection Clause. Under the Twenty-sixth Amendment, however, the vote may not be denied on account of age to anyone 18 years of age or older. Thus, while a state could deny the vote to those under 16, it could not impose an age restriction that denied the vote to 18-, 19-, or 20-year-olds or to those over 70. With the exception of residence, citizenship, and age qualifications, all "restrictions on the franchise of any character must meet a stringent test of justification." *Hill v. Stone,* 421 U.S. at 298.

EXAMPLE 7-C

A state law provides that anyone who owes back taxes or fines to the state may not vote. Elmer, who has been out of work for two years, owes the state $35 in personal property taxes on his automobile and $300 in unpaid traffic tickets. As a result, he was barred from voting in a recent election to pick members of Congress and members of the state legislature. Were Elmer's constitutional rights violated?

EXPLANATION

Insofar as the state kept Elmer from voting for the state's delegation to Congress because of his failure to pay property tax, the state violated the Twenty-fourth Amendment. That Amendment, which applies only to federal elections (i.e., a primary or regular election to select the President, Vice-President, or members of Congress), prohibits denying the vote "by reason of failure to pay any poll tax or other tax."

Though the Twenty-fourth Amendment does not protect Elmer's right to vote for state officials, Elmer can also invoke the Fourteenth Amendment Equal Protection Clause. Strict scrutiny is triggered because the state is selectively denying the vote to those who owe back taxes or fines. The state would have to show that this discrimination was necessary to achieve a compelling state interest. The state has an overriding interest in preserving the integrity of the election process, but a person's failure to pay taxes or fines in no way threatens this goal. And even if the state has a compelling interest in collecting revenue, since there are numerous other ways of attaining this goal, it is unnecessary to deny the vote as a collection device. See *Hill v. Stone*, 421 U.S. 289 (1975); *Harper v. Virginia Bd. of Elections*, 383 U.S. 663 (1966).

The rule that selective denials of the franchise are subject to strict scrutiny applies only to elections for public entities that perform "normal governmental" functions. With respect to special limited-purpose entities that do not exercise general governmental authority, the Court will apply only rational basis review under the Fourteenth Amendment to laws that restrict the vote to those persons who are principally affected by the entity's actions. *Salyer Land Co. v. Tulare Lake Basin Water Storage Dist.*, 410 U.S. 719, 726-730 (1973) (upholding California law that allowed only landowners to vote in water storage district elections). However, in *Rice v. Cayetano*, 120 S. Ct. 1044 (2000), the Court refused to extend the special-purpose-district exception to denials of the franchise based on ancestry or race. In that case, the Hawaii constitution restricted the right to vote for trustees of the Office of Hawaiian Affairs (OHA) to "native Hawaiians" and "Hawaiians," groups defined as being descendants of the "peoples" who inhabited the islands in 1778. The OHA is a statewide agency whose mission is to better the conditions of these Hawaiians. The Court held that even if the OHA qualifed as a special purpose district for purposes of an Equal Protection Clause challenge, this would not excuse compliance with the "race neutrality command of the Fifteenth Amendment. . . . The Fifteenth Amendment has independent meaning and force. A state may not deny or abridge the right to vote on account of race. . . ." Id. at 1059-1060.

§7.3.3   *Individual Vote Dilution: "One Person, One Vote"*

The Problem: Unequal Weighting of Votes

A more subtle way to abridge a person's right to vote than outright denial is by employing an electoral scheme in which some people's votes count less than others. For example, state law might provide that in a state or local election (i.e., an election to fill positions at the state or local government level), a person shall receive an *extra* ballot for every $10,000 he or she paid in state income taxes during the previous year. Under this system, no one is completely denied the right to vote, but people's votes are not weighted equally. A person who paid $40,000 in state income tax may cast five votes (one regular and four extra), while an individual who owed no state income tax may cast only one vote. This involves individual vote dilution in that some people's votes carry less weight than those of others. Such a scheme is normally unconstitutional except in rare instances where the election involves a special limited-purpose entity that does not "administer such normal functions of government as the maintenance of streets, the operation of schools, or sanitation, health, or welfare services." *Ball v. James*, 451 U.S. 355, 366 (1981) (upholding a "one acre, one vote" voting scheme for electing directors of a water reclamation district).

Individual vote dilution is not usually as blatant as the last hypothetical suggests. Instead, vote dilution typically results from the fact that electoral districts are drawn in such a way that they do not include the same number of people even though each district elects the same number of officials. As a consequence, those who live in larger population districts cast a vote that is diluted in relation to the vote of those residing in smaller districts.

EXAMPLE 7-D

A town of 60,000 people is run by a three-member town council. The town is divided into districts A, B, and C, each of which elects one member to the council. District A consists of 40,000 people, district B of 15,000 people, and district C of 5000 people. See Figure 7-1. Are some people's votes diluted in comparison with the votes of others?

EXPLANATION

Yes. The 5000 people who live in district C have the same representation and the same influence on the council as the 40,000 people in district A. When the people in district C cast ballots for a council member, they each in effect have a 1/5000th say in the outcome of the election, while the people of district A each have a 1/40,000th say. Because the votes of those who live in district C carry eight times the weight of those who live in district A, the

Figure 7-1

votes of those living in district A are *diluted* in comparison with the votes of those living in district C. To avoid individual vote dilution, each of the three districts would need to contain the same number of people, i.e., 20,000 (60,000/3 = 20,000).

The extent to which individual vote dilution has occurred is described in terms of the maximum (or overall) population deviation. This figure measures the difference between the largest district and the smallest district in terms of the percentage by which each exceeds or falls short of the ideal population. In Example 7-D, the ideal district contains 20,000 people. District A, the largest district, is 100 percent larger than it should be ((40,000 −20,000)/20,000 = 20,000/20,000 = 100 percent). District C, the smallest district, is 75 percent smaller than it should be ((20,000 − 5000)/20,000 = 15,000/20,000 = 75 percent). If you picture a thermometer on which the largest district's deviation from the ideal is marked as a temperature above zero, while the smallest district's deviation falls below zero, the maximum population deviation is the distance between these two points — in this case, 175 percent (i.e., the distance between +100 percent and −75 percent). If this example seems grotesque, the maximum population deviation between Georgia's congressional districts in 1963 was 140 percent. See *Wesberry v. Sanders*, 376 U.S. 1, 2 (1964).

The fact that voting districts contain unequal populations does not necessarily mean that there is individual vote dilution. The key lies in whether there is a disparity between districts in terms of the *ratio of elected officials to population*. Such a disparity existed in Example 7-D, since the ratio of elected officials to population was 1 to 40,000 in district A as compared with 1 to 5000 in district C.

EXAMPLE 7-E

In Example 7-D, suppose that the town was divided into only two districts, A and B. See Figure 7-2 on the following page. District A contains 40,000 people and elects two members to the town council, while district B contains 20,000 people and elects one council member. Does vote dilution occur under this districting scheme?

EXPLANATION

No. Even though the two districts are of unequal population, no vote dilution has occurred, since in both districts, the ratio of elected officials to population is the same, i.e., 2/40,000 = 1/20,000. In this example, the city

Figure 7-2

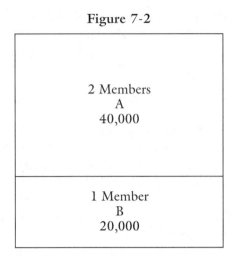

has used a combination of a single-member district and a multimember district in a manner that does not cause any individual vote dilution.

"One Person, One Vote"

Individual vote dilution is subject to strict scrutiny. Under the Constitution, each person is entitled to cast a vote that carries substantially the same weight as that of other voters in the same election. The Court has derived this principle of "one person, one vote" from two distinct sources. In the case of elections for the U.S. House of Representatives, the Court has read the requirement of Article I, §2, cl. 1—representatives are to be chosen "by the People"—as mandating substantial equality of population among the various districts established by a state legislature for the election of members of Congress. With respect to state and local elections, the Court has extracted the same principle from the Equal Protection Clause. Under that Clause, "an individual's right to vote for state [officials] is unconstitutionally impaired when its weight is in a substantial fashion diluted when compared with votes of citizens living in other parts of the State." *Reynolds v. Sims*, 377 U.S. 533, 568 (1964).

When governmental officials are elected on a district-by-district basis, compliance with the principle of "one person, one vote" requires that state and local governments "make an honest and good faith effort to construct districts . . . as nearly of equal population as is practicable." Id. at 577. In other words, each elected official must represent the same number of people. Thus, in Example 7-D, in order to cure the individual vote dilution so that each person's vote carries the same weight, the town would need to redraw the boundaries of its three election districts so that they are apportioned equally in terms of population by having roughly 20,000 people each.

At-Large Election Schemes

An alternative means of satisfying the principle of "one person, one vote" is to choose an elected body at large — i.e., on a citywide, countywide, or statewide basis—rather than on a district-by-district basis. Under an at-large election scheme, everyone in the jurisdiction votes for the same set of officials, and each official represents everyone in the jurisdiction. In Example 7-D, the town might thus have complied with "one person, one vote" by abandoning its system of electing the council on a district basis and instead electing it at large. Under an at-large system, each voter would have the right to vote for three council members, and each council member would represent the same number of persons, i.e., all 60,000 people of the city. Each person's vote would now carry equal weight, for each has a 1/60,000th interest in all three council members.

The U.S. Senate is an example of a body that is elected on an at-large basis. Each of a state's two Senators represents everyone in that state, and every qualified voter in the state has the opportunity to vote for each Senator. By contrast, members of the U.S. House of Representatives are usually chosen on a district basis. If a state has only one Representative in the House, then that state will elect its member at large. However, a state that has more than one Representative in Congress must divide itself into as many districts as it has Representatives, each district electing one member. Under the principle of "one person, one vote," it becomes imperative that the state's congressional districts be drawn so that they are apportioned on an equal population basis.

Reapportionment

Even if a districting scheme met the "one person, one vote" requirement when it was first established, individual vote dilution will gradually occur over time due to demographic changes that alter the population balance between districts. In Example 7-D, had the town initially created three council districts of 20,000 people each, this equality would eventually be destroyed as a result of an uneven pattern of births, deaths, and migration. At the congressional level, reapportionment may also be required if, as a consequence of the latest decennial census, there is a change in the number of Representatives the state is entitled to in the House. For example, as a result of the 1990 census, Georgia's authorized congressional delegation increased by 1, necessitating that the state be divided into 11 — rather than the previous 10 — congressional districts.

To remain in compliance with the Constitution, it is, therefore, necessary to reapportion electoral districts on a periodic basis. However, the Constitution does not require "daily, monthly, annual or biennial reapportionment." *Reynolds v. Sims,* 377 U.S. at 583. Any attempt to enforce compliance with the "one person, one vote" principle on such a frequent basis would be totally unworkable. Instead, it is sufficient if reapportionment at the federal, state, and local governmental levels occurs once every ten years, following the decennial census taken pursuant to Article I, §2, cl. 3.

The degree of mathematical precision that must be achieved in the reapportionment process depends on the purpose of the districting in question. When a state engages in districting to elect state or local governmental officials, the Court will tolerate greater deviations from perfect equality than it will for congressional districting. "[S]tate reapportionment statutes are not subject to the same strict standards applicable to reapportionment of congressional seats." *White v. Regester,* 412 U.S. 755, 763 (1973).

At the state and local levels, it is enough that there be "*substantial* equality of population among the various districts, so that the vote of any citizen is *approximately* equal in weight to that of any other citizen in the State. . . ." *Reynolds v. Sims,* 377 U.S. at 579 (emphasis supplied). At the state and local levels, maximum population deviations as high as 10 percent may be deemed so "minor" as to be "insufficient to make out a prima facie case of invidious discrimination" and, therefore, require no justification whatsoever. *Gaffney v. Cummings,* 412 U.S. 735, 745 (1973); and see *White v. Regester,* 412 U.S. at 763-764. More substantial deviations will be upheld if the state can show that they were necessary to realize legitimate districting goals, such as keeping districts compact and contiguous, respecting municipal boundaries, and avoiding contests between incumbents.

At the level of congressional districting, on the other hand, "there are no de minimis population variations," *Karcher v. Daggett,* 462 U.S. 725, 734 (1983), and the standard of review is always strict. The Constitution requires "that [congressional] districts be apportioned to achieve population equality 'as nearly as is practicable.'" Id. at 730. No matter how small a maximum population deviation the state may have achieved, a challenger can establish a prima facie case by showing that a smaller deviation was possible. Once this prima facie case is made, the state must "prove that the population deviations in its plan were necessary to achieve some legitimate state objective." Id. at 740. Moreover, in contrast to the state and local levels, it appears that a state will at best be able to justify only "minor population deviations" among congressional districts. Id. The Court has defended this very strict approach to congressional districting on the basis that at the national level, the need for equal representation "outweighs the local interests that a State may deem relevant in apportioning districts for representatives to state and local legislatures. . . ." Id. at 733. However, the Court had shown a somewhat greater tolerance for small deviations in congressional redistricting plans that are prepared long after the last census, rather than within a few years of it, due to the fact that census figures become increasingly inaccurate with time. See *Abrams v. Johnson*, 521 U.S. 74, 100 (1997) (approving court-imposed congressional redistricting plan, despite deviation from perfect equality, partly on basis that more than six years had elapsed since the prior census).

EXAMPLE 7-F

Following the 1990 census, the state adopted redistricting plans for the State Senate and Assembly and for the state's congressional districts. The maximum population deviations under these plans were 7 percent for the State Senate, 17 percent for the State Assembly, and 0.7 percent for the congressional districts. The plaintiffs challenged these schemes by showing that alternative plans would have more closely achieved equality in all three governmental bodies. Are the state's plans constitutional?

EXPLANATION

The maximum deviation for the State Senate plan is well below 10 percent and is thus so small as to be de minimis; the plaintiffs have thus failed to establish a prima facie equal protection violation as to this plan. The maximum population variation in the State Assembly plan is above the de minimis level and, therefore, must be justified under strict scrutiny. The same is true of the deviation in the congressional plan, which, though very small, will not be ignored as de minimis, since the plaintiffs have shown that the state could have achieved an even lower deviation. For the State Assembly and congressional plans to be upheld, the state must prove that each of the plans was necessary to achieve a legitimate districting goal, such as maintaining compactness and contiguity, respecting the integrity of political subdivisions or communities, or avoiding contests between incumbents. In the absence of such proof, either or both of these plans will be struck down. See *Karcher v. Daggett*, 462 U.S. 725 (1983).

§7.3.4   *Group Vote Dilution*

Minimizing Group Voting Strength

We have been focusing on situations in which the government has impaired an individual's right to vote by either denying the vote entirely to some people or diluting the weight of their vote in comparison to that of others. There is a third way in which the government may violate the fundamental right to vote, and that is by seeking to minimize or cancel out the voting strength of an identifiable group. Such group vote dilution defeats the "basic aim of legislative apportionment," which is "the achieving of fair and effective *representation* for all citizens." *Reynolds v. Sims*, 377 U.S. at 565-566 (emphasis supplied). Guaranteeing a citizen the right to vote and to cast an equal vote would be of little value if the government could then undermine the voting power of the groups with whom an individual has affiliated for voting purposes. Besides outlawing individual vote dilution, the Constitution bars the government from deliberately denying "a particular group . . . its chance to effectively influence the political process." *Davis v. Bandemer*, 478 U.S. 109, 132-133 (1986). Group vote dilution usually involves attempts to minimize the vote of minority racial groups. However, such claims may conceivably arise with respect to other groups that are politically cohesive, such as ethnic minorities, political parties, and religious communities.

Group vote dilution can be accomplished through any of several different mechanisms. First, a governmental body might be chosen on an at-large basis so that a majority group can outvote a minority group for every seat. Second, the body might be elected under a districting plan whose lines have been purposefully drawn so that a majority group controls the outcome in every district or in a disproportionate share of the districts. Third, a districting plan might use multimember rather than single-member districts, again with the goal of preventing a minority from realizing its voting potential. We will consider each of these group vote dilution devices initially in the context of minority racial groups. Thereafter, we will examine their application to other types of groups.

Dilution through At-Large Elections

One of the easiest ways to bring about group vote dilution is through the use of an at-large voting scheme. In an at-large scheme, as we noted earlier, the principle of "one person, one vote" is always satisfied, so there can be no individual vote dilution. Group vote dilution, however, is a very real danger.

EXAMPLE 7-G

In Example 7-D, assume that the town's racial composition is 40,000 whites and 20,000 blacks. The neighborhoods are fairly segregated, with whites living in the northern and central parts of town and blacks living in the southern part. Assume, too, that voting takes place along racial lines, with whites generally voting for white candidates and blacks voting for black candidates. How would an at-large election scheme produce group vote dilution?

EXPLANATION

Since blacks make up a third of the population, they might fairly expect to elect one member to the council. This would follow if the town used a districting scheme in which blacks had a clear majority in one of the three council districts. Thus, if the city created three council districts (A, B, and C) whose lines ran horizontally from east to west, whites would have a clear majority in the northern and central districts, while blacks would dominate the southern district. See Figure 7-3. Under this scheme, the council's membership would presumably reflect the racial composition of the city by containing two whites and one black.

However, whites could deliberately nullify the voting strength of black voters by deciding that the town council shall be elected at-large rather than from districts. Under this scheme, everyone in town would vote for all three council seats. If each candidate had to run for a specific seat and if a white opposed a black in each contest, whites would win all three seats, since they outnumber blacks in the town by a two-to-one margin. Through this purposeful scheme, blacks could be prevented from electing any candidates to the council despite the fact that they comprise a third of the town's population. See *Rogers v. Lodge*, 458 U.S. 613 (1982) (invalidating racially motivated at-large election scheme for Board of Commissioners of Burke County, Georgia).

Dilution through Gerrymandering

A second means of diluting the voting strength of a minority group is through gerrymandering, that is, purposefully drawing district lines so that the minority group will not have a majority in any district or in as many districts as it might otherwise have, or so that the group's political power is otherwise diminished.

Figure 7-3

○ white residents

◉ black residents

EXAMPLE 7-H

In Example 7-G, we noted that if the town had used a districting scheme in which district lines ran horizontally from east to west, blacks would be able to elect one member to the council. How might gerrymandering be utilized to dilute the voting strength of the town's black citizens?

EXPLANATION

The districting scheme could instead be racially gerrymandered so that whites are assured of electing all three council members. This could be accomplished by deliberately drawing district lines vertically from north to south rather than horizontally from east to west. See Figure 7-4. As long as each district contains 20,000 people, no individual vote dilution would occur. Yet by drawing district lines vertically rather than horizontally, since the northern and central portions of each district are virtually all-white, whites will have roughly a two-thirds majority in each district and thus be able to elect all three members of the council. Through this purposeful districting scheme, whites will have totally neutralized the voting strength of the town's sizable black minority.

Dilution through Use of Multimember Districts

The third method of purposefully diluting a group's voting strength is to use multimember rather than single-member districts so that a district elects more than one representative. Multimember districts combine aspects of at-large elections and districting, for while districts exist, at least some of them elect more than one representative on a districtwide or at-large basis. Like at-large schemes, multimember districts operate on a "winner-take-all" principle that submerges minorities and overrepresents the majority. Yet the mere fact that multimember districts may deprive a racial minority of representation is not

Figure 7-4

○ white residents

◉ black residents

enough to invalidate their use. It must also be shown "that the political processes leading to nomination and election were not equally open to participation by the group in question—that its members had less opportunity than did other residents in the district to participate in the political processes and to elect legislators of their choice." *White v. Regester*, 412 U.S. at 766.

EXAMPLE 7-I

In Example 7-D, suppose that the town council consists of five rather than three members and that these five members are chosen from three council districts. See Figure 7-5. District A, which contains 12,000 people, elects one member, while districts B and C contain 24,000 people apiece and each elect two members. Since each council member represents exactly 12,000 people, the principle of "one person, one vote" is satisfied, and thus there is no individual vote dilution. How does this scheme cause group vote dilution?

EXPLANATION

The districting plan makes it virtually impossible for blacks to elect a council member. District A contains 12,000 whites, while districts B and C (the two multimember districts) have each been drawn to contain 14,000 whites and 10,000 blacks. Assuming racial-bloc voting, a white candidate is certain to win the seat from all-white district A. Moreover, the two seats chosen from district B and the two seats chosen from district C are likely to go to white candidates, since whites outnumber blacks in each of these districts by a margin of roughly 58 percent to 42 percent.

To invalidate the use of these multimember districts and to force the town to use five single-member districts, the plaintiffs would have to prove not only that blacks are unable to elect council members of their choice, but also that they lack an equal opportunity to participate in the local political

Figure 7-5

1 Member A 12,000	
2 Members B 24,000 (14,000 whites)	2 Members C 24,000 (14,000 whites)
(10,000 blacks)	(10,000 blacks)

○ white residents
◉ black residents

process because, for example, their interests are consistently ignored by the town's political parties.

It is important to emphasize that none of the three devices we have discussed in connection with group vote dilution is unconstitutional per se. At-large election schemes, districting schemes, and multimember districts are subject to strict scrutiny only if it can be shown by direct or circumstantial evidence that they were adopted for a suspect purpose, such as diluting the voting strength of a racial minority. Otherwise, these electoral devices, despite their discriminatory impact on particular minority groups, will receive only rational basis scrutiny and are certain to be upheld.

Vote Dilution and Nonracial Groups

The examples of group vote dilution that we have examined so far have all involved dilution aimed at minority racial groups. However, group vote dilution is objectionable not only when it is aimed at racial groups, but also when it is applied against groups defined in nonracial terms. The constitutional right to participate equally in the political process is a right that belongs to all citizens, not just to racial minorities. If an identifiable group shares particular interests that cause its members to vote on a cohesive basis, a deliberate attempt by the majority to minimize or destroy that group's voting power should be subject to strict scrutiny, whether the group consists of Italians, the poor, environmentalists, Hasidic Jews, senior citizens, or Democrats. The Supreme Court has held that group vote dilution claims brought on behalf of political parties are justiciable and has at least suggested that members of other identifiable groups may bring similar claims, assuming that they can establish a prima facie case. *Davis v. Bandemer,* 478 U.S. at 125-126 (plurality opinion); id. at 147 (O'Connor, J., concurring).

Where the group is a political party rather than a racial minority, however, it is more difficult to establish a prima facie case of group vote dilution. This additional difficulty may also accompany challenges by other nonracial groups. Thus, while the Court has held that political gerrymandering claims are justiciable, it is not enough for a prima facie case to merely prove that district lines have been drawn with the purpose and the effect of making it more difficult for members of the complaining political party to *elect representatives.* In addition, the plaintiffs must show that the political gerrymander has destroyed the group's ability to *influence the political process.* This showing cannot be based simply on the outcome of one or two elections, for such possibly transitory results are insufficient to prove that the challenged "electoral system is arranged in a manner that will consistently degrade a voter's or a group of voters' influence on the political process as a whole." Id. at

132 (plurality opinion). Rather, there must be "evidence of continued frustration of the will of a majority of the voters or effective denial to a minority of voters of a fair chance to influence the political process." Id. at 133 (plurality opinion). The difficulty is that by the time enough elections have occurred to perhaps satisfy this standard, a new reapportionment plan will have been adopted in response to the latest decennial census. This may start the clock running all over again, for the plaintiffs must now seek to prove that the *new* plan is one that "consistently" impairs their influence on the political process. In *Bandemer,* the Court thus noted that the complaining Indiana Democrats failed to show "that the 1981 reapportionment would consign [them] to a minority status . . . throughout the 1980's or that [they] would have no hope of doing any better in the reapportionment that would occur after the 1990 census." Id. at 135-136.

EXAMPLE 7-J

Suppose that the town of 60,000 in Example 7-D is divided into three town council districts, each containing 20,000 people. The districts were designed by the council after the last decennial census. The council, which then consisted of two Democrats and one Republican, drew the districting plan with the announced purpose of minimizing the voting strength of the town's 27,000 Republicans. The plan achieved this by drawing district lines so that each district contains 11,000 Democrats and 9,000 Republicans. The three districts were so bizarre in shape that they were named "The Corkscrew," "The Pretzel," and "Frankenstein." After the first three biennial elections conducted under the plan resulted in Democrats winning all three seats on the council, the Republicans filed suit, claiming that the plan violates the Equal Protection Clause as a political gerrymander. Is the plan unconstitutional?

EXPLANATION

The plaintiffs will have no difficulty proving the intent element of the prima facie case, for the council admitted that its purpose was to discriminate against Republicans. However, it is very unlikely that even three elections are sufficient to prove the element of discriminatory impact. This is especially true given the narrow 55 percent-45 percent margin between the parties in each district. Council members probably cannot risk entirely ignoring the interests of Republican voters, for they cannot count on winning every Democratic vote in their district. A candidate's position on certain key issues may cause some Democratic voters to cross party lines. Thus, in the absence of proof that Republican voters are consistently deprived of an opportunity to influence the local political process, the mere fact that Republicans are consistently unable to elect any members to the town council will not by itself establish the discriminatory impact element of the prima facie case. The council's districting scheme is, therefore, likely to be upheld under the rational basis equal protection test.

As this example suggests, unlike most strict scrutiny equal protection cases (see §6.2.2), in the group vote dilution context the impact element of the prima facie case may be much harder to prove than the intent element. At least where political gerrymandering is involved, the legislature was almost surely aware of and intended the political consequences of its reapportionment plan. See *Davis v. Bandemer*, 478 U.S. at 128-129. The problem will be to satisfy what the Court has referred to as a "heightened effect" requirement. The Court has justified this high threshold on grounds of federalism, noting that federal courts would too often otherwise be involved "in second-guessing what has consistently been referred to as a political task for the [state] legislature." Id. at 133. The net result is that while nonracial group vote dilution claims are in theory justiciable, except in rare cases it may be impossible to establish a prima facie constitutional violation.

§7.3.5   *Nondilutional Race-Based Districting*

We have seen that the fundamental right to vote may be violated by selective denials of the franchise, by individual vote dilution, or by group vote dilution. The fourth way in which the right to vote may be infringed is through race-based districting, i.e., where race is used as the predominant factor in assigning people to voting districts. Race-based districting is typically employed for the purpose of creating so-called majority-minority districts, i.e., districts in which a racial minority group constitutes a majority of the voters, thereby enhancing the group's chances of electing a representative of its own choosing.

EXAMPLE 7-K

In Example 7-G, suppose that the three-member town council is chosen from three council districts, each containing 20,000 people. The town's population is one-third black and two-thirds white. If the town council wishes to make sure that blacks are able to elect one of the three council members, how might it achieve this goal?

EXPLANATION

The council might employ race-based districting, drawing district lines so that people are assigned to districts on the basis of their race. Thus, one of the three districts, district C, might be configured so that it consists almost entirely of blacks. District C would be a majority-minority district, for blacks —who constitute a minority of the town's population—would be a majority in this district. See Figure 7-3.

Race-based districting is sometimes referred to as a form of racial gerrymandering. Yet in contrast to traditional racial gerrymanders, race-based districting does not produce group vote dilution. Rather than minimizing or canceling out any group's *legitimate* voting strength, race-based districting has the effect of helping minorities elect representatives in numbers that more closely match their proportion of the population. While such a scheme may mean that the majority is unable to elect as many representatives as it did before, the majority's representation is typically not reduced below its proportional share. Thus, in Example 7-K, assuming that prior to race-based districting whites were able to elect all three members of the council, the new scheme still leaves whites with control of two of the three council districts, exactly matching their two-thirds makeup in the town's population. Nor does race-based districting entail individual vote dilution, for the districts are presumably of equal size, thus honoring the principle of "one person, one vote."

Nonetheless, race-based districting is subject to strict scrutiny. Even though it causes neither individual nor group vote dilution, the Court has identified three other types of injury that warrant the application of strict scrutiny. First, race-based districting may cause a *representational* harm, for if a district is created to benefit a particular racial group, this may send a message to elected officials "that their primary obligation is to represent only the members of that group, rather than their constituency as a whole." *Shaw v. Reno,* 509 U.S. 630, 648 (1993). Second, such districting may produce *stigmatic* injuries by operating on "the offensive and demeaning assumption that voters of a particular race, because of their race, 'think alike, share the same political interests, and will prefer the same candidates at the polls.'" *Miller v. Johnson,* 515 U.S. 900, 911-912 (1995). Finally, race-based districting may result in harm to society by threatening to "balkanize us into competing racial factions." Id. at 912.

To establish a prima facie case of race-based districting, the plaintiff must show that those who adopted the districting plan "subordinated traditional race-neutral districting principles," with the result "that race was the predominant factor motivating the . . . decision to place a significant number of voters within or without a particular district." Id. at 916. In race discrimination cases, it is normally enough to show that race was "a motivating factor." See §6.2.2. However, the Court has rejected this standard in the race-based districting setting because it could lead to excessive federal judicial interference in an area that is "primarily the duty and responsibility of the

State." *Miller v. Johnson*, 515 U.S. at 915. Since redistricting legislatures are invariably aware of racial demographics, the "motivating factor" standard would make it too easy for a court to subject an apportionment plan to strict scrutiny.

Proof that race was "the predominant factor" motivating the assignment of voters to election districts may at times consist of nothing more than the bizarreness of a district's shape and statistics as to its majority-minority composition. In *Shaw v. Reno*, the Court held that a prima facie case of race-based districting was established simply by the fact that a North Carolina reapportionment plan containing "lines of dramatically irregular shape," 509 U.S. at 633, was "so bizarre on its face that it is 'unexplainable on grounds other than race'. . . ." Id. at 644. As *Shaw* suggests, bizarreness of shape is not necessarily dispositive, for it may have been predominantly motivated by legitimate political concerns such as protecting incumbents or preserving partisan balance in the elected body, rather than by race. See *Hunt v. Cromartie*, 526 U.S. 541 (1999) (holding that bizarre shape, even when it coincides with racially defined precincts or neighborhoods, may be explicable in political rather than racial terms where there is a high degree of correlation between racial composition and party preference). Even regularly shaped districts are open to challenge if, by "more direct evidence going to legislative purpose," the plaintiff can show that race was the predominant factor in drawing district lines. *Miller v. Johnson*, 515 U.S. at 916. The fact that a state plan was also motivated by traditional districting considerations, such as compactness, contiguity, or incumbency protection, will not defeat the application of strict scrutiny if a court finds that these "legitimate districting principles were 'subordinated' to race." *Bush v. Vera*, 517 U.S. 952, 959 (1996) (applying strict scrutiny in a mixed motive case where race predominated over traditional goal of incumbency protection).

EXAMPLE 7-L

In Example 7-K, if blacks are concentrated in the southern end of town, district C, the majority-black district, is probably not bizarre or irregular in shape. See Figure 7-3. What is the likelihood of proving the existence of race-based districting?

EXPLANATION

Such a showing would be difficult. The plaintiffs would have to prove, through evidence other than the district's shape, that race was the predominant factor in creating district C. If the town council admitted that it had taken race into account in creating the reapportionment plan, this would still not be enough to prove that other factors were subordinated to race. The council might also have been motivated by a desire to keep districts compact or by a desire to preserve the community of interest that exists in the south end of town. A court might well find that these race-neutral factors played a large enough role to preclude a finding that race was the predominant consideration in creating district C.

If a prima facie case of race-based districting is established, the plan will be subject to strict scrutiny. The scheme will be ruled unconstitutional unless it is proved that the plan was adopted to further a compelling state interest and that it is narrowly tailored to achieve that interest.

EXAMPLE 7-M

Suppose that in Example 7-L a court found that race was the predominant factor in creating district C. How might the council defend the constitutionality of this majority-minority district?

EXPLANATION

It might be able to show that the plan was necessary to eradicate the effects of past discrimination. As we saw earlier (§6.4.7), this will constitute a compelling interest if there is proof that it was the actual goal behind the plan and that at the time the council adopted the plan it had a strong basis in evidence to support a finding of past discrimination. *Shaw v. Hunt*, 517 U.S. 899, 907-911 & n.4 (1996). The plan might thus be upheld if there is evidence that the town had previously used racial gerrymandering, literacy tests, poll taxes, or other devices to prevent blacks from electing members to the council and if it is also shown that because whites still vote as a racial bloc, creating a majority-black district is necessary to eliminate the present effects of this past discrimination.

In a number of race-based districting cases, states have defended their creation of majority-minority districts on the ground that the U.S. Department of Justice insisted this was necessary to comply with the federal Voting Rights Act. While the Justice Department is charged with enforcing this Act, the Supreme Court will not defer to the department's interpretation of it. The Court has said that even assuming compliance with the Act constitutes a compelling state interest (a matter the Court has left open), the Court will decide for itself whether the Act required race-based districting in the specific case and whether the state's use of race was narrowly tailored to that end. In *Shaw v. Hunt*, 517 U.S. 899 (1996), and *Bush v. Vera*, 517 U.S. 952 (1996), the Supreme Court thus applied strict scrutiny to invalidate race-based districting by North Carolina and Texas, in settings where the Justice

Department had demanded that the states create additional majority-black congressional districts.

§7.3.6   *Access to the Ballot*

In contrast to the fundamental right to vote, there is no fundamental right of access by a potential candidate to the ballot. Strict scrutiny, therefore, is not automatically triggered whenever the government regulates or restricts a person's ability to run for public office. Yet restrictions on candidate access will trigger heightened scrutiny if they substantially interfere with either of two other constitutional rights: (1) the fundamental equal protection right to vote for a candidate who reflects one's views or (2) the First Amendment right to associate with others for political purposes and to advance a candidate of one's choosing. In this section, we will consider limitations on candidate access in light of the Equal Protection Clause. The First Amendment right of association is discussed in §8.6.

The Court has applied strict scrutiny to laws that have the effect of conditioning ballot access on the wealth of a candidate or the candidate's supporters. In *Bullock v. Carter*, 405 U.S. 134 (1972), the Court struck down a Texas statute that imposed candidate filing fees as high as $8,900, and in *Lubin v. Panish*, 415 U.S. 709 (1974), it invalidated a California law that set candidate filing fees at 2 percent of the position's annual salary. The effect of both laws was to prevent less affluent groups from being able to vote for a candidate who shared their views. Applying strict scrutiny, the Court noted that there are less discriminatory ways to achieve the states' goals of controlling the length of the ballot and discouraging frivolous candidacies, such as requiring that candidates collect a specified number of signatures before their names may appear on the ballot. In order for such a filing fee scheme to be constitutional, the state must provide indigent candidates with alternative means of qualifying for the ballot. However, even signature requirements may trigger strict scrutiny if the number of signatures a candidate must collect is so high that it will keep independent candidates and minor parties from appearing on the ballot.

On the other hand, strict scrutiny will not be applied to ballot access restrictions that keep particular individuals off the ballot as long as they do not prevent any groups of voters from fielding a candidate of their choice. For example, an ordinance requiring that all elected city officials be residents of the city is probably constitutional, for while it will bar certain individuals from running for office, the requirement is unlikely to infringe on any group's ability to vote for a candidate of its choice. See *McCarthy v. Philadelphia Civil Serv. Commn.*, 424 U.S. 645 (1976) (upholding city requirement that all city employees be city residents).

§7.4   The Right to Travel

One of the fundamental rights protected by the Fourteenth Amendment is the right to travel, i.e., the right to move to a state and establish residence there. Laws that discourage or penalize exercise of this right by discriminating against newcomers to the state are subject to strict scrutiny either under the Equal Protection Clause or under the Fourteenth Amendment's Privileges or Immunities Clause, or both. The right to travel secured by the Fourteenth Amendment is something of a misnomer. What is protected is not the right to simply visit or pass through a state, but the right to migrate and change one's domicile and to then be treated as an equal with other residents of the state. The right to visit or pass through a state, whether for business or for pleasure, may be protected by other constitutional provisions, including the Commerce Clause, and the Privileges and Immunities Clauses of Article IV. See Christopher N. May & Allan Ides, *Constitutional Law: National Power and Federalism,* chs. 8-9 (2001).

The Supreme Court initially used the Equal Protection Clause to protect newcomers of a state against laws that discriminate against them. The right to travel was deemed to be a fundamental right for equal protection purposes. As such, not all laws discriminating against new residents of the state were subject to strict scrutiny. Rather, strict scrutiny came into play only if the state's adverse treatment of newcomers was sufficient to discourage or penalize migration to the state. Forms of discrimination that were deemed to be too incidental or insignificant did not impinge on the right to travel (see §7.2), and therefore did not trigger strict scrutiny.

Without disavowing its equal protection right to travel cases, the Court in *Saenz v. Roe,* 526 U.S. 489 (1999), recently held that the right to travel is also protected by the Privileges or Immunities Clause of the Fourteenth Amendment. See May & Ides, *Constitutional Law,* supra, at §9.3.1. One of the privileges or immunities of national citizenship is "the right of the newly arrived citizen" to be "treated like other citizens of that state." *Saenz v. Roe,* 526 U.S. at 500, 502. Under the Privileges or Immunities Clause, a state law that "discriminates against some of its citizens because they have been domiciled in the State for less than" a specified period of time is subject to strict scrutiny, regardless of how "incidental" the effect of the discrimination involved. Id. at 504-505. This is not to say that all such laws are necessarily unconstitutional.

Today, laws that discriminate against new residents of a state may thus be challenged under the Fourteenth Amendment, using either the Equal Protection Clause or the Privileges or Immunities Clause. Yet because it is more difficult to trigger strict scrutiny using the equal protection analysis due to its impingement requirement, a litigant would almost always prefer to challenge such discrimination by invoking the Privileges or Immunities

Clause. While it is too early to tell, the Court's equal protection right to travel line of cases may fall into desuetude, much like a road that is abandoned after the construction of a modern highway.

In the balance of this section we will examine the right to travel in the context of several different types of residency requirements, i.e., durational residency requirements; fixed-point and fixed-date residency requirements; and bona fide residency requirements. Not all of these implicate the right to travel protected by the Fourteenth Amendment.

§7.4.1 Durational Residency Requirements

One type of law that may trigger strict scrutiny under both the Equal Protection and the Privileges or Immunities Clauses is a durational residency requirement or waiting period. Such measures deny new residents a benefit or privilege that is available to other residents of the state until the newcomers have lived in the state and/or the county for a specified period of time. If the benefit is sufficiently vital or important, the state's discrimination between new and old residents will be deemed to impinge on the right to travel and will receive strict scrutiny under the Equal Protection Clause. Durational residency requirements for welfare benefits, medical care, and voting are thus subject to strict scrutiny, for they penalize the right to travel by imposing substantial burdens exclusively on those who recently moved to the state. Where less critical benefits are at stake, strict scrutiny is not necessarily called for under the Equal Protection Clause, although strict scrutiny will still be employed under the Privileges or Immunities Clause.

EXAMPLE 7-N

A California law provides that during their first year in the state, new residents who apply for welfare may receive a monthly grant no higher than what they would have been eligible for in the state from which they moved. The purpose of the statute is to reduce the state's welfare budget by $11 million a year. The law was challenged by several California residents who qualified for welfare benefits but who within the previous year had moved to California from states with lower benefit levels. As a result, the plaintiffs receive welfare grants that are from $200 to $400 a month less than those received by Californians who have lived in the state for a longer period of time. Does this California durational residency requirement violate the Equal Protection Clause, or the Privileges or Immunities Clause?

EXPLANATION

Even though it imposes a one-year waiting period, the California law might not be subject to strict scrutiny under the Equal Protection Clause. In contrast to the one-year durational residency requirements for welfare struck down in *Shapiro v. Thompson*, 394 U.S. 618 (1969), California does not withhold all welfare benefits from newcomers; instead, they receive the same cash benefits they were receiving or would have received in their home states. In addition, the disparity between the benefits paid new residents and older residents is partially offset by additional housing assistance and food stamp allowances. Thus, the impact on the fundamental right to travel may be too incidental to trigger strict scrutiny under the Equal Protection Clause.

Strict scrutiny would nevertheless be applied under the Privileges or Immunities Clause, which has no similar impingement requirement. Under strict scrutiny, the law is unconstitutional. The state's interest in reducing welfare costs is important but probably not compelling. Even if it were, the state's discrimination against newcomers is not necessary to achieving the state's goal. It could save the same amount of money by instead reducing all welfare grants — for new residents and old residents alike — by 72 cents a month. See *Saenz v. Roe*, 526 U.S. 489 (1999) (invalidating identical California welfare statute under Privileges or Immunities Clause).

EXAMPLE 7-O

State law provides that in order to file a divorce action, the plaintiff must have been a resident of the state for one year immediately prior to filing the action. Carol moved to the state five months ago and would like to bring a divorce action there so that she can marry Ralph. If Carol challenges the validity of the state's one-year durational residency requirement, will strict scrutiny apply under the Equal Protection Clause?

EXPLANATION

This law classifies residents based on their length of residence in the state. Carol will argue that by denying her access to the divorce court for a year, the state is penalizing her for having recently exercised her right to travel. The state will respond that unlike waiting periods for welfare benefits, medical care, and voting, a divorce decree is not a vital governmental benefit and the harm caused by the waiting period is not irreparable. Once the durational residency requirement has been satisfied, Carol will receive exactly the same benefit she seeks now — a dissolution of her marriage. By contrast, in the welfare, medical care, and voting contexts, benefits denied during the waiting period are irretrievably lost. On this basis, the state will argue that the one-year waiting period does not impinge on either the fundamental right to travel or the fundamental right to marry and that strict scrutiny should, therefore, not be applied. See *Sosna v. Iowa*, 419 U.S. 393 (1975) (upholding one-year waiting period for filing a divorce action under the Equal Protection Clause, without applying strict scrutiny).

The result in this example might have been different had the state imposed a much longer waiting period, e.g., ten years rather than one year. Even though the nature of the benefit or privilege would be the same, the harm inflicted during the interim might in many respects now become irreparable. In other words, whether or not a durational residency requirement impinges on the equal protection right to travel may be a function of both the nature of the benefit and the length of time it is withheld. For a truly vital benefit, such as welfare or medical care, even a short waiting period may be enough to trigger strict scrutiny; for less critical benefits, it may take a long waiting period before one could conclude that the right to travel was being penalized. The Court in *Sosna* implied as much, noting that most states imposed waiting periods for divorce of between six months and two years and that Iowa's one-year period was the most common period prescribed.

If the one-year waiting period for a divorce in Example 7-O were instead challenged under the Privileges or Immunities Clause, strict scrutiny would have applied since the law discriminates against new residents of the state. Yet the measure might not be found unconstitutional. In *Saenz v. Roe,* the Court suggested that a state may be allowed to impose a durational residency requirement when there is a danger that immediate eligibility "will encourage citizens of other States to establish residency for just long enough to acquire some readily portable benefit, such as divorce or a college education, that will be enjoyed after they return to their original domicile." 526 U.S. at 505. The Court contrasted the welfare benefits at issue in *Saenz,* noting that they would be entirely consumed while the new resident was still living in the state. However, as Chief Justice Rehnquist remarked in his dissent,

> this "you can't take it with you" distinction is more apparent than real. . . . Welfare payments are a form of insurance, giving impoverished individuals and their families the means to meet the demands of daily life while they receive the necessary training, education, and time to look for a job. The cash itself will no doubt be spent in California, but the benefits from receiving this income and having the opportunity to become employed or employable will stick with the welfare recipient if they stay in California or go back to their true domicile. Similarly, tuition subsidies are "consumed" in-state but the recipient takes the benefits of a college education with him wherever he goes. A welfare subsidy is thus as much an investment in human capital as is a tuition subsidy, and their attendant benefits are just as "portable." . . . [T]he line drawn by the Court borders on the metaphysical, and requires lower courts to plumb the policies animating certain benefits like welfare to define their "essence" and hence their "portability."

Id. at 519-520. It remains to be seen whether the "portability" argument will enable states to salvage some durational residency requirements despite the fact that they are subject to strict scrutiny under the Privileges or Immunities Clause.

Besides making a portability argument, a state might be able to defend a relatively short durational residency requirement on the ground that it is necessary to assure that an individual has in fact become a bone fide resident of the state. In *Saenz*, the Court expressly alluded to this possibility, noting that because it was undisputed that the plaintiffs there were citizens of California, "[w]e thus have no occasion to consider what weight might be given to a citizen's length of residence if the bona fides of her claim to state citizenship were questioned." Id. at 505.

§7.4.2 Fixed-Point and Fixed-Date Residency Requirements

Besides durational residency requirements, there are two other types of residency requirements that may trigger strict scrutiny due to their impact on the right to travel. One is a fixed-point residency requirement: In order to receive a particular governmental benefit or privilege, a person must have been a resident of the state at a specified point in time, such as when they were born, when they turned 21, or when they graduated from college. The other is a fixed-date residency requirement, which conditions a benefit or privilege on a person's having resided in the state on a specific date, such as January 1, 1975. Like durational residency requirements, both fixed-point and fixed-date residency requirements draw distinctions among residents of the state; moreover, they usually have the effect of discriminating against newer residents of the state. In contrast to durational requirements, the burdens imposed by fixed-point and fixed-date requirements are permanent, for no matter how long a person waits, he or she will never be treated the same as other state residents. Because of their permanent impact, it may be easier than with durational residency requirements to find that fixed-point or fixed-date requirements impinge on the right to travel so as to trigger strict scrutiny under the Equal Protection Clause. To the extent that they discriminate against newer state residents, they should in any event receive strict scrutiny under the Privileges or Immunities Clause.

EXAMPLE 7-P

Under State Z law, those who were residents of State Z when they graduated from high school are entitled to free tuition at the state university. Ted is 25 years old and has been a resident of State Z for the last six years. He was admitted to the state university, but was advised that he must pay tuition of $10,000/year because when he graduated from high school, he was a resident of State X. Ted has challenged State Z's tuition policy under the

Equal Protection Clause and the Privileges or Immunities Clause. Will the policy be struck down?

EXPLANATION

The state tuition policy involves a fixed-point residency requirement because in order to receive the benefit of free tuition, one must have been a state resident at a fixed point in one's life. This is not a fixed-date residency requirement, since the relevant date will vary in each individual case. Nor has the state employed a durational residency requirement or waiting period, for no matter how long Ted resides in State Z, he will never qualify for free tuition.

The Court has suggested that *durational* residency requirements for reduced tuition at a state university do not impinge on the equal protection right to travel. See, e.g., *Vlandis v. Kline*, 412 U.S. 441, 452-454 (1973); *Starns v. Malkerson*, 326 F. Supp. 234 (D. Minn. 1970), *aff'd*, 401 U.S. 985 (1971). Here, however, the state has employed a *fixed-point* requirement that has the effect of permanently relegating newcomers to a status inferior to that of older residents. The permanency of the disqualification may cause a court to find that State Z's residency requirement penalizes exercise of the right to travel and must, therefore, be subject to strict scrutiny. See *Attorney General of N.Y. v. Soto-Lopez*, 476 U.S. 898 (1986) (plurality opinion) (applying strict scrutiny to invalidate a fixed-point residency requirement for the receipt of a civil service veteran's preference, noting that while the benefit was not as important as welfare, medical care, or voting, denial of the benefit was permanent rather than temporary).

Under the Privileges or Immunities Clause, strict scrutiny should be called for since this law discriminates against Ted as a relative newcomer to the state. While the law involves a fixed-point rather than a durational residency requirement, the state is still denying a relative newcomer the right to be treated like native-born or longer-term residents of the state. However, if the Court adopts the "portability" argument discussed earlier, this law might be upheld. On the other hand, the Court's discussion of portability in *Saenz* was in the context of a temporary delay in providing newcomers with a benefit. The danger that a person will "take the benefit and run" diminishes the longer they have lived in the state. Thus, even if this concern might justify some type of durational residency requirement, "portability" should not constitute a basis for permanently denying such a benefit to a person like Ted who has resided in the state for six years.

§7.4.3   *The Equal Protection Alternative to Strict Scrutiny*

Under the Equal Protection Clause, if a state law that discriminates against newcomers impinges on the right to travel, it will be subject to strict scrutiny and invalidated unless the measure is shown to be necessary to achieve a compelling state interest. If there is no infringement of the right to travel, so that strict scrutiny is not triggered, the standard of equal protection review will not necessarily drop to the "toothless" rational basis test. As we noted earlier, discrimination against those who recently moved to the state is sometimes reviewed under an enhanced version of the rational basis test. See §6.7.2.

EXAMPLE 7-Q

State B gives residents an annual $10 recreation credit for each year they have lived in the state since reaching age 21. The credit can be used to reduce any fee charged by the state for admission to a park, beach, or campground and to reduce state fees for recreational fishing and hunting licenses. Ted, who is 51 and has lived in State B all his life, receives a $300 annual recreation credit, reflecting the fact that he has resided in the state for 30 years since reaching age 21. Sam, who is also 51, moved to the state five years ago and thus receives only a $50 credit. Has State B violated Sam's rights under the Equal Protection Clause?

EXPLANATION

The recreation credit discriminates against newer residents of State B, who receive smaller credits than their counterparts, such as Ted, who have lived in State B all their lives. The credit involves a form of durational residency requirement, for state benefits are tied to how long one has lived in the state; however, unlike typical durational residency requirements, there is no point at which the relative newcomer is treated as a full equal to longer-term residents. Yet for equal protection purposes, it is not clear that this durational residency scheme deters or penalizes exercise of the right to travel; instead, it may encourage adults to move to State B and reward them for doing so.

Even if it does not infringe on the right to travel, the credit discriminates on the basis of when a person established residence in the state; moreover, the discrimination is permanent, for Sam will never catch up with people such as Ted. The Court might, therefore, apply an enhanced version of the rational basis test. Under this standard, while the state may argue that the recreation credit scheme furthers the interest of encouraging people to move to the state and to remain there, this might not justify the creation of "fixed, permanent distinctions between . . . concededly bona fide residents, based on how long they have been in the State." *Zobel v. Williams*, 457 U.S. 55, 59 (1982) (invalidating Alaska scheme that paid annual dividends on the basis of the number of years a person had lived in the state).

Zobel was decided before the Court in *Saenz v. Roe* placed the right to travel under the umbrella of the Privileges or Immunities Clause. Today, the recreation credit scheme set forth in this example, as well as the dividend scheme challenged in *Zobel*, would most likely be subject to strict scrutiny and invalidated under the Privileges or Immunities Clause.

§7.4.4   *Bona Fide Residency Requirements*

It is important to distinguish durational, fixed-point, and fixed-date residency requirements, all of which may impinge on the right to travel, from bona fide residency requirements. A bona fide residency requirement merely insists that a person in fact be a resident of the state in order to receive a benefit or engage in some activity. Thus, whereas durational, fixed-point, and fixed-date residency requirements draw distinctions *among residents* of the state on the basis of when they took up residence there, bona fide residency requirements draw distinctions *between residents and nonresidents* of the state. Such requirements do not discourage or penalize exercise of the right to travel, but rather encourage people to move to the state and reward them for doing so. Once a person exercises this right by becoming a bona fide resident, he or she is instantly treated just like — and entitled to the same benefits as — all other residents of the state. Since bona fide residency requirements do not impinge on the right to migrate to the state, they are not subject to strict scrutiny equal protection review. Nor do they trigger scrutiny under the Privileges or Immunities Clause. However, because they do discriminate against citizens of other states in favor of the state's own citizens, bona fide residency requirements may be subject to fairly demanding review under the dormant Commerce Clause and under the Privileges and Immunities Clause of Article IV, §2. See May & Ides, *Constitutional Law*, supra, at chs. 8-9.

The fact that bona fide residency requirements do not raise right to travel concerns indicates that the right is narrower in scope than we have so far suggested. The Court has described the right to travel as the right to migrate, as opposed to the right simply to travel about. Yet even this formulation is too broad, for it is only the right to *immigrate* or *move to* the state — not the right to *emigrate* or *leave* the state — that is protected by the right to travel under the Equal Protection Clause and the Privileges or Immunities Clause. If the right to emigrate were part of the fundamental right to travel, even bona fide residency requirements might trigger strict scrutiny, since they might discourage or penalize the decision to move out of the state.

EXAMPLE 7-R

State A's medical school, which is one of the best in the nation, provides free tuition to all bona fide residents of the state. Students who attend the school, but do not maintain a permanent residence in the state, are charged full tuition. Sonya was a resident of State A when she began medical school, but during her second year, she and her family moved to State B. As a result,

Sonya has now been charged out-of-state tuition of $25,000/year. Has State A violated Sonya's constitutional right to travel?

EXPLANATION

Sonya's right to travel has not been violated. State A has merely imposed a bona fide residency requirement in order to receive free tuition. Because the requirement encourages people to move to the state, it does not burden the right to travel under either the Equal Protection Clause or the Privileges or Immunities Clause. The state has not created a classification that treats new residents less favorably than older residents, but has instead drawn a distinction between residents and nonresidents. Since the right to travel is not implicated, a court would at best apply enhanced rational basis review under the Equal Protection Clause. The residency requirement would be upheld on the ground that it rationally furthers the state's goal of underwriting the education of those most likely to provide medical care to residents of the state after graduation.

Nor does State A's residency requirement violate the Commerce Clause or Article IV's Privileges and Immunities Clause. Even if the requirement discriminates against interstate commerce because of the burden it places on out-of-state students, the state's operation of the medical school is exempt from the dormant Commerce Clause under the market participant doctrine. (See May & Ides, *Constitutional Law,* supra, at §8.11.) And under the Privileges and Immunities Clause, the state has leeway to favor its residents by giving them free access to the state-owned medical school. See id. at §9.4.2.

§7.5   Access to the Courts

Under very limited circumstances, the Equal Protection Clause may require that indigents be provided with equal access to the courts. In these situations, the government may be obligated to furnish counsel, waive fees, or pay litigation costs for those who would otherwise be unable to participate effectively in the legal process on a basis comparable to that of more affluent litigants. However, the Court has stopped far short of recognizing a broad-based fundamental right of equal access to the judicial process. Outside of the criminal context, the few cases in which the Court has required states to provide indigents with effective access to the legal system have often relied at least in part on substantive or procedural due process as well as the Equal Protection Clause.

In the criminal context, the Court has held that a state is obligated to provide indigent defendants with a free trial transcript and appointed counsel in order to take advantage of a first appeal of right. *Gideon v. Wainwright,*

372 U.S. 335 (1963); *Griffin v. Illinois,* 351 U.S. 12 (1956). Since the state is not constitutionally required to provide a system of appellate courts or a right of appellate review, these decisions are best understood as resting on a limited equal protection right of equal access to the appellate courts. *M.L.B. v. S.L.J.,* 519 U.S. 102, 120 (1997). However, the Court has construed this right narrowly, emphasizing that the Equal Protection Clause does not require the state "to duplicate the legal arsenal that may be privately retained by a criminal defendant . . . but only to assure the indigent defendant an adequate opportunity to present his claims fairly in the context of the State's appellate process." *Ross v. Moffitt,* 417 U.S. 600, 616 (1974) (holding that state need not provide counsel for taking discretionary appeals after first appeal of right).

In *M.L.B. v. S.L.J.,* the Court extended its holdings from the criminal context to a civil proceeding that terminated a parent's rights in her two minor children. In that case, the Mississippi Supreme Court dismissed the mother's appeal because she was unable to pay record preparation fees of $2,352.36. The U.S. Supreme Court reversed. It emphasized that though such proceedings may be civil in nature, they have devastating and irretrievable consequences for a parent that set them "apart from mine run civil actions, even from other domestic relations matters such as divorce, paternity, and child custody," which are usually "modifiable at the parties' will or based on changed circumstances." 519 U.S. at 127-128. Accordingly, said the Court, the Equal Protection Clause required the state to provide the indigent parent with a record of sufficient completeness to allow proper appellate consideration of her claim. Though the Court's decision rested on equal protection principles, it also noted that the case directly implicated a parent's fundamental interest in the relationship with her children. Id. at 117-118.

In most other civil contexts, the Constitution does not require a state to waive court fees or other costs for those unable to pay them. The *M.L.B.* Court stressed that it was not disturbing the "general rule . . . that fee requirements ordinarily are examined only for rationality" and that a "State's need for revenue to offset costs, in the mine run of cases, satisfies the rationality requirement. . . ." Id. at 122-123. Like *M.L.B.,* the few other civil cases that have departed from this rule have usually involved the presence of a fundamental right, and most of them have thus rested at least in part on substantive or procedural due process, as well as equal protection principles.

In *Boddie v. Connecticut,* 401 U.S. 371 (1971), for example, the Court held that a state was constitutionally obligated to waive court fees and costs for an indigent who wished to file a divorce action. Since the state retained a monopoly over the means of adjusting marital relationships, the fee requirement operated as an absolute ban on divorce and remarriage for indigents. Under substantive due process, such a direct infringement on the fundamental right to marry is invalid because fee requirements are not necessary to achieve any compelling state interest. And as a matter of procedural due process, the fee requirement impaired an indigent's fundamental liberty in the marital decision without affording an opportunity to be heard.

Any thought that *Boddie* established a general right of equal access to the courts in civil cases was put to rest by *United States v. Kras,* 409 U.S. 434 (1973). The Court there upheld a federal law requiring all bankruptcy petitioners to pay fees and costs of $50. Though the effect of this requirement was to deny indigents access to the bankruptcy court, *Boddie* did not compel the government to waive the fee. The *Kras* Court explained that, in contrast to *Boddie,* no fundamental interest was involved and thus only rational basis review was called for under substantive due process. With respect to procedural due process, while inability to pay the fee could impair a debtor's property interests, it was not clear that such a deprivation would occur. Unlike the situation in *Boddie,* the government has no monopoly over the means by which indigents may protect their property interests: "[B]ankruptcy is not the only method available to a debtor for the adjustment of his legal relationship with his creditors." Id. at 445. Finally, under the equal protection component of the Fifth Amendment, since no fundamental right was involved and since poverty is not a suspect or quasi-suspect basis of classification (see §6.7.1), only a rational basis was needed to justify the fee requirement.

M.L.B., Boddie, and *Kras* all involved the question of whether the government had to waive fees that would otherwise keep an indigent from getting into a trial or an appellate court. A related issue concerns when persons who are already in court are entitled to have the government pay certain of their litigation expenses. The issue is not one of access to the courts as such, but one of *meaningful* access. The Court has often approached this issue in terms of procedural due process rather than equal protection. If, on a case-by-case basis, a litigant's inability to pay a specific litigation expense is likely to harm an important interest, the state may be required to pay that expense. Compare *Little v. Streater,* 452 U.S. 1 (1981) (procedural due process required state to pay for blood tests in a paternity suit where, without them, an indigent faced a serious risk of erroneously being adjudged the father) with *Lassiter v. Department of Social Servs.,* 452 U.S. 18 (1981) (procedural due process did not require state to appoint counsel for indigent mother in parental termination suit where issues and evidence were such that counsel would not have made a significant difference). The question of what procedures are necessary to comport with the requirements of procedural due process is explored in §5.5.

§7.6   Welfare and Subsistence

The Supreme Court has rejected the proposition that for equal protection purposes, there is a fundamental interest in the basic necessities of life.

Though "[t]he administration of public welfare assistance . . . involves the most basic economic needs of impoverished human beings," it is, nonetheless, subject to the same standard of review as "state regulation of business or industry." *Dandridge v. Williams,* 397 U.S. 471, 485 (1970). Consequently, classifications employed in determining eligibility for welfare, food stamps, housing, and medical care typically call for only a rational basis review under the Equal Protection Clause. To be sure, governmental decisions involving the basic necessities of life must accord with procedural due process. And such decisions will be subject to strict scrutiny if they impinge on some *other* fundamental liberty—e.g., the right to travel—or discriminate on the basis of race or alienage. But the interest in subsistence itself is not fundamental for purposes of either the Due Process or the Equal Protection Clause.

EXAMPLE 7-S

A state provides monthly welfare grants to needy families. The grant is based in part on the number of unmarried children below age 21 living in the household. The Smith family's grant has been reduced by $150 per month because Sam, their 19-year-old son, was recently married. Sam and his new wife live in the Smith household. Did the state violate the Equal Protection Clause by reducing the Smiths' grant?

EXPLANATION

Since wealth or poverty is not a suspect or quasi-suspect basis of classification, heightened scrutiny is not called for on this basis. Nor is the interest in subsistence benefits a fundamental right that would trigger strict scrutiny. The Smiths may argue that strict scrutiny is required because reducing the grant discriminates against the family due to Sam's exercise of his fundamental right to marry. However, a court would probably reject this argument on the ground that the state's conduct was not sufficient to infringe on Sam's freedom to marry. The state did not directly prohibit him from marrying, and it would claim that the indirect effect of a $150/month loss does not substantially impair the exercise of this fundamental liberty. On the other hand, if the Smiths could show that the impact of this welfare rule on the fundamental liberty interest in marriage is more severe (e.g., that unless the full grant is restored, Sam and his wife will have to divorce), strict scrutiny might be triggered, and the state would have to show that its discrimination against families with married children is necessary to serve a compelling state interest. See *Bowen v. Gilliard,* 483 U.S. 587 (1987) (upholding welfare laws under rational basis equal protection test after rejecting argument that the law impinged on a fundamental liberty interest); *Lyng v. Castillo,* 477 U.S. 635 (1986) (same).

The Court's reluctance to find that the withholding of subsistence benefits impinges on a fundamental liberty interest makes it easy for government to use its control over these benefits to in effect "buy up" people's constitutional rights. The government may accomplish this by conditioning benefits such as welfare and medical care on a recipient's surrender of his or her constitutional rights. At one time, under the doctrine of unconstitutional conditions, such conditioning of governmental benefits would have been subject to strict scrutiny. However, the modern Court has sharply narrowed this doctrine. As a result, the discriminatory denial of public benefits to those who have exercised protected liberties contrary to the government's wishes will often be upheld under a rational basis standard of review.

EXAMPLE 7-T

As we saw in §2.5.4, a woman has a fundamental liberty interest to decide whether or not to abort a fetus. The Due Process Clause would thus bar a state from directly interfering with this decision by making it a crime to have an abortion during the first six months of pregnancy. *Planned Parenthood v. Casey,* 505 U.S. 833 (1992). Suppose that the state instead seeks to influence this decision indirectly by refusing to pay the medical expenses of having an abortion, while agreeing to pay the medical costs associated with childbirth. Does this discrimination against women who exercise their liberty by choosing an abortion trigger strict scrutiny under the Equal Protection Clause?

EXPLANATION

The answer depends on whether a court finds that this discriminatory denial of benefits is sufficient to impinge on a woman's fundamental right to choose between childbirth and abortion. In *Harris v. McRae,* 448 U.S. 297 (1980), the Court held that such discrimination in the administration of the federal Medicaid program did not trigger strict scrutiny even where the abortion was medically necessary. In the Court's view, while such a selective denial of medical benefits may influence an indigent woman's decision in favor of childbirth, the denial did not infringe on or penalize her exercise of the fundamental liberty to choose an abortion. The Court proceeded to uphold the discriminatory eligibility rule under the rational basis standard of review.

§7.7   Access to a Basic Education

The interest in education is a protected liberty under the Due Process Clause. *Pierce v. Society of Sisters,* 268 U.S. 510, 534-535 (1925) (parents' liberty to direct "education of children"); *Meyer v. Nebraska,* 262 U.S. 390, 399

(1923) (liberty "to acquire useful knowledge"). See §2.3.1. However, education is not a *fundamental* right under either the Due Process or the Equal Protection Clause. Consequently, state and local laws that adversely impact on an individual's ability to obtain an education generally receive only rational basis due process and equal protection review. If the situation were otherwise, federal judges might in effect become overseers of the nation's public schools. Virtually every decision by state or local education officials would be subject to judicial examination under the lens of strict scrutiny, with the result that many educational policies would be invalidated because a federal court decided they were not narrowly tailored to serve a compelling state interest. Such intrusion would be contrary to the Court's frequent recognition that education is an area that falls peculiarly within the province of local government.

However, there is a difference between the interest in education in general and the interest in acquiring a minimally adequate education. The Supreme Court has left open the possibility that the interest in acquiring "a minimally adequate education is a fundamental right" under the Equal Protection Clause, so that laws that "discriminatorily infringe that right should be accorded heightened equal protection review." *Papasan v. Allain*, 478 U.S. 265, 285 (1986). If the Court were to recognize such a fundamental right, laws that deny some children the opportunity to acquire a basic education, while affording that opportunity to other children, would be subject to strict scrutiny under the Equal Protection Clause. Under such an approach, not all laws that discriminate concerning education would be subject to strict scrutiny. Nor would heightened scrutiny apply simply because some children's educational opportunities were inferior to those of others. Strict scrutiny would come into play only where the impact of a discriminatory law is so severe as to totally deny some children the chance to acquire a minimally adequate education.

The rationale for applying heightened equal protection scrutiny in these circumstances was suggested in *Plyler v. Doe*, 457 U.S. 202 (1982), a case where the Court struck down a Texas law that excluded undocumented alien children from the public schools. The Court agreed that education is not a "fundamental right" and that, therefore, "a State need not justify by compelling necessity *every variation* in the manner in which education is provided to its population." Id. at 223 (emphasis supplied). Yet as we will see in §7.8.3, the *Plyler* Court applied intermediate rather than rational basis review, partly because of the special role that a basic education plays in promoting equality. Justice Brennan, speaking for the majority, noted that a complete "denial of education to some isolated group of children poses an affront to one of the goals of the Equal Protection Clause: the abolition of governmental barriers . . . to advancement on the basis of individual merit." Id. at 221-222. In a separate concurrence, Justice Blackmun observed that "certain interests . . . must be accorded a special place in equal protection analysis." For example, he said, the right to vote "is, in equal protection terms, an extraordinary right" because it assures "individual political equality." Id. at 233. The right to a basic education plays a similar role by helping to assure economic and social equality. Thus, a discriminatory "denial of an education is the analogue of denial of the right to vote: the former relegates the individual to second-class social status; the latter places him at a permanent political disadvantage." Id. at 234. Under this approach, while neither the Due Process nor the Equal Protection Clause would prevent a state from abolishing the right to vote for certain offices or from closing the public schools, a *discriminatory* with-drawal of either of these rights could trigger strict or intermediate equal protection scrutiny because the interests at stake — voting, and access to a basic education — are fundamental to the preservation of equality.

The cases in which the modern Court has upheld education laws under a mere rational basis standard are not inconsistent with a finding that the interest in a minimally adequate education is a fundamental equal protection right. The prior cases all involved situations where the discrimination in question, though it reduced the educational opportunities for some children, stopped short of denying anyone a minimally adequate education. See, e.g., *Kadrmas v. Dickinson Public Schools,* 487 U.S. 450, 459-460 (1988) (upholding state law allowing some school boards to charge fee for school bus transportation where this did not prevent any child from attending school); *Papasan v. Allain,* 478 U.S. 265 (1986) (upholding state law that resulted in a $75 per pupil funding disparity among schools); *San Antonio Indep. School Dist. v. Rodriguez,* 411 U.S. 1 (1973) (upholding state system of school financing that resulted in a 40 percent difference in per pupil funding among schools).

EXAMPLE 7-U

The Elm City School Board adopted a policy requiring all students attending city public schools to wear a prescribed uniform that cost $50. The policy was adopted to reduce gang violence. As a result of the policy, the three Jones children were forced to withdraw from school because their parents cannot afford to buy them uniforms. Does the city's uniform policy violate the Equal Protection Clause?

EXPLANATION

Since wealth is not a suspect classification, the fact that the policy discrimi-nates against the poor will not trigger heightened equal protection scrutiny. While the effect of the policy is to totally deny some children the opportunity to acquire a basic elementary education, the Supreme Court has yet to hold that this constitutes a fundamental equal protection right. If the court here were to conclude that such a right does exist, the policy would then be subject to strict scrutiny, for it clearly impinges on that right. Alternatively, a court following *Plyler* might subject the policy to intermediate scrutiny. Whichever the case, the policy is unlikely to pass muster as applied to children who cannot afford to buy uniforms. While the state presumably has a compelling interest in preventing gang violence, this is not the least discriminatory means of achieving that goal; the city could instead buy uniforms for those children who cannot afford them.

§7.8   A Sliding-Scale Approach to Equal Protection

§7.8.1   Problems with the Three-Tier Model

As we have seen, the Supreme Court's approach to the Equal Protection Clause generally involves application of a three-tier model. Under this model, classifications that are "suspect" or that involve discrimination with respect to a fundamental right are subject to strict scrutiny, quasi-suspect classifications based on gender or legitimacy are subject to intermediate scrutiny, and most other classifications are subject to rational basis review.

The three-tier model has become static and rigid due to the Court's unwillingness to add to the lists of suspect and quasi-suspect classifications and its reluctance to recognize new fundamental rights. To be sure, in some rational basis cases the Court has applied a slightly more demanding form of review than the model would seem to dictate, but the Court has done so without acknowledging that any change was being made to the traditional three-tier framework.

§7.8.2   Marshall's Sliding-Scale Approach

Justice Thurgood Marshall consistently urged the Court to abandon its three-tier equal protection model in favor of a more flexible analysis that would be capable of taking into account differences that are masked by a ritualistic focus on "suspect classifications" and "fundamental rights." As Marshall wrote, "All interests not 'fundamental' and all classes not 'suspect' are not the same; and it is time for the Court to drop the pretense that, for purposes of the Equal Protection Clause, they are." *Massachusetts Bd. of Retirement v. Murgia*, 427 U.S. 307, 321 (1976) (Marshall, J., dissenting). In place of the majority's stratified model, Marshall urged the Court to employ a "variable standard of review" whose intensity would depend on (1) the basis or character of the classification and (2) the importance of the interest adversely affected. The greater the significance of these factors, the greater the government's burden of justifying the classification in question.

Marshall's first factor, the character of the classification, in some ways tracks the Court's concern with whether the classifying trait is "suspect" or "quasi-suspect." However, his suggested approach is more flexible, recognizing that there are groups besides the handful that have qualified under the Court's model that, due to prejudice, stereotypes, or a history of discrimination, require added protection from the political process. On this basis, Marshall advocated giving some heightened scrutiny to laws that discriminate against groups such as the poor, the mentally retarded, and the elderly.

Marshall's second factor, the nature of the interest affected by the classification, reflects the majority's focus on "fundamental rights," but with the difference that it is more flexible than the Court's all-or-nothing approach. The fact that an interest does not qualify for the very strictest scrutiny does not necessarily mean it is worthy of no protection at all under a mere rationality test. Marshall urged that each interest be placed on a spectrum by considering the extent to which rights guarantied by the Constitution depend on it. "As the nexus between the specific constitutional guarantee and the nonconstitutional interest draws closer, the nonconstitutional interest becomes more fundamental and the degree of judicial scrutiny applied when the interest is infringed on a discriminatory basis must be adjusted accordingly." *San Antonio Indep. School Dist. v. Rodriguez*, 411 U.S. 1, 102-103 (1973) (Marshall, J., dissenting). Following this approach, Marshall would have given some special protection to interests such as subsistence, housing, medical care, employment, and education — all of which affect a person's ability to participate in a democratic society and to exercise the civil and political rights conferred by the Constitution.

§7.8.3   Plyler v. Doe

To date, the Supreme Court has not rejected the three-tier model of equal protection review; nor has it adopted the sliding-scale approach that Marshall advocated. Yet the Court has at times shown increased flexibility in resolving equal protection cases — flexibility of the type that Marshall championed. Thus, at a doctrinal level, what began as a two-tier model consisting of only strict scrutiny and rational basis review has evolved into a three-tier model with the addition of intermediate scrutiny for classifications created on the basis of gender or legitimacy. Moreover, as we have seen, the Court has at times appeared to apply an enhanced version of the rational basis test, though without acknowledging that anything other than minimal scrutiny was being employed.

Perhaps the closest the Court has come to using Marshall's flexible sliding-scale approach was in *Plyler v. Doe*, 457 U.S. 202 (1982), where the Court struck down a Texas law that denied undocumented alien children the free public education that the state provided to other children. Justice Brennan, writing for the majority, carefully set out the Court's traditional three-tier equal protection model. He agreed that the case did not qualify for strict scrutiny, since "[u]ndocumented aliens cannot be treated as a suspect class. . . . Nor is education a fundamental right. . . ." Id. at 223. Texas had also not discriminated on the basis of gender or legitimacy, criteria that would have warranted application of intermediate scrutiny. Yet, said Brennan, "more is involved in these cases than the abstract question whether [the statute] discriminates against a suspect class, or whether education is a fundamental right." The Texas statute "imposes a lifetime hardship on a discrete class of children not accountable for their disabling status." Id. The Court felt compelled to take these realities into account and, to the dissent's dismay, refused to apply the rational basis standard called for by the three-tier model. Instead, the Court employed a form of intermediate scrutiny by requiring the state to prove that its discrimination actually "furthers some substantial state interest." Id. at 230. Texas was unable to make such a showing, and the statute was accordingly held to violate the Equal Protection Clause. As Chief Justice Burger accurately observed in dissent, the majority departed from the Court's traditional approach to equal protection cases "by patching together bits and pieces of what might be termed quasi-suspect-class and quasi-fundamental-rights analysis," thus "spin[ning] out a theory custom-tailored to the facts of these cases." Id. at 244.

The *Plyler* Court came very close to employing the mode of analysis that Marshall had long advocated. The majority noted that the basis of the classification was a trait over which the law's victims had no control. Moreover, it stressed that the interest at stake, "basic education," was vitally important to both the individual and society. Justice Marshall in fact joined Brennan's majority opinion, yet Marshall wrote a one-paragraph concurrence subtly urging that the Court *formally* reject its "rigidified approach to equal protection analysis" and instead adopt "an approach that allows for varying levels of scrutiny." Id. at 231. While Brennan and the majority demonstrated the kind of flexibility and sensitivity to context that lay at the heart of Marshall's sliding-scale approach, they, nonetheless, paid continued lip service to the three-tier equal protection model.

8

The First Amendment: Freedom of Speech and of the Press

§8.1 Introduction and Overview

As usual, we begin with the text. The words are simple and straightforward: "Congress shall make no law . . . abridging the freedom of speech, or of the press." There is power in this simplicity. The blunt proscription would seem to preclude any legislation that limits or punishes the protected activities. No law. But as the length of this chapter attests, the simplicity of text does not translate into a paucity of doctrine, and the doctrines rarely, if ever, speak in terms of absolutes. Rather, the freedoms of speech and press are, like other rights protected by the Constitution, both contextual and contingent, providing a range of possibilities as varied as the human imagination. The text is not, however, meaningless. The seemingly absolute proscription, at the very least, describes a powerful constitutional commitment to the freedoms of speech and press. That is our starting point.

This commitment stems from a variety of philosophical perspectives, some emphasizing the importance of freedom of expression to human growth or self-realization, others noting the essential role of free expression within a political democracy, and still others seeing this freedom as the only method through which falsehood can be exposed and some approximation of transient truth discovered. Given the wide range of First Amendment doctrines, it is not too surprising that each of these perspectives can find some voice in the Court's opinions. The predominant theme of those opinions, however, is the centrality of political speech to the core purposes of the

First Amendment not because political speech is inherently more valuable than other types of speech, but because our system of self-governance is dependent on free inquiry and debate and because a centralized governmental power has the potential to constrict knowledge and to distort that debate through the suppression of opposing viewpoints. In the Court's words, therefore, the First Amendment represents "a profound national commitment to the principle that debate on public issues should be uninhibited, robust, and wide-open." *New York Times v. Sullivan*, 376 U.S. 254, 270 (1964).

Political speech does not, however, represent a rigidly defined category. Rather, in practice, all speech is treated with the same dignity as that afforded political speech unless the speech at issue falls into a specifically defined category of lesser protected expression — commercial speech and obscenity being the obvious examples. Thus, the freedoms of speech and press fully protect commentary and debate on an almost boundless range of topics from the profound to the mundane. Political speech is simply the nucleus around which these other categories revolve.

In terms of analysis, you will find that the doctrines of freedom of speech and press share much with the analysis applied to problems involving equal protection and due process. Thus, content-based restrictions on political speech are subject to strict scrutiny, requiring both a compelling state interest and the application of the least restrictive means test. And as speech strays from the core values of the First Amendment, the level of scrutiny will decrease in a manner similar to the three-tiered or the sliding-scale model of equal protection. Commercial speech, therefore, receives mid-level scrutiny. Moreover, the analytical tie to these other constitutional provisions applies even in those contexts in which special First Amendment doctrines have been developed to address particular types of problems. The specialized jargon of these doctrines often reflects a particular instance of strict, mid-level, or rational basis scrutiny.

Similarly, one will see the strands of substantive due process analysis in the treatment of governmental regulations that burden speech in a content-neutral fashion. Although the precise test used — time, place, and manner — speaks in terms of burdens on speech, the elements of the test are closely allied with the familiar balancing formula of due process.

§8.2   Introductory Themes

§8.2.1   *Defining Terms: Speech and Press*

The Speech and Press Clause prohibits the abridgement of "freedom of speech, or of the press." Literally this proscription includes only the spoken and the printed word. But in practice, does it embrace a wider array of expressive activities? For example, does it include the public display of a painting such as Picasso's *Guernica*? Or a public performance of Stravinsky's *Rite of Spring*? Does postmodern architecture qualify as speech? How about a protest demonstration in which blood is poured on the steps of Congress? The answer to each of these questions is yes (or at least probably yes). Each is a form of expression protected, at least to some extent, by the First Amendment. Indeed, the phrases "freedom of speech" and "freedom of the press" are often used interchangeably with the more inclusive phrase "freedom of expression."

In general, a wide variety of expressive activity or conduct, i.e., conduct intended to communicate a message and reasonably understood to communicate that message, is included within the broad reach of the Speech and Press Clause. As the Court observed in *Texas v. Johnson*, 491 U.S. 397 (1989), the protections of the First Amendment do "not end at the spoken or written word." Id. at 404. Nor do they end with the media of communication available to the founding generation. Thus, under appropriate circumstances, such diverse media as dance, music, art, architecture, photography, performance art, bumper stickers, parades, sit-ins, advertisements, motion pictures, cyberspace, and *Leave It to Beaver* reruns all qualify for First Amendment solicitude. This does not mean that such activities are absolutely protected. It means only that they are embraced within the broad concept of freedom of expression and are, therefore, entitled to the applicable doctrinal protections developed under the First Amendment.

A good example of the Court's approach to expressive activity is found in *Spence v. State of Washington*, 418 U.S. 405 (1974). In that case, a college student affixed a peace symbol to a U.S. flag and displayed the flag from the window of his apartment. His purpose was to protest the then-recent invasion of Cambodia and the killing of students at Kent State University. He was charged and convicted under a statute that criminalized the "improper use" of a U.S. flag.

The Court reversed his conviction as inconsistent with the First Amendment. In explaining why the student's actions were a form of protected expression, the Court focused on two factors: the *nature* of the conduct and the *context* within which that conduct occurred. As to the nature of the conduct, flags have been traditionally used and accepted as a form of communication, and the use here was consistent with that tradition. Id. at 410. In terms of context, given the temporal proximity of the flag display to the invasion of Cambodia and the killings at Kent State University, "it would have been difficult for the great majority of citizens to miss the drift of appellant's point at the time that he made it." Id. Given this combination of nature and context, the student's actions were clearly expressive and, therefore, would be treated as speech within the meaning of the First Amendment.

In *United States v. O'Brien*, 391 U.S. 367, 376 (1968), the Court suggested that not all expressive activity will be treated as speech: "We cannot accept the view that an apparently limitless variety of conduct can be labeled 'speech' whenever the person engaging in the conduct intends thereby to express an idea." In practice, however, the Court has not applied this limitation. Instead, the Court has either accepted the claim that the conduct at issue was sufficiently expressive to be entitled to First Amendment consideration or at least assumed such to be the case. In *O'Brien,* for example, the Court "assumed" that burning a draft card on the steps of a courthouse as a protest against the draft was speech within the meaning of the First Amendment — a fair assumption given both the nature of the activity and the context in which it occurred. See also *Clark v. Community for Creative Non-Violence,* 468 U.S. 288, 293 (1984) ("assumes" that overnight sleeping in Lafayette Park as part of a demonstration of the plight of the homeless is speech). At some point, however, the Court may well conclude that a particular activity, claimed to be expressive, is not speech within the meaning of the First Amendment.

EXAMPLE 8-A

The bombing of the Murrah Federal Building in Oklahoma City took place on the anniversary of the FBI's confrontation with the Branch Davidians in Waco, Texas. One purpose of the bombing was to protest the so-called cover-up of the Waco incident. Another was to send a message of general dissatisfaction with the federal government. Can (or should) this bombing be treated as expressive activity under the First Amendment?

EXPLANATION

Certainly the *nature* of the activity—a bombing—is not as readily associated with communication as is a flag display or an armband worn in protest. On the other hand, one could argue that a terrorist bombing is by definition meant to convey a message of terror. The context of the Murrah Building bombing also lends some credence to the communicative aspect of the incident. The choice of the Waco anniversary date was designed to and did convey a "particularized" message, at least as particularized as the flag protest in *Spence.* So was the bombing speech? In a sense, it does not matter. The First Amendment would not in any fashion protect such a horrific act regardless of how one characterizes the conduct. So a court could "assume" that the bombing was speech and easily dispose of any First Amendment contention by application of the appropriate doctrinal test. Yet treating a terrorist bombing as speech seems almost perverse. Given the morally repugnant nature of the act, a court might well conclude that even the "assumption" sometimes applied to nontraditional methods of communication is unwarranted in this context. If, as the Court has often implied, not all conduct intended to convey a message will be treated as speech, a terrorist act would seem a logical candidate for application of this exclusion.

In addressing the problem of expressive conduct, the Court has sometimes drawn a distinction between pure speech and symbolic speech, the latter being a term of art referring to nonverbal methods of communication. The distinction can be exemplified by using the facts of the *O'Brien* case. Suppose that an individual wishes to protest the draft. He can deliver a speech espousing his views, or as was done in *O'Brien*, he can burn his draft card as a symbolic gesture of opposition. The former is an example of pure speech; the latter is an example of symbolic speech (or expressive conduct). Are both forms of speech entitled to the same level of First Amendment scrutiny? The answer is yes, although there is some language in the Court's decisions that could lead one to conclude otherwise.

In *O'Brien*, the Court purported to describe a special test for the constitutional assessment of infringements on symbolic speech:

> [W]e think it clear that a government regulation is sufficiently justified if it is within the constitutional power of the Government; if it furthers an important or substantial governmental interest; if the governmental interest is unrelated to the suppression of free expression; and if the incidental restriction on alleged First Amendment freedoms is no greater than is essential to the furtherance of that interest.

391 U.S. at 377. Applying this test, the Court concluded that the First Amendment did not prevent the government from punishing O'Brien for burning his draft card. On the record before it, the Court saw the regulation as designed to advance important governmental interests in preserving the integrity of the draft and as not designed to punish draft protestors for the message they conveyed. Implicitly O'Brien was free to communicate his message in other forms that would not tread on these governmental interests. Since the government could not have punished O'Brien for simply speaking out against the draft, it would seem that pure speech is entitled to greater protection than symbolic speech. Not so.

The *O'Brien* test is nothing more than the standard time, place, and manner test (albeit worded slightly differently) that the Court generally applies to content-neutral regulations of speech. See *Clark v. Community for Creative Non-Violence*, 468 U.S. at 298 & n.8 (noting the parallels between the two tests). Both tests apply mid-level scrutiny if the governmental regulation is not directed at the content of the speech, and neither test is used if the regulation is content-based. O'Brien's burning of his draft card was punishable, in other words, because the punishment was premised not on the message O'Brien attempted to convey, but on the *manner* in which he conveyed it. Had O'Brien spray-painted the words "Stop the draft" on the walls of a courthouse, the "pure" form of his speech would no more have protected him from punishment for damaging public property than did the "symbolic" nature of his actual speech. In both cases, the focus of the government would be on the manner, and not the content, of the speech. On the other hand, if the government's reason for punishing O'Brien had stemmed from its opposition to the message he sought to convey, the fact that his speech was "symbolic" rather than pure would not allow the government to punish him. In short, the symbolic speech doctrine is merely a restatement of the time, place, and manner test that we will discuss in §8.4. Do not, therefore, fall into the trap of thinking that symbolic speech is a lesser protected form of speech.

In fact, the supposed distinction between pure speech and symbolic speech is tenuous at best. All speech is symbolic. Take the word "hippopotamus." It represents a verbal shorthand we use when referring to a rather large, herbivorous, semi-aquatic mammal with a huge head, thick skin, and short legs. Calling it a hippopotamus is easier and more fun. The word "hippopotamus," however, is not a hippopotamus; it is a verbal symbol of the animal we are trying to describe. A picture of a hippopotamus is also not a hippopotamus; it, too, is a symbol. Indeed, *Webster's New Third World Dictionary* uses both words and a picture to define the word "hippopotamus." Both the word and the picture are symbolic, and both are speech, and both are entitled to the same First Amendment protections. (Beware. Some professors and some judges still think there is a special symbolic speech doctrine. If you cannot show them the error of their ways, simply apply the *O'Brien* test, described above, and pretend that you have actually done something meaningful.)

In summary, the parts of the Speech and Press Clause work together to protect a broad realm of freedom of expression. That realm includes both conventional and unconventional modes of communication. Obviously the more conventional one's method is, the more likely it is that a court will see the expressive component of the conduct. But it remains true, nonetheless, that once the expressive activity qualifies as speech, the full range of First Amendment protections will apply.

Throughout this chapter, unless a more precise approach is warranted, we will use the word "speech" to include the vast array of communicative activities that fall within the protection of the First Amendment.

§8.2.2 *Protected and Unprotected Speech*

Not all types of speech or expression qualify for protection under the First Amendment. Certain discrete categories of speech have been held by the Court to be proscribable because they fall entirely outside the First Amendment umbrella. As a result, they are generally entitled to no constitutional protection. These proscribable categories of speech include "fighting words," obscenity, child pornography, and false or misleading commercial speech. However, as we will see, there are some circumstances under which governmental restrictions on generally proscribable speech may, nonetheless, run afoul of the First Amendment. See §8.3.8.

In approaching a First Amendment problem, it is often a good idea to first determine whether or not the speech at issue is speech that the First Amendment protects. If the result of this analysis is that the speech is of a constitutionally unprotected type — e.g., obscenity — the First Amendment analysis is normally over. If, on the other hand, the speech is of a type that falls under the First Amendment umbrella, it is then necessary to decide under the applicable First Amendment test whether the government has a right to punish or restrict it. For example, as we will see shortly, political speech, which lies at the core of the First Amendment, may be punished if the requirements of the clear and present danger test are satisfied. See §8.3.2.

When reading the Court's opinions, be alert to the fact that the term *unprotected speech* is often used in two quite different senses. The term sometimes refers to speech, such as fighting words or obscenity, that is proscribable because it does not qualify for First Amendment protection. On other occasions, however, the term is used to describe speech that is generally entitled to First Amendment protection, but that is punishable under the particular circumstances of the case. In this chapter, unless otherwise indicated, the term *unprotected speech* will be used to describe speech such as obscenity that falls entirely outside the First Amendment umbrella.

§8.2.3 *The Special Problem of Prior Restraints*

Historically courts have been more suspicious of prior restraints than they have been of other governmental restrictions on expression. Typically, prior restraints occur in one of two contexts: (1) governmental licensing or permit schemes and (2) injunctions against publication. The key to identifying a prior restraint is to focus on the timing of the government's intervention. If the government intervenes to prevent an expressive act, i.e., if the intervention takes place *before* a communication occurs, then the government's action is a prior restraint. For example, suppose that the government seeks and is granted a judicial order enjoining a newspaper from publishing certain classified information. By seeking and obtaining an injunction prior to publication, the government has interposed the force of law between a potential publisher and the act of publication. This is a classic prior restraint. The intervention precedes the communication.

An important distinction is drawn between prior restraint and subsequent punishment. The latter is a governmental restriction on expressive activity in which the government intervenes *after* the act of communication. In other words, a speech is made, and the speaker is "subsequently" punished. Suppose, for example, that a statute makes it a felony to publish classified information. A newspaper publisher who violates this proscription would be subject to a subsequent punishment, i.e., to potential criminal sanctions imposed after the act of publication. Although the statute is designed to prevent publication of classified information, the government's intervention takes place only after the publication has occurred. This subsequent punishment is not, by definition, a prior restraint.

EXAMPLE 8-B

The City of Metrolex has created a Motion Picture Licensing Board. The board is empowered to "license" the public performance of motion pictures within the city. No such performance is permitted in the absence of a board-issued license. In order to qualify for a license, a motion picture must be submitted to the board for review. A license will be denied only if the submitted motion picture is deemed to be "obscene." By way of contrast, the neighboring City of Ruralex has passed an ordinance that makes the public performance of any "obscene" motion picture a felony. This ordinance is enforced by the local city attorney through criminal prosecution. Does the Metrolex scheme operate as a prior restraint?

EXPLANATION

Yes. The reason is simple. Before a motion picture can be performed in public, it must be submitted to the board for review and approval. Since the intervention by the government precedes any public performance of the motion picture, the licensing scheme is a prior restraint. The Ruralex ordinance, on the other hand, operates only as a subsequent punishment. Although the ordinance is designed to prevent the screening of obscene motion pictures and although it may be quite effective in doing so, the governmental intervention comes only after an obscene motion picture has been screened. The restriction on speech is, therefore, subsequent.

In short, the critical distinction between a prior restraint and a subsequent punishment is the timing of the governmental intervention vis-à-vis the act of communication. Only an intervention that precedes an act of communication is a prior restraint.

Although both prior restraints and subsequent punishments are subject to First Amendment scrutiny, it is generally presumed that prior restraints present the more serious invasion of First Amendment liberties. While it remains in effect, a prior restraint completely suppresses the attempted communication. In essence, the government acts as a censor when it issues a prior restraint. Of course, the threat of criminal sanctions presumably operates as a strong and effective deterrent on speech or publication, and under some circumstances, the threat of prosecution may just as effectively prevent publication as would a prior restraint. Nonetheless, the deterrent effect is not considered a prior restraint, and prior restraints remain the most disfavored type of restriction on expressive activity.

One reason prior restraints are particularly disfavored is that a person who violates an injunction or other prior restraint on speech is ordinarily subject to punishment even if the speech activity was constitutionally protected; in other words, it is usually no defense to the violation of a prior restraint that the restraint was unconstitutional. Ordinarily, the only way to challenge the constitutionality of a prior restraint is to comply with it while challenging its validity in court; this may, of course, result in a lengthy postponement of the desired speech activity. By contrast, a statute that merely criminalizes certain speech may be violated by a speaker who is confident that the statute is unconstitutional. In the subsequent criminal prosecution, the First Amendment may be raised as a complete defense. In other words, while the First Amendment may shield a speaker who violates a criminal proscription on speech, the Amendment usually will not protect one who violates a prior restraint.

The judicial antipathy toward prior restraints is demonstrated in two leading cases. The first is *Near v. Minnesota,* 283 U.S. 697 (1931). In that case, a county attorney brought an action to enjoin the publication of a "malicious, scandalous and defamatory newspaper" known as *The Saturday Press.* Id. at 703. The newspaper had published a series of highly charged, possibly defamatory articles accusing local police and governmental officials of various derelictions, including corruption in office. After a trial, the publication of the newspaper was abated as a public nuisance, and its publishers were "perpetually enjoined . . . from producing, editing, publishing, circulating, having in their possession, selling or giving away any publication whatsoever which is a malicious, scandalous or defamatory newspaper." Id. at 706. Any violations of the injunction would subject the publishers to being held in contempt of court.

Although the injunction was a product of the previously published issues of the newspaper, the order of the lower court was not a punishment for those publications. Rather, it was directed toward the future publishing activities of the defendants. With respect to those future publications, the government's intervention preceded the publication. It suppressed any such publications. The order was, therefore, a prior restraint, and as such, the lower court's order was highly suspect. This was so because, in the Supreme Court's view, both historically and as a matter of sound jurisprudence, prior restraints were highly disfavored, particularly in the context of critical commentary on public officials. Id. at 714-717. Subsequent punishments did not, however, receive that same disapproval from the *Near* Court.

> The fact that for approximately one hundred and fifty years there has been almost an entire absence of attempts to impose previous restraints upon publications relating to the malfeasance of public officers is significant [evidence] of the deep-seated conviction that such restraints would violate constitutional right. Public officers, whose character and conduct remain open to debate and free discussion in the press, find their remedies for false accusations in actions under libel laws providing for redress and punishment, and not in proceedings to restrain the publication of newspapers and periodicals.

Id. at 718-719. In short, while a subsequent punishment might pass constitutional muster, only under the most exceptional circumstances will a prior restraint do so. To this end, the Court described what is now referred to as the troopship exception for prior restraints: "No one would question but that a government might prevent actual obstruction to its recruiting service or the publication of the sailing dates of transports or the number and location of troops." Id. at 716. By analogy, this "exception" can be seen as the rough equivalent of a very strict scrutiny test.

New York Times v. United States, 403 U.S. 713 (1971), presents a much more dramatic application of the heavy presumption against prior restraints. In that case, commonly referred to as the *Pentagon Papers Case*, the executive branch of the U.S. government sought to enjoin the *New York Times* and the *Washington Post* from publishing the contents of a classified study entitled *History of U.S. Decision-making Process on Viet Nam Policy*. At the time, the Vietnam War was far from over, and the government claimed that publication of the study would jeopardize the United States's war efforts. The Court, however, refused to sanction the injunction. In a cryptic three-paragraph per curiam opinion, the Court noted the "heavy presumption" against the constitutional validity of prior restraints and declared that the government had not met its "heavy burden of showing justification for the imposition of such a restraint." Id. at 714. Thus, even the government's claims of national security in the context of an ongoing military action were insufficient to satisfy the so-called troopship exception. Despite this ruling, several Justices suggested that this same judicial reluctance would not necessarily apply to postpublication criminal prosecutions. Id. at 732 (White, J., with whom Stewart, J., joined, concurring); id. at 748 (Burger, C.J., dissenting); id. at 759 (Blackmun, J., dissenting).

The per curiam opinion in the *Pentagon Papers Case* was crafted to resolve that precise case and virtually no others. Separate opinions by the Justices do, however, shed some light on the appropriate standards. Two Justices, Black and Douglas, endorsed what was tantamount to an absolute prohibition against prior restraints. Id. at 714, 720. Justice Brennan used language suggestive of a very strict scrutiny: "Thus, only governmental allegation and proof that publication must inevitably, directly, and immediately cause the occurrence of an event kindred to imperiling the safety of a transport already at sea can support even the issuance of an interim restraining order." Id. at 726-727. Other Justices were somewhat less solicitous. While both Justices White and Stewart agreed that publication could not be enjoined under the facts presented because of the "extraordinary protection against prior restraints enjoyed by the press under our constitutional system," their reluctance stemmed in part from the absence of a statute authorizing the requested injunction. Id. at 730-731. Justice Marshall's opinion also emphasized the lack of statutory authorization. Id. at 740. Of course, the three dissenters were willing to endorse the injunction against publication. The numbers certainly do not add up to anything like an absolute prohibition against prior restraints. The judgment does, however, represent a recognition of the "heavy presumption" against prior restraints. Yet how that standard is to be interpreted and applied remains somewhat vague.

EXAMPLE 8-C

Modern Mercenary, a monthly periodical, is about to publish an article entitled "Five Easy Steps to Making Your Own Thermonuclear Device." The author of the piece, G.I. Jones, is a nuclear physicist who gathered most of his information from nonclassified sources. The article does, however, disclose for the first time how a number of seemingly unrelated concepts must be brought together in order to construct a thermonuclear device. The government seeks to enjoin this publication pursuant to a section of the Atomic Energy Act that authorizes injunctive relief against anyone who would disclose "restricted data with reason to believe such data will be utilized to injure the United States or to secure an advantage to any foreign nation." Although the government doubts that Jones's article will lead to the basement construction of nuclear weapons, governmental experts claim that publication will possibly provide sufficient information to allow a medium-sized nation to move faster in developing a thermonuclear weapon. Assuming Jones's article contains "restricted data" within the meaning of the Atomic Energy Act, should the district court grant the requested relief?

EXPLANATION

Since the government's intervention precedes the publication of the article, the injunction, if granted, would be a prior restraint. Like all prior restraints, this one comes with a heavy presumption against its validity. If one adopts an absolutist position, this case is relatively simple — no prior restraints. However, the absolutist position has never commanded a majority of the Court. Yet a similar result would probably obtain under Justice Brennan's near-absolute position. At best the government has shown that "possibly" a medium-sized nation will speed up its nuclear capabilities because of this article. This speculative outcome can hardly be described as inevitable, direct, and immediate. Some current members of the Court might well adopt Justice Brennan's approach. On the other hand, the injunction is authorized by statute, and the potential harm is quite serious. A district court judge could reasonably conclude that under such circumstances, the troopship exception has been satisfied, and that conclusion *might* be upheld by the Court. See *United States v. Progressive, Inc.,* 467 F. Supp. 990 (W.D. Wis.), *appeal dismissed,* 610 F.2d 819 (7th Cir. 1979) (issuing an injunction under similar circumstances). Arguably there were at least five votes in the *Pentagon Papers Case* supportive of this conclusion.

The vagaries of the "heavy presumption" standard were somewhat ameliorated in *Nebraska Press Assn. v. Stuart,* 427 U.S. 539 (1976). A state trial court judge, in anticipation of a trial for multiple murders, issued an order restraining the news media "from publishing or broadcasting accounts of confessions or admissions made by the accused." Id. at 541. The purpose of the gag order was to preserve the accused's Sixth Amendment right to a fair and impartial jury. The Court held that despite this strong state interest, the judge's order could not withstand constitutional scrutiny. Prior restraints are highly disfavored, particularly in the context of reporting the news in a timely fashion. Id. at 560-561. As a consequence, and in a manner strikingly similar to an intense strict scrutiny analysis, the Court examined the state's interest, the scope of the judge's order, and alternatives to that order that were less intrusive on First Amendment principles. In essence, the Court concluded that the order was not necessary to advance the purported state interest.

Outside of the news-reporting context, the formidability of the presumption against prior restraints depends on the nature of the speech activity being restrained. Recall Example 8-B — the Metrolex licensing scheme designed to prevent the public performance of obscene motion pictures. The licensing procedure described in that example is a prior restraint. However, as we will learn, obscenity, as defined by the Supreme Court, is a genre of speech that is unprotected by the First Amendment. Hence, local communities are afforded substantial leeway in the manner in which they may choose to regulate or proscribe matters deemed obscene. Accordingly, a prior restraint such as that described in the Metrolex scheme would be upheld if certain procedural safeguards were incorporated into the scheme: (1) The board must have the burden of proving that the motion picture is obscene under constitutional standards; (2) the procedure for making that determination must be of the shortest possible duration; and (3) immediate judicial review of the obscenity decision must be available. *Freedman v. Maryland,* 380 U.S. 51, 58-60 (1965). In essence, the presumption against prior restraints may be rebutted by a combination of the disfavored status of the speech and the presence of procedural safeguards designed to ensure that only disfavored speech will be suppressed.

§8.2.4   The Overbreadth and Vagueness Doctrines

The overbreadth doctrine creates a special First Amendment exception to the normal rules of standing, which bar a litigant from asserting the constitutional rights of third parties. The overbreadth doctrine allows an individual as to whom the application of a law may be constitutional to challenge the constitutionality of the law on the theory that as applied to other persons or under other circumstances the law violates the First Amendment. The essence of an overbreadth argument is that even though the challenged law may have some constitutional applications, its broad sweep encompasses protected speech activities and chills the First Amendment rights of persons not before the Court to such an extent that the entire law must be struck down. See *Los Angeles Police Dept. v. United Reporting Publishing Corp.*, 120 S. Ct. 483 (1999) (overbreadth not available in a challenge to a statute that limits access to certain police records since the claim is not premised on "speech").

Since application of overbreadth requires the complete invalidation of a law that may have some constitutional applications, the courts are reluctant to apply the "strong medicine" of this doctrine. Accordingly, there are a number of restrictions on application of the overbreadth doctrine. First, if a law is subject to a reasonable, limiting construction that comports with the Constitution and that avoids the overbreadth concern, the law will not be invalidated. The Court will not, however, accept a narrowing construction that appears to be fabricated for purposes of the pending case. (Note that while the Supreme Court may limit the statutory scope of a federal law, any narrowing construction of state law must be premised on state court decisions.) Second, the law in question must be *substantially* overbroad; while this is a vague requirement, it means that a law will not be struck down under the overbreadth doctrine if there are only a handful of circumstances in which its application would be unconstitutional.

The void for vagueness doctrine requires that all criminal statutes adequately describe the activities they prohibit. The doctrine is premised on two due process concerns — that persons potentially subject to the proscription be given fair notice of that which is proscribed and that officers charged with enforcing the law not be vested with arbitrary enforcement discretion. *Papachristou v. City of Jacksonville*, 405 U.S. 156, 162 (1972). In the context of statutes that may tread on First Amendment rights, these due process concerns take on special significance. A vague statute that may include protected speech activity within its amorphous scope potentially runs afoul of the overbreadth doctrine by chilling that protected speech. Under such circumstances, the overbreadth and void for vagueness arguments are essentially identical—the vagueness creates the overbreadth. Next, a vague statute that may be applied to speech activity and that vests enforcement officers with arbitrary authority to define the scope of the proscription runs a risk of permitting discriminatory enforcement on the basis of the favored or disfavored content of the speech. The vesting of such arbitrary authority is itself unconstitutional.

In *NAACP v. Button,* 371 U.S. 415 (1963), the Court described the constitutional significance of these doctrines to the First Amendment:

> The objectionable quality of vagueness and overbreadth does not depend upon absence of fair notice to a criminally accused or upon unchanneled delegation of legislative powers, but upon the danger of tolerating, in the area of First Amendment freedoms, the existence of a penal statute susceptible of sweeping and improper application. These freedoms are delicate and vulnerable, as well as supremely precious in our society. The threat of sanctions may deter their exercise almost as potently as the actual application of sanctions. Because First Amendment freedoms need breathing space to survive, government may regulate in the area only with narrow specificity.

Id. at 432-433.

EXAMPLE 8-D

A City of Rockville ordinance prohibits "any person from engaging in any disturbing or offensive conduct" while on the grounds of City Park. On a crisp autumn afternoon, while strolling through the park, Billy decides to express his oneness with nature by tearing his clothes off and prancing through the falling leaves. He is arrested for violating the city ordinance. Assuming that a precisely drawn law, such as the prohibition of public nudity, could proscribe the expressive activity engaged in by Billy, may Billy, nonetheless, mount a successful overbreadth or vagueness challenge to this ordinance?

EXPLANATION

To successfully invoke the overbreadth doctrine, Billy must establish that the ordinance is substantially overbroad. He may well succeed on this score. The words "disturbing or offensive" are subject to very broad applications that would include much protected speech. For example, a Republican may find almost any speech by a Democrat disturbing or offensive even though the Democrat has every right to engage in such speech. In addition, this potential overbreadth is a product of vagueness. Given the words used — "disturbing or offensive"—the actual scope of the proscription is unclear, providing both inadequate notice to potential violators and an opportunity for discriminatory, content-based enforcement. Therefore, in the absence of a reasonable and narrowing construction that would confine the scope of the ordinance to unprotected speech, the statute violates the principle of overbreadth and is void for vagueness.

§8.3   Content-Based Restrictions on Speech

§8.3.1   *What Constitutes a Content-Based Restriction?*

A content-based restriction on speech is one in which the applicability of the law is triggered by the substance or content of the message being conveyed. In *Near v. Minnesota,* for example, the lower court's injunction was directed toward the future publication of any "malicious, scandalous, or defamatory" newspaper, characterizations that can only emanate from the substance or content of an intended publication. Similarly, in the *Pentagon Papers Case,* the injunction sought by the government was directed toward preventing the defendant newspapers from publishing specific factual information — a content-based imposition. Content-based restrictions are considered a most serious infringement of First Amendment liberties, since the government is using the force of law to distort public discourse by suppressing, through either prior restraint or subsequent punishment, those messages perceived by the government to be somehow objectionable. Always begin with the presumption that a content-based restriction on speech is suspect. The strength of that presumption (and scrutiny) may diminish, however, if the type of expression at issue falls into a less protected category of speech. Or the Court may avoid the strict scrutiny triggered by a content-based restriction by interpreting statutory language in a manner that eliminates the content-based issue. See, e.g., *National Endowment for the Arts v. Finley,* 524 U.S. 569 (1998) (construing as merely advisory and not regulatory a statutory directive to the National Endowment for the Arts to consider "general standards of decency" in awarding grants).

Restrictions on speech may qualify as content-based in a number of different ways. One involves restrictions aimed at particular subjects or topics, e.g., a statute barring public utilities from including political messages in their billing envelopes or barring the disclosure of classified information. A second type of content-based regulation involves restrictions aimed at specific viewpoints, e.g., a law prohibiting criticism of the war effort or banning the teaching of evolution. Another type of content regulation involves restrictions resulting from the speaker's identity, e.g., a law barring labor organizers or religious groups from using a public auditorium. This list is not exclusive; content-based restrictions can take other forms as well.

It may be difficult to decide what type of content-based restriction is involved in a particular case. For example, is a law that outlaws the showing of indecent films a subject or topic restriction, or does it entail a viewpoint restriction, on the theory that it seeks to restrict the expression of a certain attitude toward sex? As we will see later, it is sometimes necessary to decide what type of content-based restriction is involved, for viewpoint restrictions in certain circumstances are treated more severely by the Court than other types of content restrictions. See §8.5.

A law that would otherwise appear to be content-based in any of the senses we have just described may, nonetheless, be treated by the Court as being content neutral if the government can show that the law was aimed at the secondary effects of the speech. Secondary effects are those other than the impact of the speech on a listener. For example, a law prohibiting the showing of indecent movies because such films are thought to promote marital infidelity imposes a content-based restriction, since it is aimed at the impact on those who view them. If, on the other hand, the same law had been enacted to protect surrounding neighborhoods from the crime that sometimes accompanies so-called adult theaters, then under the secondary effects doctrine the law would be deemed content neutral, since it was enacted to combat the secondary effects of indecent movies. The extent to which this doctrine will be applied in contexts other than those that involve pornography remains to be seen. Compare *City of Renton v. Playtime Theatres, Inc.*, 475 U.S. 41 (1986) (applying secondary effects doctrine to uphold prohibition against adult theaters) with *Boos v. Barry*, 485 U.S. 312 (1988) (rejecting application of secondary effects doctrine in case involving political speech).

In the sections that follow, we will examine a number of doctrines designed to assess the constitutionality of various content-based restrictions on speech. These doctrines are the product of the Court's treatment of recurring problems that arise in the context of freedom of speech. Keep in mind that each of these doctrines is a reflection of the underlying First Amendment values at stake, creating variable standards of scrutiny depending on the proximity of the speech to what the Court perceives as core values of the First Amendment.

As we will see, there are basically three different types of tests the Court employs in assessing the validity of content-based restrictions on speech. The first involves application of a *specialized* or *doctrinal test* that has been created for a particular type of protected speech. For example, the clear and present danger test is used to assess restrictions on speech that advocates unlawful conduct, while the commercial speech test is used mainly for restrictions on commercial advertising. A second approach involves determining whether the speech in question falls into a category of constitutionally *unprotected or proscribable speech;* examples of this approach include the "fighting words" doctrine and the test for obscenity. Finally, if no specialized or doctrinal test exists and if the speech is of a type entitled to First Amendment protection, the Court may employ an *ad hoc balancing test* in which it determines whether or not the restriction can be defended on the ground that it is narrowly tailored to achieve a compelling governmental interest.

§8.3.2 *Advocacy of Unlawful Conduct: The Clear and Present Danger Test*

The clear and present danger test is the original First Amendment doctrine. It is most clearly applicable to laws restricting advocacy of unlawful conduct, but it has also been applied in the more general contexts of laws restricting either social protest or commentary on public issues. As now configured, the clear and present danger test operates as a specialized form of strict scrutiny, permitting restrictions on speech only when necessary to advance a substantial, overriding governmental interest and only when the danger presented by the speech is such that the government has no other option but to punish the speaker.

The doctrine began inauspiciously. In *Schenck v. United States*, 249 U.S. 47 (1919), two defendants were charged with various violations of the Espionage Act of 1917. The charges stemmed from their distribution of leaflets exhorting potential conscripts to resist the draft. At trial, the defendants claimed a First Amendment right to distribute the leaflets. They were, nonetheless, convicted. The Supreme Court affirmed, treating their First Amendment defense with almost casual indifference. In the words of Justice Holmes:

> We admit that in many places and in ordinary times the defendants in saying all that was said in the circular would have been within their constitutional rights. But the character of every act depends upon the circumstances in which it is done. . . . The most stringent protection of free speech would not protect a man in falsely shouting fire in a theatre and causing a panic. . . . The question in every case is whether the words used are used in such circumstances and are of such a nature as to create a clear and present danger that they will bring about the substantive evils that Congress has a right to prevent. It is a question of proximity and degree. When a nation is at war many things that might be said in time of peace are such a hindrance to its effort that their utterance will not be endured so long as men fight and that no Court could regard them as protected by any constitutional right. The statute of 1917 in §4 punishes conspiracies to obstruct as well as actual obstruction. If the act, (speaking, or circulating a paper,) its tendency and the intent with which it is done are the same, we perceive no ground for saying that success alone warrants making the act a crime.

Id. at 52. The Court did not apply any clear and present danger standards to the facts before it. There was no examination of proximity, degree, or context. Rather, the Court simply assumed that the circumstances warranted the conviction and punishment. It was apparently enough that the leaflets may have had a bad tendency.

The week after deciding *Schenck,* the Court issued two more opinions upholding similar convictions under the Espionage Act. Justice Holmes authored both opinions, and in neither did he allude to the clear and present danger language he had used in *Schenck.* In the first, *Frohwerk v. United States,* 249 U.S. 204 (1919), it was sufficient to uphold the defendant's conviction that it "*might* . . . have been found that the circulation of the paper was in quarters where a little breath would be enough to kindle a flame and that the fact was known and relied upon by those who sent the paper out." Id. at 209 (emphasis supplied). And in the second, *Debs v. United States,* 249 U.S. 211 (1919), the defendant was convicted for delivering a speech in which he praised individual draft resisters for their courage and sacrifice. His criminality derived from the inference that his listeners should follow the same course of conduct. The First Amendment discussion was relegated to a cryptic citation to *Schenck.*

At this point, "clear and present danger" would seem to have been no more than a passing phrase in an opinion that gave little regard to the freedom of expression. A significant change was, however, on the horizon. Hints of that change appeared just six months after the decisions in *Schenck, Frohwerk,* and *Debs.* The vehicle was yet another Espionage Act case — *Abrams v. United States,* 250 U.S. 616 (1919). Again, the Court rejected the proffered First Amendment defense. Yet despite the parallels between the facts of *Abrams* and those of the preceding cases, Justice Holmes, joined by Justice Brandeis, dissented:

> Every year if not every day we have to wager our salvation upon some prophecy based upon imperfect knowledge. While that experiment is part of our system I think that we should be eternally vigilant against attempts to check the expression of opinions that we loathe and believe to be fraught with death, unless they so *imminently* threaten *immediate* interference with the *lawful and pressing purposes* of the law that an immediate check is required to save the country. . . . Only the emergency that makes it immediately dangerous to leave the correction of evil counsels to time warrants making any exception to the sweeping command, "Congress shall make no law . . . abridging the freedom of speech."

Id. at 630-631 (emphasis supplied). Despite his protestation to the contrary, id. at 627, Holmes's dissent reflected a new, speech-protective perspective on the freedom of expression. From this new perspective, speech advocating unlawful conduct would be protected unless that speech "imminently" threatened "immediate" interference with a "lawful and pressing" governmental purpose. In other words, unless the restrictive law is narrowly tailored to advance an important purpose, the freedom of speech must prevail.

Justice Brandeis took these emerging themes a step further in his eloquent concurring opinion in *Whitney v. California*, 274 U.S. 357, 372 (1927) (Brandeis, J., joined by Holmes, J., concurring). See also *Gitlow v. New York*, 268 U.S. 652, 672 (1925) (Holmes, J., joined by Brandeis, J., dissenting). Brandeis proposed a test that was highly speech-protective and, most important, enforceable by courts on an as-applied basis. 274 U.S. at 374-378.

> To justify suppression of free speech there must be reasonable ground to fear that serious evil will result if free speech is practiced. There must be reasonable ground to believe that the danger apprehended is imminent. There must be reasonable ground to believe that the evil to be prevented is a serious one. . . . [E]ven advocacy of [law] violation, however reprehensible morally, is not a justification for denying free speech where the advocacy falls short of incitement and there is nothing to indicate that the advocacy would be immediately acted on. The wide difference between advocacy and incitement, between preparation and attempt, between assembling and conspiracy, must be borne in mind. In order to support a finding of clear and present danger it must be shown either that immediate serious violence was to be expected or was advocated, or that the past conduct furnished reason to believe that such advocacy was then contemplated.

Id. at 376.

The standards suggested by Brandeis in *Whitney*—incitement, immediacy or imminence, and seriousness of harm—were adopted and applied by the Court in *Herndon v. Lowry*, 301 U.S. 242 (1937). In *Herndon*, the defendant was convicted for soliciting membership in the Communist Party, an organization whose aim was, in part, the forcible overthrow of the government, admittedly a serious evil. While the defendant had participated in public meetings and had distributed communist literature, there was no evidence that he had in any fashion endorsed *immediate* unlawful action. Thus, although the evidence established that the defendant had engaged in *advocacy* of a doctrine that itself embraced unlawful action, there was no evidence that he had *incited* anyone to take such action or that as an *immediate* result of his activities such unlawful action was *imminent*. The Supreme Court reversed his conviction, finding that the absence of incitement and imminence was fatal to the conviction. Id. at 260-264. In short, there was no clear and present danger sufficient to overcome the presumptive protection for speech provided by the First Amendment.

After *Herndon*, the Court began to apply the clear and present danger test beyond the context of unlawful advocacy. See, e.g., *Terminiello v. Chicago*, 337 U.S. 1, 4-5 (1949) (breach of peace); *West Virginia State Bd. of Educ. v. Barnette*, 319 U.S. 624, 633-634 (1943) (refusing to salute the flag); *Cantwell v. Connecticut*, 310 U.S. 296, 308-309 (1940) (religious proselytizing); *Thornhill v. Alabama*, 310 U.S. 88, 104-105 (1940) (labor picketing). In one such case, the Court described the "minimum compulsion" of the First Amendment as requiring that "the substantive evil must be extremely serious and the degree of imminence extremely high before utterances can be punished." *Bridges v. California*, 314 U.S. 252, 263 (1941). Holmes's passing observation in *Schenck* had thus become a relatively formidable and widely applicable doctrine, inherent in which was a strong presumption in favor of freedom of expression.

EXAMPLE 8-E

Shannon was convicted of assaulting nonunion truck drivers as part of an effort to force those truck drivers to join a union. In a presentencing hearing, Shannon's lawyer requested that Shannon be placed on probation as a first-time offender. In response to this request and prior to sentencing, the leading local newspaper ran an editorial describing Shannon as a "goon and a thug" and calling for imposition of the maximum sentence. The editorial ended with this observation: "Judge Scott will make a serious mistake if he grants probation to Shannon. The community needs the example of his assignment to the rock pile." Based on this editorial, Judge Scott held the newspaper in contempt and assessed a fine of $1,000. In so ruling, Judge Scott explained that the editorial threatened the "impartial adjudication of a pending case." Applying the modern clear and present danger test, may this contempt citation be upheld?

EXPLANATION

Probably not. Although interference with the impartial adjudication of a pending case is a most serious evil and one that the government is fully empowered to prevent, on these facts there is little evidence that the cited newspaper editorial would cause the occurrence of this evil, much less that the evil was imminent. To say that a judge will make a "serious mistake" would seem to fall well within the right of a newspaper to comment on matters of public interest. Stated somewhat differently, one should be able to assume that a judge is sufficiently hearty to be able to withstand such criticism. See *Bridges v. California*, 314 U.S. at 271-275 (arriving at a similar conclusion under similar facts); accord *Craig v. Harney*, 331 U.S. 367 (1947); *Pennekamp v. Florida*, 328 U.S. 331 (1946).

Yet one can certainly argue to the contrary. The purpose of the editorial was clearly to put pressure on the judge, and if one adds the fact that the judge was soon to be up for reelection, the potential for interference becomes more plausible and the threat more imminent. This is especially true if the newspaper enjoys either prestige or power within the community. So, too, if the trial had been particularly notorious. From this perspective, there may well be a clear and present danger to the administration of justice — a substantial possibility that the judge will conform his or her decision to the dictates of the editorial. *Bridges v. California*, 314 U.S. at 299-300 (Frankfurter, J., dissenting). The presumptive strength of the First Amendment, however, has generally prevailed over such arguments.

The foregoing example should demonstrate at least two important points. First, as evolved, the modern clear and present danger test values freedom of expression over even very weighty government interests. Only specific facts proving an imminent danger to such an interest will permit interference with the freedom of expression. The parallel with strict scrutiny is obvious. Speech may be restricted only to prevent an extremely serious evil — a compelling government interest — and only if the occurrence of that evil is an imminent result of the speech. Moreover, the law must be narrowly drawn to advance the government's interest in the least restrictive or least intrusive manner. Second, and closely related, the clear and present danger test, and, therefore, implicitly any protection afforded by the First Amendment, is intensely fact driven. Context is everything; therefore, what is said in any particular case must be filtered through the facts of that case.

The critical importance of context can be seen in *Dennis v. United States*, 341 U.S. 494 (1951), a case in which the clear and present danger test seemed to veer away from the speech-protective model described above. The defendants in *Dennis* were convicted under the Smith Act of conspiring to create an organization, the Communist Party of the United States, that advocated the unlawful overthrow of the U.S. government. There was no evidence, however, that the defendants were devising specific plans to overthrow the government or to engage in acts of sabotage. Rather, the evidence established only that the defendants had conspired to form a group to teach and advocate the creed of communism as espoused by Marx, Lenin, and Stalin, included within which was the propriety and inevitability of violent overthrow and industrial revolution. The defendants claimed a First Amendment right to teach these doctrines.

In a plurality opinion, which has been treated by the Court as authoritative on a number of occasions, Chief Justice Vinson purported to endorse what he described as the Holmes-Brandeis version of clear and present danger, but in fact applied a formula that was more deferential to governmental interests. "In each case [courts] must ask whether the gravity of the 'evil,' discounted by its improbability, justifies such invasion of free speech as is necessary to avoid the danger." 341 U.S. at 510 (quoting *United States v. Dennis*, 183 F.2d 201, 212 (2d Cir. 1950)). In other words, under this formula, the more substantial the potential evil is, the less likely its realization must be for the government to restrict speech promoting that evil.

Quite obviously, the violent overthrow of governmental and social institutions is a substantial evil. Id. at 509. In the plurality's words, "[T]his is the ultimate value of any society, for if a society cannot protect its very structure from armed internal attack, it must follow that no subordinate value can be protected." Id. As to imminence, any lack of immediacy — indeed, there was no showing of immediacy—was far outweighed by a combination of the substantiality of the evil and the perception that the illegal action would occur whenever the time for action was deemed propitious. In the plurality's words, clear and present danger "cannot mean that before the Government may act, it must wait until the *putsch* is about to be executed, the plans have been laid and the signal is awaited." Id. Given the context of the emerging Cold War and the perceived threat posed by the worldwide communist movement, the Court found that a clear and present danger existed sufficient to affirm the defendants' convictions. The Court made no attempt to distinguish *Herndon v. Lowry*, but presumably the defendant there was seen as an isolated actor, and not part of a nationwide conspiracy. Presumably, too, the context of the Cold War altered perceptions about the threat posed by the communist movement.

EXAMPLE 8-F

Lester is an anti-government man. He believes that all forms of government are a massive conspiracy designed to suppress freedom and individualism. Lester also believes that violence is a legitimate method to combat the forces of this unconscionable leviathan. To promote his views, Lester has written a pamphlet that describes his philosophy, and in it, he advocates the use of stealth and violence to combat the forces of government. He gives, as an example, the bombing of public buildings. At least once every week Lester stands outside public buildings and hands out free copies of his pamphlet. Based on this activity, Lester is charged with violating a statute that makes it a crime "to advocate the use of violence to overthrow or physically attack any institution of government." Does the clear and present danger test protect Lester under these circumstances?

EXPLANATION

If one applies the pre-*Dennis* version of clear and present danger, requiring both an extremely serious evil and an extremely high probability of imminence, then, in the absence of more evidence, Lester's activities would seem to be protected. Although the evil is extremely serious, the facts do not show any degree of imminence. At best there is the possibility that someone in the future may act on Lester's proselytizing. Stated somewhat differently, Lester has engaged not in incitement, but in protected advocacy. Thus, this would appear to be an instance in which the remedy of more speech remains readily available. On the other hand, if one applies the *Dennis* balancing formula, a contrary result may obtain. Given the seriousness of the evil, combined with very real concerns about domestic terrorism, the relative lack of probability may not sufficiently "discount" the evil to prevent prosecution for this advocacy.

But should *Dennis* apply to facts such as those described in Example 8-F? Some insight into a potential answer can be found in Justice Jackson's concurring opinion in *Dennis*. 341 U.S. at 561. Justice Jackson thought that the clear and present danger test was useful as a judicial tool to measure the constitutionality of prosecutions of discrete acts of protest: "a hot-headed speech on a street corner, or circulation of a few incendiary pamphlets, or parading by some zealots behind a red flag, or refusal of a handful of school children to salute our flag." Id. at 568. Under such circumstances, a judge can examine the facts and make the appropriate determination of evil and immediacy. But with respect to a "well-organized, nation-wide conspiracy," such as the Communist Party, the "verbal trap" of clear and present danger requires the appraisal of "imponderables." Id. at 570. As a consequence, Jackson thought the test was simply inapplicable under such circumstances. If one adopts Jackson's approach, Lester's circulation of incendiary pamphlets would seem to qualify for application of the pre-*Dennis* clear and present danger test—his activities were not part of a well-organized, nation-wide conspiracy. If this is true, it suggests that there are two somewhat different strains of the clear and present danger test.

That this may be the case is suggested by the Court's decision in *Brandenburg v. Ohio*, 395 U.S. 444 (1969). In that case, the Court returned to the version of clear and present danger described by Justice Brandeis in *Whitney*, though, oddly enough, without ever using the phrase "clear and present danger." In *Brandenburg*, a Ku Klux Klan leader was convicted of violating a state law that made it unlawful to advocate "the duty, necessity, or propriety of crime, sabotage, violence, or unlawful methods of terrorism as a means of accomplishing industrial or political reform." Id. at 444-445. The conviction was premised on two speeches made by the defendant at Klan gatherings. In one, he stated, "We're not a revengent organization, but if our President, our Congress, our Supreme Court, continues to suppress the white, Caucasian race, it's possible that there might have to be some re-vengeance taken." Id. at 446. And in the other, he made racist comments about blacks and Jews. The Court reversed. In the Court's view, the advocacy of unlawful conduct could not be punished "except where such advocacy is directed to inciting or producing imminent lawless action and is likely to incite or produce such action." Id. at 447.

Brandenburg did not, however, overrule *Dennis*. Instead, *Brandenburg* represents an application of the distinction recognized by Justice Jackson in his *Dennis* concurring opinion. In those contexts in which the speech is *public and overt*, the formula of Justice Brandeis's *Whitney* concurrence provides a good judicial measure of constitutionality. In contexts in which the speech is *covert*—i.e., part of some type of an organized, clandestine conspiracy— the balancing test applied by the *Dennis* majority may well provide the most serviceable method for assessing the countervailing interests at stake. Of course, one could argue that a case involving the Klan should fit into the latter category. But the charges against the defendant in *Brandenburg* did not involve covert or clandestine operations; rather, they were premised on the defendant's public declarations of his organization's philosophy, made in the presence of a television film crew.

EXAMPLE 8-G

Suppose that instead of being a lone pamphleteer, Lester was the leader of American Liberation Now (ALN), an organization whose purpose was to establish, through crime and violence, an independent state within the United States. Suppose, too, that ALN had several hundred members who met in secret to discuss philosophy and strategy and to train for independence. These members were pledged to achieve their goal of independent statehood as soon as the circumstances were propitious. If, based on his leadership of this organization, Lester were charged with conspiring to advocate the unlawful overthrow of the government of state X and if he relied on the First Amendment as a defense to those charges, which version of clear and present danger should (or would) a court apply?

EXPLANATION

One argument would be that there is only one version of clear and present danger—namely, the one applied in *Brandenburg*, the Court's most recent foray into this context. Under that test, Lester's potential conviction could be upheld only if imminence of unlawful conduct were established. In the absence of such a showing, the appropriate remedy is more speech. This is true regardless of whether the speech on which the charges rest is public or clandestine. The other argument would look to the *Dennis* balancing formula as presenting the more appropriate measure. This argument is founded on the assumption that the charges are premised not on public statements made by Lester (such as those at issue in *Brandenburg*), but on Lester's speech-related involvement in the covert and clandestine activities of the ALN. According to this view—which is similar to that espoused by Justice Jackson in *Dennis*—the covert and clandestine nature of the activities at issue makes application of the more traditional clear and present danger test both impractical and unsound. The government should not have to wait "until the *putsch* is about to be executed." Rather, in determining whether Lester may be punished, the court must balance the substantiality of the evil against its improbability. The outcome is obviously both subjective and fact dependent.

To sum up, the clear and present danger test is contextual. The formulas described in *Dennis* and *Brandenburg* are both designed to balance the weightiness of the government's interest against the individual's right of free expression. Which test to apply and how rigorously to apply it will depend on the facts, the perceived dangers, and the government's opportunities to prevent the very real harms that may be caused by the advocacy of unlawful conduct.

§8.3.3   *Fighting Words and Hate Speech*

Fighting words are defined as those words "which by their very utterance inflict injury or tend to incite an immediate breach of the peace." *Chaplinsky v. New Hampshire,* 315 U.S. 568, 572 (1942). Such words are presumed to play little or no part in the exposition of ideas and are, therefore, deemed to be a type of speech that falls outside the First Amendment umbrella. Id. Yet despite a definition that focuses on the inherently harmful or provocative nature of the words themselves, in practice the applicability of the fighting words doctrine depends largely, if not completely, on the context in which the presumably harmful or provocative words are used. There are, therefore, no words that automatically fall into this category. *Cohen v. California,* 403 U.S. 15, 22-26 (1971) (the word "fuck" may not be excised from the lexicon on the theory that it is "inherently likely to cause violent reaction"). More-over, words that one normally would not consider to be fighting words may warrant that label if delivered under particularly volatile circumstances and in a manner likely to cause a violent reaction.

EXAMPLE 8-H

Al is a card-carrying liberal. He has a strong aversion to anything to the right of the New Deal, and he finds conservative talk show hosts particularly loathsome. One evening while taking a stroll, Al happens upon Bush Limbo, the well-known (and sometimes rotund) host of a conservative call-in radio show. Al races up to Bush and screams in his face, "You're a big fat idiot!" Just before Bush is about to land the first blow, a police officer intervenes and arrests Al for causing a breach of the peace. Were the words uttered by Al "fighting words" and, therefore, unprotected by the First Amendment?

EXPLANATION

Perhaps. The mere offensiveness of the words used will not automatically qualify them as fighting words, but given the circumstances and the manner of delivery, a court might find that Al's intemperate epithet was delivered in a manner likely to invite an unthinking, violent response. See *Chaplinsky v. New Hampshire*, 315 U.S. 568 (1942) (epithets "God damned racketeer" and "damned Fascist" delivered in a face-to-face confrontation with a police officer held to be fighting words). If so, the "fighting words" label may be applied, and the speech will be unprotected. The relatively mild nature of Al's invective may, however, render the application of the doctrine somewhat questionable. Had the words used been more provocative, however (e.g., so-called four-letter words), the "fighting words" label would more easily attach due to the increased likelihood that the use of such words in an angry face-to-face confrontation would lead to a breach of the peace.

Suppose, however, that Al publishes a book entitled *Bush Limbo Is a Big Fat Idiot*. Even if this pejorative epithet would qualify as fighting words in a face-to-face confrontation, it would not be so considered as the title to a book. The context simply lacks the necessary immediacy associated with the fighting words doctrine. This would remain true even if the book title contained highly provocative four-letter words.

As one can discern from the above example, the fighting words doctrine may be thought of as merely a specific application of the clear and present danger test. *Feiner v. New York*, 340 U.S. 315, 319-320 (1951); *Terminiello v. Chicago*, 337 U.S. 1, 2 (1949). The use of offensive or provocative language will be punishable according to that doctrine only if words are delivered in a manner and under circumstances likely to cause an immediate and serious harm—typically, a violent reaction stemming from a face-to-face confrontation. Given this reality, a number of commentators have suggested that the fighting words nomenclature should be abandoned. They argue that instead of treating fighting words as a form of speech that falls outside the First Amendment, such words should be recognized as a form of speech that falls under the First Amendment umbrella, but that is, nonetheless, punishable where the requirements of the clear and present danger test are met. The Court, however, continues to refer to "fighting words" as a separate category of unprotected speech.

Closely related to the fighting words doctrine is the problem of hate speech. In recent years, a number of communities — particularly college communities—have attempted to regulate the use of language that ridicules or demeans racial minorities, women, gays and lesbians, and other groups deemed particularly susceptible to verbal abuse. Proponents of such regulations argue that the designated groups are victims of deeply ingrained patterns of prejudice, patterns that are only exacerbated by a permissive attitude toward verbal abuse. Hate speech as such is not, however, an unprotected category of speech, and since state-imposed limitations on hate speech are by definition content-based, they must satisfy rigorous First Amendment standards. As a consequence, courts have been reluctant to uphold such measures. See, e.g., *Doe v. University of Mich.*, 721 F. Supp. 852 (E.D. Mich. 1989) (striking down the University of Michigan's speech code). Similarly, in *R.A.V. v. City of St. Paul*, 505 U.S. 377 (1992), the Supreme Court struck down a city ordinance that prohibited the display of any symbol that "arouses anger, alarm or resentment in others on the basis of race, color, creed, religion or gender." Id. at 380. Even though the state limited the scope of the ordinance to fighting words, an unprotected category of speech, the Court held that the law was facially invalid as a content-based restriction on speech, since the proscription depended on the message being communicated by the fighting words. Id. at 391-393.

§8.3.4   Free Speech Limitations on Defamation (and Related Torts)

The Court's landmark decision in *New York Times v. Sullivan*, 376 U.S. 254 (1964), rejected an entrenched judicial assumption that the common law of defamation was categorically exempt from limits imposed by the First Amendment. In the post-*Sullivan* jurisprudence of the First Amendment, the law of defamation is no longer the sole bailiwick of the states. Instead, the *Sullivan* Court proclaimed "a profound national commitment to the principle that debate on public issues should be uninhibited, robust, and wide-open, and that it may well include vehement, caustic, and sometimes unpleasantly sharp attacks on government and public officials," id. at 270, under which the common law of defamation and other speech-premised torts (e.g., intentional infliction of emotional distress) must at times give way to the expanding constitutional law of free speech.

The decision in *Sullivan* grew out of a controversy surrounding a full-page advertisement published in the *New York Times*. The ad solicited support for the civil rights movement and described, among other things, certain anti-civil rights actions said to have taken place in Montgomery, Alabama, under the auspices of the local sheriff's department. In response, the Sheriff of the City of Montgomery sued the *New York Times* (and others) for defamation, alleging that he had been libeled by certain factual errors contained in the ad. Under Alabama law as it stood, a publication was deemed "libelous per se" if the publication was "of and concerning" the plaintiff and if it tended to injure the plaintiff "in his reputation" or "bring [him] into public contempt." Id. at 267. Once libel per se was established, the defendant could prevail only on proof that the matters published were true. The ad at issue in *Sullivan* did contain factual errors regarding the events said to have occurred in Montgomery, and under Alabama law, those falsehoods could be treated as pertaining to the sheriff. After a trial, a jury awarded the sheriff $500,000 in damages.

The Supreme Court reversed, holding that the First Amendment prohibits a "public official from recovering damages for a defamatory falsehood relating to his official conduct unless he proves that the statement was made with 'actual malice'—that is, with knowledge that it was false or with reckless disregard of whether it was false or not." Id. at 279-280. Moreover, the actual malice element must be established with "convincing clarity." Id. at 285-286.

The Court's rationale for this relatively tough standard focused on the importance of public debate in a democratic society. If that debate is to be uninhibited, robust, and wide-open, the participants must be free to risk the publication of factual error in their exploration for truth or consensus and in their quest for democratic accountability. To conclude otherwise would be to impose a dangerous chill on both the terms and the scope of public discourse. In short, the risk of transient error was far outweighed by the risk of enforced silence.

This risk of error does not, however, encompass the knowing or reckless falsehood, since neither contributes to a good-faith willingness to participate in public discourse. Thus, under *Sullivan,* in the context of criticism of public officials, the knowing or reckless falsehood is without First Amendment value and hence without First Amendment protection. The actual malice standard was designed to ensure that, in the context of public debate, only this unprotected speech remained subject to the law of defamation.

The Burdens Imposed by the Actual Malice Standard

In cases in which it applies (a subject to which we will return), the actual malice standard injects a scienter element into the plaintiff's prima facie case. The standard has nothing to do with "malice" as that word is commonly understood. Rather, it requires only that a plaintiff alleging defamation prove that the defendant published a defamatory falsehood with knowledge of falsity or with reckless disregard for the truth. The phrase "knowledge of falsity" means what it says — the defendant must have known that the published defamation was false. "Reckless disregard for the truth" is only a small step removed. That language requires proof that the defendant "entertained serious doubts as to the truth of his publication," *St. Amant v. Thompson,* 390 U.S. 727, 731 (1968) or that the publication was made with "'a high degree of awareness of . . . probable falsity.'" *Harte-Hanks Communications v. Connaughton,* 491 U.S. 657, 667 (1989) (quoting *Garrison v. Louisiana,* 379 U.S. 64, 74 (1964)). Mere negligence or failure to follow professional standards is not enough to satisfy either standard. 491 U.S.

664-666. Proof of actual malice must be clear and convincing, id. at 657, a standard that falls somewhere between a preponderance of the evidence and proof beyond a reasonable doubt.

EXAMPLE 8-I

Olive was a candidate for the position of city court judge. The local newspaper, the *Blade-Gazette*, supported her rival, the incumbent. One week prior to the election, the incumbent's clerk was indicted on several counts of bribery in connection with cases pending before the city court. The next day, the *Blade-Gazette* published an article in which it quoted "an anonymous informant" as claiming to have been bribed by Olive to make false accusations against the indicted clerk. The informant was quoted accurately, but her description of Olive's complicity was completely false. Olive had never spoken to her and was not involved with any type of bribery. With a limited amount of investigation, the *Blade-Gazette* would have discovered these facts. Among other things, the prosecutor would have told the newspaper that there was both physical evidence and several other witnesses that corroborated the informant's testimony against the clerk and that Olive had played no role in the affair. Was the falsehood regarding Olive published "knowingly" or with "reckless disregard for the truth"?

EXPLANATION

It depends. The fact that the *Blade-Gazette* was careless and even unprofessional in its investigation will not, standing alone, be sufficient to establish actual malice. The limited (or nonexistent) investigation may, however, support an inference that the newspaper doubted the veracity of the informant and did not wish to have those doubts verified. This inference, standing alone, is still not *clear and convincing* evidence of actual malice. If, on the other hand, Olive can prove that the *Blade-Gazette* was aware of facts tending to discredit the informant's story and failed to pursue obvious leads to that effect, the case for actual malice would be much stronger. This is especially true when one factors in the *Blade-Gazette*'s support for the incumbent. Under such circumstances, it might fairly be said that the *Blade-Gazette* published the falsehood with a high degree of awareness of its probable falsity. See *Harte-Hanks Communications*, 491 U.S. at 685-693 (affirming a finding of actual malice on similar grounds).

Implicit in the actual malice standard is a requirement that the plaintiff prove the falsity of the defamatory statement. Knowledge of falsity can only be established if the defamatory assertion was in fact false; reckless disregard for the truth also implies the publication of a false statement. In other words, truth is not a defense in an actual malice case; instead, lack of truth, i.e., falsity, is an element of the plaintiff's cause of action. The burden of proof on this element, however, is merely a preponderance of the evidence. In Example 8-I, therefore, Olive would be required to prove by a preponderance of the evidence that she had not bribed the informant.

The falsity element also requires that the alleged defamation involve an assertion of *fact* and not a mere statement of *opinion*. While a factual assertion can be false, an opinion, regardless of how ridiculous or pernicious, cannot be. As a consequence, statements of opinion are absolutely protected. If, however, the supposed opinion reasonably implies the existence of certain false and defamatory facts, it will be treated as a factual assertion. In other words, courts will not allow a defendant to disguise a factual assertion as an opinion. The claim in Example 8-I that Olive bribed a potential witness is a statement of fact. Had the published account quoted the informant as "being of the opinion" that Olive was involved in such a scheme, the conclusion would be the same. The former asserts the fact of bribery; the latter reasonably implies it. See *Milkovich v. Lorain Journal Co.*, 497 U.S. 1 (1990).

A similar treatment is given to hyperbole and parody. In those contexts in which the actual malice standard applies, both genres are absolutely protected unless the publication can be reasonably said to imply a false statement of facts. Thus, in *Hustler Magazine v. Falwell*, 485 U.S. 46 (1988), a particularly nasty parody regarding a well-known televangelist and his mother was held not actionable, since no reasonable person could have interpreted the parody—which was labeled as such—as making any assertion of fact, implied or otherwise. The *Hustler* case is also noteworthy because the underlying tort was not defamation, but intentional infliction of emotional distress. Nonetheless, the *Sullivan* standard applied, and recovery could be premised only on the plaintiff's proof of falsity and actual malice.

The Contexts in Which the Actual Malice Standard Applies

First, the actual malice standard applies to speech-premised tort claims, such as defamation or intentional infliction of emotion distress, when such claims are brought by public officials. The latter term is broadly defined to include all elected officials as well as any individual running for elective office—such as Olive in the example above. It includes as well any person employed by the government who holds a position that permits him or her to exercise discretion over the conduct of governmental affairs or whose position is such that the public would have "an independent interest in the qualifications and performance of the person who holds it." *Rosenblatt v. Baer*, 383 U.S. 75, 85-86 (1966) (supervisor of a county-owned ski resort deemed a public official). This definition excludes public employees such as custodians, filing clerks, and typists, but it just as clearly includes public school teachers, police officers, playground supervisors, social workers, and the like.

The actual malice standard also applies when such claims are brought by public figures, i.e., persons who are "intimately involved in the resolution of important public questions or, by reason of their fame, shape events in areas of concern to society at large." *Curtis Publishing Co. v. Butts*, 388 U.S. 130, 164 (1967) (Warren, C.J., concurring). The Court has subsequently recognized two types of public figures for purposes of this rule:

> [First are those who] occupy positions of such persuasive power and influence that they are deemed public figures for all purposes. More commonly, those classed as public figures have thrust themselves to the forefront of particular public controversies in order to influence the resolution of the issues involved.

Gertz v. Robert Welch, Inc., 418 U.S. 323, 345 (1974). Notice that under this standard, the status of being a public figure derives largely from a personal choice by the "public figure" to become involved in public affairs. The Court has stated that the case of the truly involuntary public figure will be rare indeed.

EXAMPLE 8-J

Bill "Big Boy" Butz is the head coach of the New York Knockablockers, a newly franchised NFL football team. A New York sportswriter has written several articles about Butz and his unorthodox training methods, including an accusation that Butz promotes the use of illegal steroids. If Butz sues the sportswriter for defamation, will Butz be deemed a public figure?

EXPLANATION

Probably. A person who has accepted a high-profile position such as that occupied by Butz is a public figure for purposes of any publications pertaining to the position from which that status derives. See *Curtis Publishing Co. v. Butts*, 388 U.S. 130 (1967).

Suppose, however, that Butz's wife, Beverly, files for divorce and that the same reporter writes an article describing Beverly as a "prime candidate for the Bette Ford Clinic." Suppose, too, that Beverly holds a news conference explaining why she has decided to leave Butz. Is Beverly a public figure? Not likely. Beverly's marriage to a public figure does not automatically make her a public figure, and this is true regardless of how interesting the public or the press may find her marriage and divorce. What is important is that nothing in these facts indicates that Beverly occupies a position of persuasive power and influence. Nor has she thrust herself to the forefront of a *public* controversy. As long as the news conference is not being used to influence the outcome of the divorce proceedings, it will not transform Beverly into a public figure. See *Time, Inc. v. Firestone*, 424 U.S. 448 (1976).

The Standards for Private-Plaintiff Lawsuits

At one time, some members of the Court sought to extend the actual malice standard to any speech related to a matter "of public or general interest." *Rosenbloom v. Metromedia, Inc.*, 403 U.S. 29, 43 (1971) (plurality opinion). Thus, the standard would apply regardless of the status of the plaintiff. The Court, however, has rejected that view, limiting the application of actual malice to cases in which the plaintiff is either a public official or a public figure. *Gertz v. Robert Welch, Inc.*, 418 U.S. 323 (1974). Specifically, in *Gertz v. Robert Welch*, the Court held that in defamation suits brought by private plaintiffs, i.e., plaintiffs who are neither public officials nor public figures, liability for *actual damages* could be established, consistent with the First Amendment, if the plaintiff proves that the defendant had, with negligence, published a false statement of fact regarding the plaintiff. See also *Philadelphia Newspapers, Inc. v. Hepps*, 475 U.S. 767, 768 (1986). The award of punitive damages or presumed damages, however, would require a showing of actual malice. *Gertz*, 418 U.S. at 349.

There is one final wrinkle in private-plaintiff lawsuits (and it is a wrinkle that could potentially spread to the public official/public figure context). The requirement that actual malice be satisfied in order for a private plaintiff to receive presumed or punitive damages applies only when the defamation at issue involves a matter of public concern. Otherwise, presumed and punitive damages can be imposed under a less strict, but unspecified standard. *Dun & Bradstreet, Inc. v. Greenmoss Builders, Inc.*, 472 U.S. 749 (1985) (plurality and concurring opinions). The *Dun & Bradstreet* Court did not opine on whether the *Gertz* negligence standard should also be jettisoned under such circumstances. But see *Dun & Bradstreet*, 472 U.S. at 774 (White, J., concurring) (suggesting that the fault standard of *Gertz* should not apply). Nor did the Court discuss whether public officials and public figures could avoid the requisites of *New York Times v. Sullivan* by arguing that an alleged defamation did not involve a matter of public concern. Both questions remain open.

Another open question after *Dun & Bradstreet* involves what is meant by the phrase "a matter of public concern." In that case, the Court held that a private credit report falsely impugning the credit of a business was not a matter of public concern, but in so holding, the Court provided no method for applying this standard. See 472 U.S. at 789 (Brennan, J., dissenting) (arguing that a credit report on a local business is a matter of public concern, since it contains information of interest to the community at large). The only measure is a comparison with the facts in *Gertz*. There, the Court implicitly held that a published accusation that a lawyer was the architect of a communist plot to frame a police officer was a matter of public concern. Although one can sense a difference between the facts of *Dun & Bradstreet* and those of *Gertz*—a private report versus a public accusation—there is, as of yet, no doctrinal way to measure this distinction, leading some commentators to suggest that the distinction will and ought to be abandoned.

Reconsider Example 8-J. Could Beverly Butz, a private plaintiff, be awarded presumed or punitive damages without satisfying the actual malice standard? That depends on whether the defamation involves a matter of public concern. Recall that the defamation against Beverly arose from the implied fact that she had a substance abuse problem. Surely, from Beverly's perspective, whether the implied fact is true or false, the topic of the defamation involves a purely private matter and not one that should be subjected to public scrutiny. One's personal life can be likened to the private credit report at issue in *Dun & Bradstreet*—for the eyes and ears of a limited few. On the other hand, the prevalence of substance abuse within all classes of our society is surely a matter of public concern. The more we keep such matters hush-hush, the more likely it is that greater numbers will suffer from this widespread problem. In short, there is no obvious dividing line between matters that are of public concern and matters that are not.

§8.3.5   *Campaign Financing and Restrictions on the Initiative Process*

Campaign Financing

The First Amendment has been interpreted as limiting the authority of the government to regulate the financing of political campaigns. See generally *Buckley v. Valeo*, 424 U.S. 1 (1976). In particular, expenditures in support of candidates for elective office are thought to be inextricably tied to the underlying message of the campaign. They are, therefore, treated as political speech. As a consequence, such expenditures (e.g., taking out a newspaper ad supporting the candidate) are entitled to the most stringent protections of the First Amendment. These same protections apply to expenditures made in support of referendum measures. *Citizens against Rent Control v. Berkeley*, 454 U.S. 290 (1981). As one Justice cynically observed, for purposes of the First Amendment, "[M]oney talks." 424 U.S. at 262 (White, J., concurring and dissenting).

Although the Court has recognized the importance and legitimacy of the government's interest in preventing corruption or the appearance of corruption in the electoral and referendum processes, the Court has rarely found that interest sufficient to justify restrictions on direct expenditures. The net result is that no government—federal, state, or local—may limit the amount of money a political candidate may spend toward his or her own election. Similarly, direct expenditures by individuals or independent political groups in support of a candidate (or a cause) may not be restricted as long as the expenditures are "independent" and not disguised contributions. *Federal Election Commn. v. National Conservative Political Action Comm.,* 470 U.S. 480, 493 (1985). This means the expenditures may not be made at the request of or coordinated with the endorsed candidate.

The Court has, however, permitted the government to restrict political expenditures made by profit-based corporations. See *Austin v. Michigan State Chamber of Commerce,* 494 U.S. 652 (1990) (allowing the government to require such corporations to make any such expenditures from "segregated" funds generated by voluntary contributions). If, however, the purpose of a nonprofit corporation is not to amass wealth, but to promote ideas, then the freedom to spend money in support of those ideas cannot be restricted. *Federal Election Commn. v. Massachusetts Citizens for Life,* 479 U.S. 238 (1986).

EXAMPLE 8-K

The Federal Election Campaign Act (FECA) prohibits any corporation from spending funds from its corporate treasury in support of a candidate for federal elective office. Citizens for Life, Inc., a nonprofit corporation whose purpose is to promote a pro-life philosophy, used funds from its treasury to publish a flier in support of a pro-life candidate for Congress. The expenditures were independent in the sense that they were neither requested by nor coordinated with the candidate. Can FECA be constitutionally applied to this expenditure?

EXPLANATION

No. While Congress may restrict "non-segregated" expenditures by for-profit corporations, Congress may not do so with respect to expenditures by a nonprofit, such as Citizens for Life, whose purpose is not to amass economic wealth, but to promote an idea. *Federal Election Commn. v. Massachusetts Citizens for Life,* 479 U.S. 238 (1986).

There is an important distinction, however, between political expenditures and political contributions. While the authority of the government to restrict expenditures in political campaigns is severely limited by the First Amendment, the authority to impose restrictions on the amount of a person's contributions to political campaigns is not. *Buckley v. Valeo,* 424 U.S. at 20-21; see also *Nixon v. Shrink Missouri Government PAC,* 120 S. Ct. 897 (2000) (upholding state contribution limitations under the *Buckley* standard). The Court has determined that the relationship between speech and contributions is marginal. The political message conveyed by a monetary contribution is at best opaque, and in terms of the impact on speech by the candidate, the restriction on contributions does no more than force that candidate to rely on a broader base of support. The interest in preventing corruption or the appearance of corruption is sufficiently strong to override these marginal effects on the freedom of speech. Note, however, that the protections afforded independent expenditures have created a rather easy method for circumventing any restriction on contributions. Amounts that cannot be contributed *to* a candidate can be spent *in support of* that candidate as long as the expenditures are "independent." *Federal Election Commn. v. National Conservative Political Action Comm.*, 470 U.S. 480 (1985); see also *Colorado Republican Federal Campaign Comm. v. Federal Election Commn.*, 518 U.S. 604 (1996) (expenditures by a political party used to attack rival party's candidate, but before its own candidate's nomination, deemed independent and fully protected).

Restrictions on the Initiative Process

The Constitution is neutral with respect to whether a state may implement a ballot initiative process, and if a state chooses to adopt such a process, it retains "considerable leeway to protect the integrity and reliability of the initiative process." *Buckley v. American Constitutional Law Foundation*, 525 U.S. 182, 191 (1999). However, to the extent that state restrictions on the initiative process interfere with political expression, those restrictions are subject to strict scrutiny under the First Amendment. Id. at 191 & n.12. We have already noted that state-imposed contribution limitations in this context are subject to First Amendment scrutiny. *Citizens against Rent Control v. Berkeley*, 454 U.S. 290 (1981). Similarly, certain restrictions on the process through which a measure qualifies for the ballot may also be subjected to strict scrutiny if those restrictions limit core political speech.

The two leading cases are *Meyer v. Grant*, 486 U.S. 414 (1988), and *Buckley v. American Constitutional Law Foundation*, supra. In *Meyer*, the Court invalidated a ban on the use of paid petition circulators, concluding that the ban unconstitutionally diminished core political speech by inhibiting the ability of the measure's supporters to communicate their message. Id. at 422-423. The state's justifications for this imposition — promoting grass roots support for initiatives, and leveling the playing field — did not survive the standards of strict scrutiny. Id. at 425-428. In *Buckley*, the Court also applied strict scrutiny to invalidate three restrictions on the signature-gathering process: a requirement that petition circulators be registered voters, a requirement that they wear personal identification badges displaying their names, and a reporting requirement that mandated disclosure of each circulator's name, address, and the total amount paid to that circulator. The Court found that each of these requirements restricted political speech by substantially diminishing the number of persons willing to circulate petitions, thus reducing the initiative's proponents' ability to convey their message. The Court further concluded that the state's primary justification for these measures — protecting the integrity of the initiative process — was either inadequately advanced or could be served by less restrictive means. Id. at 195-196, 203-204. The *Buckley* Court did conclude, however, that a state may "legitimately [require] sponsors of ballot initiatives to disclose who pays petition circulators, and how much." Id. at 205.

§8.3.6   *Commercial Speech*

At one time, commercial speech, i.e., speech whose purpose is to propose a commercial transaction, was completely unprotected by the First Amendment. In essence, commercial speech was equated with commercial activity, and as a consequence, federal, state, and local governments were free to restrict commercial speech to the same extent they could restrict commercial activity. In *Valentine v. Chrestensen,* 316 U.S. 52 (1942), for example, the Court saw no constitutional objection to a content-based ordinance that completely prohibited the distribution of leaflets advertising a for-profit exhibition. The state was free to regulate this "occupation" without reference to any countervailing First Amendment concerns. Id. at 54.

The Court's categorical exclusion of commercial speech from the protection of the First Amendment was eventually criticized, then limited, and finally rejected. *Virginia Bd. of Pharmacy v. Virginia Consumer Council,* 425 U.S. 748 (1976); *Bigelow v. Virginia,* 421 U.S. 809 (1975); *Cammarano v. United States,* 358 U.S. 498, 514 (1959) (Douglas, J., concurring). Today, as will be developed below, the Court exercises what is essentially a mid-level scrutiny when examining laws that restrict speech because of its commercial content. Thus, although the Court no longer treats commercial speech as unprotected, commercial speech still receives less protection than that accorded political speech, apparently on the presumption that commercial speech is at least somewhat removed from the core values protected by the First Amendment. By labeling speech "commercial," therefore, one lowers the level of scrutiny protecting that speech.

The Definition of Commercial Speech

The mere fact that a speaker seeks to profit from expressive activity, however, does not necessarily transform that activity into commercial speech. For example, a good many motion pictures are made for the primary purpose of economic gain. Yet motion pictures are not automatically treated as commercial speech. *Joseph Burstyn, Inc. v. Wilson,* 343 U.S. 496, 501 (1952). Nor are books or newspapers, most of which are published with a profit motive, deemed to involve commercial speech. *New York Times v. Sullivan,* 376 U.S. 254, 266 (1964); *Smith v. California,* 361 U.S. 147, 150 (1959). With respect to these media, the profit motive usually runs parallel with an expressive content that is not necessarily commercial. Thus, a movie made for profit may tell the story of a little pig and her friends on the farm. It is that expressive content that defines the character of the speech.

The Court has had difficulty coming up with a satisfactory definition of commercial speech. It has variously described commercial speech as "expression related *solely* to the economic interests of the speaker and its audience," *Central Hudson Gas & Elec. v. Public Serv. Commn.,* 447 U.S. 557, 561 (1980) (emphasis supplied), or as speech that "*does no more than* propose a commercial transaction," *Virginia Bd. of Pharmacy v. Virginia Consumer Council,* 425 U.S. 748, 762 (1976) (emphasis supplied). More recently it has sought to narrow the definition by stating that "the proposal of a commercial transaction [is] '*the test* for identifying commercial speech.'" *City of Cincinnati v. Discovery Network, Inc.,* 507 U.S. 410, 423 (1993) (emphasis in original). Yet none of these descriptions is meant to be technical; rather, they provide a common-sense basis for determining whether any particular speech can be deemed commercial. Essentially, if the *purpose and content* of a message, taken as a whole, are "strictly business," i.e., designed to propose a commercial transaction, then the speech conveying that message is commercial. *Friedman v. Rogers,* 440 U.S. 1, 11 (1979). If not, the commercial label, as well as the lower level of scrutiny, may be inappropriate.

Price advertising for a specific product is an obvious instance of this category, just as political advertising, even when it seeks monetary contributions, is not. The former invites the listener or reader to buy a product; the latter invites the recipient to invest in a political debate. Between these alternatives are a number of subtle variations in which the invitation to transact business may not be explicit, but is, nonetheless, at the heart of the speech; or in which that invitation is so closely tied to a matter of public import as to negate any inference that the speech is merely commercial; or in which clearly commercial speech is combined with speech that is noncommercial in nature. There is no precise test for measuring these variations, and unfortunately the Court often applies the "commercial speech" label in a question-begging fashion. As mere mortals, however, we must assess the facts of each case with an eye toward discovering the precise speech values at stake. Common sense is often the key.

EXAMPLE 8-L

Mercury, Inc., is in the business of producing and marketing an extensive line of athletic shoes and apparel. The company's logo is a slashing bolt of lightning; its motto is "Your turn." Currently Mercury is running three different types of advertisements on television. The first features a well-known professional basketball player. In the ad, he talks about the special line of shoes Mercury has developed for him. As the ad ends, he holds one of the shoes toward the camera and says, "Your turn." The second ad features a series of visually stunning vignettes of athletes engaged in fierce competition. The only direct allusion to Mercury comes at the end of the ad, with a cut to a graphic of the Mercury logo and motto. The third ad features scenes of several young girls involved in different sports. The voice-over talks about the importance of athletic competition for young girls, stressing such things as building self-esteem, avoiding teen pregnancy, achieving good grades, and maintaining personal health. The ad ends with the same graphic of the Mercury logo and motto. Which, if any, of these ads is commercial speech?

EXPLANATION

The first advertisement is commercial speech. Although the celebrity does not expressly invite the viewer to purchase the shoes, the message of the commercial is plainly to propose a commercial transaction: Buy these shoes. Nor is there any doubt that the purpose of this ad is to promote sales of the new line of shoes. In short, there is a common-sense congruity between content and purpose, both being "strictly business."

The second advertisement is more subtle in its sales pitch. Standing alone the vignettes propose no business transaction. They are artistic depictions of athleticism. As such, they should be entitled to the full protection of the First Amendment. But does the juxtaposition of the vignettes with the Mercury logo and motto alter this conclusion? In other words, does the commercial character of this advertisement overwhelm the artistic character? Probably so. When one considers both the implicit message created by the juxtaposition and the clear overall purpose to promote the Mercury label, a conclusion that the advertisement as a whole is commercial speech seems sensible. In *Board of Trustees of the State University of New York v. Fox*, 492 U.S. 469 (1989), for example, the Court held that the presence of noncommercial speech at a commercial Tupperware party — the speech involved financial responsibility and efficient homemaking — did not sanitize the commercial nature of the enterprise. The party was in essence a sales pitch. Id. at 473-475. Moreover, the commercial and noncommercial aspects of the speech at the party were not "inextricably intertwined" such that the one could not be communicated without the other. Id.

The third advertisement is more subtle still. It does promote the Mercury company, but it does so only by associating the company with what is in essence a public service announcement. There is no direct sales pitch. And although Mercury may profit from this advertised association, that does not necessarily transform the communication into commercial speech. In *Bigelow v. Virginia*, 421 U.S. 809 (1975), for example, the Court held that the for-profit aspects of an advertisement for abortion services did not transform the ad into commercial speech, since the advertisement also included non-commercial information of "public interest" regarding the general availability of abortions. Id. at 822. The third Mercury ad likewise contains information of public interest. Arguably, therefore, this ad is not commercial speech. The proposal of a commercial transaction, if any, is at best an indirect product of the public service provided by the message. On the other hand, the non-commercial and commercial aspects of the ad are not inextricably inter-twined. The importance of girls participating in athletics can be communicated without any reference to Mercury. One could certainly argue, therefore, that the use of a public service message as a prologue to the real ad — the familiar logo and motto — should not be allowed to transform the commercial nature of this ad into a more protected form of speech. Yet if one takes the latter approach, a television documentary on world hunger might be relegated to the category of commercial speech by virtue of the fact that it is sponsored by General Foods Corporation. Ultimately, you must decide whether the third ad is closer to the Tupperware party in *Fox* or the abortion ad in *Bigelow*. The "correct" answer is at best elusive.

The foregoing examples should illustrate that commercial speech is relatively easy to spot in those situations in which the "strictly business" aspect of the speech is more or less obvious and is not interwoven with other types of speech — e.g., the free-standing offer to sell or purchase goods or services for a fee, the publication of prices, and so on. As the content or context of the message becomes more ambiguous and more complex, the commercial components of the speech may be outweighed by First Amend-ment concerns that require a more exacting level of scrutiny. The only measure here is one of careful judgment, common sense, and effective argument.

The Rationale for Protecting Commercial Speech

Having defined commercial speech (to the extent a definition is possible), we must next examine the constitutional standard against which restrictions on commercial speech are measured. The two leading cases are *Virginia Board of Pharmacy v. Virginia Consumer Council*, 425 U.S. 748 (1976), and *Central Hudson Gas & Electric v. Public Service Commission*, 447 U.S. 557 (1980). The first established commercial speech as a constitutionally pro-tected form of speech and provided a rationale for that protection; while the second examined the law that had developed under *Virginia Board* and organized that law into a test for measuring the constitutionality of laws restricting commercial speech.

At issue in *Virginia Board* was a state law that prohibited licensed pharmacists from publishing the prices of prescription drugs. The prohibited speech was commercial. As the Court phrased it, "Our pharmacist does not wish to editorialize on any subject, cultural, philosophical, or political. . . . The 'idea' he wishes to communicate is simply this: 'I will sell you the X prescription drug at the Y price.'" 425 U.S. at 761. The question before the Court was whether the commercial character of this speech automatically divested it of the protections of the First Amendment.

The Court examined this question from three perspectives: the advertiser, the consumer, and society at large. As to the first, the mere fact that the speaker had an economic motivation did not deprive the speech of First Amendment protection. In numerous other contexts, speech that was economically motivated was, nonetheless, protected — labor disputes being a prime example. Id. at 762-763. Second, "[a]s to the particular consumer's interest in the free flow of commercial information, that interest may be as keen, if not keener by far, than his interest in the day's most urgent political debate." Id. at 763. The Court noted that "the poor, the sick, and particularly the aged" would find this information not only useful, but perhaps critically important. Id. at 763-764. Finally, from the perspective of society at large, much commercial advertising contains information of interest to the general public, and even more important, the free flow of commercial information is indispensable to making intelligent economic choices in our free enterprise economy. Id. at 764-765. In short, commercial speech plays an important role within our socioeconomic system, and as a consequence, such speech is entitled to the protections of the First Amendment.

In holding that commercial speech was protected by the First Amendment, the Court did not completely insulate commercial speech from governmental regulation. For example, the Court saw "no obstacle to a State's dealing effectively with" the problem of false or misleading advertising. Id. at 771-772. Similarly, the Court emphasized that the price advertisements at issue before it did not propose transactions that were illegal in any way. Id. at 772. The Court in *Virginia Board* did not, however, propose any standard for measuring the constitutionality of commercial speech that was not false or misleading or that did not propose an illegal transaction. Some Justices and commentators have taken this to mean that commercial speech not falling into either category should be fully protected. See *44 Liquormart, Inc. v. Rhode Island*, 517 U.S. 484, 518 (1996) (Thomas, J., concurring). The Court, however, has not adopted this view.

The *Central Hudson* Test

Laws that regulate commercial speech are now measured under the *Central Hudson* test, a "four-part analysis" described by the Court in *Central Hudson*

Gas & Electric v. Public Service Commission, 447 U.S. at 561-566. The test is essentially a modified version of mid-level scrutiny. Under the first part of the test, one asks whether the commercial speech at issue is either misleading or related to an unlawful activity. Id. at 563-564. If the speech is either, it is not protected by the First Amendment, and the government may regulate or even prohibit it entirely. Thus, a law that prohibits newspapers from running advertisements for prostitution would be upheld without resort to First Amendment analysis (assuming prostitution is illegal within the jurisdiction). If, however, the commercial speech is neither misleading nor related to unlawful activity, it is protected by the First Amendment, and the government may regulate it only if three additional standards are satisfied:

- The government interest in doing so must be substantial;
- The regulation must directly advance that interest; *and*
- A more limited restriction on speech will not serve that interest.

Id. at 564. In *Central Hudson,* for example, public utilities were banned from advertising to promote the use of electricity. Since the ban was not directed toward misleading advertisements or the promotion of unlawful activity, the constitutionality of the ban depended on the satisfaction of the above three standards.

The substantial governmental interest requirement invites a value judgment regarding the relative importance of the governmental interest. This prong can be satisfied by any nontrivial governmental interest. In *Central Hudson,* the interests in energy conservation and the maintenance of a fair utility rate structure were both deemed substantial. More generally, laws designed to protect the health, safety, or welfare of citizens and residents will easily satisfy this standard. If, however, the Court deems the asserted interest illusory or a *post hoc* rationalization, this element will not be satisfied. *Linmark Assoc., Inc. v. Township of Willingboro,* 431 U.S. 85 (1977) (record did not support government's claim of white flight). Few laws are struck down for failure to satisfy the substantial governmental interest requirement.

The third and fourth requirements of *Central Hudson* measure the "fit" of the law. Under the directly advances requirement, a regulation of commercial speech will not be upheld if it is either ineffective or remote in sustaining the government's interest. There is no mathematical measure for this requirement. Again referring to *Central Hudson,* the Court found that the ban on promotional advertising did directly advance the state's interest in energy conservation, citing what the Court perceived as an "immediate connection between advertising and demand for electricity." 447 U.S. at 569. However, the connection between promotional advertising and the goal of maintaining a fair rate structure was deemed far too speculative. Id. There was simply no showing that increased demand would alter the fairness of the rate structure.

The fourth element requires that the law be narrowly tailored to advance the government's interest. If the law is perceived as excessively sweeping in its coverage or if there are other equally effective, but substantially less speech-restrictive alternatives, the law will not be upheld. The advertising ban in *Central Hudson* was struck down under this standard, since the ban prohibited the promotion of energy-efficient uses of electricity; i.e., it was broader than necessary to advance the goal of energy conservation, and there were less speech-restrictive alternatives to a complete ban on promotional advertising. This fourth element does not, however, require that the state employ the "least restrictive means." *Board of Trustees of the State Univ. of N.Y. v. Fox*, 492 U.S. 469, 475-481 (1989). Rather, the standard is one of reasonable fit, a measure that is more flexible than least restrictive means, but less deferential than rational basis. *Florida Bar v. Went for It, Inc.*, 515 U.S. 618 (1995).

As a general matter, the Court has not been consistent in the manner in which it has applied the *Central Hudson* standards. At times, the Court has used a "reasonableness" overlay to permit states broader leeway in the regulation of commercial speech, and at other times, the Court has approached the standards as creating a strong presumption against such regulations. Thus, the Court's relatively straightforward application of the "four-part analysis" in *Central Hudson* should not lead you to conclude that this test has led to obvious results or even to a coherent body of results. As was true in the context of equal protection, mid-level scrutiny is somewhat more malleable than its strict scrutiny and rational basis counterparts, and the commercial speech case law bears this out.

EXAMPLE 8-M

Puerto Rico permits gambling in licensed casinos. While the casinos are allowed to advertise to promote tourism, they are not allowed to engage in promotional advertising "to the public of Puerto Rico." The purpose of this limitation is to reduce the demand for gambling by Puerto Rican residents and to thereby protect their health, safety, and welfare. More specifically, the goal of the limitation is to prevent increases in local crime, such as prostitution and public corruption; to avoid the infiltration of organized crime; and to preserve the moral and cultural identity of Puerto Rico. Is this limitation a legitimate regulation of commercial speech?

EXPLANATION

The answer depends on the rigor with which one applies the *Central Hudson* test. The first two steps in the analysis would be noncontroversial. Since the ban applies to advertisements that are neither misleading nor related to unlawful activities, Puerto Rico could not premise its defense of the regulation on this element of the test. Similarly, there would be general agreement that the interests asserted by Puerto Rico are substantial. The prevention of crime is one of the paramount purposes of government. The difficulty arises in the application of the third and fourth elements. Does the regulation directly serve the interests asserted by Puerto Rico? And if so, would a more limited restriction on speech advance those interests?

From a perspective that is more deferential to governmental preroga- tives, one could argue that the advertising ban *directly advances* the interests asserted by the government. If, as was recognized in *Central Hudson,* adver- tising increases demand for a product, the ban on local advertising should prevent increased demand for casino gambling by residents, and the absence of that increased demand should diminish the pressure to commit those crimes associated with casino gambling. Next, since "some" advertising would diminish the effectiveness of the across-the-board ban, a more limited restriction on speech would not adequately advance the government's inter- est. This is essentially the approach a five-person majority of the Court took in upholding such a ban in *Posadas de Puerto Rico Assocs. v. Tourism Co.,* 478 U.S. 328, 340-344 (1986).

On the other hand, from a more speech-protective perspective, the relationship between the government's aims and the advertising ban is "re- mote" at best. There is simply no way to know whether the ban will affect the amount of resident casino gambling, much less prevent in any significant way the types of crimes that are associated with casino gambling. Indeed, given the popularity of casino gambling and the fact that it will be promoted and developed for the tourist trade, the ban may be completely ineffective in reaching its goals. In addition, with respect to the fourth requirement, there are a number of less speech-restrictive ways in which Puerto Rico could advance its goals, among them an outright ban on casino gambling by residents. See *44 Liquormart, Inc. v. Rhode Island,* 517 U.S. 484, 509-510, 531-532 (1996) (majority of the Court disapproves the *Posadas* analysis in two separate opinions).

In a recent decision, the Court endorsed reasoning similar to that in the preceding paragraph when it held that a federal ban on casino advertising over the broadcast media could not be constitutionally applied to advertise- ments that were broadcast in a state in which casino gambling was legal. *Greater New Orleans Broadcasting Assoc., Inc. v. United States,* 527 U.S. 173 (1999). Applying the "directly advance" element of *Central Hudson,* the Court noted that the government had failed to produce evidence that a ban on casino gambling advertising would actually reduce the demand for gam- bling and thereby ameliorate problems associated with gambling. Although the Court's holding did not rest on this point, the opinion did suggest that the government must do something more than speculate about a potential relationship between an advertising ban and the interest the government seeks to promote. Id. at 189. The more fundamental flaw in this particular advertising ban, however, was the fact that it "and its attendant regulatory regime is so pierced by exemptions and inconsistencies that the Government cannot hope to exonerate it." Id. at 190. For example, the ban did not apply to gaming on Indian reservations. In essence, the lack of coherence in the ban made it impossible to conclude that it was properly tailored to advance the government's asserted interests. As such, *Greater New Orleans Broadcasting* represents another example of the Court's recent move toward a stricter application of the *Central Hudson* test.

Thus, although the *Central Hudson* test is easily described — at least as a verbal formula — its application remains subject to substantial variations, depending on the circumstances of the case and on one's perception of how strictly the test ought to be applied. Currently the Court seems inclined to a more speech-protective application of the test. In *44 Liquormart,* for example, the Court unanimously struck down a state law that banned the advertising of retail liquor prices. While there was no majority opinion, the overall tenor of the principal opinions was toward a relatively rigorous application of the *Central Hudson* standards. See also *Rubin v. Coors Brewing Co.,* 514 U.S. 476 (1995) (striking down federal ban on the disclosure of alcohol content on beer labels as not directly advancing government's interest in preventing strength wars).

EXAMPLE 8-N

A state bar regulation prohibits personal injury lawyers from sending direct-mail solicitations to accident victims or their relatives for 30 days following the accident. The regulation is designed to protect the "flagging" reputation of the legal profession by preventing members of that profession from engaging in a "deplorable" practice that intrudes on the "special vulnerability and private grief of victims or their families." Is this regulation constitutional under the First Amendment?

EXPLANATION

We must first decide whether the state here is regulating commercial speech. Since direct-mail solicitations propose a commercial transaction between the lawyer and the potential client — essentially a business arrangement — the speech at issue is at least arguably commercial. Would the "commercial" label be appropriate, however, if the solicitation included language describing the legal rights of the victim or explaining the importance of a prompt investigation or the wisdom of avoiding a precipitous settlement? Aren't the "solicitation" and the .pertinent noncommercial information "inextricably intertwined," as was the case in *Bigelow v. Virginia?* Suppose, for example, that the solicitation arises out of an airline disaster. The airline will certainly procure legal counsel immediately and may even attempt to gain quick settlements. Under such circumstances, is the victim's interest in legal representation purely commercial? In *Florida Bar v. Went for It, Inc.*, 515 U.S. 618 (1995), a five-person majority concluded without any discussion that such direct-mail "advertisements" were commercial speech entitled only to "intermediate" scrutiny. Id. at 622-623. The dissent argued, however, that given the potential noncommercial overlay and the vital interest of victims in receiving that information, at the very least *Central Hudson* should be applied with additional rigor. Id. at 636-637.

Assuming the speech is commercial, we must next determine if the speech is either misleading or related to an illegal transaction. Since the regulation draws no distinction between solicitations that are misleading and those that are not, or between legal and illegal transactions, the regulated speech cannot be characterized as either misleading or related to an illegal transaction. We must, therefore, apply the remaining three parts of the test described in *Central Hudson*.

Is the state's interest *substantial*? Certainly the interest in enhancing the reputation of the legal profession by preventing members of that profession from engaging in an odious practice is nontrivial. Of course, this begs the question of whether direct-mail solicitations are odious, and one's answer to that question depends on the relative importance one places on the information victims may receive from such solicitations. In other words, substantiality is premised on an assumption about the intrinsic value of the speech. Nonetheless, the majority of the Court in *Florida Bar* concluded that the state's interest was substantial, since, in general, states have a compelling interest in the practice of professions within their boundaries. Id. at 625. The dissent provided a more detailed discussion of the issue and concluded that the circularity of the state's argument was evidence that the regulation was "censorship pure and simple." Id. at 640. As such, the element of substantiality was not satisfied.

Whether the regulation *directly advances* the state's interest depends on proof of the relationship between means and ends. If the state can establish that direct-mail solicitations of accident victims harm the reputation of the legal profession, then it would follow that a ban on such solicitations would ameliorate that harm. In *Florida Bar,* the majority and the dissent disagreed over whether the proof on this point was adequate, the majority finding that it was. Id. at 627-629, 640-641.

Finally, the regulation must be *narrowly tailored* to advance the established purpose. The standard here is one of *reasonable fit*. Certainly there are numerous other ways to overcome the "ambulance chasing" image of lawyers. Among other things, the state bar could place restrictions on the content of the direct mailings to ensure that any solicitation is consistent with professional standards. The majority in *Florida Bar* seemed to soft-pedal this issue by taking a relatively deferential approach to the judgment of the state bar. The limited temporal scope of the rule, combined with other channels of communication through which victims could learn of their rights, convinced the majority that the fit between the means and the end was reasonable. The dissent, on the other hand, argued that the regulation cast a broad net that captured commercial as well as noncommercial speech, thereby establishing the unreasonableness of the fit between means and ends.

This last example highlights what the Court has described as "the difficulty of drawing bright lines that will clearly cabin commercial speech in a distinct category." *City of Cincinnati v. Discovery Network, Inc.,* 507 U.S. 410, 419 (1993). Because commercial speech receives only mid-level scrutiny, the inability to distinguish commercial from noncommercial speech threatens to dilute the protection afforded noncommercial speech. It is perhaps in response to this danger that the Court in recent years has both narrowed the definition of commercial speech and strengthened the rigor with which the *Central Hudson* test is applied. See *Greater New Orleans Broadcasting Assoc., Inc. v. United States,* 527 U.S. 173 (1999) (striking down federal ban on broadcast advertising of casino gambling in those jurisdictions in which such gambling is legal). Moreover, a number of Justices have urged that truthful and nonmisleading commercial speech about lawful activities should be fully protected under the First Amendment. See *44 Liquormart, Inc. v. Rhode Island,* 517 U.S. 484, 518 (1996) (Thomas, J., concurring); *City of Cincinnati v. Discovery Network, Inc.,* 507 U.S. at 431-438 (Blackmun, J., concurring).

§8.3.7   Sexually Explicit Speech—Obscenity and Pornography

Sexually explicit speech, whether it be in the form of visual depiction (live performance, motion pictures, photography, etc.) or verbal description (books, magazines, songs, etc.), has been relegated by the Court to a relatively low rung on the First Amendment hierarchy. Various reasons have been asserted. Most typically, sexually explicit speech is said to contribute little or nothing to the exposition of ideas. Indeed, some would say that sexually explicit speech more often than not conveys no ideas whatsoever, but merely operates as a sensual stimulus designed to generate an animalistic response. Critics have noted the obvious cultural bias in these assertions and suggest that the sexual content of speech should not diminish the protections of the First Amendment. See *Roth v. United States,* 354 U.S. 476, 508-514 (1957) (Douglas, J., & Black, J., dissenting). This more libertine attitude, however, has never commanded a majority of the Court.

A Definition of Obscenity

From a doctrinal perspective, a legal distinction is drawn between obscenity and pornography. Obscenity, which is defined below, is completely unprotected by the First Amendment, while pornography, i.e., sexually explicit speech that is not legally "obscene," is entitled to constitutional protection. As you can imagine, the distinction between these categories is somewhat elusive, but quite important, since it often defines what separates the criminal from the just naughty.

In *Miller v. California*, 413 U.S. 15 (1973), after many years of doctrinal confusion, the Court adopted the following definition of obscenity:

> (a) whether "the average person, applying contemporary community standards" would find that the work, taken as a whole, appeals to the prurient interest; (b) whether the work depicts or describes, in a patently offensive way, sexual conduct specifically defined by the applicable state law; and (c) whether the work, taken as a whole, lacks serious literary, artistic, political, or scientific value.

Id. at 24. Note that the complete focus of this definition is on the quality of the speech and not on its effect or dangerous tendency. No clear and present danger of anything need be established — no actual malice, no substantial relationship, nothing. Rather, the harm is assumed to be implicit in the nature of the speech itself. The "doctrinal test" for the regulation of obscenity, therefore, simply defines a category of speech that falls completely outside the First Amendment. If the speech fits the definition, it may be regulated without further recourse to constitutional analysis. Understanding the definition is, therefore, critical.

The first two elements of the *Miller* definition are measured from the perspective of contemporary community standards, which are themselves defined as the standards of an average person residing within the *local*, not the national, community. These local standards, as a consequence, are largely a product of the geographic reach of the jury pool and of the perceptions of the selected venire. Those perceptions can be informed by the evidence at trial as well as by the court's instructions to the jury. However, the prosecution is not required to introduce expert testimony on the question of local standards.

In applying contemporary community standards, one must assess two things: whether the material appeals to the prurient interest in sex and whether it is patently offensive. Appeal to the prurient interest connotes the promotion of lasciviousness or lustful desire. The standard is satisfied if a reasonable juror, applying contemporary community standards, could conclude that the material induces inappropriate sexual longing — obviously a subjective and elastic standard. Similarly, whether the material describes or depicts sexual conduct in a patently offensive manner requires an equally subjective judgment by this same reasonable juror. Thus, what is quite acceptable in a large, urban community may well be "patently offensive" to the members of a small, insular community.

The "prurient interest" and "patently offensive" elements of *Miller* are tempered somewhat by the further requirement that the material be fairly classifiable as "hard-core" pornography, i.e., the graphic and explicit representation of ultimate sex acts and the like. 413 U.S. at 25. In other words, the sensitivity of the local community is moderated by a nationally applicable minimum of tolerance. For example, in *Jenkins v. Georgia*, 418 U.S. 153 (1974), the Court held that a local jury could not, consistent with the *Miller* standard, conclude that the Mike Nichols film *Carnal Knowledge* was patently offensive. Although sex was the theme of the film, the treatment of the subject was far removed from the graphic style of hard-core pornography, thus precluding a finding that the film was obscene. Id. at 160-161.

The third element of *Miller*—whether the material lacks serious literary, artistic, political, or scientific value— is measured by a *national* reasonable person standard for which expert testimony is permissible, but not required. *Pope v. Illinois*, 481 U.S. 497 (1987). This standard quite often trumps the local community's perceptions of prurient interest and patent offensiveness. In *Luke Records, Inc. v. Navarro*, 960 F.2d 134 (11th Cir. 1992), for example, a district court found that 2 Live Crew's recording of "As Nasty as They Wanna Be" was obscene under *Miller*, but the court of appeals reversed. The state had failed to meet its burden of proof on the third element of the *Miller* test. The state's only evidence of obscenity was the recording itself. The defense, however, presented expert testimony by two pop music critics and a political science professor, all of whom endorsed the artistic and political value of the recording.

Note also that in determining whether the first and third elements of *Miller* are satisfied, the material must be "taken as a whole." That is, the work as a whole must appeal to a prurient interest in sex. Therefore, an allegedly obscene segment of a larger artistic endeavor cannot be excised from the whole. Thus, in *Navarro*, the lyrics of "As Nasty as They Wanna Be" could not be isolated from the accompanying music. At the same time, an otherwise obscene motion picture will not be saved by a scene in which a couple fornicates while listening to a medley of John Philip Sousa's greatest hits, since the work as a whole must have serious value. The distinction is between the sham inclusion of "art" and a fully integrated artistic endeavor.

EXAMPLE 8-O

The newly released film *Terminator 2001: A Violent Odyssey* is a box office smash. It stars Arnold Swartzenlocker, the popular body-building hunk, in a sci-fi thriller about the past, the future, and a lot of stuff in between. In one scene, Arnold runs around naked, and in another, he makes love to an androgenous android. The scene, however, is filmed in a manner that makes it impossible to see anything but two large shapes bouncing around in what appears to be a rather large hamster habitat. The film does have plenty of violence though, including one scene of graphic and gruesome mayhem, at the end of which Arnold reprises his famous line, "I have every intention of returning to this locale, if the opportunity presents itself." The film is rated PG-13. The city attorney for the small town of Omigosh went to the local premiere of *Terminator 2001*. He has now charged the owner of the theater with violation of the town's anti-obscenity ordinance. Consistent with the *Miller* test, may a jury convict on these charges?

EXPLANATION

Most likely not. Although the Court has adopted a local community standard to measure prurience and patent offensiveness, there remains a national minimum standard of explicitness that even a sensitive local community must tolerate. Regardless of what one thinks of Arnold's film, it is simply not the type of material the Court was considering when it created the *Miller* standard. Although the film may appeal to various base instincts, nothing in the above description suggests that the appeal is to a prurient interest in sex. Nor does the patent offensiveness of the film have anything to do with the graphic depiction of sexual conduct. Violence, no matter how gruesome, is not obscene (in the absence of a graphic sexual context). Similarly, nudity, in and of itself, is not obscene. *Schad v. Borough of Mount Ephraim*, 452 U.S. 61, 66 (1981). In short, the local community standards, even if offended, would quite likely be trumped by the national minimum of tolerance. Finally, although one need not decide the point, given Arnold's earlier work, it seems quite likely that, taken as a whole, the film has tremendous literary, artistic, political, and even scientific value. Two thumbs up.

EXAMPLE 8-P

Imagine, however, a somewhat different film — *Penetrator 2001: A Sexual Oddity*. It stars Jonny Hot, a cult hero among aficionados of pornography. The film has little plot. Mostly it is about sex, sex, and more sex, all of which is graphically portrayed in intimate detail. Several of the scenes are somewhat humorous as spoofs of popular sci-fi classics. But mostly the film is about Jonny Hot's never ending sexual unions. Is this film obscene?

EXPLANATION

Perhaps. It would seem that *Penetrator 2001* is surely meant to appeal to the viewer's interest in sex. Whether that interest is "prurient" will depend on the jury's perception of contemporary standards within the relevant local community. Similarly, patent offensiveness is also a question for the jury, applying contemporary community standards. However, the city's ordinance must have specifically defined the sexual conduct that allegedly is depicted in a patently offensive way. Moreover, in both determinations, the jury's judgment is limited by a national standard of minimal tolerance. But if the film is fairly characterized as hard-core pornography—we would have to see it to know for sure — this national standard will not trump the jury's determinations. Finally, the third element asks whether the work, taken as a whole, lacks serious literary, artistic, political, or scientific value. This is a national standard under which the jury would have to determine if the limited humor (or other production values) makes the film something other than raw, hard-core pornography.

It should be clear that the *Miller* definition of obscenity provides little more than a verbal screen for a highly subjective judgment. Justice Stewart's offhanded remark regarding obscenity — "I know it when I see it"—would seem to be equally as useful and, at the same time, less legally pretentious. *Jacobellis v. Ohio,* 378 U.S. 184, 197 (1964). Nevertheless, the *Miller* three-part formula remains both the definition and the standard for the regulation of obscenity.

Because speech that qualifies as obscenity under *Miller* is completely unprotected by the First Amendment, it may, therefore, be suppressed through either the threat of subsequent punishment or the imposition of prior restraints. As to the former, there is a narrow (and shrinking) consti-tutional privilege for the possession of obscene material within one's own home. *Stanley v. Georgia,* 394 U.S. 557 (1969); but see *Osborne v. Ohio,* 495 U.S. 103 (1990) (refusing to extend the privilege to the possession of child pornography). Beyond that limited privilege, however, the government need only comply with applicable principles of criminal procedure in order to punish the production or dissemination of obscene material. In attempting to secure a prior restraint against the dissemination of obscene speech, the government must provide a prompt hearing in which it carries the burden of establishing obscenity. *Freedman v. Maryland,* 380 U.S. 51, 58-59 (1965). If the hearing is administrative in nature, the prior restraint may be continued only if the finding of obscenity is promptly affirmed by a judicial body. Id.

Nonobscene Sexually Explicit Speech — Pornography

Pornography, i.e., communicative material that is sexually explicit but not legally obscene, is speech within the meaning and protections of the First Amendment. This remains true regardless of how "shabby, offensive, or even ugly" one may find it. *United States v. Playboy Entertainment Group Inc.,* 120 S. Ct. 1878, 1894 (2000). Thus, content-based restrictions on pornog-raphy will generally be evaluated under the traditional standards of strict scrutiny. Id. at 1886.

In *Playboy Entertainment Group,* for example, the Court struck down a federal statute that as a practical matter required cable channels primarily dedicated to sexually oriented programming to limit their transmissions to hours when children were unlikely to be viewing (i.e., between 10 P.M. and 6 A.M.). The regulation was content-based since it was triggered by the subject matter of the material being transmitted. Id. at 1885. As a consequence, the government was required to establish that the regulation was narrowly tailored to advance a compelling government interest. Id. at 1886. The government's goal was to prevent viewing of sexually oriented material by children whose parents might object to such viewing. The problem arose from the possibility that even nonsubscribers to the sexually oriented channel might occasionally experience "signal bleed," allowing the viewer to receive all or part of the programming. In the Court's view, however, the government failed to quantify the actual extent of the problem generated by signal bleed, and, in any event, had not selected the least restrictive means of accomplishing its goal. As to the latter, cable customers could be provided with blocking devices to prevent all transmission of the unwanted signal, leaving the channels free to transmit twenty-four hours a day. Id. at 1891. Having failed to satisfy this element of strict scrutiny, the statute was declared unconstitutional.

In two contexts, however, the Court has not applied strict scrutiny to content-based restrictions on nonobscene pornography. The first involves zoning laws that regulate the location of pornographic movie houses and bookstores. In essence, cities are free to impose restrictions on the location of such businesses, either forcing their dispersal in order to avoid creating a "red-light" district, *Young v. American Mini Theatres, Inc.*, 427 U.S. 50 (1976), or requiring their concentration in order to avoid the spread of perceived blight, *City of Renton v. Playtime Theatres, Inc.*, 475 U.S. 41 (1986). In short, as long as the city does not completely suppress so-called adult entertainment, it may impose special zoning requirements on purveyors of the medium. Quite obviously neither type of regulation would be acceptable if it were applied to political speech. A zoning ordinance that required politically oriented bookstores to locate no closer than 1000 feet from one another in order to avoid potential clashes between patrons would be subjected to the strictest scrutiny and easily struck down.

The second context involves a form of nonobscene pornography that is completely unprotected by the First Amendment. In *New York v. Ferber*, 458 U.S. 747 (1982), the Court held that the distribution of child pornography, i.e., sexually explicit motion pictures or photographs that are not legally obscene, but that depict *actual children* engaged in sex acts, could be subject to criminal prosecution. The Court reasoned that given the "modest, if not de minimis," value of the speech—the portrayal of children engaged in lewd sexual conduct—and the substantial harm and abuse suffered by the actual children who are being photographed, "it is permissible to consider these materials as without the protection of the First Amendment." Id. at 764. Child pornography, therefore, even when not technically obscene under *Miller*, is entitled to no protection under the First Amendment. See *United*

States v. Hilton, 167 F.3d 61 (1st Cir. 1999) (rejecting facial challenge to the constitutionality of the Child Pornography Prevention Act, which criminalizes the knowing possession of "virtual" child pornography).

Indecent or Vulgar Speech

The use of indecent or vulgar language is protected by the First Amendment as long as the context in which the language is used does not trigger some other limiting First Amendment principle. Thus, if, taken as a whole, the material in which the indecent language appears is obscene under the *Miller* test, the protection is lost. Similarly, if the indecent language is uttered in a context likely to cause a public disturbance, the "fighting words" doctrine may come into play. On the other hand, if the language is merely offensive or used in a context that is deemed socially inappropriate, the full protections of the First Amendment should apply. As we shall see, however, special rules apply to the use of indecent language in the broadcast media.

The leading case is *Cohen v. California,* 403 U.S. 15 (1971). There, the defendant was convicted of disturbing the peace for wearing a jacket bearing the words "Fuck the Draft." At the time of the incident, the defendant was in a corridor of a county courthouse and in the presence of women and children. Id. at 16. Although some observers may have been offended, there was no evidence of any potential altercation. The Court reversed. In so doing, it alluded to a fairly sophisticated model of speech:

> [M]uch linguistic expression serves a dual communicative function: it conveys not only ideas capable of relatively precise, detached explication, but otherwise inexpressible emotions as well. In fact, words are often chosen as much for their emotive as their cognitive force. We cannot sanction the view that the Constitution, while solicitous of the cognitive content of individual speech, has little or no regard for that emotive function which practically speaking, may often be the more important element of the overall message sought to be communicated.

Id. at 26. Premised on this view, the Court held that a state is not empowered "to cleanse public debate to the point where it is grammatically palatable to the most squeamish among us. . . . For, while the particular four-letter word being litigated here is perhaps more distasteful than most others of its genre, it is nevertheless often true that one man's vulgarity is another's lyric." Id. at 25.

The Court's solicitude for lyrical vulgarity was less charitable in *FCC v. Pacifica Foundation,* 438 U.S. 726 (1978). There, the Court adopted a particularly squeamish approach to an afternoon radio broadcast of George Carlin's satirical monologue on "dirty words." Based on a listener's complaint, the FCC issued a "declaratory order" against the station for having broadcast an "indecent" monologue at a time when children were in the audience. The order put the station on notice that any further similar broadcasts could subject it to sanctions, including license revocation. The Court upheld the constitutionality of the order on the basis of a combination of factors. Chief among them were the more limited First Amendment protections accorded the broadcast media, see §8.7.1; the fact that children were in the audience at the time the broadcast occurred; the relative modesty of the sanction imposed; and from the Court's perspective, the sheer offensiveness and de minimis value of the language used. 438 U.S. at 742-751.

§8.3.8   Content Discrimination within Categories of Unprotected Speech

We have noted that there are certain categories of speech — e.g., fighting words, obscenity, and child pornography—that fall outside the First Amendment and that, therefore, normally receive no constitutional protection. However, the Court has held that the government may not discriminate within a category of otherwise proscribable speech so as to favor some viewpoints or ideas over others. If the government does so, the First Amendment will come into play, and the measure will be struck down unless it is shown that the discrimination is necessary to achieve a compelling governmental interest.

It was on this basis that the Court in *R.A.V. v. City of St. Paul*, 505 U.S. 377 (1992), struck down a city ordinance that outlawed certain types of hate speech. Though the ordinance was limited to "fighting words," a category of generally unprotected speech, the city banned only those fighting words that provoked anger "on the basis of race, color, creed, religion or gender." By thus discriminating within the category of fighting words so as to disfavor some ideas and viewpoints over others, the ordinance triggered application of the First Amendment. Applying an ad hoc balancing test, the Court concluded that the ordinance was not necessary to achieve the city's compelling goal of combating racism, sexism, and bigotry, since a blanket ban on all fighting words would have achieved that goal equally well.

EXAMPLE 8-Q

Jones was convicted of violating a state obscenity statute for having exhibited a film entitled *Strange Bedfellows*. In the film, various well-known politicians are depicted engaging in a continuous orgy of sexual acts on a farm in North Dakota. The film satisfied the *Miller* test for obscenity: The work as a whole appeals to a prurient interest in sex; it depicts statutorily defined sexual acts in a patently offensive manner; and it lacks any serious political, literary, artistic, or other value. Jones has appealed on the ground that the state has violated his First Amendment rights. Is the court of appeals likely to reverse his conviction?

EXPLANATION

Because obscenity is a constitutionally unprotected, proscribable category of speech, Jones cannot raise a First Amendment objection to his conviction unless the state has discriminated within the category of obscene speech so as to favor or disfavor certain views over others. If the law under which he was convicted only bars obscenity that depicts politicians in an unfavorable light, Jones could invoke the First Amendment, but if the law bars all obscenity, this argument will fail. However, Jones might still be able to invoke the First Amendment if he can show that the obscenity statute is seldom enforced and that he was prosecuted because he made fun of certain local politicians. In the latter case, though the law is facially neutral with respect to the type of obscenity that is prohibited, it is not viewpoint neutral as applied. Even though the state has a compelling interest in protecting its citizens against obscene films, since it has available the less discriminatory alternative of prosecuting all instances of obscenity, its viewpoint discrimination within the class of obscenity violates the First Amendment.

Under this principle, not all discrimination within a class of otherwise unprotected speech triggers First Amendment scrutiny. The First Amendment will come into play only if there is "content discrimination" of a type that "'raises the specter that the Government may effectively drive certain ideas or viewpoints from the marketplace'. . . ." *R.A.V. v. City of St. Paul,* 505 U.S. at 387. Thus, an obscenity statute that applies to films, but not books raises no First Amendment concern, since the discrimination is based on the medium rather than on the content of the expression.

§8.3.9   *Compelled Speech*

In addition to imposing limitations on the government's authority to prevent or punish speech, the First Amendment restricts governmental efforts to compel speech. Thus, the government may not force anyone to affirm a particular ideological belief. See *West Virginia State Bd. of Educ. v. Barnette,* 319 U.S. 624 (1943) (holding compelled flag salute unconstitutional), discussed further in §9.5.2. Similarly, the government may not force an individual to use his or her property to convey an ideological message with which that person disagrees. In *Wooley v. Maynard,* 430 U.S. 705 (1977), for example, the Court upheld the First Amendment right of a Jehovah's Witness couple to refuse to display the state motto, "Live Free or Die," on their state-issued license plate. The couple cited religious, moral, and political objections to the motto. The Court held that the state could not compel them to be an instrument of the state's ideological message.

These same principles apply in the context of laws that compel an individual to provide financial support for another's speech. Accordingly, in *Abood v. Detroit Board of Education,* 431 U.S. 209 (1977), the Court held that although government employees could be required to pay union dues, those dues could not be used for political or ideological purposes outside of the collective bargaining context. See also *Keller v. State Bar of Cal.,* 496 U.S. 1 (1990) (compulsory bar dues may not be used for political or ideological purposes).

The Court distinguished *Abood* and *Keller* in *University of Wisconsin System v. Southworth,* 120 S. Ct. 1346 (2000). At issue in that case was a challenge to a mandatory student fee imposed by a state university, a portion of which went to fund a variety of student organizations, some of which engaged in political or ideological advocacy. Students challenging the fee claimed that they were being forced to support political and ideological positions with which they disagreed, in violation of the principles applied in *Abood* and *Keller.* The Court, however, explained that the rules developed under the particular circumstances of those cases did not translate well into the public university context where the fees were being used to subsidize the speech of student organizations and not the university itself. The Court concluded that as long as the funds generated from mandatory student fees were distributed among the various groups on a viewpoint-neutral basis, there was no constitutional violation of the students' associational or free speech rights. Id. at 1354. The Court did note, however, that a referendum procedure through which the student body could vote to approve or disapprove of fee allocations might well violate the viewpoint-neutrality principle. Id. at 1357. The case was remanded for further consideration of that issue.

§8.4 Content-Neutral Restrictions on Speech: The Time, Place, and Manner Test

The government sometimes regulates speech indirectly by imposing limitations that do not pertain to the content of speech, but that do affect the circumstances under which expressive activity may occur. These so-called time, place, and manner restrictions are, by definition, content neutral. Thus, they are focused not on the message of the speech, but on factors related to the circumstances under which the speech may be delivered. For example, an ordinance that prohibits the use of loudspeakers on city streets is a time, place, and manner restriction. It prohibits, at all *times*, in specified *places*, a particular *manner* of communicating, and the prohibition applies regardless of the content of the message the speaker wishes to convey. Similarly, if a law that makes it a crime to deface governmental property is applied to an individual who spray paints a graffiti message on the walls of a governmental building, this law is properly characterized as a time, place, and manner restriction as long as the punishment is not premised on the message of the graffiti.

§8.4.1 Content Neutrality

Time, place, and manner restrictions are constitutional as long as they "are [1] justified without reference to the content of the regulated speech, . . . are [2] narrowly tailored to serve a significant governmental interest, and . . . [3] leave open ample alternative channels for communication of the information." *Clark v. Community for Creative Non-Violence*, 468 U.S. 288, 293 (1984). The first element of the test, content neutrality, is a key component of the analysis. A law is content neutral if its application is not dependent in any manner on the message being conveyed by the speaker. Stated somewhat differently, a content-neutral law focuses only on the time, place, or manner of a communication. See *City of Erie v. Pap's A.M.*, 120 S. Ct. 1382 (2000) (plurality treats ban on public nudity as a content-neutral regulation of expressive conduct). However, as noted earlier, a law that appears to be content-based may be treated as content neutral if it falls within the secondary effects doctrine. See §8.3.1.

Frequently one will encounter statutes or regulations that appear to be focused on time, place, and manner concerns, but that also include a content-based trigger. Suppose, for example, that a state law prohibits the distribution of campaign literature within 100 feet of a polling place on election day. In a colloquial sense, this prohibition regulates the time (election day), the place (polling place), and the manner (distribution of literature) of the affected speech. But the trigger of the law's application is dependent on the political content of the literature being distributed. Therefore, the law cannot properly be characterized as a time, place, and manner restriction. Rather, it is a content-based restriction on political speech. See *Burson v. Freeman*, 504 U.S. 191 (1992).

EXAMPLE 8-R

A city ordinance prohibits picketing on public streets or sidewalks within 150 feet of a grade school or high school during hours when school is in session. Excluded from the ordinance is peaceful labor picketing. Is this ordinance properly characterized as a time, place, and manner restriction?

EXPLANATION

No. Even though the ordinance does regulate the time, place, and manner of expression, the applicability of the ordinance is dependent on the content of the message conveyed by the picketing. Labor picketing will be allowed, while picketing with other messages will not. The ordinance, therefore, must be analyzed as a content-based restriction on speech. *Carey v. Brown*, 447 U.S. 455, 460-461 (1980); *Police Dept. of Chicago v. Mosley*, 408 U.S. 92, 95-96 (1972).

EXAMPLE 8-S

A Colorado statute makes it unlawful for any person within 100 feet of a health care facility's entrance to "knowingly approach" within 8 feet of another person, without that person's consent, in order to pass "a leaflet or handbill to, display a sign to, or engage in oral protest, education, or counseling with [that] person. . . ." The measure was passed, in part, as a response to problems of access to health care facilities caused by abortion protestors. The measure was designed, however, to apply to all health care facilities, including those having nothing to do with family planning, on the theory that the state has a strong interest in protecting ingress and egress to and from those facilities. Is this statute content neutral?

EXPLANATION

The measure appears to be content neutral. The statute applies regardless of the general subject matter of the speech, the specific topic of that speech, or the speaker's particular viewpoint. Nor does this appear to be a situation in which the government is seeking to suppress a particular message. Rather Colorado has imposed a "place" regulation that applies regardless of the underlying message the speaker wishes to convey. Thus, unlike the situation presented in Example 8-R, the statute's applicability here is not dependent on the content of the message being conveyed. One could argue, however, that the phrase, "oral protest, education, or counseling" creates a content-based restriction since only these forms of speech are covered by the statute. A friendly greeting, therefore, would not be covered. In a similar case, the Court held that such language was not a content restriction, but merely designed to ensure that the statute applied only to the types of speech activity most likely to cause the consequences the government sought to prevent, namely, the harm caused by in-your-face harassment of patients and health care givers. *Hill v. Colorado*, 120 S. Ct. 2480 (2000).

The principle of content neutrality is also violated by facially neutral time, place, and manner restrictions that grant excessive discretion to administrators. "[S]uch discretion has the potential for becoming a means of suppressing a particular point of view." *Heffron v. International Soc. for Krishna Consciousness*, 452 U.S. 640, 649 (1981). In *Shuttlesworth v. Birmingham*, 394 U.S. 147 (1969), for example, the Court struck down a city ordinance that granted a city commission the authority to grant or deny a parade permit on the basis of the commission's perception of the "public welfare, peace, safety, health, decency, good order, morals or convenience." In the Court's view, these vague and subjective standards vested the commission with a "virtually unbridled and absolute power" over the granting of parade permits. Id. at 150. The potential for abuse passed the limits of constitutional tolerance. On the other hand, the Court has upheld parade permit requirements that limit the discretion of the issuing administrator to the imposition of reasonable time, place, and manner constraints designed to accommodate public safety and convenience. *Cox v. New Hampshire*, 312 U.S. 569 (1941).

§8.4.2 Narrowly Tailored to Advance a Significant Governmental Interest

The second element of the time, place, and manner test requires a familiar means/ends analysis with something of a variable bite—not unlike mid-level scrutiny. Is the restriction narrowly tailored to advance a significant governmental interest? The answer depends on a variety of fact-driven considerations, including

- the nature of the speech activity being regulated;
- the perceived significance of the governmental interest;
- the scope of the restriction;
- the availability of effective, but less restrictive alternatives; and
- the court's judgment as to the actual effectiveness of the restriction in advancing the proffered interest.

As to the nature of the speech activity being regulated, be aware that the more traditional a mode of communication is, the more likely it is that the Court will be sympathetic to the claimed violation of First Amendment rights. The other considerations are more or less self-evident in application.

EXAMPLE 8-T

The City of Lost Angels prohibits the distribution of "handbills" on any street, sidewalk, or park within the city. "Handbill" is defined to encompass all forms of written literature, including circulars, leaflets, booklets, pamphlets, posters, and the like. The prohibition applies regardless of the content of the handbill. The asserted governmental interest is the prevention of

littering. Is this ordinance narrowly tailored to advance a significant governmental interest?

EXPLANATION

No. While the prevention of littering within the city may well be a significant
governmental interest, the ordinance completely bans a time-honored mode
of communication and does so in a manner much more intrusive than
necessary to advance the proffered interest. Laws that punish a party who
litters provide an effective and a substantially less restrictive method to
advance the city's goal. Given the breadth of the prohibition, the nature of
the speech activity affected, and the availability of substantially less restrictive
alternatives, this ordinance is unconstitutional. See *Schneider v. State*, 308
U.S. 147 (1939).

EXAMPLE 8-U

A federal regulation prohibits all forms of peaceful picketing on the public
sidewalks that surround the grounds of the Supreme Court building. The
purpose of the ban is to preserve the integrity of the Supreme Court grounds,
to protect individuals having business with the Court, and to maintain proper
order and decorum on those grounds. Is this regulation narrowly tailored to
advance a significant governmental interest?

EXPLANATION

Given the nature, function, and prestige of the Supreme Court, it certainly
follows that the government has a strong and, therefore, significant interest
in promoting safety, order, and decorum on the grounds surrounding the
Supreme Court building. The question then is whether the total ban on
peaceful picketing is "narrowly tailored" to advance those interests. It does
not seem to be. The total ban is far more sweeping than necessary to advance
the stated goals. Peaceful picketing, by definition, threatens neither persons
nor property, nor would it seem to detract from the decorum of the Court,
at least when practiced on the otherwise public sidewalks surrounding the
Court. Moreover, there are numerous less restrictive alternatives to the total
ban, such as limitations on the number of picketers, the size of signs, and so
on. See *United States v. Grace*, 461 U.S. 171, 181-184 (1983) (arriving at
an identical conclusion under virtually the same facts).

Despite the apparent rigor of this mid-level scrutiny, application of the
test is not always fatal to the government's position. For example, *Clark v.
Community for Creative Non-Violence*, 468 U.S. 288 (1984), involved a First
Amendment challenge to a National Park Service (NPS) regulation that

prohibited camping in national parks except in designated camping areas. No such areas are designated in the memorial parks located in Washington, D.C., including Layfayette Park and the Mall. The Community for Creative Non-Violence (CCNV), seeking to demonstrate the plight of the homeless, was granted a permit by NPS to erect temporary tent cities in Layfayette Park and the Mall. However, CCNV's request to sleep in the "symbolic tents" was denied on the basis of the content-neutral camping ban. The Supreme Court, assuming that sleeping in a symbolic tent was expression protected by the First Amendment, upheld the NPS regulation as being a valid time, place, and manner restriction. In the Court's words, "It is . . . apparent to us that the regulation narrowly focuses on the Government's substantial interest in maintaining the parks in the heart of our Capital in an attractive and intact condition, readily available to the millions of people who wish to see and enjoy them by their presence." Id. at 296. See also *Heffron v. International Socy. for Krishna Consciousness,* 452 U.S. at 650-656 (upholding regulation that prohibited face-to-face solicitations at state fair except in designated booths).

In essence, application of this means/ends analysis requires a careful marshaling of facts and a dose of common sense.

EXAMPLE 8-V

Reconsider the facts of Example 8-S. Assume that the measure was passed pursuant to the state's traditional police powers to protect the health and safety of its citizens. More particularly, the state wished to ensure unimpeded access to health care facilities and to avoid potential trauma to patients caused by in-your-face confrontational protests. Is this measure narrowly tailored to advance a significant government interest?

EXPLANATION

The interests asserted by the state are undoubtedly significant. Individuals entering health care facilities often are struggling with a wide range of physical and emotional concerns. Eliminating the additional trauma of a personal confrontation would seem to be quite significant from a health perspective. (A good lawyer would, of course, want to present evidence on this point.) The speech being regulated, however, is political speech. A court must, therefore, carefully examine the restrictions to determine if they are narrowly tailored to advance the asserted interest. This depends largely on the scope of the restriction. Here the restriction operates only within a specifically defined zone, namely, a 100-foot radius from the entrance of any health care facility. Moreover, the restriction does not prohibit all forms of speech within that zone. There are no restrictions on the content or manner of one's verbal communications or on the type of signs one might use. The only restriction is the 8-foot limitation on approach, and even this limitation does not prevent the speaker from offering a passerby a leaflet. The passerby is free, of course, to reject the offer or to reach into the 8-foot zone and accept the leaflet. It would seem then that within the zone itself there are ample opportunities to communicate virtually any message, and there is nothing in the statute or in the facts that suggest any limitation on one's ability to communicate messages outside of the zone. Given the limited intrusion on the speaker's ability to convey a message and given that the statute effectively eliminates the problems caused by in-your-face confrontational communications, in the absence of some creative alternative that is equally effective the measure would seem to be narrowly tailored to advance a significant interest. *Hill v. Colorado,* 120 S. Ct. 2480 (2000) (so holding under similar facts). Compare this conclusion with that described in Example 8-X. Do you see the distinction?

§8.4.3   *Alternate Channels for Communication*

The third element of the time, place, and manner test requires that the restriction leave open ample alternative channels for speech activity. Certainly if the effect of a law is to leave no time, no place, and no manner under which the subject information can be communicated, this element of the test is not satisfied. Beyond this certainty, there is no set formula for determining exactly what range of alternatives will satisfy the standard. It appears, however, that the general availability of traditional means of communication will suffice. For example, in *Clark v. Community for Creative Non-Violence,* the Court seemed to resolve this element by offhandedly observing that nothing in the record suggested that the "message concerning the plight of the homeless" could not be communicated through either the media or other means. 468 U.S. at 295.

EXAMPLE 8-W

The Minnesota State Fair is an annual event designed to exhibit to the public a wide array of goods, services, entertainments, and other matters of interest. Exhibitors, of which there are approximately 1400, are not allowed to sell goods or solicit funds anywhere in the fair except at their designated booths. The Krishnas have rented a booth at the fair; however, in addition to solicitations at the booth, they seek permission to engage in solicitations throughout the 125 acres of the fairgrounds. The fair administrators, relying on the neutral rule described above, decline to grant the requested permission. Assuming that this limitation on peripatetic solicitations is narrowly tailored to advance a significant state interest, does the restriction leave open ample alternative channels of communication?

EXPLANATION

Yes. The restriction does not apply to any areas outside the fair, leaving a wide array of communicative opportunities available to the Krishnas, and even within the fair, the Krishnas remain free to make solicitations at their booth. This may not be the ideal system from the perspective of the Krishnas, but in the absence of a showing that the alternative channels are either illusory or demonstrably inadequate, this factor of the time, place, and manner test should be easily satisfied. See *Heffron v. International Socy. for Krishna Consciousness*, 452 U.S. at 654-655.

Where the speech in question is of a type that the Court treats as having relatively low value, the requirement that there be alternative channels of communication may be so diluted as to be meaningless. For example, in *City of Renton v. Playtime Theatres, Inc.*, 475 U.S. 41 (1986), a zoning ordinance relegated theaters that showed adult films to the outlying portions of the city. Even though application of the ordinance turned on the content of the movies being shown, the Court deemed the law to be content neutral on the basis that it was aimed at the secondary effects of such theaters on the surrounding neighborhoods. See §8.3.1. Applying the time, place, and manner test, the Court found that the third part of the test was satisfied even though the theaters proved that as a practical matter, the 5 percent of the city where they were legally permitted to locate was not commercially viable. Thus, in the particular context of this adult pornography, the alternative channels of communication did not need to be ample or even available.

§8.4.4   Prior Restraints

Some time, place, and manner restrictions operate as prior restraints. For example, many cities have ordinances that allow parades on city streets only after the sponsors of the parade have received a permit from a designated city office. The Court has upheld such ordinances as long as the discretion of the person assigned to administer them is limited to the application of reasonable time, place, and manner considerations. On the other hand, if the ordinance grants the administrator arbitrary discretion with the potential for content-based discriminations, the ordinance will be struck down.

§8.4.5   Injunctions

A court may issue an injunction that regulates the time, place, and manner of speech as long as the "provisions of the injunction burden no more speech than necessary to serve a significant government interest," *Madsen v. Women's Health Center, Inc.*, 512 U.S. 753, 765 (1994), and as long as the purpose of the injunction is not to suppress the message of the speakers, id. at 763. The Court has described this test as requiring a "somewhat more stringent application" of First Amendment principles than would be required by the standard time, place, and manner analysis. The most recent applications of this test have involved injunctions issued against protestors at abortion clinics.

EXAMPLE 8-X

The Family Planning Clinic (FPC) is a privately owned health care facility that performs abortions. For the past several years, FPC has been involved in an ongoing conflict with abortion protestors who demonstrate daily on the grounds surrounding the clinic. The protests have included the blocking of driveways and entrances, aggressive confrontations with employees and patients, and occasional physical assaults. FPC sought an injunction against the protestors to prevent them from interfering with the operations of the clinic. The trial court issued an injunction that imposed a 15-foot floating buffer zone around persons and vehicles seeking access to the clinic and a fixed 15-foot buffer zone around clinic doorways, driveways, and parking lot entrances. Protestors entering either of these zones would be subject to contempt. Are these two aspects of the injunction acceptable time, place, and manner restrictions?

EXPLANATION

Although the injunction focuses only on the activities of abortion protestors, the purpose of the injunction appears to be not the suppression of their point of view, but the regulation of their conduct. The injunction will, therefore, be treated as content neutral.

As to the significance of the governmental interest, the standard is akin to that used in mid-level scrutiny, requiring that the government show that there is some important interest at stake. The interests in maintaining public safety and in protecting a woman's right to seek "pregnancy-related services" have been deemed significant in the particular context of abortion protests. *Schenck v. Pro-Choice Network of Western N.Y.*, 519 U.S. 357, 375-376 (1997).

The question then becomes whether either the floating buffer zone or the fixed buffer zone burdens more speech than necessary to advance these significant interests. Under similar facts, the Court in *Schenck* concluded that a floating buffer zone unduly intruded on basic speech rights by making it impossible to engage in a normal conversation or to hand out leaflets without potentially running afoul of the injunction. The fixed buffer zones were upheld, however, as appropriate devices to ensure safe and free access to the facility.

§8.5   The Nature of the Public Forum

The previous discussion of content-based and content-neutral restrictions on speech assumed that the speech in question occurred in a setting where the First Amendment operates at full strength. Yet before one can proceed on that assumption, it is necessary to make a preliminary determination as to the nature of the property on which the expressive activity occurs. For these purposes, it is necessary to distinguish between private property and public property.

Where the government seeks to restrict speech on (or involving the use of) property that is privately owned — e.g., books, newspapers, billboards, movie theaters, or the front lawn of one's home — speech is protected to the fullest extent called for by the appropriate First Amendment test. In other words, content-based restrictions on protected speech are subject to strict scrutiny or to a specifically applicable doctrinal test, while content-neutral restrictions are subject to the standard time, place, and manner analysis.

On the other hand, where the expressive activity occurs on property owned by the government, the level of First Amendment protection depends on how the particular property is classified, i.e., as a *public forum*, a *designated public forum*, or a *nonpublic forum*. How a piece of public property is classified under this so-called forum doctrine is critical. While First Amendment protections operate at full strength in public fora and in designated public fora (as they do with respect to private property), the protections are substantially diluted where the property in question is deemed to be a nonpublic forum.

A traditional public forum is a public facility that has, by long tradition, been dedicated to "the free exchange of ideas." *Cornelius v. NAACP Legal Defense & Educ. Fund*, 473 U.S. 788, 800-802 (1985). Falling squarely within this category are streets, sidewalks, and parks that "have immemorially been held in trust for the use of the public and, time out of mind, have been used for purposes of assembly, communicating thoughts between citizens, and discussing public questions." *Hague v. CIO*, 307 U.S. 496, 515 (1939); see also *Frisby v. Schultz*, 487 U.S. 474, 481 (1988).

A designated public forum is a public facility that is not a traditional public forum, but one that the government has intentionally dedicated to expressive activity, such as a college meeting room or a municipal auditorium. While the government may limit the scope of the designated public forum (e.g., use by enrolled students only), in which case it may be described as a limited public forum, or rescind the designation altogether, as long as the facility remains dedicated to expressive activity the full protections of the First Amendment apply within the legitimately defined scope.

A public facility, such as a welfare office or a courtroom, in which some expressive activity occurs, but which is neither a traditional nor a designated public forum is, by definition, a nonpublic forum, to which the protections of the First Amendment apply in only a limited fashion. In the words of the Court:

> Public property which is not by tradition or designation a forum for public communication is governed by different standards. We have recognized that the First Amendment does not guarantee access to property simply because it is owned or controlled by the government. In addition to time, place, and manner regulations, the State may reserve the forum for its intended purposes, communicative or otherwise, as long as the regulation on speech is reasonable and not an effort to suppress expression merely because public officials oppose the speaker's view.

Perry Educ. Assn. v. Perry Local Educators' Assn., 460 U.S. 37, 46 (1983). In short, within a nonpublic forum, the government is free to impose reasonable restrictions on speech, including most content-based restrictions, as long as the government maintains viewpoint neutrality, i.e., as long as the government does not grant or deny access on the basis of the favored or disfavored status of any particular message.

§8.5.1   *The Traditional Public Forum*

Given the more limited First Amendment protection applied to speech in a nonpublic forum, the determination of whether any particular facility is a public forum or a nonpublic forum is critical. Indeed, public forum analysis often presents a threshold issue in First Amendment cases. Examination of that issue begins with determining whether the forum qualifies as a traditional public forum. This breaks down into two propositions: The first covers those fora that are almost automatically included; the second focuses on the potential for further expansion of the category into more novel realms.

First, streets, sidewalks, and parks are generally considered traditional public fora to which the protections of the First Amendment fully apply. See *Frisby v. Schultz*, 487 U.S. 474, 481 (1988) (reaffirming standard as to residential streets). Therefore, if a case involves expressive activity on a street or a sidewalk or in a park, the public forum threshold is usually easily crossed. The generalization must, however, be qualified. If the street, sidewalk, or park has a special or limited use, i.e., it is not a generalized public thoroughfare or a general-use park, the traditional "public forum" label may not attach. Thus, a street on a military base is not a traditional public forum. *Greer v. Spock*, 424 U.S. 828, 835-837 (1976). Nor is a limited-use sidewalk resting completely on post office property and designed solely to provide access from a post office parking lot to a post office building. *United States v. Kokinda*, 497 U.S. 720, 727-728 (1990). Perhaps the same can be said of historic national parks designed for the special purpose of preserving our environment or heritage. Those qualifications aside, however, in general, public streets, sidewalks, and parks are traditional public fora.

Next, while the category of traditional public fora may theoretically include a much wider array of public facilities than streets, sidewalks, and parks, in practice it does not, largely because the Court has been reluctant to expand the category beyond those specific contexts. But see *Edwards v. South Carolina*, 372 U.S. 229, 235 (1963) (arguably treating the grounds surrounding a state legislative house as a traditional public forum). The theoretical threshold for entree into the category is a showing that the property or facility at issue is of a type whose *principal and historical purpose* is the free exchange of ideas. *Cornelius v. NAACP Legal Defense & Educ. Fund*, 473 U.S. at 801-802. Of course, this is a somewhat peculiar test given that streets, sidewalks, and parks do not themselves meet this standard other than by *ipse dixit*—for example, one would think that the principal purpose of a street is to provide a thoroughfare for traveling from one place to another. The Court has also noted that one indicium of a traditional public forum is "unfettered access" by the public. *Arkansas Educ. Television Commn. v. Forbes*, 523 U.S. 666, 678 (1998). As long as "principal and historical purpose" and "unfettered access" remain the standard, one should not expect any major additions to the category of traditional public forum.

EXAMPLE 8-Y

Members of the Intergalactic Society of Enlightenment, known as Izzies, seek to promote their views by proselytizing wherever crowds gather. Their proselytizing includes the distribution of free literature and the solicitation of contributions. They have found airports to be particularly attractive venues for these activities, and several Izzies have regularly solicited funds at the Buena Vista International Airport, a city-owned facility located in Virginia. After complaints from numerous patrons of the airport, the city adopted an ordinance that prohibited all face-to-face solicitations on airport property. The Izzies challenged this ordinance, arguing that the airport is a traditional public forum. They premise their argument on a combination of factors: the similarity of airport thoroughfares to streets and sidewalks, the history of expressive activity at airports, and the similar history and tradition of expressive activity at other transportation centers, such as train and bus stations. In essence, they argue that freedom of speech is consistent with the general character of airports and that this consistency compels a finding that airports are traditional public fora. Evaluate these arguments.

EXPLANATION

The arguments are certainly plausible. Anyone who has traveled by air transportation knows that expressive interactions, including the distribution of literature and face-to-face solicitations, do occur in airports in much the same fashion as those solicitations occur on city streets. Moreover, the analogy to city streets and sidewalks is especially strong given the plethora of shops and vendors that now line airport walkways. This argument, however, does not adequately address the somewhat more rigid focus of the traditional public forum inquiry. Applying the principal and historical purpose test, it would be difficult to sustain the proposition that one of the principal purposes of an airport is the free exchange of ideas. Although expressive activity clearly takes place in an airport—e.g., commercial advertising by airlines and conversations among travelers—*the* principal purpose of an airport is the profitable facilitation of air travel. That being the test, the analogies to streets and sidewalks and to bus and train stations would seem inapt. See *International Socy. for Krishna Consciousness, Inc. v. Lee*, 505 U.S. 672, 679-683 (1992).

There is one potential wrinkle to the analysis described in Example 8-Y. Since the decision in *International Society for Krishna Consciousness, Inc.*, the personnel of the Court has changed in a manner that may lead to a somewhat more flexible approach to traditional public forum analysis, more akin to that argued by the Izzies in Example 8-Y. See *International Socy. for Krishna Consciousness, Inc.*, 505 U.S. at 693-703 (Kennedy, J., concurring). One should not, therefore, assume that traditional public forum analysis will remain narrowly focused on the principal and historical purpose test. In short, your arguments in this context should consider the possibility of a more inclusive approach.

§8.5.2   Designated Public Forum

A public facility that does not qualify as a traditional public forum may, nonetheless, be characterized as a *designated* public forum. The test here focuses on the intent of the government. But here, too, the current Court has erected a somewhat substantial (and murky) barrier. If and only if the government *intends* to open a nontraditional public forum to a wide class of persons for expressive activity will the designated public forum status attach. As a consequence, a designated public forum cannot be created by inaction or by general public access to the forum, see *International Socy. for Krishna Consciousness, Inc. v. Lee*, 505 U.S. at 680, or even by a "selective" opening of the forum for expressive activity, *Perry Educ. Assn. v. Perry Local Educators' Assn.*, 460 U.S. at 47. Thus, if a state university develops a policy under which classrooms are made available as meeting places for student clubs, the requisite intent to designate a public forum has been established. *Widmar v. Vincent,* 454 U.S. 263, 267 (1981). However, because the intent of the university was to open its classrooms only to student groups, the property is a limited public forum available only to those groups. Moreover, if student groups just happen to use classrooms without objection from the university, no public forum has been designated even as to them. Nor has such a forum been established if the university permits selective, nonsystematic use by student groups, though the difference between what is selective and what reflects a standing policy is far from clear.

The facts of *Perry Education Association v. Perry Local Educators' Association,* 460 U.S. 37 (1983), are instructive. At issue in that case was the "forum" status of a school district's internal mail system. The system was dedicated largely to school purposes. Access was, however, granted to a labor union that had been elected as the exclusive bargaining agent for the teachers. In addition, certain civic groups, such as the Girl Scouts, the Cub Scouts, and the YMCA, were occasionally allowed access to the system. A rival union sought access to the internal mail system on the theory that the school district had created a designated public forum. The Court disagreed. The "selective access" granted to civic groups did not transform the internal mail system into a designated public forum. Id. at 47. The Court provided no elaboration, but presumably something more systematic would be required to establish the necessary intent to created a designated public forum. This judicial reluctance underscores the nature of the inquiry. A designated public forum will not be created by accident or by occasional practices that permit expressive activity to occur within the forum. Rather, a designated public forum will be created only if the government consciously and affirmatively intends to create one. In addition, even if a designated public forum has been created, the government may limit the scope of that designation, thereby establishing a *limited* public forum. Thus, the *Perry* Court explained that even if access by the various civic groups had created a designated public forum, the scope of that forum would be limited to access by like groups. Id.

As with traditional public forum analysis, the somewhat rigid designated public forum test should not be seen as a definitive and permanent standard. It does, however, represent the Court's most recent foray into this realm.

EXAMPLE 8-Z

AETC is a public broadcasting station owned by the State of Arkansas. During the 1992 elections, the station decided to air a series of debates involving the candidates for various federal and state offices. One of the debates was to focus on the candidates for the Third Congressional District. AETC invited the Republican and Democratic candidates for that district, but declined to invite Ralph Forbes, an independent candidate from the Third Congressional District. In declining to invite Forbes, AETC cited his overall lack of support among the voters of the district. The AETC believed that the limited amount of time available for the debate would be better served by focusing attention on the candidates from the two major parties. Are the AETC *debates* a traditional or a designated public forum?

EXPLANATION

One could certainly argue in the abstract that the "principal and historical purpose" of a public broadcasting station is the free exchange of ideas. Of course, the historical vintage and operation of such stations bears only the most remote comparison to streets, sidewalks, and parks. And the free exchange of ideas on such stations has always been tempered by the editorial judgment of the stations' managers. Perhaps most importantly, the public has never enjoyed "unfettered access" to airtime on public broadcasting stations. Similarly, even if we focus solely on the televised debates as traditional public fora, there is nothing in the history of such debates to suggest a generalized public right of access. It is quite unlikely that the Court would declare debates aired on public broadcasting stations to be a traditional public forum. That brings us to the question of a designated public forum. Focusing solely on the televised debates, it would not seem that AETC's actions evidence an intent to open these debates to a wide class of persons for expressive purposes. Rather, at most AETC has selectively invited certain parties to engage in expressive activity in what would appear to be a nonpublic forum. The debates are neither a traditional nor a designated public forum. See *Arkansas Educ. Television Commn. v. Forbes*, 523 U.S. 666 (1998) (so holding under similar facts).

§8.5.3   *Nonpublic Forum and Viewpoint Neutrality*

Finally, if the public facility at which expressive activity occurs is neither a traditional public forum nor a designated public forum, it is by default a nonpublic forum. Thus, whether governmental property falls into this latter category is answered through a process of elimination. Speech in a nonpublic forum may be limited under a mere reasonableness standard tied to the underlying purpose of the forum as long as the restrictions imposed are viewpoint neutral. *Arkansas Educ. Television Commn. v. Forbes*, 523 U.S. at 682.

EXAMPLE 8-AA

The Combined Way (CW) is a charity drive aimed at federal employees. Money raised through the program is distributed to participating organizations. Participation is limited to nonprofit charitable agencies that provide direct health and welfare services to individuals. Each such organization is permitted to "advertise" its needs in a CW circular that is published as a part of the drive. Specifically excluded from the drive are legal defense and political advocacy organizations. The reason given for this exclusion is that "a dollar spent on food and shelter is more beneficial than a dollar spent on litigation or political advocacy." In addition, the government argues that the exclusion avoids the appearance of political favoritism. A political advocacy group challenges the constitutionality of the exclusion as a restriction on political speech. Assuming that the CW drive is a *nonpublic forum*, will this content-based restriction withstand judicial scrutiny?

EXPLANATION

Probably. Although the exclusion of political advocacy from the forum is a content-based restriction of political speech, the nonpublic status of the forum significantly lowers the level of judicial scrutiny. As long as the restriction is reasonable and viewpoint neutral, it will be upheld. This restriction appears to satisfy both standards. It is certainly reasonable to conclude that money spent directly on food and shelter is more beneficial than money spent on litigation or advocacy. This remains true even if there is an equally reasonable argument to the contrary. The same can be said of the political favoritism rationale. As to the requirement of viewpoint neutrality, nothing on the face of the exclusion indicates that the CW is favoring one side or the other of a political controversy. An orientation toward litigation or political advocacy is not itself a viewpoint, but a means to advance a particular viewpoint. Therefore, unless it can be demonstrated that the restriction, either by design or as applied, reflects a bias against disfavored viewpoints, the restriction will be upheld. See *Cornelius v. NAACP Legal Defense & Educ. Fund,* 473 U.S. 788, 806-813 (1985) (holding, on similar facts, that the forum was nonpublic and, therefore, subject to the lower level of scrutiny).

The viewpoint-neutrality standard was violated in *Lamb's Chapel v. Center Moriches Union Free School Dist.,* 508 U.S. 384, 394 (1993), by an access policy that permitted a wide array of expressive uses, but only as long as the speaker did not adopt a religious viewpoint.

§8.6   The First Amendment Right of Association

The Court has referred to the right of association in two separate contexts. The first involves those intimate relationships that are protected by the right of privacy under the due process clauses — e.g., marriage, parent and child, and extended family. The second, which is the topic of this section, protects the freedom of individuals to gather in small groups or to unite in large organizations in order to engage in activities protected by the First Amendment, such as "speech, assembly, petition for the redress of grievances, and the exercise of religion." *Roberts v. United States Jaycees*, 468 U.S. 609, 618 (1984).

This First Amendment right of association, although not mentioned in the text of the Constitution, is implicit in the textual freedoms protected by the First Amendment. The exercise of those freedoms presumes the availability of opportunities for human dialogue and united action, without which the expressly provided rights would be meaningless. The right of association thus assures individuals the freedom to choose with whom and for what causes they will gather to exercise their First Amendment freedoms.

Potential infringements on the right of expressive association may include such governmental action as making membership in a particular organization a crime, imposing special hardships on those who join a disfavored group, forcing disclosure of otherwise secret membership lists, interfering with the internal operations of an organization, and creating barriers to an organization's participation in the political process. Keep in mind, however, that these potential infringements are only relevant to the extent that the burden imposed adversely affects expressive activity. In addition, implicit in the right to associate is the right not to associate. Thus, while the government may require an individual engaged in a specific occupation to join a labor union, the government may not require that individual to support the union's political advocacy. Nor, in the absence of a compelling justification, may the government force an organization to accept as members individuals whose expressive activity is inconsistent with the tenets of the organization.

Like freedom of speech itself, while the right of association is not absolute, it is, nonetheless, deemed *fundamental*. As a consequence, infringements on this right may only "be justified by regulations adopted to serve compelling state interests, unrelated to the suppression of ideas, that cannot be achieved through means significantly less restrictive of associational freedoms." *Roberts*, 468 U.S. at 623. In applying this ad hoc balancing test, the terms "least restrictive means" and "narrowly tailored" are sometimes substituted for the latter phrase. Yet regardless of the language used, the standard of review is strict scrutiny.

EXAMPLE 8-BB

In the midst of the civil rights movement, the Attorney General (AG) of Alabama brought an equity suit to enjoin the NAACP from conducting activities within the state. The AG argued that the organization had failed to qualify to do business within the state as required by Alabama law. The NAACP claimed a First Amendment right to engage in the contested activities. As part of the AG's lawsuit, a state court ordered the NAACP to turn over its membership lists to the AG. Fearing reprisal against its members, the organization refused to comply with the order. For this refusal, the NAACP was held in contempt. Would enforced disclosure, under the above circumstances, violate the right of association of NAACP members?

EXPLANATION

Yes. The compelled disclosure of affiliation with a group engaged in advocacy can have a chilling effect on a prospective member's willingness to join the group as well as on the group's ability to convey its message. Under circumstances in which the potential for reprisal is real, the forced disclosure violates the right of association unless the state can demonstrate that the disclosure is necessary to advance a compelling state interest. In *NAACP v. Alabama*, 357 U.S. 449 (1958), under similar facts, the Court concluded that there was no compelling interest justifying the enforced disclosure.

In the special context of state regulation of elections, the Court has adopted a variable standard of review. If the burden imposed on associational rights is deemed severe, the state regulation must be narrowly tailored to advance a compelling state interest. If, however, the burden is of a lesser character, "important regulatory interests" will be sufficient to sustain the measure. *Timmons v. Twin Cities New Party*, 520 U.S. 351, 358-359 (1997). There is no bright-line test to measure the difference between a "severe" and a "lesser" burden. Rather, the distinction turns on the degree to which a state regulation impairs the ability of a political party or candidate to exercise core First Amendment functions.

EXAMPLE 8-CC

The Republican Party of Connecticut permits independent voters — voters not registered in either party — to vote in Republican primaries for federal and state office. The state, however, requires persons voting in a party's primary to be members of that party. Does the state law impose a severe burden on Republican Party members' right of association?

EXPLANATION

Yes. Party members are free to associate politically with whomever they choose, and their effort to broaden their base of support by inviting independent voters to participate in the party's primary falls squarely within the right of association. The state's prohibition will be deemed severe, since it directly impacts a core function of a political party, namely, the ability to attract new members. The state may prohibit this practice only if it uses a means narrowly tailored to advance a compelling state interest. *Tashjian v. Republican Party of Conn.*, 479 U.S. 208, 217 (1986). In *Tashjian,* the state asserted four interests in defense of a similar prohibition: administrative burden, the prevention of interparty raiding, voter confusion, and protection of the two-party system. The Court found that the first was inadequate, while the latter three were insufficiently implicated. Id. at 217-225. See *Eu v. San Francisco County Democratic Central Comm.*, 489 U.S. 214 (1989) (applying the compelling state interest standard in striking down provisions of state law that prohibited governing bodies of political parties from endorsing primary candidates and that dictated the organization and composition of a party's governing body).

EXAMPLE 8-DD

In 1996, a California ballot proposition, Proposition 198, changed the state's primary election from a closed primary, in which only a political party's members can vote on its nominees, to an open primary, in which nonmembers of a party can cross over and vote for that party's nominee. Thus, a person registered in one party can participate in the nomination of a candidate for another party. The candidate of each party who wins the most votes is that party's nominee for the general election. Four political parties filed suit challenging the practice. Each party prohibits nonmembers from voting in its primary, the purpose of this requirement being to allow only party members to select the candidate who will then represent the views of the party in the general election. Does Proposition 198 impose a severe burden on the associational rights of these parties?

EXPLANATION

Yes. Proposition 198 forces a political party to alter its candidate-selection process in a manner that allows nonmembers of the party, who may have different views from that of the party, to participate in the selection of the party's candidate for office. Since a nominee represents the collective views of those who vote for her, the open primary system could well have a severe impact on the party's ability to convey its viewpoint to the electorate during the general election. In fact, participation by nonparty members may alter the views of the party by nominating a candidate who does not share the views of the party's majority. Proposition 198, therefore, must be narrowly tailored to advance a compelling state interest. See *California Democratic Party v. Jones,* 120 S. Ct. 2402, 2411 (2000) (so holding under similar facts). The Court in *California Democratic Party* also went on to hold that the asserted interests of the state — producing elected officials who better represent the electorate, expanding candidate debate beyond the scope of partisan concerns, ensuring that disenfranchised persons enjoy the right to an effective vote, promoting fairness, affording voters greater choice, increasing voter participation, and protecting privacy — were not compelling under the circumstances. Id. at 2412-2414.

By way of contrast with the preceding examples, in *Timmons v. Twin Cities Area New Party,* the Court concluded that a state law that prohibited a candidate from appearing on the ballot as the nominee of more than one political party did not impose a severe burden on the party's associational rights.

> Minnesota's laws do not restrict the ability of the New Party and its members to endorse, support, or vote for anyone they like. The laws do not directly limit the Party's access to the ballot. They are silent on parties' internal structure, governance, and policy-making. Instead, these provisions reduce the universe of potential candidates who may appear on the ballot as the Party's nominee only by ruling out those few individuals who both have already agreed to be another party's candidate and also, if forced to choose, themselves prefer that other party. . . . We conclude that the burdens Minnesota imposes on the Party's First and Fourteenth Amendment associational rights — though not trivial — are not severe.

520 U.S. at 363. The state's "anti-fusion" statute was then upheld under the less rigorous standard of review described above.

In some recurring right of association contexts, the Court has adopted more specific doctrinal tests to address the particular type of problem presented. Yet even in those contexts, the analysis parallels the strict scrutiny formula.

EXAMPLE 8-EE

The Hillside Board of Education requires all teachers to take an oath that they do not belong to any organization that "advocates the unlawful overthrow of the government." Hayes, a member of the Masked Militia Movement (MMM), was fired from his job as a high school physical education teacher because of his refusal to take this oath. The MMM does advocate the violent overthrow of all government. Does Hayes's dismissal violate his right of association?

EXPLANATION

It does unless the oath is interpreted to apply only to active membership in such organizations and only when the individual has actual knowledge of the illegal aims of the organization and the specific intent to further those illegal aims. *Keyishian v. Board of Regents,* 385 U.S. 589, 606-610 (1967). Only under such circumstances would the oath represent the "least restrictive means" to advance a compelling state interest. See *United States v. Robel,* 389 U.S. 258, 265-268 (1967).

The right of association does not, however, protect all associations, but only those related to First Amendment protected activity. Thus, a law partnership designed solely to promote the economic interests of its partners is not protected by the right of association, at least not to the extent that the partnership is engaged in for-profit economic activity. The right to associate for economic gain has not been recognized as a First Amendment right, although the First Amendment does protect rights of commercial speech. On the other hand, if the purpose of the partnership were to engage in political advocacy through litigation, the protections would attach. Political advocacy is a quintessential First Amendment right, and the right of association is tailor-made to protect collective efforts to engage in that expressive activity. See, e.g., *NAACP v. Button,* 371 U.S. 415 (1963) (NAACP's sponsorship of civil rights litigation was expressive activity protected by the First Amendment).

But suppose our law partnership is somewhat more complicated. Although created primarily for economic purposes, it also engages in significant expressive advocacy by performing a substantial amount of pro bono litigation for the homeless. Does the firm's dominant economic purpose preclude application of the right of association, or does its expressive advocacy transform the economic enterprise into an expressive association? This same question applies to other groups that associate for a combination of economic, social, and expressive activities.

The Court has not provided a measure for resolving these issues. Instead, as long as the organization engages in any protected expressive activity, the Court asks whether the alleged government infringement on associational rights actually impinges on that protected activity. Justice O'Connor has argued, however, for more of a bright-line test. In *Roberts,* for example, she suggested that the right of association should attach only to those organizations whose activities are *predominantly expressive.* 468 U.S. at 635. This approach would seem to run the risk of underprotecting First Amendment associational activities, although in most cases the results under O'Connor's approach and that adopted by the Court should be roughly similar.

EXAMPLE 8-FF

The Junior Chamber of Commerce (JCC) is an all-male membership organization that promotes and practices the arts of good salesmanship and sound management. The JCC claims that the training provided its members in these areas gives them an advantage in the business world. Aside from these training programs, one of the major activities of the JCC is the recruitment and sale of memberships in the organization. Over 80 percent of the national officers' time is devoted to recruiting new members, referred to generally as customers. A JCC bylaw does, however, provide that one aim of the organization is to promote "genuine Americanism and civic virtue" in young men. In addition, the JCC does from time to time take advocacy positions on political and public issues. The State of Minnesota, applying its public accommodations law, has ordered the JCC to admit women members. The JCC argues that the forced admission of women violates its male members' rights of association by impairing their right not to associate with women. Assuming that rules of standing are satisfied, may the JCC claim a First Amendment right of expressive association? Would that right be violated by application of the Minnesota public accommodations law?

EXPLANATION

If one applies the approach endorsed by Justice O'Connor in *Roberts*, given the largely commercial nature of the JCC, the collateral expressive activities of the organization would seem insufficient to qualify the JCC as a group to which the First Amendment right of association attaches. 468 U.S. at 638-640. Under the more elastic approach adopted by the Court, however, one can presume that the right of association is at least implicated, since the organization engages in some protected First Amendment activity. Under this approach, the question is not whether the JCC qualifies as an expressive association, but whether the forced association with women impermissibly infringes on the expressive component of the JCC's mission. In *Roberts*, under similar facts, the Court found no violation of the right of association. First, any infringement on the expressive activities of the JCC was minimal. Moreover, to the extent that associational rights were implicated, the state's interest in eradicating gender discrimination was compelling and not related to the suppression of ideas, and the means chosen represented the least restrictive means of advancing the state's interest. See also *Board of Directors of Rotary Intl. v. Rotary Club of Duarte*, 481 U.S. 537, 548-549 (1987) (applying approach adopted in *Roberts*).

EXAMPLE 8-GG

The Boy Scouts of America (BSA) is a private, not-for-profit organization engaged in instilling its system of values in young people. The BSA seeks to instill these values by having its adult leaders spend time with the youth members, instructing and engaging them in activities like camping, archery, and fishing. The organization asserts that homosexual conduct is inconsistent with those values, and in particular with the Scout Oath, which requires a scout to be "morally straight" (no pun intended), and with the Scout Law, which requires a scout to be "clean." The BSA does not specifically teach youth members about sex — no merit badge on this subject! Rather, scouts are instructed to receive guidance on this topic from their parents, their spiritual leaders, or from professionals. The Boy Scouts do, however, have a written policy against avowed homosexuals as adult leaders. That policy is based on the view that homosexuality is inconsistent with the Scout Oath and Law. Dale is an adult whose position as assistant scoutmaster of a New Jersey troop was revoked when the BSA learned that he is an avowed homosexual and gay rights activist. He filed suit in the New Jersey Superior Court, alleging that his dismissal violated New Jersey's public accommodations law, which prohibits discrimination on the basis of sexual orientation. The State Supreme Court upheld his claim under state law and further ruled that application of that law did not violate the BSA's First Amendment right of expressive association. Is the BSA's right of expressive association implicated by these facts? Assuming an affirmative answer, would that right be violated by application of the New Jersey law requiring the BSA to accept Dale as an adult leader?

EXPLANATION

The BSA clearly engages in expressive activity as part of its efforts to instill values in its young members. For example, the Scout Oath provides, "On my honor I will do my best to do my duty to God and my country and to obey the Scout Law; To help other people at all times; To keep myself physically strong, mentally awake, and morally straight." Similarly, the Scout Law states, "A Scout is: Trustworthy, Loyal, Helpful, Friendly, Courteous, Kind, Obedient, Cheerful, Thrifty, Brave, Clean, and Reverent." Many scout activities center around promoting these ideals. The BSA also claims that the ideals of being "morally straight" and "clean" include an admonition against homosexuality. Furthermore, the organization claims that the policy against homosexual adult leaders is premised on that admonition. Thus, if a homosexual were allowed to be a scout leader, the implied endorsement of homosexuality would run counter to the message the BSA wishes to convey on that topic. In this way, Dale's inclusion as a leader would substantially burden the BSA's right of expressive association.

A contrary view stems from the fact that the BSA does not engage in any expressive activity regarding sexuality. Nothing in the Scout Oath or the Scout Law addresses sexuality; nor does the organization in any manner attempt to instill the value of heterosexuality through its scouting activities. Essentially, the BSA is silent on this matter, instructing scout leaders to refer scouts with questions on these topics to parents, spiritual leaders, or professionals. That being the case, the sexual orientation of an adult leader would have no discernible impact on the expressive activities of the scouts. From this perspective, application of the New Jersey public accommodations law would not burden or even implicate the BSA's expressive right of association.

In the case from which these facts were derived, the Court split five-four on this issue, the majority deferring to the Boy Scouts' characterization of its expressive mission as including an admonition against homosexuality. *Boy Scouts of America v. Dale,* 120 S. Ct. 2446 (2000). The dissent focused on the fact that the BSA engaged in no expressive activity on the topic of sexuality, a view that was also adopted by the New Jersey Supreme Court. *Dale v. Boy Scouts of America,* 160 N.J. 562, 613, 734 A.2d 1196, 1223-1224 (1999).

Since the majority found that BSA's right of expressive association was burdened, the Court was required to apply the compelling state interest test. On this issue, the New Jersey Supreme Court had described the state's interest as being to eliminate "the destructive consequences of discrimination from our society." 160 N.J. at 619-620, 734 A.2d at 1227-1228. The New Jersey Supreme Court also concluded that the state had abridged no more speech than that necessary to accomplish that goal. Id. In addressing this issue, the U.S. Supreme Court described the applicable standards of review and then simply concluded with no elaboration, "The state interests embodied in New Jersey's public accommodations law do not justify such a severe intrusion on the Boy Scouts' rights to freedom of expressive association." 120 S. Ct. at 2457. Of course, the Supreme Court can get away with such a lack of analysis, but a student might want to consider and explain why New Jersey's asserted interest was or was not compelling, and whether the public accommodations law advanced that interest in a manner that was the least restrictive of the speech interests at stake.

§8.7   Special Problems of the Media

The text of the First Amendment refers to the freedoms of speech and "of the press." Although one Justice has suggested that the specific reference to the press indicates that the press should be entitled to special protections beyond those afforded the general public, the Court has never adopted this approach. Potter Stewart, "Or of the Press," 26 *Hastings L.J.* 631 (1975).

Rather, both freedoms are seen as part of a more encompassing freedom of expression. In cases specifically involving the press, however, the Court has not ignored the special role played by the press in our system of freedom of expression. In this section, we will examine some specific problems that arise in the context of freedom of the press.

§8.7.1   Access to Information

From time to time, members of the press have argued for a right of access to information over which the government may enjoy a monopoly. The Court's decisions have made it clear, however, that the press enjoys no greater access to government-controlled information than that enjoyed by the public at large. *Saxbe v. Washington Post Co.*, 417 U.S. 843 (1974); *Pell v. Procunier*, 417 U.S. 817 (1974). In *Houchins v. KQED, Inc.*, 438 U.S. 1 (1978), however, the Court, in a three-one-three decision, held that the "equal" access granted the press and public must afford the press "effective" access and must, therefore, take into account the special needs of the press. For example, press access might include the use of microphones or other equipment under circumstances where the use of such equipment is denied to the public. This result, however, was a product of Justice Stewart's swing vote between the plurality and the dissent; as a consequence, the decision may be of very limited precedential value.

§8.7.2   Access to Criminal Proceedings

Despite the Court's reluctance to enforce a general right of access to government-controlled information, in *Richmond Newspapers, Inc. v. Virginia*, 448 U.S. 555 (1980), the Court held that both the public and the press have a First Amendment right to attend criminal trials. This right is premised on the historical tradition of open criminal trials and on the public's right to know what transpires in a criminal proceeding. As a consequence of this right, a criminal trial cannot be closed to the public or the press in the absence of specific findings that establish both a compelling governmental interest in closure — typically, fairness to the defendant or the protection of a witness — and a means narrowly tailored to advance that interest. *Globe Newspaper Co. v. Superior Court*, 457 U.S. 596, 606-607 (1982).

In *Globe Newspaper*, for example, the Court struck down a state law that required trial court judges to exclude the press and public from all criminal trials involving sexual offenses against persons under 18 years of age. The Court agreed that the state's interest in protecting minor victims of sex crimes from further trauma and embarrassment was compelling, but concluded that the interest could be adequately served by a nonmandatory law that assessed the propriety of closing trials on a case-by-case basis. Id. at 608. See also *Press-Enterprise Co. v. Superior Court*, 464 U.S. 501, 510-513 (1984) (applying same standard to jury voir dire).

Several commentators have suggested that the right of access to criminal trials established in *Richmond Newspapers* could serve as the foundation for a more inclusive "right to know" directed toward providing the public with the fullest possible access to government-controlled information. See, e.g., Anthony Lewis, "A Public Right to Know about Public Institutions: The First Amendment as Sword," 1980 Sup. Ct. Rev. 1. The Court has yet to accept that invitation.

§8.7.3   *Gag Orders in Criminal Proceedings*

A concomitant to the right of access to criminal trials is the right to publish information procured through that access. As a consequence, gag orders that prohibit the press from publishing accounts of ongoing criminal proceedings are highly suspect, this despite the potential conflict between the right to publish and the defendant's right to a fair trial. As the Court recognized in *Nebraska Press Assn. v. Stuart*, 427 U.S. 539 (1976), a judicially imposed gag order is a prior restraint and is, therefore, subject to the strictest scrutiny — "prior restraints on speech and publication are the most serious and the least tolerable infringement on First Amendment rights." Id. at 559.

Although the *Nebraska Press* Court did not hold that such orders are per se invalid, the tenor of the Court's opinion, along with that of concurring opinions, suggests that the circumstances under which such an order will be permitted are rare to nonexistent. This does not mean that the First Amendment right to publish trumps the Sixth Amendment guarantee of a fair trial. Rather, the heavy presumption against prior restraints requires that the trial court seek measures that will accommodate both rights. At a minimum, therefore, a trial court is required to make specific findings that there are no less intrusive means for protecting the integrity of the trial process, and the *Nebraska Press* Court announced a litany of such alternatives: change of venue, postponement of the trial, searching questioning of prospective jurors, the use of emphatic and clear instructions, and sequestration of jurors. Id. at 563-564. In the vast majority of cases, these alternatives will obviate any necessity to impose a gag order on the press.

The Court has not applied the rule of *Nebraska Press* to civil proceedings, and, therefore, gag orders *may* be more easily sustained in the civil context. See *Seattle Times Co. v. Rhinehart*, 467 U.S. 20 (1984) (upholding order restricting newspaper from disclosing information it had received as part of discovery in defamation case).

§8.7.4   *The Publication of Truthful Information Contained in Public Records*

The Court has consistently upheld the right of the press to publish truthful information lawfully obtained from public records. While the right is not absolute, any potential infringement on that right will be subject to what is in essence strict scrutiny. Thus, a newspaper or other instrument of mass media may be punished for such a publication only when the proscription on publication is "narrowly tailored to a state interest of the highest order." *Florida Star v. B.J.F.,* 491 U.S. 524, 541 (1989).

This is a difficult standard to satisfy. In *Florida Star,* for example, the state attempted to impose civil liability—negligence per se—for publication of the identity of a rape victim whose name had accidentally appeared in a police report. The Court agreed that protecting the privacy of a rape victim was an interest of the "highest order," but found that the means chosen by the state were not sufficiently tailored to meet the constitutional standard. Three reasons were given. First, the state could have protected the victim's privacy interest by excluding her name from the police report. Next, the negligence per se standard swept too broadly by imposing liability even when the victim's identity was well known throughout the community. And finally, the proscription was underinclusive, since it applied only to the mass media. See *Smith v. Daily Mail Publishing Co.,* 443 U.S. 97 (1979) (upholding right of press to publish lawfully obtained name of youth charged as a juvenile offender); *Cox Broadcasting v. Cohn,* 420 U.S. 469 (1975) (upholding right of press to publish name of rape-murder victim that had been lawfully obtained from court records).

§8.7.5   *The Protection of Confidential Sources*

In *Branzburg v. Hayes,* 408 U.S. 665 (1972), the Court rejected claims by news reporters that they had a First Amendment privilege to shield confidential sources when subpoenaed to testify before a grand jury engaged in a criminal investigation. The reporters argued that enforced disclosure violated their First Amendment right to gather information. Although they did not seek an absolute privilege, the reporters argued that the government could breach the privilege only by satisfying what was in essence the compelling state interest test. The Court completely rejected their claim, finding no such privilege in the context of good-faith grand jury investigations.

Post-*Branzburg,* therefore, reporters have no *constitutional* privilege to refuse to reveal confidential sources before a grand jury that is engaged in a good-faith criminal investigation. The Court did observe, however, that "wholly different issues" would be presented if the grand jury investigation were "conducted other than in good faith. . . . Official harassment of the press undertaken not for purposes of law enforcement but to disrupt a reporter's relationship with his news sources would have no justification." Id. at 707-708. Beyond this, any privilege enjoyed by reporters must be based on statutory "shield" laws enacted by state or federal governments.

§8.7.6   Forced Access to the Press: Print Media

At issue in *Miami Herald Publishing Co. v. Tornillo*, 418 U.S. 241 (1974), was a state law requiring newspapers to provide reply space to political candidates they had criticized in their editorial pages. Proponents of the right of access had argued that modern newspapers, along with their television and radio counterparts, exercise vast and almost monopolistic control over the information available to the public. Moreover, given economic realities, competition with these information magnates was all but impossible. The statutorily conferred right of access was designed to ensure that the public received a wider array of information than would otherwise be available through what was essentially a monopoly over information. The Court concluded, however, that the forced access operated as a substantial content-based restriction on the editorial judgment of the press, the net effect of which would be to dampen public debate by inducing the press to avoid controversy on important public issues. Id. at 257-258. Without further consideration, the Court held the statute invalid.

The Court's opinion in *Tornillo* ended with the somewhat enigmatic observation, "It has yet to be demonstrated how governmental regulation of this crucial process can be exercised consistent with First Amendment guarantees of a free press as they have evolved to this time." Id. at 258. But despite this seeming invitation for further consideration, the doctrine of *Tornillo* has been treated as firmly established and relatively absolute, quite likely on the theory that governmental supervision of editorial judgment is simply inconsistent with the First Amendment. The government may not force the press to publish that which it does not wish to publish. The one possible exception arises in the context of defamation. Although the Supreme Court has not addressed the issue, it may be that a court-ordered retraction is a permissible remedy against the press once liability for defamation has been established under a fault standard. See id. (Brennan, J., concurring). Arguably the government has a compelling interest to provide relief for the harm incurred, and recognizing that the victim has a right of retraction may be a narrowly tailored means to that end.

One final point: The opinion in *Tornillo* made no reference to an earlier decision in which the Court had upheld a very similar right of access requirement as applied to the broadcast media, *Red Lion Broadcasting Co. v. FCC*,

395 U.S. 367 (1969). The differential treatment of these two media is presumably the result of characteristics peculiar to the broadcast media, a topic to which we now turn.

§8.7.7   *The First Amendment and Modern Technologies*

The Broadcast Media

The broadcast media, both radio and television, rely on electromagnetic frequencies to transmit their messages across the airwaves. On the basis of the theory that these frequencies represent a scarce commodity held in trust for the public, the federal government has developed a regulatory scheme through which the use of these frequencies is regulated to promote the "public interest, convenience or necessity." Communications Act of 1934, 47 U.S.C. §309(a) (1988). The Court has accepted this scarcity theory, *National Broadcasting Co. v. United States,* 319 U.S. 190, 213 (1943), the consequence being that the broadcast media can be regulated in ways that would be unconstitutional if applied to the traditional print media. The Court has also accepted the theory that the "pervasive" nature of the broadcast media may raise privacy concerns not evident in other forms of communication. In essence, broadcast messages intrude on one's privacy by invading the home with little or no choice by the viewer other than to change the channel. This intrusive potential is of special concern when children may be in the audience.

The most obvious difference in treatment between broadcast and print media is that the former may be subjected to content-based licensing requirements that would violate the doctrine of prior restraints if imposed on the print media. See *City of Lakewood v. Plain Dealer Publishing Co.,* 486 U.S. 750 (1988) (upholding facial challenge to a permit scheme that granted mayor broad discretion to deny permits for use of news racks on city streets). Moreover, once a license is granted, the broadcaster is not free to use the assigned frequency in any manner it chooses, but is subject to content-based regulations designed to promote the public interest, convenience, and necessity. See *FCC v. Pacifica Found.,* 438 U.S. 726 (1978) (upholding FCC authority to regulate indecent language in radio broadcasts).

A good example of this disparate treatment can be seen by contrasting the Court's decision in *Miami Herald Publishing Co. v. Tornillo,* 418 U.S. 241 (1974), with its decision in *Red Lion Broadcasting v. FCC,* 395 U.S. 367 (1969). In the former case, the Court held that a state could not require a newspaper to print a response to a political editorial. Forced access was antithetical to the right of a newspaper to control the editorial content of its pages. In *Red Lion,* however, the Court had no difficulty in upholding the Federal Communications Commission's authority to impose a similar right of reply requirement on the broadcast media — specifically, the right to respond to personal attacks and to certain political editorials under the "fairness doctrine." In the Court's words, "Although broadcasting is clearly a medium affected by a First Amendment interest . . . differences in the characteristics of news media justify differences in the First Amendment standards applied to them." Id. at 386. The primary difference the Court relied on was the presumed scarcity of available frequencies. Because of that scarcity, the privilege of a broadcast license carried with it the responsibility to act in the public interest, and the FCC could reasonably conclude that a right of reply for personal attacks and political editorials reflected a proper balance of First Amendment concerns by ensuring that the fullest range of information is made available to the public with only a limited intrusion on the editorial prerogative of the broadcasters.

The *administrative* right of access upheld in *Red Lion* did not translate, however, into a *constitutionally mandated* right of access. Thus, in *Columbia Broadcasting Co. v. Democratic National Committee,* 412 U.S. 94 (1973), the Court held that a broadcaster could, consistent with the First Amendment, adopt a policy of refusing to accept paid editorial advertisements on issues of public importance. Nothing in the First Amendment created a constitutionally mandated right of access. Id. at 121-132. Taken together with *Red Lion,* this means that while a broadcaster may be required to provide access under statutorily derived administrative regulations — the personal attack component of the fairness doctrine, for example — in the absence of such regulations, the broadcaster enjoys a relatively uninhibited editorial freedom to deny access to the use of its facilities.

EXAMPLE 8-HH

A federal statute provides that a broadcaster's license may be revoked "for willful or repeated failure to allow reasonable access to or to permit purchase of reasonable amounts of broadcast time by a legally qualified candidate for federal elective office on behalf of his or her candidacy." Frederica S. is the Republican candidate for the Eighty-fifth Congressional District in the State of California. She has repeatedly attempted to purchase air time from a local television station, but has been rebuffed in each instance. Upon Ms. S.'s complaint, the FCC held an open hearing and, on completion of that hearing, held that the station had violated the above statutory proscription. As part of its judgment, the FCC ordered the station to sell Ms. S. a "reasonable amount of air time." Evaluate the station's claim that the order violates its First Amendment right to control the content of its programming.

EXPLANATION

Ms. S. is not seeking a constitutional right of access. Rather, she is seeking access on the basis of a congressional enactment. The most appropriate precedent, therefore, is *Red Lion*. Under that decision, the question is whether Congress has acted reasonably in balancing the First Amendment rights of the broadcaster, the candidate, and the public. Given the limited nature of the desired access — reasonable access for legally qualified candidates for federal elective office — along with the importance of the information involved — political speech — it would seem that Congress has made a fair accommodation of the interests at stake by limiting the scope of the intrusion to the significance of the public's interest. See *CBS, Inc. v. FCC*, 453 U.S. 367 (1981).

One should not take the foregoing discussion to mean that the government's power to impose content-based restrictions on the broadcast media is without limit. Aside from the federal government's authority to impose limited rights of access or to promote the discussion of public affairs, and excluding the special problem of indecent speech, other content-based restrictions on the broadcast media may well be subject to the same standards of review applicable to the print media. In *FCC v. League of Women Voters of California*, 468 U.S. 364 (1984), for example, the Court applied what was in essence strict scrutiny in striking down a federal statute that prohibited noncommercial television stations funded by the Corporation for Public Broadcasting from engaging in "editorializing" on issues of public importance. Id. at 381-384. The heightened standard of review was mandated by the nature of the speech being regulated, namely, commentary on issues of public importance. The medium of communication did not in any fashion alter that standard. The Court distinguished the more deferential approach it had adopted in *Red Lion* as arising in a context in which the governmental intervention promoted more speech rather than less. Id. at 398.

Developing Technologies

The scarcity rationale, which is at the heart of the Court's broadcast media jurisprudence, has never been accepted uncritically. Today, the factual premise for that rationale is even more suspect. With the advent of cable television, fiber optics, and the ever-expanding information superhighway, the idea that there is a scarcity of "frequencies" on which broadcasters must rely is no longer tenable. Ultimately, this new factual reality should lead to a new jurisprudence, the most likely characteristic of which will be a merging of the standards applicable to electronic and print media, although one can expect some divergence on the basis of the different characteristics of the new technologies and the theory that old habits die hard. See Note, "The Message in the Medium: The First Amendment on the Information Superhighway," 107 *Harv. L. Rev.* 1062 (1994).

Turner Broadcasting System, Inc. v. FCC, 512 U.S. 622 (1994)

(*Turner I*), addresses some preliminary issues in the First Amendment juris-prudence to be applied to emerging speech technologies. In that case, cable operators challenged the "must-carry" provisions of the Cable Television Consumer Protection and Competition Act of 1992. Those provisions re-quired cable operators to devote a specific number of their available channels to local broadcast stations, the so-called must-carry provisions. The govern-ment argued that cable operators should be subject to the more relaxed First Amendment standards applicable to the broadcast media under *Red Lion*. The operators countered that the regulation operated as a content-based restriction thereby requiring application of strict scrutiny. The Court rejected both arguments.

The Court first held that cable operators did not share the physical characteristics that justified the more intrusive regulation of the broadcast media. Neither the scarcity rationale nor a frequency interference rationale applied. As a consequence, any restriction on the speech engaged in by cable operators would be examined under "settled principles of our First Amend-ment jurisprudence," id. at 639, rather than under relaxed standards. That did not mean, however, that the special characteristics of cable would be ignored in applying those principles. Thus, the Court rejected the argument that *Miami Herald Publishing Co. v. Tornillo* required automatic rejection of the must-carry provisions. The Court found the analogy between the print media and cable media inapt.

> [T]he asserted analogy to *Tornillo* ignores an important technologi-cal difference between newspapers and cable television. Although a daily newspaper and a cable operator both may enjoy monopoly status in a given locale, the cable operator exercises far greater con-trol over access to the relevant medium. A daily newspaper, no mat-ter how secure its local monopoly, does not possess the power to obstruct readers' access to other competing publications — whether they be weekly local newspapers, or daily newspapers published in other cities. Thus, when a newspaper asserts exclusive control over its own news copy, it does not thereby prevent other newspapers from being distributed to willing recipients in the same locale.
>
> The same is not true of cable. When an individual subscribes to cable, the physical connection between the television set and the ca-ble network gives the cable operator bottleneck, or gatekeeper, con-trol over most (if not all) of the television programming that is channeled into the subscriber's home. Hence, simply by virtue of its ownership of the essential pathway for cable speech, a cable operator can prevent its subscribers from obtaining access to programming it chooses to exclude. A cable operator, unlike speakers in other media, can thus silence the voice of competing speakers with a mere flick of the switch.

512 U.S. at 656. Ultimately, the Court concluded that as applied to cable operators, the must-carry provisions were content-neutral regulations of the

manner of speech and that they were, therefore, subject to mid-level scrutiny under the time, place, and manner test. Id. at 642. The case was remanded for application of that standard. On remand, the trial court upheld the must-carry provisions and the Supreme Court affirmed. *Turner Broadcasting System, Inc. v. FCC*, 520 U.S. 180 (1997) (*Turner II*).

For our purposes, the essential message of the *Turner Broadcasting* decisions is that settled principles of First Amendment law will be applied to emerging technologies, but with an eye toward applying those principles in a fashion that takes into account any special characteristics of the new technologies. Just as print is not broadcasting, cable is neither broadcasting nor print, and the Internet combines features of all these media as well as unique features of its own. In short, analogies with other forms of speech will be useful only to the extent that the old and new forms of speech share relevant First Amendment characteristics pertinent to the problem presented. Otherwise, the First Amendment principles to be applied must be considered in light of the special characteristics of the new medium. See *Denver Area Educ. Telecommunications Consortium, Inc. v. FCC*, 518 U.S. 727, 744-745 (1996) (plurality views the analogy between cable and broadcast media as sufficiently precise in the context of viewing by children to permit the regulation of indecency on cable access channels to a degree similar to that permitted over broadcast stations).

9

The First Amendment: Freedom of Religion

§9.1 Introduction and Overview

The First Amendment provides, "Congress shall make no law respecting an establishment of religion, or prohibiting the free exercise thereof. . . ." The two clauses of this sentence, commonly referred to as the Establishment Clause and the Free Exercise Clause, ostensibly divide the constitutional principle of religious freedom into two doctrinal realms, each with its own particular principles and methods. Stated very generally, the Establishment Clause precludes the government from favoring any particular religion or group of religions or from preferring religion over nonreligion (though the scope of this limitation is evolving rapidly), while the Free Exercise Clause limits the government's authority to interfere with religious beliefs and practices. Taken together, both Clauses are designed to promote religious freedom by limiting the capacity of the government to become excessively involved in religious matters. Both Clauses apply to the states through the Fourteenth Amendment.

As a preliminary matter, although "religion" is the protected subject under both the Establishment Clause and the Free Exercise Clause, the Court has never defined religion in a constitutional context. Typically, a court will accept any nonfrivolous claim that a particular set of beliefs constitutes a religion. Certainly the term *religion* includes all organized systems of faith premised on either a supreme being or some similar transcendent authority. This is true regardless of how bizarre the belief system or how recent the heritage of that system. In a sense, religion is in the heart of the believer. Thus, although a court may inquire into the sincerity of one's religious beliefs, a court will not inquire into the legitimacy or believability of those beliefs. The Court has stated that merely philosophic or personal beliefs do not qualify as a religion; however, the difference between a philosophy and a religion is far from clear, and the Court has never applied this distinction. Presumably, therefore, something like existentialism is not a religion, although one could certainly make a case to the contrary.

In what follows, we will examine the various doctrines the Court has developed under the religion clauses, focusing first on the Establishment Clause and then on the Free Exercise Clause. We will also note significant areas in which the clauses seem to overlap. The primary difficulty the student will confront in this area derives from the Court's inability to settle on a relatively consistent interpretation of the religion clauses. As a consequence of this recurring instability, religion clause cases cannot be reduced to a simple formula, but must be examined from a variety of jurisprudential perspectives.

§9.2 The Establishment Clause: Themes, Theories, and Tests

The Establishment Clause provides, "Congress shall make no law respecting an establishment of religion." These words have been interpreted as limiting governmental action of two types:

- action that discriminates between religions, and
- action that promotes religion in general.

The various subdivisions of these general categories will be discussed below. At this point, it is important to note, however, that the scope and content of the second category are the subjects of sharp debate on the Court. At the heart of that debate are two competing interpretations of the Establishment Clause — separationism and nonpreferentialism. That debate is further complicated by a number of compromise approaches that borrow from each of these interpretive theories. While a student need not become immersed in theory in order to understand the Court's Establishment Clause jurisprudence, some familiarity with these particular theories and their variations will provide a more thorough appreciation of that jurisprudence. A brief overview follows.

§9.2.1 Separationist Theory

Separationism, which is sometimes referred to as the separation of church and state, provided the dominant theme of Establishment Clause jurisprudence for almost 50 years. The basic premise of separationism is that religion and government do not mix well, each presenting dangers to the other. *Everson v. Board of Educ.*, 330 U.S. 1, 9-16 (1947). In *Everson*, the Court relied heavily on the history of religious persecution and intolerance toward minority religions as support for the separationist thesis. From the perspective of this thesis, the Establishment Clause is sometimes described as creating a "wall of separation" between church and state—a metaphor borrowed from Thomas Jefferson.

The Court's reliance on separationism has not, however, created an impregnable barrier between church and state. From a realistic perspective, some interaction between government and religion is inevitable, and the developed separationist jurisprudence recognizes that inevitability. Thus, parochial schools are surely entitled to police and fire protection even though such protection assists, at least indirectly, the sectarian mission of the school. Overall, however, the theme of separationism is to keep separate, as much as reasonably possible, the realms of church and state. See *Lee v. Weisman*, 505 U.S. 577, 609 (1992) (Souter, J., concurring) (defending the separationist model). As applied, this means that the government has no power to create an officially recognized church; to prefer one religion over another; to pass laws specifically designed to aid one religion or all religions; or to support, financially or otherwise, the teaching or practice of religion. *Everson*, 330 U.S. at 15-16.

§9.2.2 *Nonpreferentialist Theory*

Nonpreferentialist theory, on the other hand, rejects the "wall of separation" metaphor and is premised instead on the idea that the government may provide aid to religion and religious institutions as long as the government does not prefer any one religion or group of religions over others. Proponents of nonpreferentialism read the history of religious persecution and intolerance as indicative of a need to prevent discriminations between religions or religious sects, but not as requiring government to separate itself completely from the sphere of religion. They note that from the time of the First Congress — the Congress that proposed the First Amendment — the United States has promoted various religious activities, thus placing a gloss on the meaning of the Establishment Clause; for example, the First Congress through joint resolution created the Thanksgiving holiday as "a day of public thanksgiving and prayer, to be observed by acknowledging with grateful hearts the many and signal favors of Almighty God." In short, according to proponents of nonpreferentialism, while the government may not discriminate between religions, it is free to promote religion in general. See *Wallace v. Jaffree*, 472 U.S. 38, 91 (1985) (Rehnquist, J., dissenting) (defending nonpreferential model). Over the last several years, nonpreferentialist theory has become increasingly influential on the Court.

§9.2.3 *Compromise Approaches*

The Court has applied at least three compromise approaches to the Establishment Clause that borrow, more or less, from the competing theories of separationism and nonpreferentialism. First, the Court has, on occasion, tempered strictures of separationism by limiting its scope to those governmental actions that can be described as creating an endorsement of religion. *Wallace v. Jaffree,* 472 U.S. at 56. Thus, governmental action that assists religion in general, but that does not place the government's stamp of approval on religion will not violate this variation of separationism. See also *Lynch v. Donnelly,* 465 U.S. 668, 690 (1984) (O'Connor, J., concurring). From this perspective, a moment of silence at the beginning of the school day would provide an opportunity for students to pray, but would not necessarily indicate any governmental endorsement of prayer.

Next, the Court has also applied a coercion test to measure the extent to which the government may promote a seemingly neutral religious practice. In *Lee v. Weisman,* 505 U.S. 577 (1992), the Court held that a public high school could not invite a religious cleric to recite a nondenominational prayer at a high school graduation because, given the context and the age of the participants, the recital of the prayer would coerce unwilling students into participating in a religious practice. See *Santa Fe Independent School Dist. v. Doe,* 120 S. Ct. 2266 (2000) (applying coercion test to strike down school-sponsored prayer at high school football games).

Finally, the Court has sometimes used tradition and historical practice to define the scope of the Establishment Clause, the idea being that the Establishment Clause should not be interpreted to void practices that have long been an accepted part of our social customs. For example, since the days of John Marshall, all sessions of the Supreme Court have opened with the proclamation, "God save the United States and this Honorable Court." It is quite unlikely that the Court would hold that this traditional practice violates the Establishment Clause. See *Marsh v. Chambers,* 463 U.S. 783 (1983) (upholding state's power to pay a chaplain to open sessions of the legislature with a prayer).

§9.2.4 *The Lemon Test (The Remains of a Separationist Model)*

In the early 1970s, the Court attempted to reduce its Establishment Clause jurisprudence to a simple three-part formula, which is now commonly referred to as the *Lemon* test. *Lemon v. Kurtzman,* 403 U.S. 602 (1971). Under the *Lemon* test, governmental action

- *must* have a secular purpose;
- *must* have a primary effect that neither advances nor inhibits religion; and
- *may not* foster an excessive entanglement with religion.

The *Lemon* test is largely a product of separationist theory and, hence, a matter of considerable controversy with those members of the Court who prefer the nonpreferential model. Moreover, as will be discussed below, the *Lemon* test has been applied in an inconsistent fashion even by separationists, thus rendering the test less than dispositive. Nonetheless, the *Lemon* test remains an important part of the Court's overall Establishment Clause jurisprudence.

The secular purpose element of the *Lemon* test requires that a law have a nonreligious purpose. This does not mean that the sole purpose of a challenged law must be secular, but only that the government must articulate a nonfrivolous secular purpose for the law. Thus, a law that is passed, in part, to advance religious doctrine is not necessarily invalid under this element if there is also a secular purpose for the law. In general, the Court tends to be deferential toward the government in applying this element. However, if the facts establish that the sole or predominant purpose of a law is religious, the Court will strike down the law on this basis. Thus, in *Epperson v. Arkansas,* 393 U.S. 97 (1968), the Court struck down an Arkansas law that made it unlawful for public school teachers to teach the theory of human evolution, the Court having concluded that under the facts presented, there was "no doubt" that the law was enacted to prevent the teaching of a theory thought to be contrary to the Book of Genesis. Id. at 107. See also *Santa Fe Independent School Dist. v. Doe,* 120 S. Ct. at 2279 (drawing inference that the purpose of a school district's policy regarding the selection of a student to deliver an invocation before home football games was to promote public prayer); *Stone v. Graham,* 449 U.S. 39, 41 (1980) ("pre-eminent" purpose of a law requiring the posting of the Ten Commandments in public classrooms was religious).

EXAMPLE 9-A

State X has adopted a statute mandating a moment of silence at the beginning of each school day. One of the purposes of this statute is to provide students with an opportunity to pray in school. Another purpose is to create a calming atmosphere in the classroom in order to better promote learning. Does this statute violate the first element of the *Lemon* test?

EXPLANATION

No. Although passage of the statute was partially motivated by religious considerations, there was also a secular purpose sufficient to meet the deferential standards applicable to this first element of the *Lemon* test. On the other hand, had the state passed a statute simply mandating a moment for silent prayer, the secular purpose requirement would probably be violated, there being no reasonably discernible secular purpose for such a law. See *Wallace v. Jaffree,* 472 U.S. 38 (1985).

By way of contrast, the second element of the *Lemon* test, i.e., that a law not have the primary effect of either advancing or inhibiting religion, often has served as a basis for invalidating laws thought to violate the Establishment Clause. There is no specific way to determine whether the effect of a law is "primary." As a consequence, this aspect of the *Lemon* test is quite subjective, making it a convenient surrogate for a more generalized judgment that a particular law or governmental action goes too far in advancing nonsecular ends. For example, what is the primary effect of a law that permits a public school district to loan mathematics textbooks to students attending parochial schools? A strict separationist might argue that the primary effect is to advance the mission of a sectarian institution by making it less expensive for that institution to operate. A less strict view, however, might contend that the primary effect is to advance the state's interest in promoting a sound secular education for all its young citizens. Neither argument is inherently correct or incorrect given the overall elasticity of the test. In general, the more substantial and the more direct the aid is, the more likely it is that the Court will find a primary effect to advance religion.

Finally, the excessive entanglement prong of the *Lemon* test is designed to ensure that any interaction between church and state is not such that the state becomes too heavily involved in the affairs of a church or religious institution. In determining whether there is an excessive entanglement, the Court has examined the character of the religious institution involved; the nature of the governmental assistance, i.e., whether the aid is financial or "in-kind" services; and the resulting interaction between the religious institution and the government.

EXAMPLE 9-B

State X has adopted legislation providing salary supplements to parochial school teachers who teach purely secular subjects (e.g., mathematics) in otherwise sectarian schools. The purpose of the supplement is to achieve parity between the salaries of such teachers and their public school counterparts. In order to ensure that the state money is not being used to advance sectarian goals, such as the teaching of religion, all parochial schools with teachers participating in this program must agree to intermittent inspections by state officers. Does this inspection program foster an excessive entanglement between church and state?

EXPLANATION

Arguably yes. By injecting the state into the operations of a sectarian institution and by requiring the state to make judgments about whether particular classes are being taught in a secular or sectarian fashion, there appears to be an excessive entanglement. The fact that the aid is financial will tip the balance toward a finding of excessive entanglement, since the Court has generally presumed that the Establishment Clause precludes direct financial aid to religious institutions. See *Lemon v. Kurtzman,* 403 U.S. at 614-622.

Notice that the excessive entanglement element puts a state between a rock and a hard place when it comes to assisting religious institutions. If the state does not take action to ensure that its monies are being spent only for secular purposes, then there is a distinct possibility that a court will find that the primary effect of the state's program is to advance religion. Yet if the state does attempt to oversee public expenditures, the potential for excessive entanglement looms large.

A final word on the *Lemon* test: Although one can find numerous applications of the *Lemon* test in the case reports, the current tendency of the Court is to either ignore or downplay the significance of this test. Certainly those who espouse nonpreferentialism are not likely to place strong reliance on *Lemon.* On the other hand, lower court judges, some members of the Supreme Court, and sometimes a majority of the Court continue to use *Lemon* as a framework for analyzing Establishment Clause problems. See *Santa Fe Independent School Dist. v. Doe,* 120 S. Ct. at 2279 (using "secular purpose" prong of *Lemon* to invalidate a school policy promoting prayer at high school football games); *Agostini v. Felton,* 521 U.S. 203 (1997) (applying, but modifying *Lemon* in a manner more in accord with the nonpreferentialist model).

§9.3 The Establishment Clause Applied: Discrimination between Religions

In the context of governmental action that discriminates between religions, there is general agreement that the government may not create an official religion, prefer one religion over others (which is tantamount to the same thing), or treat any religion less favorably than it does others. A separationist would easily conclude that any such action violates the *Lemon* test, while a proponent of nonpreferentialism would deem the discriminatory practice inconsistent with the basic principle of nonpreference. This congruence of theory will be evident as we examine each of the ways in which a law may be said to discriminate between religions.

§9.3.1   *The Ban on Officially "Established" Religions*

First, the language of the Establishment Clause divests Congress of any power to designate or adopt an official religion for the United States. Any such law would be a "law respecting an establishment of religion." In addition, the Establishment Clause appears to prevent the United States from interfering with state-established religions, of which there were several at the time the Bill of Rights was adopted. Indeed, one of the purposes of the Establishment Clause was to prevent such interferences. Thus, a congressional enactment *disestablishing* the official religion of Virginia would be a "law respecting an establishment of religion" in violation of the Establishment Clause.

This latter aspect of the Establishment Clause is no longer relevant. With the incorporation of the Establishment Clause through the Fourteenth Amendment, the protection of the state's authority to establish an official religion has been transformed into a constitutional barrier that prevents the exercise of such an authority. Thus, just as Congress may not create an official religion for the United States, neither may state or local governments do the same within their respective jurisdictions. In short, under the Establishment Clause, federal, state, and local governments may not create, sponsor, or promote an official or established religion. Any attempt to do so is invalid per se.

§9.3.2   *The Limitation on Conferring a Preferred Status*

As one might suspect, problems involving the actual establishment of an official government religion are rare to nonexistent. Congress, for example, has never passed a law expressly establishing an official national religion. Modern instances in which states or local governments have attempted to do so are idiosyncratic at best. The Establishment Clause, however, goes beyond proscribing the creation of an official religion. It also prohibits the government from granting a preferred status to any religion or group of religions. Thus, the government may not impose a tax to support the ministers of any particular faith, or spend money to promote certain religious practices or beliefs, or pass laws designed to conform government practices to the tenets of any particular religion. In each such case, the government would be conferring a preferred status on the religion so favored, which, although not accomplished through an express "establishment" of an official religion, is tantamount to the same thing.

EXAMPLE 9-C

The Unity City School Board has decided, with overwhelming community support, to promote the religious doctrines of Christianity within its school system. Although students attending Unity City schools will not be required to profess their acceptance of Christianity, all students will be required to take courses on New Testament theology, and all classes will be taught with an underlying theme of Christian faith. Does this program violate the Establishment Clause?

EXPLANATION

Yes. The Establishment Clause precludes the school board from taking this action. Although the school board has not expressly designated Christianity as the official local religion, it has granted Christianity a preferred status in violation of the Establishment Clause.

The result in Example 9-C is the same under either a separationist or a nonpreferentialist approach. In terms of separationist theory, the action taken by the school board violates the primary effect element of the *Lemon* test by actively promoting a particular religious perspective. Moreover, it might violate the first element of the *Lemon* test, since the city would have a difficult time articulating a secular purpose for the law. From the perspective of nonpreferentialism, the school board's policy creates an unconstitutional preference for Christianity over other religions, such as Judaism and Buddhism, thereby violating the nonpreferential premise of that theory. Compromise approaches, such as endorsement and coercion, generate the same result. The school board has endorsed Christianity and has coerced conformity to the doctrines of that religion. Finally, there is no convincing argument on the basis of traditional or historical practices that limits the applicability of the Establishment Clause in this context.

As the foregoing discussion suggests, in the context of governmental action that confers a preferred status on a religion, there is in a sense only one theory. The government's conferral of a preferred status violates the Establishment Clause. To this extent, the analysis of "preferred status" problems is relatively simple. Once a preference is established, unconstitutionality is essentially a foregone conclusion.

The only difficulty in this context is in determining whether a challenged statute or governmental action does in fact grant a preferred status to a religion. There is no particular test for making such a determination. In fact, the label of "preferred status" is merely a conclusion that is placed on a court's interpretation of the facts and circumstances presented. In approaching this issue, however, it may be helpful to frame the inquiry in terms of the *Lemon* test by asking whether the government's sole purpose in enacting a measure was to favor one religion or whether this is the primary effect of the law.

EXAMPLE 9-D

Unity City has adopted a Sunday closing law that prohibits the operation of any "nonessential" businesses on Sundays. Most retail operations are included within the prohibition. Does this law violate the Establishment Clause on the ground that it grants a preferred status to a particular religion or group of religions?

EXPLANATION

Arguably it does. Historically, Sunday closing laws were passed for the avowed purpose of promoting Sunday worship—a potential violation of the secular purpose requirement. Moreover, those religions that recognize Sunday as a day set aside for religious worship are seemingly preferred over those religions that do not by conferring a special benefit on Sunday worshipers—a potential violation of the primary effect requirement. A combination of the foregoing factors does seem to give religions that espouse Sunday worship a preferred status.

On the other hand, a court could construe the Sunday closing law as promoting the secular purpose of rest and recuperation and as not directly preferring any particular religious practice. And even though such laws were at one time religiously premised, the modern basis for these laws has been secularized by practice, habit, and cultural change. Similarly, although some religions will benefit from this law, one could certainly argue that the primary effect is as secularized as the purpose, namely, the promotion of rest and recuperation. Under this interpretation of the facts, no religion is granted a preferred status, and neither separationist nor nonpreferentialist theories would be violated by the practice. See *McGowan v. Maryland*, 366 U.S. 420 (1961) (upholding Sunday closing law against an Establishment Clause challenge).

§9.3.3   *The Limitation on Imposing a Disfavored Status*

Just as the government may not grant one religion a preferred status, the government may not impose a disfavored status on any religion. Such action is typically referred to as action discriminating against a religion. The underlying principle is virtually identical to that described in the discussion of preferred status. A law that grants one religion a preferred status obviously discriminates against all other religions. So, too, a law that discriminates against certain religions creates a preferred status for those religions not so burdened. Yet the two approaches serve distinct ends. The focus of preferred status cases is on a religion receiving a special benefit, while the focus of discrimination cases is on a religion receiving less favored treatment. The problem is the same, for the government has established a preference. Since the problem is the same, it follows that the solution is the same whether we think of the matter in terms of preferred status or discriminatory treatment. This is true under both separationist and nonpreferentialist theories. Hence, a law that discriminates against a religion must satisfy the *Lemon* test to pass separationist theory, and this same law must satisfy the principle of nonpreference to pass nonpreferentialist theory. Compromise approaches achieve the same result.

This anti-discrimination principle was applied by the Court in *Fowler v. Rhode Island*, 345 U.S. 67 (1953). At issue in *Fowler* was a local ordinance that had been construed to prohibit preaching in a public park by a Jehovah's Witnesses minister, but to permit Catholics and Protestants to hold religious services in that same park. The Court found that this discrimination violated the First Amendment because it was "merely an indirect way of preferring one religion over another." Id. at 70. The decision in *Fowler* underscores the similarity between governmental action that discriminates against a religion and governmental action that confers a preferred status on a religion. Each presents another perspective from which to examine the other.

Discrimination problems in which one religion is subjected to less favored treatment can also be analyzed as potential violations of the Equal Protection Clause. *Larson v. Valente*, 456 U.S. 228 (1982). Since religion is a fundamental right, a law that discriminates against a religion must be subject to strict scrutiny and the compelling interest test. In *Larson*, the Court applied these equal protection standards to a state law that exempted religious organizations from reporting under the state's charitable solicitations act, but only if the organization received more than half of its contributions from members or affiliated organizations. Since the Unification Church received the bulk of its contributions from nonmembers, it was deemed ineligible for the exemption. The Court concluded that the state law created a denominational preference by providing a selective exemption for certain religious organizations. As a consequence, the Court applied strict scrutiny and found the state's justifications for the discrimination inadequate under that standard.

§9.4 The Establishment Clause Applied: The Nondiscriminatory Promotion of Religion

The second way in which the government may run afoul of the Establishment Clause is through action that neither favors nor disfavors any particular religion or group of religions, but that, nonetheless, provides support or assistance to religion in general. Unlike the contexts of preferred status and discrimination, in which there is a harmony of views, this context involving the nondiscriminatory promotion of religion is fraught with conflict and disharmony. As will be noted below, theory matters.

Nondiscriminatory promotion may come in either of two forms. The first involves governmental action designed to promote the value of religion generally. An example of this type of governmental assistance would be a state law that mandates a moment of silence for prayer in public schools. Even though such a law is denominationally neutral, it still promotes religion and thus falls within this category. Second, governmental assistance to religion may be the product of a program that is not designed to promote religion in any manner, but that, nonetheless, has the effect of doing so. An example of this form of assistance would be a state-funded program that permits public schools to lend textbooks to private schools regardless of the private school's religious or nonreligious character. While religion is seemingly irrelevant to the state's plan, if private *sectarian* schools participate in the program, the government can be fairly described as providing support or assistance to those religious institutions. In short, this final category includes laws that deliberately promote religion as well as laws that provide support for religion through otherwise neutral criteria.

The question to be resolved in this category is whether governmental action that promotes religion in either of the above fashions runs afoul of the Establishment Clause. The answer to that question depends in large part on which theory one applies to the particular controversy at issue.

The conflict between the separationist and the nonpreferentialist models is particularly striking. According to strict separationist theory, the government may not support, assist, or otherwise promote religion or religious institutions; and although there is significant moderation in some applications of this theory, the overall effect of the theory is to discourage such support. Thus, the government may not promote the value of religion over nonreligion; nor may the government provide direct support to religious institutions. Under nonpreferentialist theory, however, there is no limitation on the power of government to promote religion or to support religious institutions. The government is free to promote religion generally — i.e., to discriminate against nonreligion and to support religious institutions as long as the government does not create a preference for any particular religion or religious institution.

EXAMPLE 9-E

The Unity City School Board has adopted a policy that mandates "a moment of silent meditation or prayer" at the beginning of each school day. A student who is an atheist challenges this policy on the grounds that it is designed to promote prayer in public schools in violation of the Establishment Clause.

Invoking the *Lemon* test, she argues that although a mandated moment of silent meditation may have a secular purpose, the "or prayer" language has no purpose other than to promote religion in a public school setting. She also argues that the primary effect of this additional language is to advance a religious practice.

EXPLANATION

The student has a reasonably good argument under separationist theory and the *Lemon* test. Under nonpreferentialist theory, however, her argument is unavailing. Even if the law does promote prayer in public school, it does so in a neutral manner without preferring any particular religion. If the court adopts a nonpreferentialist approach, our student's only hope is to somehow convince the court that a policy promoting silent prayer is not in fact neutral and that it does confer a preferred or disfavored status on certain religions.

The most effective way to study this category of Establishment Clause jurisprudence is to examine some of the contexts in which issues involving the promotion of religion have arisen. The two contexts chosen—public aid to parochial schools and prayer in public schools—provide a fair overview of this category in action as well as a hint of the direction the Court may be heading within this realm of governmental assistance to religion. The key to understanding this area will be found not in memorizing specific results—a process certain to trigger migraine headaches and dizzy spells — but in recognizing how particular results are the product of underlying theories and of subjective judgments regarding the proper scope of the Establishment Clause.

§9.4.1 *Public Aid to Parochial Schools*

For nearly 50 years, some form of separationism provided the dominant theme within the Court's decisions involving public aid to elementary and secondary parochial schools. *Everson v. Board of Educ.*, 330 U.S. 1 (1947). Of course, under an absolutely strict application of separationist theory, no such aid would be permitted under any circumstances. After all, so the argument goes, if one purpose of the Establishment Clause is to prevent the government from taxing and spending in support of religious institutions, then that purpose is potentially subverted whenever the government provides public assistance to sectarian institutions.

But the Court has never adopted such a rigid view. Instead, separationist principles have been moderated to permit some degree of governmental support for parochial schools, particularly when that support is either part of a general health and safety program or clearly directed toward the students and not the school itself. In short, separationism has been tempered by a desire to avoid hostility toward religion.

EXAMPLE 9-F

Unity City reimburses parents for the cost of their children's bus transportation to and from school. This reimbursement is available regardless of whether the children attend public or private school. A substantial portion of the money expended under this program will be used to reimburse parents who send their children to a local Catholic school. Does this program violate the Establishment Clause?

EXPLANATION

Under a separationist approach using the *Lemon* test, the city's reimbursement plan does not violate the Establishment Clause. The plan has a secular purpose — the promotion of safe transportation for school-aged children — and its primary effect is to provide that transportation, not to aid religion. Nor is there an excessive entanglement, since the aid is directed to the parents, making the state's involvement with the schools minimal. See *Everson v. Board of Educ.*, 330 U.S. 1 (1947).

———————

One should not take Example 9-F to suggest that public assistance to parochial schools will always or even generally meet with the Court's approval; nor should one assume that the simplicity of Example 9-F reflects the overall simplicity of the Court's jurisprudence in this sphere. Indeed, one result of the Court's acceptance of less than strict separationism is a body of case law in which compromise may be as important as the underlying theory espoused. Moreover, the emerging theory of nonpreferentialism and the presence of significant compromise theories between that theory and separationism have made for a somewhat complicated jurisprudence and a plethora of seemingly chaotic results.

The Court's decision in *Wolman v. Walter*, 433 U.S. 229 (1977), presents a good example of this phenomenon. At issue in *Wolman* was the constitutionality of a state statute that provided various forms of aid to parochial schools — a program for lending textbooks and instructional materials and equipment, a program for providing standardized testing and scoring services, a program to provide diagnostic and therapeutic services for students, and the provision of bus transportation for field trips. The Court invalidated some of these programs (the lending of instructional materials and equipment and the provision of bus transportation for field trips) and upheld others (the lending of textbooks, the provision of standardized testing and scoring services, and the provision of diagnostic and therapeutic services). Only two Justices agreed with all of these results; the other seven Justices concurred and dissented to various parts of this disposition. As Justice Blackmun, author of the Court's opinion, observed, "[T]he wall of separation that must be maintained between church and state 'is a blurred, indistinct, and variable barrier depending on all the circumstances of a particular relationship.'" Id. at 236 (quoting *Lemon v. Kurtzman*, 403 U.S. at 614).

This indeterminacy does not mean that the separationist theory is wrong. It does suggest, however, that the Court has not been successful in developing a consistent and coherent method for applying that theory in the specific context of public aid to parochial schools. One potential antidote to this failure is adoption of a stricter model of separation of church and state, permitting virtually no public assistance to parochial schools beyond that provided by general public services related to health and safety. The current Court is certainly not headed in that direction.

Another approach, which some members of the current Court have urged, would be to adopt some version of the nonpreferentialist model. Application of that model would create a very different jurisprudential landscape, allowing public aid to parochial schools as long as that aid did not establish a preference for any particular religion or group of religions. A state could lend textbooks, films, projectors, and nonreusable workbooks; a state could provide assistance for trips to the zoo or the museum; a state could provide salary assistance for teachers; and so forth. See *Mitchell v. Helms*, 120 S. Ct. 2530 (2000) (upholding the constitutionality of such a program). Compromise theories of endorsement and coercion also support a wider availability of government assistance to parochial schools. Id. at 2556 (O'Connor, J., concurring).

However, the cost of this coherency would be the potential expenditure of large sums of public money in support of sectarian institutions. To the extent that this is of concern to a proponent of nonpreferentialism, the theory is subject to modification. Thus, while one who espouses nonpreferentialism certainly would allow more governmental assistance to parochial schools than would a separationist, that liberality could be tempered by a reluctance to permit direct financial aid to such institutions. Under this modified nonpreferential theory, a direct subsidy to a parochial school might not be permitted, while a subsidy granted to a parent whose child attended the school would be allowed. Indeed, some Justices of the nonpreferential school have hinted at such a possibility. *Lee v. Weisman*, 505 U.S. 577, 631 (1992) (Scalia, J., dissenting).

At the present time, the Court appears to be moving toward a nonpreferentialist model, at least under circumstances in which the governmental assistance is directed toward the student (or parent) and not conferred directly on the school itself. In *Zobrest v. Catalina Foothills School District*,

509 U.S. 1 (1993), for example, the Court held that the Establishment Clause would not be violated by a governmental program that paid for a sign-language interpreter to be used by a hearing-impaired student attending a "pervasively sectarian" Catholic school. Two factors were deemed dispositive. First, the program was neutral from a religious perspective; i.e., it was nonpreferential. Second, the governmental aid went not to the school directly, but to the student. In essence, the private choice of the individual acted as a buffer between the government and the sectarian institution. That individual's choice to spend the government aid in a sectarian context was not, therefore, attributable to the government. See *Rosenberger v. Rector & Visitors of the Univ. of Va.*, 515 U.S. 819 (1995) (Establishment Clause not violated when state university pays for the printing of a sectarian student newspaper, in part because direct payment went to the printer and not to a religious organization).

EXAMPLE 9-G

The State of Grace has adopted a voucher system for funding all public and private schools, including parochial schools. Under this system, the parent of every school-aged child is entitled to a financial voucher that can be used to pay all or part of the tuition at whatever school the child attends. In essence, the voucher operates as an educational grant, the amount of which is equivalent to what it would cost to educate the child in a public school. A public school's budget will be the sum of the vouchers it receives from parents who send their children to that school. The vouchers will operate in the same way and provide the same per-child benefit for children enrolled in private schools. Does this voucher system violate the Establishment Clause?

EXPLANATION

Under separationist theory, applying the *Lemon* test, this voucher system might well run afoul of the Establishment Clause. A court could invalidate the scheme under the second part of the *Lemon* test by concluding that the voucher plan has the primary effect of advancing religion, since some governmental money would be used to finance sectarian studies. Or a court might find that the plan violates the third prong of the *Lemon* test, since the necessity of monitoring the school's expenditures to ensure that public money was not being spent to support religious studies would foster an excessive entanglement between church and state.

Under a nonpreferentialist approach, however, the voucher system might well be constitutional. The law creates no preferred status for a religion, and at least arguably, it does not provide direct aid to a religious institution. Rather, the aid is filtered through the parent; it is the parent, not the state, who decides whether any aid will be received by a sectarian institution. See *Mueller v. Allen*, 463 U.S. 388 (1983) (upholding neutral tax credit for expenses incurred by parents in providing tuition, textbooks, and transportation for their children attending public or private schools).

On the other hand, the amount of aid granted here is substantially greater than the amount involved in *Zobrest*, where the government paid only for the services of a sign language interpreter. Here the vouchers could be used to cover the entire operating expense of a sectarian school. Members of the Court who place themselves between the separationists and the non-preferentialists might well find this distinction significant. In other words, the fact that the aid is neutral and indirect may not itself be dispositive for these members of the Court. We will explore that possibility further below.

The Court made another nod toward nonpreferentialism in *Agostini v. Felton*, 521 U.S. 203 (1997). The essential question in *Agostini* was whether public employees could provide on-site remedial instruction to students attending sectarian schools. The program at issue was designed to provide students attending sectarian schools the same opportunities for remedial instruction that were available to public school students. In other words, the program was neutral from a religious point of view. The Court, however, had previously held that the precise program at issue in *Agostini* violated the Establishment Clause under the primary effect and excessive entanglement elements of the *Lemon* test. *Aguilar v. Felton*, 473 U.S. 402 (1985); *School Dist. of Grand Rapids v. Ball*, 473 U.S. 373 (1985). In *Agostini*, the parties argued that the jurisprudential basis for those decisions had been eroded by subsequent case law. The Court agreed, overruling both *Aguilar* and *Ball*. In so doing, the Court reaffirmed all three elements of the *Lemon* test, but reinterpreted the second and third elements, primary effect and excessive entanglement, in a manner that jettisoned much of their previous separation-ist character.

In order to fully appreciate the *Agostini* decision, some further elabo-ration of *Aguilar* and *Ball* is necessary. In *Ball*, the Court examined an analogous "shared time" program adopted by a Michigan school district. In finding that the program violated the Establishment Clause, the Court cited three factors that created an impermissible primary effect: (1) The presence of a public school teacher in a sectarian school created a substantial risk that the teacher would become subtly or overtly involved in the religious indoc-trination of her students; (2) the presence of the teacher created a symbolic union between church and state; and (3) the aid advanced the religious mission of sectarian schools by making it easier for those schools to pursue their sectarian goals. The program at issue in *Aguilar* suffered from the additional defect of excessive entanglement because the school board there had adopted a monitoring system designed to ensure that its public employ-ees did not inculcate religion while teaching at sectarian schools.

As to *Ball,* the *Agostini* Court explained that the factors relied on in that case were no longer deemed sufficient to establish an impermissible primary effect. To do so would exalt form over substance and would ignore jurisprudential developments subsequent to the *Ball* decision, particularly as applied in *Zobrest v. Catalina Foothills School District,* discussed above. In short, no longer will it be presumed that state-employed teachers who teach nonsectarian subjects in sectarian institutions will engage in religious inculcation; nor will it be presumed that their presence creates a symbolic union between government and religion. Finally, the fact that sectarian schools indirectly benefit from a government-sponsored remedial instruction program does not create a primary effect that advances religion. This is so for two reasons. First, the aid, i.e., the remedial instruction, goes directly to the student. Second, as long as the remedial program does not replicate services already provided by the benefited institutions, thereby relieving those schools of costs they would have otherwise borne, the primary effect remains secular.

As to *Aguilar* and excessive entanglement, the *Agostini* Court explained that this element was "an aspect of the inquiry into a statute's effect," essentially equating the second and third elements of the *Lemon* test. 521 U.S. at 233. Thus, it appears that only entanglements that have the effect of advancing or inhibiting religion will run afoul of the Establishment Clause. From this perspective, neither administrative cooperation between the state and sectarian institutions nor the potential for political divisiveness caused by such a cooperative program is sufficient, standing alone, to establish an excessive entanglement. There must be some showing that the governmental involvement has the effect of advancing or inhibiting religion in a manner sufficient to satisfy the "effects" test. Moreover, although the Court hinted that "pervasive" monitoring by the state might lead to an excessive entanglement by either advancing or inhibiting religion, a reasonable amount of monitoring to ensure that state employees do not engage in religious inculcation is well within constitutional bounds.

Having thus rejected the jurisprudential foundations of *Ball* and *Aguilar,* the Court overruled both cases and affirmed the constitutionality of the on-site remedial instruction program it had struck down in *Aguilar.* In so ruling, the Court emphasized that the program was neutral from the perspective of religion, was directed at supporting students and not institutions, and was carefully designed to avoid promoting the sectarian goals of the schools at which the program operated.

The Court's most recent foray into the realm of public aid to parochial schools revealed the fault lines of the emerging jurisprudence. *Mitchell v. Helms,* 120 S. Ct. 2530 (2000). At issue in *Mitchell* was a federal program under which state and local educational agencies received federal money to purchase educational materials and equipment which they could then loan to public and private elementary and secondary schools within their respective jurisdictions. The federal funds could not be used to supplant current programs, but only to supplement the overall curriculum. The range of items that could be purchased included library materials such as general circulation books, reference materials, and computer software and hardware for instructional use. All items purchased under the program were required to be secular in nature and no item purchased under the program could be used for sectarian purposes. Thus if a computer were purchased under the program, the computer could be lent to a parochial school, but the school was forbidden to use the computer to teach sectarian matters.

The precise issue before the Court was whether the federal program ran afoul of *Lemon*'s second prong, the primary effect test. The parties apparently conceded that the program had a secular purpose, and they did not raise excessive entanglement as an issue before the Court.

The Court upheld the program, but without a majority opinion. A four-person plurality opinion, which was authored by Justice Thomas and joined by Chief Justice Rehnquist, and Justices Scalia and Kennedy, adopted a distinctly nonpreferentialist perspective. In the plurality's view, the effects test was to be measured solely by a consideration of two questions derived from the *Agostini* decision, both of which focused on the issue of "neutrality." Did the government program seek to indoctrinate religion? And were the recipients of the aid selected by reference to religion? If either question was answered in the affirmative, the effects test and the principle of neutrality would be violated. If not, the program would be deemed neutral (i.e., nonpreferential) and within constitutional bounds. Given that the equipment and materials purchased under the program were themselves secular and that sectarian uses were forbidden, the first question was answered in the negative. The program itself did not indoctrinate religion. Nor was there any evidence that the recipients of the aid were chosen on religious criteria. In fact, the aid was dispersed based solely on the number of students enrolled at the school. In short, the government program was neutral and therefore within constitutional bounds.

The plurality also concluded that the potential for diversion of the equipment to sectarian uses by the parochial schools was constitutionally irrelevant. As long as the government itself did not participate in that diversion there was no violation of the Establishment Clause. "[A] government computer or overhead projector does not itself inculcate a religious message, even when it is conveying one." Id. at 2548. In essence, the plurality concluded that a diverted sectarian use was not attributable to the government but to private actors. Finally, although not an issue in the case, the plurality hinted that even direct financial aid to sectarian schools might be permissible as long as the government itself was not promoting the sectarian mission of the school. Id. at 2547 n.8.

Justice O'Connor's concurring opinion, which was joined by Justice Breyer, described the plurality's rationale as one of "unprecedented breadth." Id. at 2556. She agreed that the aid program was constitutional, but strongly disagreed with the "singular importance" the plurality had placed on neutrality, and with the plurality's assertion that the diversion of government aid to sectarian use was constitutionally permissible. The former was but one factor to consider in the "impermissible effect" analysis, and the latter would, in her estimation, amount to an unconstitutional endorsement of religion. For O'Connor, the constitutionality of the aid program resulted from the confluence of several factors: the neutral, secular criteria under which the aid was awarded; the fact that the aid supplemented and did not supplant the existing curriculum; the fact that no religious schools received government funds; the fact that the items purchased and loaned were secular; the fact that evidence of actual diversion was de minimis; and the inclusion in the program of adequate safeguards against diversion. Based on the foregoing, O'Connor concluded that the aid program neither advanced nor endorsed religion.

The dissent, authored by Justice Souter and joined by Justices Stevens and Ginsburg, provided a detailed rejection of the plurality's neutrality model and of the proposition that diversion of government aid to sectarian purposes was ever constitutionally permissible. The key question for the dissent was whether the aid supported the religious or the secular mission of the school. Resolution of that question required the consideration of a number of factors, including the government's neutrality in distributing the aid, the form of the aid (e.g., money, services, textbooks, equipment, etc.), the direct or indirect path from government to religious institution, the divertibility of the aid to sectarian uses, the potential of aid to reduce traditional expenditures of religious institutions, and the relative importance of the aid to the recipient. In short, the dissent called for a multi-factored analysis similar to that adopted by Justice O'Connor. The primary difference between the concurrence and the dissent was that the dissent placed dispositive significance on the divertibility of the aid to sectarian uses. In other words, the fact that a computer could be diverted to a religious use led the dissent to conclude that the provision of this type of aid was unconstitutional.

What can we say for certain about the *Mitchell* decision and the current state of the law regarding government aid to parochial schools? Combining the plurality and the concurrence, it seems clear that the government may under some circumstances provide parochial schools with aid that is potentially divertible to sectarian uses. To this extent the contrary impression left by *Wolman v. Walter,* supra, is overruled. Combining the concurrence and the dissent, however, it is equally clear that the Court has not adopted the nonpreferentialist model when the aid goes directly to the school, and that actual diversion of government aid to sectarian purposes is unconstitutional. Moreover, this same concurring and dissenting majority continues to be concerned about the form of the aid and the manner through which it is funneled to the religious institution. Thus, the majority of the Court — the concurrence and the dissent — requires a multi-factored assessment to determine whether the provision of aid to a religious institution has the impermissible effect of advancing or inhibiting religion. Here, the concurrence, which has a slightly more relaxed standard for assessing the potential unconstitutional effects, will likely provide the key to resolving borderline cases.

Reconsider Example 9-G. Do *Agostini* and *Mitchell* reveal how the Court will assess the constitutionality of a system in which government-issued vouchers are used to pay tuition in private, sectarian schools? Certainly the *Agostini* Court's emphasis on the neutrality of the remedial instruction program and on the fact that the aid went to students and not to secular institutions would suggest a charitable view toward a religiously neutral voucher system in which the aid was filtered through the private choices of parents. On the other hand, *Agostini,* which was decided on a five-four vote, does not necessarily resolve this question. And the concurring and dissenting opinions in *Mitchell* make the outcome far from obvious. One element deemed significant by the *Agostini* Court and the concurring and dissenting "majority" in *Mitchell* was the fact that the remedial instruction program at issue did not replicate programs already available at the sectarian institutions. Rather, it was a supplemental program on which those institutions did not depend for their survival. A system of vouchers may well be deemed more than supplemental, since the vouchers will be used to support, perhaps fully, the overall teaching mission of the sectarian schools. Some members of the Court, perhaps a majority, may consider this factor as indicative of direct aid that has the primary effect of advancing or endorsing religion.

§9.4.2   *Prayer in Public Schools*

Suppose that the Unity City School Board composes a prayer to be recited at the beginning of each school day by all students and faculty members who are willing to participate in the recital. The prayer is designed to be nondenominational: "Almighty God, we acknowledge our dependence upon Thee, and we beg Thy blessings upon us, our parents, our teachers, and our Country." Does the school board's action violate the Establishment Clause?

Under a strict application of separationist theory, the answer is yes, and the Court so held in *Engle v. Vitale,* 370 U.S. 421 (1962). The reason is simple: The law directly promotes a religious practice and in so doing lays waste to the wall of separation between church and state. It does not matter that the prayer is designated nondenominational or that students are not compelled to join in the recital. The school board's promotion of a religious practice is enough to offend the principles of the Establishment Clause. The *Lemon* test, which was adopted after the decision in *Engle,* would provide the same result. There is no discernible secular purpose to the school board's action, and even if there were such a purpose, the primary effect of promoting public school prayer is to advance religion.

Under a nonpreferentialist approach, the constitutionality of the school board's action depends on how one construes the board's prayer. If the prayer is assumed to be nondenominational, i.e., to create no preferred status for any particular religion or group of religions, then the school board's action would be constitutional. The board is free to promote religion as long as it does not discriminate against any particular religion. On the other hand, if the prayer were construed as promoting only a particular set of religious beliefs, then the school board's action would run afoul of the principle of nonpreference. In other words, the latter construction of the facts would take the problem out of this category and place it in the category of discrimination among religions, which was discussed earlier. As such, the school-endorsed recital of the prayer would be unconstitutional. See *Epperson v. Arkansas,* 393 U.S. 97 (1968) (invalidating religiously motivated law that prohibits teaching of evolution in public schools as inconsistent with the secular purpose element of *Lemon*); *Abington School Dist. v. Schemp,* 374 U.S. 203 (1963) (holding that public school may not require that the Lord's Prayer or passages from the Bible be recited at the beginning of each school day).

Unlike its decisions regarding public aid to parochial schools, the Court in this context has been reasonably consistent in following precedent. School prayer, at least government-sponsored school prayer, is simply not permitted. Thus, with respect to this particular subcategory, the theory of separationism, bolstered by stare decisis, is likely to remain the controlling principle. But see *Lee v. Weisman,* 505 U.S. at 632-636 (Scalia, J., dissenting) (arguing on historical grounds that the Establishment Clause should not be construed to prohibit a religious invocation at a public school graduation).

But suppose that our school board does not endorse or promote any particular prayer, but promotes prayer in general by providing students an opportunity to pray if they wish to do so and in any manner they choose. Would this action run afoul of the Establishment Clause? In *Wallace v. Jaffree,* 472 U.S. 38 (1985), the Court was confronted with an Alabama statute that authorized public schools to conduct a period of silence "for meditation or voluntary prayer." Although the statute endorsed no particular religion and authorized no particular prayer, the Court, nonetheless, held that the statute violated the Establishment Clause. The majority's analysis focused on the secular purpose element of the *Lemon* test. After analyzing the legislative history of this statute and predecessor statutes, the Court concluded that the purpose of the law was to promote religion. Indeed, the Court concluded that the statute "had no secular purpose." As a consequence, the Court invalidated the statute as an impermissible endorsement of religion.

The dissent, authored by Justice Rehnquist, challenged the underlying separationist model relied on by the majority. In the dissent's view, the Establishment Clause was not designed to prevent the government from taking action that favored religion over "irreligion." Rather, the purpose of the Clause was to prevent the creation of a government-sponsored religion and to preclude discrimination among sects. Since the Alabama statute did neither, but merely promoted religion generally, the Establishment Clause provided no basis for striking down the law. Rehnquist's opinion presents a classic statement and application of the nonpreferential model, and when compared with the majority opinion, it underscores the pragmatic distinction between separationist and nonpreferentialist theories.

This same tension arises in the context of prayer at public school graduations. In *Lee v. Weisman,* 505 U.S. 577 (1992), the Court held that the practice of inviting a cleric to recite a nonsectarian prayer at a high school or middle school graduation violated the Establishment Clause. This conclusion flows directly from separationist theory. The challenged practice had the primary effect of promoting religion and, given the school district's guidelines for the composition of nonsectarian prayers, fostered an excessive entanglement between church and state. The majority opinion, however, ignored *Lemon* and relied instead on the coercion model noted above, concluding that students at the graduation were psychologically coerced to join in the prayer.

The "rule" to be derived from the *Lee* decision is somewhat difficult to discern. Four of the five Justices in the majority joined concurring opinions that struck decidedly separationist themes and saw "coercion" as a sufficient, though not a necessary, element of an Establishment Clause violation. Id. at 599 (Blackmun, J., concurring); id. at 609 (Souter, J., concurring). Those same Justices have tended to be favorably disposed toward the *Lemon* test. The four dissenters, on the other hand, provided a scathing critique of what they described as the majority's "ersatz, 'peer-pressure' psycho-coercion" test. Id. at 641 (Scalia, J., dissenting). The dissent also argued that the Establishment Clause should not be construed to invalidate historical practices that are an accepted part of our cultural heritage. In the dissent's estimation, the invocation of God at public ceremonies, including at public school graduations, was precisely such a historical practice. In addition, the dissent sounded a theme of nonpreferentialism by arguing that the recital of a nondenominational prayer did not violate any true principles of the Establishment Clause — in essence, no religion was granted a preferred status.

The sole proponent of the notion that "coercion" was the essence of an Establishment Clause violation was Justice Kennedy, the author of the majority opinion. Presumably, in the absence of coercion, he would have joined the dissent, thus making coercion a necessary component of the result in *Lee.* The decision in *Lee,* therefore, is an example of a case in which a compromise was struck between the principles of separationism and nonpreferentialism.

Under that compromise, governmental action that both promotes *and* co-erces participation in a religious practice will violate the Establishment Clause.

EXAMPLE 9-H

Prior to 1995, a student elected as Santa Fe High School's student council chaplain delivered a prayer, sometimes overtly Christian, over the school's public address system before each home varsity football game. This practice was sanctioned and promoted by the school district itself and was part of school-sponsored pre-game activities. Santa Fe High School is a public school and the school district is a political subdivision of the state. The school's population is heavily Southern Baptist. Mormon and Catholic students ob-jected to the practice and filed a suit challenging it under the Establishment Clause. While the suit was pending, the school district revised its policy to authorize two student elections, the first to determine by majority vote whether prayers should be delivered at football games, and the second to choose the individual who would select and deliver those prayers. Is the new policy unconstitutional?

EXPLANATION

Let's begin with the *Lemon* test. First, does the new policy have a secular purpose? One could argue that the secular purpose of the policy is to foster good sportsmanship and a positive environment for competition. Yet nothing in the policy itself or in the history of its adoption suggests that the prayer was ever intended to promote either of these ideals. Moreover, given that the new policy grew out of a prior practice in which the school district directly promoted prayer at high school football games, it would appear that the purpose of the new policy was simply to preserve that practice and at the same time avoid an Establishment Clause challenge to it. If the sole purpose was to promote prayer, the policy is unconstitutional, i.e., there is no secular purpose. Second, even if there is a secular purpose, the primary effect of the new policy would appear to be the promotion of prayer by intentionally creating a vehicle through which that end and that end alone could be accomplished. Third, given that the policy was created and supervised by the school district, the process of dual elections may well foster an excessive entanglement between church and state. A classic separationist would, there-fore, find the policy unconstitutional.

A similar conclusion derives from both the endorsement and coercion models. Under the former, the school district has placed its imprimatur on a religious practice, namely, prayer, perhaps even Christian prayer, by creating a system through which prayer will be promoted with the use of school facilities at school-sponsored events and under circumstances in which those attending the event are likely to presume the school's endorsement of the prayer. A contrary argument would be that the school district has not endorsed prayer, but merely given students the choice of whether they wish to engage in that activity. But again, it is the school district that is purposefully providing this religious opportunity through the use of school facilities. This is not a case of students spontaneously praying at a football game. As to coercion, one must ask whether students attending or participating in the game are being coerced into joining the prayer. The case for coercion is probably not as strong as that in *Lee v. Weisman,* where the activity was a graduation ceremony in which attendance was essentially mandatory. On the other hand, for those attending the football game, including players, cheerleaders, band members, and team supporters, the pressure to conform may be just as great as it would be at a graduation. It would seem, therefore, that even under these middle ground positions, the policy violates the Establishment Clause.

Finally, under a nonpreferentialist model, one might want more facts regarding the nature of the prayers recited. If the prayers are sufficiently nondenominational, a nonpreferentialist would be unlikely to find a violation of the Establishment Clause. On the other hand, if the prayers were overtly Christian, the principle of nonpreferentialism might well be violated. Yet even if the prayers are distinctly sectarian, as Justice Thomas suggested in *Mitchell v. Helms,* supra, there might be no violation of the principle of government neutrality. Under this view of nonpreferentialism, the choice of prayer would not be attributable to school but to the private individual reciting it. Similarly, some members of the Court might find prayers at high school football games to be part of our historical culture in which the name of God is invoked at public ceremonies. For them there would be no violation of the Establishment Clause.

The Court, confronted with similar circumstances, held that the school district's dual election system violated the Establishment Clause. In the Court's view, the school district's policy had three major flaws. First, applying the *Lemon* test, the Court concluded that there was no secular purpose behind the policy. Looking at the face of the policy and the circumstances under which it was adopted, the Court concluded that the sole purpose of the policy was to promote a religious practice. Next, the Court held that by granting a majority of the students the power to select prayers to be recited at a school-sponsored event, the school district had endorsed a religious practice. Moreover, those attending the football games would reasonably assume that the prayer was endorsed by the school district. Finally, relying on *Lee v. Weisman,* the Court concluded that the recital of school-sponsored prayers prior to football games would coerce participation by other students attending the game, some of whom were compelled to be there by virtue of their extra-curricular responsibilities. *Santa Fe Independent School District v. Doe,* 120 S. Ct. 2266 (2000). The three dissenters (Chief Justice Rehnquist, joined by Justices Scalia and Thomas) criticized the majority for relying on *Lemon,* for refusing to credit the school district's secular purpose, and for failing to recognize that the prayer was to be recited by a student and not by a representative of the school district itself. Id. at 2283.

Suppose that a class valedictorian presents an address to the graduating class in which she gives thanks to God and asks her fellow students to join in that thanksgiving. Would such a speech violate the Establishment Clause? Under the Court's current jurisprudence, there is a strong argument that it would not. Applying the *Lemon* test, separationists on the Court would probably find no violation of the Establishment Clause. First, as long as the choice of the valedictorian is on the basis of nonreligious criteria, the secular purpose requirement of *Lemon* will be easily satisfied. Second, one could certainly argue that the primary effect of the school's participation in that speech is to recognize a student whose nonreligious achievements have entitled her to the honor of addressing her class, though that argument would be slightly less persuasive if the speech were completely sectarian. Third, unless the school dictates the content of the speech, there will be no excessive entanglement between church and state.

The same result is achieved under either an endorsement or a coercion approach. The school has not endorsed the content of the speech, and there is no state-imposed coercion to join the speaker in giving thanks to God. Of course, additional facts could alter one's conclusions on these points. Thus, if the school made it clear that the speaker was speaking for the school, a very different conclusion might well emerge. Finally, proponents of nonpreferentialism would have no objection whatsoever to a speech that gave thanks to God, and they certainly would not object to a religiously neutral school policy that permitted an outstanding student to address the graduating class. See *Westside Community Bd. of Educ. v. Mergens,* 496 U.S. 226 (1990) (a plurality of the Court found no violation of the *Lemon* test in a school policy that would allow the Christian Club to meet on a public high school campus under the same rules applicable to nonreligious clubs, while two other members of the Court concluded that the neutrality of the policy satisfied the Establishment Clause).

In sum, the Court's jurisprudence in the context of prayer in public schools has been relatively consistent. The Court will not allow a public school to sponsor prayer in the classroom or at other school events, including those prayers that can be characterized as nondenominational. Separationist theory has been and remains the dominant theory in this context. On the other hand, truly voluntary student-led prayers on public school campuses will not run afoul of the Establishment Clause.

§9.4.3   Other Contexts

Establishment Clause challenges to governmental action that promotes or provides aid to religion or religious institutions may also arise in a variety of other contexts, including the public display of religious symbols (particularly during the holiday seasons), tax exemptions for religious institutions, released time from public school for religious studies, aid to sectarian colleges and universities, the participation of religious institutions in secular governmental programs, and the delegation of governmental power to religious institutions. The themes, techniques, and debates that arise in the contexts of public school prayer and public aid to elementary and secondary schools arise as well in these other contexts. One can expect, therefore, that the move toward nonpreferentialism will have an impact on the jurisprudence of these various subcategories and that the *Lemon* test will continue to be subject to criticism and intermittent expendability. One can also expect, however, that stare decisis will continue to have some influence over the direction the Court will take in each of these subcategories.

EXAMPLE 9-I

Several taxpayers have filed suit in federal court, challenging, on Establishment Clause grounds, the display of a nativity scene and a menorah in the rotunda of City Hall during the winter holiday season. The city permits such displays as long as the costs of constructing, maintaining, and dismantling them are not borne by the city. How will a court rule?

EXPLANATION

From the perspective of separationism, the display could well violate the first and second elements of the *Lemon* test. It is difficult to discern a secular purpose for the display of these two deeply religious symbols, and one would think that the primary effect of the display is to advance religion. Similarly, under the endorsement model, the city appears to be endorsing the two religions represented by closely associating the government with what is clearly a religious message. On the other hand, a coercion model would not necessarily lead to the same conclusion. Passersby in City Hall are not required to acknowledge this display in any manner. And from the perspective of nonpreferentialism, as long as the city's policy is neutral with respect to the religious symbols that may be displayed, there is no violation of the Establishment Clause. Similarly, using tradition and history as a measure of the Establishment Clause, one might well conclude that such displays are within an acceptable range of governmental action. In short, the answer depends on the controlling perspective from which the problem is analyzed. Compare *Lynch v. Donnelly*, 465 U.S. 668 (1984) (upholding constitutionality of municipal policy that permitted a holiday display that included both sectarian and secular symbols) with *County of Allegheny v. American Civil Liberties Union,* 492 U.S. 573 (1989) (holding that display of creche on county courthouse grounds violates Establishment Clause).

§9.5   The Free Exercise Clause

The Free Exercise Clause provides, "Congress shall make no law . . . prohibiting the free exercise" of religion. This language has been interpreted as protecting the right of an individual to adhere to whatever religious doctrine or faith that individual chooses to believe. This protection of religious belief is, as a practical matter, absolute. A corollary of this freedom to believe is the right to profess one's chosen beliefs. Incursions on this right are generally examined under traditional, rigorous free speech standards.

The Free Exercise Clause also protects religiously motivated conduct, but not to the same extent as it does the rights to believe and to profess those beliefs. Although religiously motivated conduct was once protected under a strict scrutiny test, the current Court has adopted a less solicitous attitude toward most such conduct. Only laws that are specifically directed toward regulating conduct *because of* its religious nature are subject to heightened scrutiny. Laws that regulate conduct *despite* its religious nature are not subject to such exacting review.

§9.5.1   *The Distinction between Belief and Conduct*

While the distinction between belief and conduct often plays a critical role in determining the appropriate level of judicial scrutiny to be applied under the Free Exercise Clause, there is no bright-line test for determining whether a law regulates belief or conduct. At times the distinction between belief and conduct is less than obvious. For example, in *McDaniel v. Paty,* 435 U.S. 618 (1978), a state law disqualified "ministers of the Gospel" from participating in a state constitutional convention. Although seven members of the Court agreed that the provision violated the Free Exercise Clause, there was no majority opinion for the Court. Three Justices thought that the law impinged on an individual's beliefs, since its application depended on the intensity of those beliefs, i.e., beliefs that were sufficiently intense to cause one to choose the ministry. These Justices, therefore, concluded that the law transgressed the absolute protection afforded religious belief. Four Justices, however, thought that the law was directed primarily toward religious conduct, i.e., action taken in the capacity as a minister, and that it was, therefore, not subject to the same strict level of protection as that afforded religious belief. Yet they did agree that the law violated the Free Exercise Clause, but under a slightly more deferential standard.

Although there is no bright-line test for determining whether a particular law regulates belief or conduct, an effective way to measure the distinction is to examine the regulatory focus of the law being challenged. If the regulatory focus of the law is on an individual's *thought processes* or on the *mental conclusions* the individual may have derived from those processes, then the law is belief-centered and subject to the absolute prohibition imposed by the Free Exercise Clause. On the other hand, if the regulatory focus of the law is directed toward *external actions* triggered by those thought processes and mental conclusions, the law is conduct-centered and not subject to the absolute prohibition. In most cases, the distinction between thought processes and external action will be apparent from the interaction between the challenged law and the particular facts presented.

EXAMPLE 9-J

Dickie is a member of a religious group that absolutely prohibits the use of violence toward fellow human beings. On the basis of his religious beliefs, Dickie refused to sign an oath affirming the duty of all citizens to defend with arms the Constitution of the United States. Due to this refusal, Dickie was denied a position as a public school teacher. If Dickie were to challenge the government's action under the Free Exercise Clause, would the case be treated as involving a regulation of belief or conduct?

EXPLANATION

Although the act of signing the oath can be fairly characterized as conduct, the government's attention is focused not so much on the refusal to sign as on what that refusal signifies, namely, a particular belief. Ultimately, Dickie is being denied a job because of what he believes. The government's action, therefore, runs afoul of the absolute prohibition against the regulation of belief.

On the other hand, if Dickie were drafted to fight in a war (assuming that he was not entitled to statutory conscientious objector status) and refused to serve on the basis of his religious beliefs, any punishment for that refusal to fight would presumably involve a regulation of his conduct. Although Dickie's refusal was premised on belief, the focus of the government's attention is not on Dickie's beliefs, but on his external action. The punishment for refusing to fight applies regardless of a person's motivation and would have been the same had Dickie's refusal stemmed from cowardice. The government's action, therefore, would not run afoul of the absolute prohibition against the regulation of belief and would be evaluated under the less stringent standard that applies to religiously motivated conduct.

§9.5.2   *The Protection of Religious Belief*

The protection afforded religious belief is essentially absolute. Individuals or groups are entitled to believe anything they choose to believe, no matter how improbable, pernicious, or plain silly that belief may be. As the Court recently observed, "The free exercise of religion means, first and foremost, the right to believe and profess whatever religious doctrine one desires. Thus, the First Amendment obviously excludes all 'governmental regulation of religious *beliefs* as such.' The government may not compel affirmation of religious belief, punish the expression of religious doctrines it believes to be false, impose special disabilities on the basis of religious views or religious status, or lend its power to one or the other side in controversies over religious authority or dogma." *Employment Div. v. Smith,* 494 U.S. 872, 877 (1990).

One of the most important cases arising in this context is *West Virginia State Board of Education v. Barnette,* 319 U.S. 624 (1943). In that case, a group of Jehovah's Witnesses brought suit, seeking to enjoin a West Virginia law that required all public school students to participate daily in the salute to the flag and in the recital of the Pledge of Allegiance. The Witnesses objected to the compelled flag salute and Pledge as contravening the Bible's Exodus, Chapter 20, verses 4 and 5, which states: "Thou shalt not make unto thee any graven image, or any likeness of anything that is in heaven above, or that is in the earth beneath, or that is in the water under the earth; thou shalt not bow down thyself to them nor serve them." The Witnesses believed that both the salute and the Pledge violated these Biblical admonitions.

Although the challenged law was in a sense directed toward conduct — saluting the flag and reciting the Pledge — the Court interpreted the state law as primarily directed toward the public affirmation of what an individual believed. As a consequence, the Court held that the state law violated the First Amendment by compelling the Witnesses to affirm a belief they did not share with the community. The Court declared:

> If there is any fixed star in our constitutional constellation, it is that no official, high or petty, can prescribe what shall be orthodox in politics, nationalism, religion, or other matters of opinion or force citizens to confess by word or act their faith therein. If there are any circumstances which permit an exception, they do not now occur to us.

Id. at 642. The holding and principles of *Barnette* have been consistently followed, particularly in the context of religious belief. See *Torcaso v. Watkins,* 367 U.S. 488, 495-496 (1961) (holding unconstitutional a state law that required an individual to affirm a belief in God in order to obtain a governmental commission).

EXAMPLE 9-K

Pete was indicted for mail fraud. The indictment charged a scheme to defraud on the basis of Pete's promotion of the "I Can" movement and his asserted belief that he was the appointed messenger of God, that he had shaken hands with Jesus, and that he had the divine power to cure incurable diseases. Could the jury, consistent with the First Amendment, convict Pete on the basis of its conclusion that his claimed religious beliefs were in fact false?

EXPLANATION

No. Although a jury could examine Pete's good faith in asserting these beliefs, i.e., whether Pete actually entertained the professed beliefs, it could not attempt to determine the truth or falsity of those beliefs. To do so would undermine the freedom of religion by giving government the power to determine the truth of religious belief and doctrine and to then punish those found to hold "false" beliefs. See *United States v. Ballard*, 322 U.S. 78 (1944).

In this example, as in *Barnette*, the determination of unconstitutionality was premised on a single inquiry, i.e., whether the contested governmental action was aimed at a religious belief. An affirmative answer to that inquiry led directly to a finding of unconstitutionality. There was no balancing of interests, strict or otherwise. The protection of belief is, in this sense, absolute.

The Right to Profess Religious Beliefs

The protection of religious belief also includes the right to profess one's beliefs freely and openly. In *Cantwell v. Connecticut*, 310 U.S. 296, 304 (1940), the Court observed, "No one would contest the proposition that a State may not, by statute, wholly deny the right to preach or to disseminate religious views." And just as the government may not declare any particular religious belief to be false or heretical, the government may not outlaw the expression of unpopular or offensive religious views merely because those views do not comport with some generally accepted notion of what is true from a religious perspective.

However, the right to profess one's religious beliefs is not absolute. It stands on the same footing as the First Amendment right to profess one's political beliefs. In neither case may the government suppress the expression of those beliefs simply because the beliefs are deemed to be false, pernicious, or even dangerous. Yet the government may, as we saw in Chapter 8, sometimes restrict such expression if it is able to satisfy a very strict standard of judicial review. Speech professing one's religious beliefs or promoting religious dogma is thus not protected under all circumstances. In general, the protection afforded religious expression differs little, if at all, from the protection afforded speech generally, and a content-based restriction on an individual's ability to express religious ideas will be subject to the same searching scrutiny as would a content-based restriction on political speech

EXAMPLE 9-L

Cantwell is a Jehovah's Witness. He believes it is his duty to proselytize his faith and to demonstrate the corruption of organized religions. Consistent with these beliefs, Cantwell introduced himself to two strangers on a street corner and with their permission played a recording for them that was highly critical of the Catholic Church. Though both individuals were highly incensed by what was said on the recording, no violence ensued. Cantwell was, nonetheless, convicted of inciting a breach of the peace. Did Cantwell's conviction violate his free speech or free exercise rights?

EXPLANATION

The conviction violated Cantwell's free speech rights. In a case with similar facts, the Supreme Court reversed the defendant's conviction, holding that since he had done no more than express an idea that his listeners found offensive, he could not be convicted consistent with the free speech guarantee of the First Amendment. The Free Exercise Clause, though mentioned by the Court in passing, added nothing to its analysis. *Cantwell v. Connecticut,* 310 U.S. at 307-311.

However, religious speech that does present a clear and present danger to public safety may, like political speech, be subject to governmental restriction.

EXAMPLE 9-M

The Cult of the Avenging Angel is a modern apocalyptic religion that believes the path to salvation will be found in swift vengeance on its enemies. Members of the cult are taught that each one of them has a duty to seek vengeance on any person who harms the cult in any manner. May the government outlaw the teaching of this belief?

EXPLANATION

It depends. The government may not outlaw the teaching of this belief merely because it represents an evil or pernicious doctrine. But if the government can show that the circumstances under which this doctrine is being taught are such as to create a clear and present danger of an imminent harm, such as specific harm to a particular individual, then consistent with both the

Free Speech and the Free Exercise Clauses, that particular dissemination of this idea can be proscribed or punished. See §8.3.2.

Similarly, just as content-based restrictions on religious speech must satisfy strict scrutiny, content-neutral restrictions are subject to time, place, and manner standards.

EXAMPLE 9-N

The Knights of Columbus, a religious organization affiliated with the Roman Catholic Church, wish to sponsor an interfaith parade celebrating the theme "Religion in America." The city in which the Knights hope to hold the parade requires parade sponsors to apply for and obtain a parade permit and, should the permit be granted, to comply with various regulations designed to promote the safe and efficient use of city streets while the parade is in progress. What First Amendment standards should be applied to assess the constitutionality of the parade permit requirement?

EXPLANATION

Because both the permit application process and the regulations are content neutral, the proper standards for assessing the city's permit procedures and regulations are those developed under the time, place, and manner test applicable to parades generally. The religious nature of the message to be conveyed by this planned parade does not alter those standards.

The congruity between the freedom of speech and the freedom to profess one's religious beliefs also means that religious speech cannot be treated less favorably than other protected speech. Thus, in *Rosenberger v. Rector & Visitors of the University of Virginia*, 515 U.S. 819 (1995), the Court held that a state university cannot refuse to fund a student publication merely because that publication espouses a religious viewpoint. The religious nature of the proposed publication does not lessen the protections afforded by the First Amendment guarantee of free speech. Here, the state's refusal was not viewpoint neutral and, as a consequence, violated the strict standards that protect speech in a limited public forum. See §8.5. The Court also found that funding the publication, under neutral principles, does not violate the Establishment Clause.

Ecclesiastical Disputes

The protection afforded religious belief is also implicated when the government attempts to insinuate itself into an ecclesiastical dispute within a church hierarchy. For example, in *Presbyterian Church v. Hull Church*, 393 U.S. 440 (1969), a general church organization became involved in a dispute with two local churches that had been members of the general church. The dispute involved the ownership of certain property that the local churches held in trust for the general church. The controversy arose when the local churches withdrew from the general church and thereafter claimed ownership of the property, their theory being that the general church had abandoned certain doctrinal tenets, thereby relinquishing its interest in the property. This theory was consistent with state law, and after a trial in state court, the position of the local churches was sustained by a jury. The Supreme Court reversed, holding that a court may not become embroiled in a property dispute within a church if resolution of that dispute requires the court to resolve a controversy over religious doctrine. Whether the general church had abandoned previously held doctrinal tenets fell directly within that category and was not, therefore, subject to judicial resolution.

Similarly, the Free Exercise Clause precludes courts from becoming embroiled in conflicts involving the internal operations of a church or religion, at least in the absence of some showing of fraud or deceit.

EXAMPLE 9-O

The Holy Synod of the Serbian Orthodox Church removed and defrocked the Bishop for the American Canadian Diocese of that church. The removed bishop challenged this action as arbitrary under the internal regulations of the church. He filed suit in state court, seeking reinstatement. May a court grant the requested relief?

EXPLANATION

Even assuming that the church did act arbitrarily in applying its own internal regulations, the First Amendment precludes a court from interfering with the church's decision, at least in the absence of some showing of fraud or deceit. *Serbian Orthodox Diocese v. Milivojevich*, 426 U.S. 696 (1976).

Of course, the mere fact that a church is involved in a legal controversy does not disable the judiciary or the government generally from resolving that controversy. The First Amendment is only implicated when the resolution of such a controversy requires the judiciary or the government to become embroiled in a religious doctrinal dispute or in a dispute over the application of the internal rules and regulations of a church.

§9.5.3 The Protection of Religiously Motivated Conduct

As we noted earlier, the Free Exercise Clause also protects religiously motivated conduct, though the protection may not be as strong as that afforded
religious beliefs. The phrase "religiously motivated conduct" denotes action
taken in compliance with one's religious beliefs, such as drinking wine as part
of a Catholic mass or ingesting peyote in compliance with the tenets of the
Native American Church. A Quaker's scripture-based refusal to bear arms
against a fellow human being is another example of religiously motivated
conduct. The key factor in each of these examples is the presence of a
religious motivation for the action undertaken or refused. In the absence of
such a motivation, the consumption of wine, the ingestion of peyote, and
the refusal to bear arms would constitute purely secular conduct and would
be entitled to no protection under the Free Exercise Clause.

The protection afforded religiously motivated conduct is dependent on
the type of law involved. For these purposes, laws that potentially infringe
on religious conduct can be divided into three categories: (1) laws that
regulate or prohibit religious conduct *because of* its religious nature or only
when that conduct is engaged in for religious purposes; (2) laws that regulate
religious conduct *despite* its religious nature; and (3) laws that regulate
nonreligious conduct, but that incidentally *burden* religious practices. The
Free Exercise consequences of each of these types of laws will be discussed
below.

The Purposeful Suppression of Religiously Motivated Conduct

The Free Exercise Clause severely limits the government's authority to enact
a law that regulates religiously motivated conduct specifically *because of* that
conduct's religious nature or only when that conduct is engaged in for
religious purposes. Such a law is not neutral within the meaning of the Free
Exercise Clause, since the law uses religion as a criterion for the application
of governmental power. This lack of neutrality creates a presumption of
invalidity that can only be rebutted through satisfaction of the strict scrutiny
test. Thus, only if the government can demonstrate that the challenged law
advances a compelling interest through the least restrictive means available
will the law be upheld. The instances in which this test will be satisfied under
the Free Exercise Clause are extraordinarily rare.

Not all laws that regulate religiously motivated conduct fall into this
category. The key question is whether the government's action is purposefully aimed at religion. For example, a law that by its specific terms prohibits
the *sacramental* drinking of wine regulates conduct because of its religious

nature, while a law that prohibits the consumption of wine regardless of the circumstances under which it is consumed does not. The first example describes a law that is purposefully directed toward the suppression of a religious practice, while the second describes a neutral law that happens to sweep a religious practice within its scope. The free exercise implications for this latter type of law are discussed in the next subsection.

The leading case involving the deliberate regulation of religious conduct is *Church of the Lukumi Babalu Aye, Inc. v. City of Hialeah*, 508 U.S. 520 (1993). At issue in that case was a series of city ordinances that prohibited the ritual or sacrificial killing of animals within city limits. The ordinances were adopted in response to the Santeria religion, whose religious ceremonies include the ritual sacrifice of animals. A Santerian church brought suit in federal court, seeking to enjoin enforcement of the ordinance. The church claimed a violation of the Free Exercise Clause. The key question for the Court was whether these ordinances were adopted *because of* the religious nature of the practices at issue. If they were, then the ordinances would be subjected to a rigorous and presumptively fatal application of the strict scrutiny test.

The Court approached this "because of" inquiry from two perspectives, each designed to determine whether the laws' real purpose was to suppress a religious practice. First, the Court considered whether the city ordinances were neutral in the sense that their adoption was independent of the religious nature of the practice being prohibited. The ordinances did not satisfy this test. Both the text of the ordinances, which used religious terms such as *ritual* and *sacrifice*, and the events leading up to their adoption, which indicated an animosity for the Santeria religion, made it clear that the object of these ordinances was the suppression of a religious practice. The ordinances also included an exemption for licenced slaughterhouses, seeming to favor the secular killing of animals and further demonstrating a lack of neutral purpose.

Second, the Court considered whether, in terms of their practical effect, the ordinances could be considered laws of general applicability. In other words, the Court asked whether the scope of these ordinances encompassed a wide array of related activities in order to advance a legitimate legislative purpose or whether it placed the entire burden of the law on activities of a religious nature. In the latter case, it could be inferred that the measures were enacted because of their impact on this religious practice. Here, the Court noted that if, as the city suggested, the purpose of these ordinances was to prevent the inhumane treatment of animals and promote public health, the ordinances were substantially underinclusive, since the proscription of the law only applied when those interests were threatened by religiously motivated conduct. As a consequence, the ordinances could not be fairly characterized as laws of general applicability.

Since the ordinances were neither neutral nor of general applicability, the Court concluded that they were enacted because of, not despite, the impact on a religious practice. The Court, therefore, applied the strict scrutiny test. The purported interests of the city—the humane treatment of animals and public health — although perhaps compelling in the abstract, were not deemed compelling under the circumstances, since the ordinances did so little to advance those interests. So, too, the ordinances were overbroad and underinclusive, and hence not narrowly tailored to advance the city's purported interests. In short, the ordinances failed the strict scrutiny test.

The *Church of the Lukumi Babalu Aye* was an unusual case, for the facts and circumstances made it obvious that the city's action was designed to suppress the religious practices of the Santeria religion. More typically, free exercise challenges to governmental action that proscribes religiously motivated conduct arise in contexts where it is more difficult to prove that the government was deliberately aiming at a religious practice.

EXAMPLE 9-P

Imagine yourself in the nineteenth century. The Territory of Utah has been settled by adherents to the Mormon religion. Members of that religion are admonished to practice polygamy or else risk eternal damnation. Congress passes a law proscribing the practice of polygamy in the territories. A practicing Mormon who has taken a second wife is prosecuted and convicted under this law. He defends, arguing that his conduct was motivated by his sincere religious beliefs and is, therefore, protected by the Free Exercise Clause. Can the government argue that the law is neutral or of general applicability?

EXPLANATION

Yes. The proscription applies regardless of one's religious motivation: It proscribes polygamy under all circumstances. This example is, therefore, quite unlike *Church of the Lukumi Babalu Aye*, where the lack of neutrality and general applicability was plain. One could argue, however, that the anti-polygamy law was not neutral if it could be shown that its specific purpose was to outlaw a practice engaged in by members of what was at that time considered a radical and dangerous religion. Given the law's appearance of neutrality and general applicability, however, the burden of establishing this illicit motive would be substantial. See *Reynolds v. United States*, 98 U.S. (8 Otto) 145 (1878) (upholding anti-polygamy law against a free exercise challenge).

In sum, if an individual can establish that the government has taken action specifically designed to suppress a religious practice, then the governmental action will be subject to strict scrutiny, requiring both a compelling governmental interest and the least restrictive means to advance that interest. If, however, the challenged action can be fairly described as neutral or of general applicability, this rigorous constitutional standard will not apply.

The Nonpurposeful Regulation of Religiously Motivated Conduct

As discussed in the prior section, a law specifically directed toward the proscription of a religious practice "prohibits" the free exercise of religion within the meaning of the Free Exercise Clause. But can a law that is neutral from the perspective of the Free Exercise Clause, but that, nonetheless, sweeps within its proscription some conduct of a religious nature, also be deemed to be a law "prohibiting" the free exercise of religion?

For example, suppose that a law proscribes the ingestion of peyote under any and all circumstances. If one wishes to ingest peyote for religious purposes, as would a member of the Native American Church, the law prohibits that ingestion. Thus, the law literally "prohibits" a religious practice even if the purpose of the law is not to suppress a religious practice as such. But does this type of nonpurposeful prohibition, i.e., one emanating from an otherwise neutral law of general applicability, run afoul of the Free Exercise Clause?

The Court has not been consistent in its answer to this question. The two most important cases are *Wisconsin v. Yoder*, 406 U.S. 205 (1972), and *Employment Division v. Smith*, 494 U.S. 872 (1990). In *Yoder*, the Court applied strict scrutiny to a neutral statute that punished religiously motivated conduct, while in *Smith*, the Court concluded that strict scrutiny was not warranted for such a statute. We will examine each case in turn. As the law now stands, however, a neutral law of general applicability will not be subject to strict scrutiny as a matter of constitutional law merely because that law sweeps religiously motivated conduct within its coverage.

Wisconsin v. Yoder involved a free exercise challenge to a Wisconsin compulsory school-attendance law that required all children residing within the state to attend public or private school until age 16. Amish parents whose children were subject to this law refused to send their children to school past the eighth grade, claiming that to do otherwise would violate fundamental principles of their religion by risking the spiritual salvation of their children. The Supreme Court held that enforcement of the compulsory school-attendance law against the Amish parents violated their free exercise rights.

Yoder involved neither the regulation of belief nor the purposeful suppression of religiously motivated conduct. Nonetheless, the Court held that the Wisconsin compulsory school-attendance law could not be applied to Amish children unless the state established that doing so would advance "interests of the highest order" that could not be "otherwise served" by measures that did not encroach on the religious freedom of the Amish — in essence, unless the state could overcome the standards of strict scrutiny.

Yoder and the cases following it did not, however, establish a blanket immunity for all religiously motivated conduct. The heightened scrutiny described in *Yoder* was not necessarily fatal to the law being challenged. For example, in *United States v. Lee*, 455 U.S. 252 (1982), a member of the Old Order Amish claimed that paying Social Security taxes as an employer violated principles of his religion. Despite the clash between religion and state, the Court found no violation of the Free Exercise Clause. "The state may justify a limitation on religious liberty by showing that it is essential to accomplish an overriding governmental interest." Id. at 257. In general, however, in the post-*Yoder* world, governmental action that regulated or prohibited conduct of a religious nature was subject to some form of strict scrutiny under the Free Exercise Clause even if the government did not purposefully target religious activity.

EXAMPLE 9-Q

The Unity City School Board has voted to expand the school week from five to six days in order to make better use of overcrowded school facilities. Under the new plan, all students will be required to attend classes on Saturdays at least two-thirds of the school year. In order to avoid charges of favoritism, the board has refused to recognize any exceptions to this Saturday attendance rule. Several students have objected to the new policy on the grounds that their religion commands that they do no work on Saturday, their Sabbath. Does the board's policy violate the Free Exercise Clause?

EXPLANATION

Although the board's policy regulates conduct and not belief, and is neutral and of general application, the policy, nonetheless, impairs the free exercise of religion by requiring the students to take action inconsistent with their religious beliefs. Under *Yoder*, the policy can be applied to these students only if the board can establish that the law serves an interest of the highest order and does so in a manner essential to advance that interest. It is unlikely that the board could make such a showing in this case.

All of this changed with the Court's decision in *Employment Division v. Smith*, 494 U.S. 872 (1990). *Smith* involved an Oregon statute that criminalized the possession of peyote, a hallucinogenic drug derived from certain cactus plants. Members of the Native American Church challenged the constitutionality of this statute as applied to their religious use of peyote within the church's religious ceremonies. There was no claim that the law was specifically designed to suppress the religious practices of the Native American Church. The law in question was concededly neutral and of general applicability. The religious practices of the church just happened to fall within the general proscription of the law, just as had the practices of the Amish parents in *Yoder*. The *Smith* Court held that the Free Exercise Clause was not implicated, since the law being challenged was "not specifically directed" at the religious practices of the Native American Church. Under *Smith,* the free exercise protection for religiously motivated conduct is limited to circumstances such as those present in *Church of the Lukumi Babalu Aye*, where a law is specifically directed at the suppression of a religious practice.

Smith's reinterpretation of the Free Exercise Clause was premised in part on a policy judgment regarding the proper scope of that Clause within a pluralistic society. According to the Court, "[B]ecause 'we are a cosmopolitan nation made up of people of almost every conceivable religious preference,' and precisely because we value and protect that religious divergence, we cannot afford the luxury of deeming *presumptively invalid,* as applied to the religious objector, every regulation of conduct that does not protect an interest of the highest order." 494 U.S. at 888 (quoting *Braunfeld v. Brown*, 366 U.S. 599, 606 (1961)). The price of this policy judgment is that the values and practices of a minority religion — such as the Native American Church — may be ignored in the majoritarian political process. Thus, although under *Smith* the practices of a minority religion may not be deliberately suppressed, such practices may fall victim to the majority's unwitting interference with a religious practice that the members of that majority do not share.

EXAMPLE 9-R

The City of Vegen has passed a law prohibiting the intentional killing of any animal regardless of the circumstances under which the killing takes place. The purpose of the ordinance is to protect animals and promote a healthy, vegetarian life style. In passing this law, the city council was aware that members of the Santerian Church engaged in animal sacrifice within the city limits. Does the ordinance violate the Free Exercise Clause?

EXPLANATION

Under *Smith*, the Free Exercise Clause will provide no protection for members of the Santerian Church unless they can establish that the ordinance was specifically designed to prohibit their religious practices. The city council's mere awareness that the ordinance would apply to the Santerians is not adequate to establish such a lack of neutrality. Given the apparent neutrality and general applicability of the ordinance, the Free Exercise Clause does not come into play and will not prevent application of this ordinance to the practices of the Santerian Church.

Smith thus radically changed the law. Until that 1990 ruling, neutral laws of general applicability that unintentionally prohibited religious practices were generally subject to strict scrutiny, while after *Smith*, the Free Exercise Clause is no longer even triggered by such laws. Oddly enough, *Yoder* was not overruled. Instead, the Court distinguished *Yoder* as involving a hybrid situation in which the Free Exercise Clause was joined with another constitutional right—the right of parents to direct the education of their children —a rather obvious revision of the rationale of the *Yoder* decision. Under *Smith*, free exercise claims challenging neutral laws that happen to regulate or prohibit religiously motivated conduct will be subject to heightened scrutiny only if such claims are joined with the claimed violation of another fundamental right.

EXAMPLE 9-S

Revising the facts of Example 9-Q, public school students seek an exemption from a school district requirement that they attend classes on Saturday. They assert that such attendance would conflict with their religious beliefs and practices. Assuming that an appropriate case is filed on their behalf, will they prevail on this claim?

EXPLANATION

Under *Smith*, the students have no free exercise claim, since the school policy requiring them to attend school on Saturdays is neutral and of general applicability, and the district's requirement does not impair any of the students' fundamental constitutional rights.

However, if the parents of these same students sought to prevent their children from attending school on Saturdays, the parents' fundamental right to direct the education of their children, coupled with the underlying free exercise claim, might well trigger heightened scrutiny as a "hybrid" case under the *Smith* revision of *Yoder*.

In sum, while at one time a neutral law of general applicability would be subjected to strict scrutiny if that law had the effect of prohibiting a religious practice, today heightened scrutiny is available only if the parties challenging such a law also assert the infringement of a separate fundamental right. While some members of the Court have called for a reconsideration of *Smith,* as of this date there is no indication that five members of the Court are willing to overrule that decision.

The Incidental Burdening of Religiously Motivated Conduct

A law that does not itself *prohibit* or *regulate* religiously motivated conduct may, nonetheless, make it more difficult for an individual to engage in a religious practice. Such a law can be said to indirectly burden the free exercise of religion. For example, a state law that requires an individual seeking unemployment compensation to be available for work Monday through Saturday burdens the religious practices of anyone whose religion requires abstinence from work on Saturdays. While the law does not require anyone to work on Saturdays, it does impose a burden on individuals whose religion deems Saturday to be a sacred day reserved for rest and worship. That burden is a product of the choice forced by the law — the individual must either violate religious principles or forgo a valuable governmental benefit. Is such a burden tantamount to the "prohibition" of a religious practice and, therefore, sufficient to trigger the protections of the Free Exercise Clause?

In *Sherbert v. Verner,* 374 U.S. 398 (1963), the Court answered this question in the affirmative. The facts of *Sherbert* were those described in the preceding paragraph. The suit was brought by a Seventh-Day Adventist who claimed that the state violated the Free Exercise Clause by forcing her to violate the precepts of her religion in order to be eligible for unemployment compensation. The Court agreed that this choice imposed a *substantial burden* on the claimant's free exercise rights and that it could be justified only by a "compelling state interest." Finding no such interest at stake, the Court held that the plaintiff could not be denied unemployment compensation solely on the basis of her unavailability to work on Saturdays. Cf. *Bob Jones Univ. v. United States,* 461 U.S. 574 (1983) (Court finds that interest in eradicating racial discrimination is sufficiently compelling to justify burden imposed on religious organization that claims a religious right to maintain racially discriminatory policies).

EXAMPLE 9-T

Thomas, a Jehovah's Witness, was employed in a foundry that fabricated sheet metal for industrial uses. When the foundry was closed, he was transferred to a department that produced military weapons. Thomas believed that he could not work in that department consistent with his religious convictions. Since all remaining departments of the company were involved in the production of military weapons, he asked to be laid off. When this request was denied, Thomas quit and applied for unemployment insurance. His application was denied, despite a finding that he quit his job for religious reasons, because his religious motivation was not considered "good cause" for voluntary termination within the meaning of state law. Applying *Sherbert,* does Thomas have a good claim?

EXPLANATION

Under *Sherbert,* the state's refusal to grant Thomas unemployment compensation burdened his ability to honor his religious convictions. In order to justify this denial of benefits, the state must demonstrate that it has chosen "the least restrictive means of achieving some compelling state interest." *Thomas v. Review Bd.,* 450 U.S. 707, 718 (1981).

However, the approach adopted in *Sherbert* does not apply every time the government takes action that is inconsistent with an individual's religious beliefs. Rather, *Sherbert* applies only if the effect of the government's action is to coerce an individual to violate his or her religious principles. The Free Exercise Clause does not require the government to conduct its purely internal operations in a way that conforms with or promotes an individual's religious precepts. See *Bowen v. Roy,* 476 U.S. 693 (1986) (government may use an individual's Social Security number even if the individual insists that in doing so the government violates precepts of his religion).

EXAMPLE 9-U

The U.S. Forest Service has announced plans to construct a paved road through a national forest. The road will cause serious damage to sacred areas necessary to the religious practices of several Native American tribes. The tribes claim that the construction of the road will violate the Free Exercise Clause by making it impossible for their members to engage in sacred religious ceremonies. Will the tribes' claim be upheld?

EXPLANATION

Their claim will be denied. Despite the substantial impact on the sacred practices of these tribes, the Free Exercise Clause does not limit the government's power to use its own land in a manner that may happen to conflict with a body of religious principles. The government has not regulated or prohibited any religious practices, nor has it coerced anyone to violate their religious beliefs as a condition of receiving a governmental benefit. *Lyng v. Northwest Indian Cemetery Protection Assn.,* 485 U.S. 439 (1988).

In sum, under *Sherbert,* a law will be subjected to strict scrutiny only if it burdens an individual's ability to comply with religious precepts by forcing the individual to choose between receiving a valuable governmental benefit and adhering to religious principle. Otherwise, governmental action that does not itself prohibit or regulate religious practices is not subject to review under the Free Exercise Clause even though it may make it more difficult for an individual to practice his or her religion.

The question remains whether *Sherbert* and the line of cases following it survive the decision in *Employment Division v. Smith*. Logic would seem to dictate that they do not. If neutral laws that actually *prohibit* religiously motivated conduct are no longer subject to the Free Exercise Clause, then neutral laws that merely *burden* the practice of one's religion would seem unlikely candidates for free exercise protection. Indeed, the impact of a prohibition will usually be more severe than that of a burden, and it would be odd if the lesser intrusion were given the greater protection. Yet the *Smith* Court did not overrule *Sherbert*. Instead, it avoided the potential applicability of *Sherbert* by suggesting, contrary to a vast body of case law, that *Sherbert* and its progeny are limited to the unemployment compensation context or, more generally, to similar situations in which the government has designed a program compatible with individualized exemptions. One can perhaps safely assume that *Sherbert* is still a valid precedent within the unemployment compensation context, but beyond that, *Sherbert's* continuing vitality remains subject to grave doubt.

§9.6   The Accommodation of Religion

Under *Smith v. Employment Division*, the First Amendment does not require the government to provide exemptions from laws of general applicability for individuals who claim a religiously premised right to engage in conduct otherwise prohibited by those laws. However, the Court in *Smith* also made it clear that the government is free to create such religious exemptions if it chooses to do so. Thus, the Constitution neither requires nor precludes the reasonable accommodation of religious beliefs and practices. In the context of the *Smith* decision, this means that while the Constitution did not require Oregon to recognize an exemption from its criminal drug laws for Native American Church members who ingested peyote, Oregon could, nonetheless, grant an exemption for the religious use of peyote.

However, although the accommodation of a religious practice may be generated by a desire to promote the free exercise of religion, any accommodation of a religious practice runs the risk of violating the Establishment Clause by granting the accommodated religion a preferred status. In order for the government's voluntary accommodation of religion to pass muster under the Establishment Clause, three requirements must be satisfied, each of which will be discussed in turn.

First, the accommodation of religion must do no more than offset or alleviate a special burden that the government has imposed by law. *Board of Educ. of Kiryas Joel v. Grumet*, 512 U.S. 687, 705-707 (1994). An exemption for the religious use of peyote would satisfy this principle, since the exemption merely removes a burden that the state itself imposed by the criminal law.

EXAMPLE 9-V

All residents of the Village of Hasidim are members of a strict, orthodox Jewish sect. Most of the children who live there attend private sectarian schools within the village. A few children with learning disorders attend a nearby public school where special education programs are available, but their parents have expressed concern that attendance at the public school will have an adverse impact on the children's religious upbringing. In response to these concerns, the state has created a new school district just for the village. The purpose of this new school district is to create a state-funded special education program for village children with learning disabilities. Does the creation of this new school district represent an acceptable accommodation of religion, or does it violate the Establishment Clause?

EXPLANATION

The state's action is probably unconstitutional. Rather than alleviating a burden imposed by the state, this governmental action appears to confer a special benefit on a particular religious sect by granting that sect governmental powers in order to advance the religious aims of the sect. *Board of Educ. of Kiryas Joel v. Grumet*, 512 U.S. at 706 (holding that a similar arrangement violated the Establishment Clause).

Second, the accommodation must be denominationally neutral. *Larson v. Valente*, 456 U.S. 228 (1982). To do otherwise would violate the nondiscrimination principle of the Establishment Clause. A denominational discrimination is quite unlikely to satisfy either the *Lemon* test or the principle of nonpreference. Similarly, it is unlikely that such a discrimination would satisfy the equal protection standard of strict scrutiny. Thus, an exemption for the religious use of peyote that applied only to the Native American Church would potentially violate this principle by discriminating against other religions that used peyote as part of their religious ceremonies. But see *Peyote Way Church of God, Inc. v. Thornburgh*, 922 F.2d 1210 (5th Cir. 1991) (finding no violation of the Establishment Clause or equal protection in refusing to extend exemption from laws proscribing peyote use to religions other than the Native American Church).

Finally, the Court has sometimes insisted that in order not to violate the

Establishment Clause, the accommodation must be neutral as between relig-ion and nonreligion. See *Texas Monthly, Inc. v. Bullock,* 489 U.S. 1 (1989) (holding unconstitutional a tax exemption that only applied to religious publications). However, in *Corporation of Presiding Bishop v. Amos,* 483 U.S. 327 (1987), the Court, applying a relaxed version of the *Lemon* test, upheld an exemption to Title VII of the 1964 Civil Rights Act that permitted religious organizations, unlike other employers, to use religion as a criterion for hiring and firing employees. In the Court's words, "Where . . . govern-ment acts with the proper purpose of lifting a regulation that burdens the exercise of religion, we see no reason to require that the exemption come packaged with benefits to secular entities." Id. at 338. The Court focused on the first two elements of the *Lemon* test, concluding, first, that the alleviation of a governmentally imposed burden on a religious practice was a permissible secular purpose and, second, that the primary effect of the Title VII exemption was not to advance a religion, but rather to permit religious organizations to function without governmental interference. A proponent of nonpreferentialist theory would come to the same conclusion, since an exemption that favors all religions creates no preference for any particular religion.

EXAMPLE 9-W

The Unity City School Board has adopted a "released time" program to permit public school students to leave public school premises each day in order to receive religious instruction. Only students who will attend a pro-gram of religious instruction are released. Is this program a lawful accom-modation of religion?

EXPLANATION

First, does the program alleviate a state-imposed burden on religion? Perhaps. Since students are required to attend school and since students who attend public schools may not receive religious instruction on the public school campus, a program that permits public school students to leave campus for religious instruction does alleviate a burden imposed by the mandatory attendance requirement. The burden, however, does not prevent students from practicing their religions; it merely restricts the time during which they can receive religious instruction. The burden is, therefore, rather slight.

Second, does the program discriminate between religions? No, the program appears to be denominationally neutral.

Finally, does the program favor religion over nonreligion? Yes, for stu-dents cannot be released to attend nonreligious functions. However, applying *Lemon* as it was applied in *Amos* or following nonpreferentialist theory, this discrimination would probably not be fatal to the program. See *Zorach v.*

Clauson, 343 U.S. 306 (1952) (upholding a similar program). Yet under a strict application of the *Lemon* test, this program would appear to be unconstitutional. Students who do not participate in this program are in essence held captive on the school premises due to their failure to participate in an off-campus program of religious instruction, a seeming violation of the separationist principle, embodied in the first and second elements of the *Lemon* test, that the government should not promote religion generally.

In short, the government may accommodate a religious belief or practice in order to permit the free exercise of religion, but in so doing, the government may not violate the underlying principles of the Establishment Clause. The Court has adopted a nonpreferentialist approach to the Establishment Clause in this context by permitting the government to accommodate a religious practice, while at the same time not requiring that similar benefits be granted to parallel secular practices.

Table of Cases

Index